studio pottery

Twentieth Century British Ceramics in the Victoria and Albert Museum Collection

Oliver Watson

Photography by Ian Thomas and Mike Kitcatt

Published in association with the Victoria and Albert Museum

The original publication of this catalogue was made
possible through generous support from Christie's
Fine Art Auctioneers, London, and from the Ceramica-
Stiftung, Basel

Phaidon Press Limited
2 Kensington Square
London W8 5EZ

First paperback edition 1993, reprinted 1994
First published as *British Studio Pottery* 1990

Published in association with the Victoria and
Albert Museum
© 1993 Phaidon Press Limited
Text and illustrations © 1990 the Victoria and
Albert Museum

ISBN 0 7148 2948 X

A CIP catalogue record for this book is available from
the British Library

Printed in Spain

Note: Prices are given in the catalogue in decimal
currency. The old sixpence (2.5p) has been rounded
down to 2p. Most prices before the war, and some
afterwards, were expressed in guineas (one pound and
one shilling = £1.05). The museum has often enjoyed
the benefit of a discount, usually 10 per cent, but
ranging from 5 to 20 per cent. The price given in the
catalogue is that actually paid, not the listed price.
The discount, especially when of prices in guineas or
of those fractionally below a rounded figure (e.g.
£19.95 rather than £20), can give rise to some rather
bizarre sums.

In the 1993 edition, some attribution dates have
been revised. Although this affects the chronology of
the catalogue, the original entry numbers have been
retained, for reasons of consistency.

Frontispiece illustrations:
half-title page Ewen Henderson, teabowl, 1987 (cat. 272);
title page Bernard Leach, vase, *c.*1957 (cat. 346)

studio pottery

Contents

Acknowledgements

My greatest debt of gratitude is to John Mallet, Keeper of the Department of Ceramics until 1989. He encouraged me to take up an interest in studio pottery when I joined the Museum, primarily as an Islamicist, in 1979. I have benefited immensely from his great knowledge and stimulating ideas. A sharp critic, his penetrating eye has helped me to identify quality and to spot the overblown or insubstantial, as much in my own thoughts and writing as when looking at ceramics.

This catalogue, put together in less than a year, would not have been possible without the sterling help of Francesca Hyman, Museum Assistant in the Department of Ceramics, and Susan McCormack, a volunteer from Australia, who, with great efficiency and calm, helped catalogue the pots, organised the photographic programme, burrowed in the library and tracked down and pestered potters to compile biographies and bibliographies. Ian Thomas and Mike Kitcatt of the Museum's photographic studio undertook a demanding photographic schedule and produced remarkable results, with noble help from Sarah Hodges in the darkroom.

Mick Casson, Emmanuel Cooper, Henry Hammond, Bill Ismay, Eileen Lewenstein, Tatjana Marsden and Henry Rothschild have been particularly generous with time and information, as have Marta Donaghey, Tanya Harrod, Sarah Riddick, Barley Roscoe and Mary Bride Nicholson. Craig Clunas, Malcolm Baker, Rowan Watson, Jennifer Opie and Alison Britton have all suggested improvements to the manuscript and helped in the formulation of my ideas.

My thanks are of course due to the potters themselves who answered sometimes repeated requests for information, often at short notice.

Finally, my thanks go to Dan Klein and Hugo Morley-Fletcher for their enthusiastic support.

Oliver Watson
Victoria and Albert Museum   December 1989

PL. 1 Michael Cardew, bowl, earthenware, c. 1936 (cat. 83)

Preface

If a sure way exists to tell whether a pot is 'good', I do not know it. We may adapt to ceramic circumstances the old recipe for *well-building*, 'Commodity, Firmness and Delight'; yet these conditions hold only with ware destined for use and, even then, who shall determine for us a matter so personal as 'Delight'? It is no accident that as the computer and microchip finally assume all responsibility for industrial design and production, so that hygiene and hard-wearing qualities can be taken for granted, we crave all the more in pottery those traces, preserved like the dinosaur's footprints, of the skilled human hand pressing on mud.

Industrial ceramics have their own virtues and can yield their own Delights. Though they too are collected by the Victoria and Albert Museum, they are excluded from this catalogue. For Dr Watson's present purposes they are off-stage; yet their presence is everywhere felt. Do not forget, either, the work of artist potters overseas. British studio pottery was born of a love-affair with the Far East, and has lately extended its embrace to the USA. Yet Europe, and France in particular, has often shown from the late nineteenth century onwards an admirable contempt both for the distinction between studio and factory and for the hierarchies of 'fine' and 'decorative' art. Remember Deck, Delaherche, Carriès, Gauguin, Bindesbøll, Metthey, Kåge, Picasso and Zauli. The Omega workshops, snuffed out by the 1914–18 War, had offered an escape from insularity; even during that War Proust's friend, Antoine Bibesco, gave the V&A a group of French pottery which, if better publicised, might have helped set the inter-war generation on a different track.

At about the time I was appointed Keeper of the Department of Ceramics, in June 1976, we were given the responsibility, previously exercised by the Museum's Circulation Department, for collecting modern ceramics and glass. This was an exhilarating new responsibility, but a heavy one, particularly because we received no extra staff and were for some months left short of two senior posts, Michael Archer and I being the only two left in the Keeper grades. None the less we were determined that the demise of the Circulation Department should mark no failure of nerve in the Museum's collecting of modern ceramics, and in this we had support from our Director, Roy Strong. It is fascinating to learn now, from Oliver Watson's text, that in little more than a decade under my Keepership we added to the collection about a third of the objects in the present catalogue.

Continuity with the Circulation Department's experience of modern collecting was ensured when Barbara Morris joined the Department for the year or two before she reached retiring age, but we also benefited from David Coachworth's informal suggestions. In *Ceramic Review* for July and August 1981 I tried to explain our then methods of collecting. Most of what I wrote in 1981 reflects the policies and methods of collecting we pursued throughout my time, but there is an important exception: even as I wrote I had begun, more and more, to delegate responsibility for collecting studio pottery to Oliver Watson, who had recently joined us after a brief spell at Farnham Art School, where his knowledge of early Islamic pottery had been placed at the disposal of the ceramic students. Often Oliver and I would visit exhibitions, or more rarely studios or collections, together. As my confidence in his judgment of studio pottery grew, he became our acknowledged expert in this field. Sometimes, when Oliver was not available, I would make a purchase on my own, or take advice from another member of staff or from an outsider; but in later years I allowed Oliver's voice to preponderate. Above all, we never had any truck with selection committees.

Those who read this catalogue or visit the collection will judge, sometimes harshly perhaps, the results of our expenditure of public money. Often we missed desirable things because they presented themselves at the wrong time of the financial year; sometimes we may have been slow in spotting major talents. But what we did buy we bought because somebody, not always one of ourselves, *liked* the work. If, at some future date, rude hands stretch out to prune this collection, let their owner reflect on these words by Geoffrey Scott: 'whatever has once genuinely pleased is likely to be again found pleasing'.

J.V.G. Mallet

PL. 3 Colin Pearson, winged pot, stoneware, 1981 (cat. 463)

Introduction

Studio pottery is today an easily recognisable movement. It has grown steadily larger and more diverse over the decades, encompassing not just more people but a greater range of styles, aims and ideals. In the United Kingdom alone there are hundreds of potters who earn a living by making pots or teaching others to do so; there are thousands of serious amateurs and semi-professionals, and many more thousands enjoy making pottery in schools and evening classes. This activity is matched, to a greater or lesser extent, throughout the industrialised world.[1]

Studio potters have never been a group with fixed boundaries and complete unanimity of purpose. To call them a 'movement' may be misleading, for they encompass a wide range of aims and purposes often seemingly opposed. Michael Cardew (1901–83) and Hans Coper (1920–81) are two figures who are of undisputed significance in the history of studio pottery. Cardew wanted only to produce functional ware, believing the true task of the potter was to make '…domestic, useful, usable pottery, which is what pottery is all about… Potters make things you can eat and drink from, in considerable quantities'.[2] He asserted that the real qualities of pottery were controlled by the clay, and only to a tiny extent by the potter. Coper, on the other hand, was a sculptor for whom a vestige of function was a self-imposed constraint. He called clay a 'most unresponsive material' and claimed he did not enjoy working with it; he only used it because he could not achieve the effects he wanted in any other material. The studio pottery movement is only a movement in so far as it holds both these men with their opposing views within its main stream.

In England, its beginnings are to be found in the early decades of this century, when the term 'studio pottery' was first used to describe a certain type of ceramic. It was seen essentially as work produced on a relatively small scale by a single person or small team, where the individual hand-made nature of the product and a consciously non-industrial stance were important characteristics. This description is still valid today, though it applies to potters who have greatly differing styles, interests and methods of production. The term became current in the mid-1920s when it was used to distinguish a certain kind of potter's work from industrial 'art pottery'.[3] Art pottery, a term used from the last quarter of the 19th century up to the 1930s, describes a wide variety of decorative wares made for their consciously 'artistic' qualities by a range of manufacturers. These varied from studios within enormous industrial concerns such as Minton's and Doulton's to smaller factories such as Howson Taylor's Ruskin Pottery and teams of individuals such as the Martin Brothers. The styles of work varied and covered a wide range of contemporary fashions.[4] Studio pottery was distinguished as a definite and particular enterprise by virtue of the fact that the designer was also the maker of the objects. This was not the case in the art potteries, where work was generally carried out by professional throwers and decorators, not by the designers. It took a number of years for critics, exhibition organisers and the general public to appreciate fully this difference in attitude; studio potters and art potteries tended to be mixed together well into the 1930s.

Much has been written about studio potters and their works. This literature divides into several distinct categories. There are many technical and Do-It-Yourself books which often include a range of illustrations of different potters' work. Individual potters have been described in articles and reviews in magazines such as *Pottery Quarterly*, *Ceramic Review* and *Crafts*, in exhibition catalogues and pamphlets, and occasionally in the more general press. Substantial monographs are very few, and only exist for the biggest names – Leach, Cardew, Coper and Rie.[5] A number of other books survey, more or less broadly, a contemporary scene.[6] Very few attempts have been made to write a connected history of studio pottery. Bernard Leach has on several occasions written an account of his own life in a persuasive and seductively anecdotal form. He writes as a passionate crusader for a certain philosophy of the role and significance of the potter and the potter's art. It is perhaps unfortunate that the most influential history – Muriel Rose's *The Artist Potter in England*, 1955 (second edn. *Artist Potters in Britain*, 1970) – is partisan in the same direction. She sees Leach as a heroic figure who virtually single-handed resurrected a long dead craft. Other potters, apart from Lucie Rie and Hans Coper, are given short shrift. Her writing is elegant and perceptive, but her outlook today seems narrow, subjective and partial.

There has been an accelerating growth of interest in the last few years in the past story of the crafts. The Crafts Study Centre was opened in Bath in 1977 specifically to preserve objects and archival papers from the disappearing generations of pre-war craftworkers. In the 1980s, historical and retrospective exhibitions have begun to be more frequently organised; the journal *Craft History* has appeared as writers now turn their attention to earlier periods and figures.[7]

Nevertheless, it now becomes apparent that we know very little about a range of topics which are indispensable to a deeper understanding of the crafts. These reach beyond the lives of individual potters to the broader world in which potters work and in which their pots are purchased and used. Virtually all writing to date has been concerned with the making of pots: who made what, when and in what style.[8] The consumers and the mechanisms of marketing have been ignored: what sort of person was buying what sort of pot and for how much? How were the pots used and in what settings? What were the main outlets at different periods? What role did the private galleries have in determining individual success or popular taste? Little serious consideration has been given to the way in which organisations and institutions define and promote the crafts: the Victoria and Albert Museum, the Crafts Council, the Craftsmen Potters Association, the Arts and Crafts Exhibition Society, the Rural Industries Bureau. It is not easy to judge the real impact of the legion Schools of Art and the different courses with different teachers they offered at different times. Lastly, and perhaps most surprisingly, there has been little assessment of the relationships between studio pottery and contemporary ideas in industrial production, in interior decoration or in the fine arts; this in spite of the fact that these very relationships have been the most hotly debated issues within the studio pottery movement since it came to life.[9]

The task of developing a history of studio pottery is just beginning. The aim of this present catalogue is to make the basic documentation of the Museum's collections more easily available in the hope that it may encourage a more historical analysis of the subject; it does not pretend to be a history. The following sections are intended to air some of the issues that will underlie any history that may be written in the future. These discussions, inevitably somewhat idiosyncratic and personal, are set out as a number of separate topics, and aim to put into context the individual life stories that are outlined in the biographies in the catalogue proper.

A Definition of Craft

There is continual debate among potters and their critics about what exactly defines the studio potters' field of endeavour. It is seen to be bounded by two distinct and separate domains – that of industry and that of art. Their own field is 'craft'. The concept of craft as a defined area or type of work, rather than as a skill applicable to many areas of work, came into being during the course of the 19th century. The founders of the 'Arts and Crafts' movement were concerned by the loss of traditional manual skills as industry mechanised its production. This loss of skill was accompanied by appalling material poverty and spiritual deprivation. The workers were seen as nothing more than minders of machines, alienated from the things that they made. The solution lay not in simply rectifying their poverty, but in changing the nature of the way they worked. By returning to an earlier, pre-industrial organisation of work and society, by restoring manual skills and giving the worker a personal responsibility in the manufacture of the product, dignity and spiritual satisfaction would be restored. Neither the horrors of industry nor the élitism of the fine arts were needed. The model

that they adopted was a highly romanticised interpretation of mediaeval society. From the very beginning, therefore, the interest in preserving manual skills was part of a political and social movement to rectify the squalor that industry imposed on its workforce; it was a moral crusade driven by a view of an earlier, better world, and adopting in its practice a somewhat paternalistic concern for the conditions of the 'working man'.

The view of the past adopted by the Arts and Crafts world and shared by sections of the later craft movement is demonstrably a wild sentimentalisation of history: pre-industrial and industrial workers alike generally lived a brutalised life of poverty and deprivation. It is furthermore arguable whether industrialisation actually does deskill the labour force or merely redistributes skill in different areas, creating new skills while disposing of 'traditional' ones. Thus the manual skills of hand-weaving were replaced by design, engineering and metalworking skills required to produce and maintain the machines which displaced the handweavers. However, such work was not viewed by the Arts and Crafts movement as in any way dignified or spiritually rewarding. From the wide range of disappearing traditional manual skills only a certain number were thought fit for salvation. The selected skills had to fit into a particular perception of the ideal world: they needed to be in some way morally uplifting, they needed a 'tradition' going back to mediaeval and earlier times, and they had to be capable of exciting enough interest among the wealthy to entice them to pay the premium for hand-crafted work in an industrial age. The chosen crafts included furniture-making, weaving, book-production, potting and certain types of metalworking.

It is interesting to note that certain industrial skills which once caused the loss of manual skills are now themselves being re-evaluated as precious and threatened 'crafts' as they in turn are displaced by yet more modern technology. The potter Emmanuel Cooper exhibited a modern Triumph Bonneville motorcycle in his selection for the exhibition *The Maker's Eye* shown at the Crafts Council in London in 1981; he says of it: 'The ... bike, much of which is built by hand, is a fine and handsome object, yet it is not "craft" by our definition. To me this is a superb example of twentieth-century as opposed to traditional craft and deserves recognition as such.' The British motorcycle industry, once the foremost in the world, has long been overtaken by the Japanese who have invested in more up-to-date means of production; the British machines are now seen as 'hand-crafted' collectors' items, especially sought after in Japan. The nostalgic interest in steam-trains and other steam-powered machines similarly focuses on a technology once responsible for displacing traditional means of manufacturing.[10]

The First World War obliterated the remnants of the Arts

and Crafts organisation though the ideas lingered on; traditional skills were even more marginal to the economy of the country than they had been at the end of the previous century.[11] The space left by industry as it abandoned working-class manual skills could be entirely occupied by middle-class artists for their own expressive or vocational ends: 'Craft' was born. In the Arts and Crafts world, there had been a distinct class difference between the directors or designers and the employees who produced the work. It would have been unorthodox for the middle-class artist to do the manual labour.[12] But now 'artist-craftsmen' potters could make the pottery themselves and get their hands dirty with clay. The actual touch of the artist's hand on the material becomes an important part of the artistic expression and an important mark for the owner in pointing to the object's uniqueness and worth. Design and making, art and craft, are unified in the single individual.[13]

We can see today a whole range of skills that are still in the process of transformation into 'craft': in the first three years of *Crafts* magazine, from 1973 to 1976, articles appeared on thatching, saddlemaking, stone-masonry, rope-making, barrel-making, hand-made paper, hand-made chimney pots and the casting of bells. All were featured as threatened crafts: the rope-maker's craft would die unless someone took up an apprenticeship with him before his impending retirement.[14] All are presented as worthy vocations, which have an expressive and spiritual side, as well as embodying manual skill.

Having been released by industry, it is possible that hand-made pottery might have been adopted as an expressive medium in the fine-art world, such as happened to graphic techniques. Engraving, etching and lithography were originally reproductive techniques with little artistic status. As they were displaced by photo-mechanical methods of reproduction during the course of the 19th century, they were gradually absorbed into the fine-art world: etchers were finally admitted to the Royal Academy as the equals of painters and sculptors in 1928.[15] However, in pottery, the moral overtones of Arts and Crafts continued to

PL. 4 William Staite Murray, bowl, stoneware, 1924; vase, stoneware, 1927 (cat. 590–591)

resonate, and they coloured the general perception of the material itself. Many became interested in pottery precisely because of its moral stance: pottery as craft offered a vocation with ethical and social interests in which a strong critique of contemporary fine-art practice, as much as of industrial processes, was important. But there were also those who saw the potential of pottery simply as an art-form with none of the wider social and moral overtones; they wished to pull pottery from the craft world into that of fine art. This is roughly the situation during the 1920s and 1930s. The two protagonists were Bernard Leach (1887–1979) and William Staite Murray (1881–1962).[16]

William Staite Murray, Head of Pottery at the Royal College of Art, London, from 1925 to 1939, was an artist. He considered pottery to be the link between painting and sculpture, and in no way inferior to either. He disdained the crafts world, exhibiting in Bond Street galleries along with contemporary painters and sculptors. Though a deeply spiritual man, a Buddhist with a great interest in oriental mysticism, he shared none of the Arts and Crafts ideas of craft as a means of social reform. Leach was equally spiritual, and explored Zen Buddhism before finally converting to the Baha'i faith. He disliked the products of the Arts and Crafts movement, but had absorbed many of their ideas. During his stay in Japan from 1910 to 1920, his views had developed in discussion with his Japanese colleagues. The state of contemporary art and design was to them proof of the degrading and debilitating effect of the separation of the intellectual, spiritual and practical aspects of life (the head, heart and hand) in modern industrial society. They fought against the individualism of the Western-style artist, claiming a surer path to truth lay through oriental religious attitudes, particularly Zen Buddhism, which encouraged selfless humility as a means to greater understanding. As the beliefs of the Japanese *mingei* 'folk-craft' movement gradually evolved in the 1920s, its leader Soetsu Yanagi introduced the notion of appreciation of art by 'direct perception': a work of art spoke directly to the soul, by-passing the confused, cluttered and misleading intellect. True beauty is seen in humble and selfless objects made for use. They took as their standard of beauty anonymous 'folk craft', of which Chinese and Korean pots of the mediaeval period were the classic standards in ceramics. The foundation of good work, they came to believe, should be the making of useful things at modest prices, objects that would bring true beauty into people's everyday lives. Repetition work enabled the artist to suppress the ego and allow deeper values to emerge. Many of these ideas find their origin in the ideals of William Morris and the Arts and Crafts movement, which had arrived in Japan early in the century, and were now absorbed into the *mingei* philosophy.[17] What was new was the way Leach and Yanagi coupled William

Morris's concern with spiritual degradation of industrialised life with oriental religious beliefs.

The pot made by a potter following the criteria of Leach and Yanagi carries a message whose importance goes beyond mere looks. When lovingly made in the correct way and with the correct attitudes, it contains, for those who are open to the message, a spiritual and moral dimension. It is, in effect, an 'ethical' pot. The ethical pot is remarkably successful and persistent. It is what characterises the 'craft' of pottery and distinguishes it from pottery as fine-art. It informs the production of most domestic studio pottery – a type of ware that has been produced continually from the 1950s to the present. Its claim to be 'natural' and 'traditional' has helped its longevity, for these associations place it at the heart of social concerns that have regularly surfaced in Britain. 'Traditional' English town and village life was a notion consciously fostered during the war as one of the values the nation was fighting to defend against fascism. In later years, other issues arose in response to the effects of increasing industrialisation: the preservation of wildlife, concern over the destruction of hedgerows and the traditional rural landscape, the back-to-the-land and self-sufficiency movements, organic farming, 'small is beautiful', 'heritage' and, most recently, the environment, ecology and the Green movement.

PL. 5 Jim Malone, covered jar, stoneware, 1980 (cat. 418)

15

To all those involved in these questions, the ethical pot could appeal; it was individual and personal, small-scale, non-industrial, made of natural materials, country-based, useful, traditional and not damaging to the environment. The power of the appeal of such values is shown by their constant use in contemporary advertising, even of the most inappropriate of products.[18] In popular perception, the ethical pot is still the very essence of studio pottery; Alison Britton, even in the 1980s, felt she had to justify and defend her work against the 'round, brown and shiny pot', even though large numbers of studio potters had for decades also been making decidedly non-ethical pots.

The success of the ethical pot has a further effect on potters and perceptions of their work. The ethical tradition stresses functionality as the basis of all good work: ceramic practice should be rooted in the making of useful wares. Wheel-made stoneware in 'natural' ceramic shapes derived from the mediaeval orient sets the standard for the proper work of the potter. Work which deviates from this may be viewed with suspicion as being 'non-traditional', 'non-ceramic' and by implication somehow 'immoral'. These views, expressed forcibly by many potters and critics, should in fairness be set against a wider history of ceramic production. Ceramics have never been a purely 'useful art': ever since the earliest recorded use of fired clay, non-functional items have been made: the mother-earth figures of prehistory; funerary, ceremonial and decorative vessels produced throughout the prehistoric, ancient and mediaeval worlds, both east and west; garnitures of Meissen or Chelsea porcelain; porcelain figures and Staffordshire flatbacks, and the Victorian obsession with the vase as art. All these examples serve to indicate that a major function of ceramics has been for ritual, to decorate an environment, to act as social signals of taste or wealth or power, to be contemplated as art in their own right. In short, ceramics through history have been significant in a way that extends far beyond mere practical use. Ceramics form part of a larger material environment, including the fine arts, with which people surround themselves and through which they identify themselves. Cooking pots and functional wares are only one facet of ceramic production.

Similarly, the notion of 'natural' and 'traditional' ceramic shapes and methods of forming must be measured against the vast number of sources to which potters have looked for inspiration over the centuries and the wide range of forming techniques they have used. Clay is an incredibly versatile material that can be worked in every state from a dry powder to a liquid or a hard-fired solid: throwing of clay on the wheel is only one of a number of possible techniques; indeed, moulding and handbuilding have longer pedigrees in ceramic history. The versatility of clay means that it allows an almost infinite variety of shapes to be made. More intractable materials, such as wood, metal and glass, have a restricted range of shapes imposed by the difficulties of the techniques required to work them. Clay has very few such restrictions; indeed, in the absence of 'naturally' imposed shapes, potters through history have turned to other materials for their sources of inspiration. From the very beginning we see the influence of natural gourd shapes, basket-work, wooden and leather vessels, glass and architectural decoration in stone or plaster. However, metal forms predominate: cast bronze or beaten brass, but particularly worked silver. Here ceramics are operating as low-cost substitutes for high-status materials.[19]

The ethical tradition in British studio pottery is, in effect, not very traditional. It dates only from the beginning of this century, and in its view on what is natural and proper to ceramics, it recognises only a small sample of the previous history of pottery production. By claiming to represent the only true tradition in potting, it robs the non-ethical potters of their legitimate ancestors in ceramic history. It is not perhaps surprising that 'expressive' potters who wish to extend beyond the parameters laid down by 'craft' in the Leach tradition, often feel somewhat trapped.[20] They are accused, incorrectly, of abandoning the real tradition of pottery. Some fight for recognition as artists, and are disturbed and hurt at their separate categorisation. Others occupy a middle ground, happy with the ethical tradition, puzzled at their exclusion from consideration as serious artists.

Fine pottery has not always had to struggle for acceptance as art, and indeed in the 19th century it was often so considered.[21] The distinction between craft and fine art has been to no little extent created, maintained and reinforced by the crafts world itself. It has succeeded in establishing its own philosophical identity, it has created an independent system of marketing through its own shops and galleries; it has achieved separate funding, eventually through its own Crafts Council; and, in the art colleges, it has helped institute distinct and separate courses for potters. In the 1920s and 1930s most potters in art colleges came from a background in the fine arts; this ceased to be the case in the 1960s when the new Diploma of Art and Design instituted in the Schools of Art clearly separated Departments of Fine Art from those of Three-Dimensional Design, where pottery was taught. It is not just the undoubted élitism and snobbery of the fine-art world that has maintained the barriers.

The Pre-War Period[22]

The story of studio pottery is often constructed round the life of Bernard Leach. While he is undoubtedly the single most important figure in the movement, a considerable body of myth

PL. 6 Reginald Wells, three vases, stoneware or high-fired earthenware, *c.* 1910–1914 (cat. 687–689)

has grown up around him which tends to obscure the real story and the real nature of Leach's contribution. For example, it is not the case that Leach was the first studio potter, nor that he alone first recognised and valued mediaeval British earthenwares and oriental stonewares as sources of inspiration. He was not a popular success until after the war and he was not interested in starting a production pottery until driven to it by near-bankruptcy in the 1930s. His success in the post-war period depended on the skills learnt by his son David from a technical college in Stoke-on-Trent (home of the 'industrial devils' so castigated by Leach). The struggles Leach had in obtaining raw materials, fuel and customers even show that St Ives, now the Mecca for studio potters world-wide, was a most unsuitable place for a pottery; indeed Leach planned throughout the 1930s to move to Devon.[23] Leach's real contribution, apart from the pots that he made, lay in the dedication and fervour that he inspired in his students and through his writings, and his powerful proselytising for pottery as an ethical craft. By 1920, when Bernard Leach returned to the UK from Japan, there were already a number of potters at work who formed the nucleus of the budding studio pottery movement. The earliest of these was Reginald Wells (1877–1951) who by 1900 had set up a pottery at Coldrum, near Wrotham in Kent. He intended to make slipwares inspired by the 17th century products of the same area and using the same materials (cat. 673–4). By 1910 he had returned to London, setting up his pottery in Chelsea and embarking on the production of wares inspired by Chinese stonewares (cat. 682–698). He was not alone in this interest. A neighbour in Chelsea, Charles Vyse (1882–1971), had also started in the 1920s to experiment with similar Chinese wares alongside his popular figure models, and William Staite Murray was working in Rotherhithe with a similar interest in oriental stonewares. Other studio potters were at work. Dora Billington (1890–1968) was teaching at the Royal College of Art, Denise Wren (1891–1979) was setting up in Oxshott, Frances E. Richards (c.1869–1931) had been working for some time in North London and Dora Lunn's Ravenscourt Pottery in Hammersmith had already gained a certain amount of recognition. These latter potters were less committed to a direct exploration of Chinese or Old English wares. Wren followed the celtic-inspired designs of her teacher Archibald Knox, while the work of Billington, Richard and Lunn was more related to the simpler forms of contemporary industrial art-pottery. Alfred Hopkins, the ceramics tutor at Camberwell School of Art, was working with saltglazes. Little relevant instruction for independent studio potters was to be had at the Art Schools. Their courses were directed towards training designers for industry and emphasis was placed on designing on paper, modelling and the making of plaster moulds for casting. Throwing, when needed, was done by a professional tradesman to designs provided by the students; it was not thought necessary for students to learn such basic working-class skills. Thus in many respects all these early potters were self-taught. Wren and Lunn both sought out professional throwers to teach them the skill, and had difficulty in obtaining their own wheels. There were no kilns suitable for the small independent potter available commercially, though advice could be had from industrial experts; Wren and Staite Murray designed their own, and Wren sold designs for a coke-fired kiln for studio use.

Leach's attention had first been drawn to the English tradition in the book *Quaint Old English Pottery* published by Charles J. Lomax in 1910 which he had seen while in Japan. This book was an indication of the growing interest among collectors, museums and the ceramic industry itself in periods earlier than the previously fashionable 18th century. This interest was fuelled by a desire to find a true 'English' artistic character, free of the foreign influences which were thought to have arrived with tin-glazed delftware and porcelain in the 17th and 18th centuries, a desire prompted in large part by the political rivalry with Germany. A major exhibition of early English pottery was held by the Burlington Fine Arts Club at the Royal Academy in 1914 and Bernard Rackham and Herbert Read in their magisterial work *English Pottery*, published in 1925, described the 17th century slipwares as 'The English Tradition' while tin-glazed wares were characterised as 'Foreign Strains'.[24] This pressure to rediscover the English national style continued through the 1930s, when the Victoria and Albert Museum held an exhibition entitled *English Pottery, Old and New*.[25] The interest in Chinese mediaeval wares came from different stimuli. Until the turn of the century, Chinese porcelains had mostly meant late Ming and Qing wares decorated in underglaze-blue, polychrome enamels or the brilliant sang-de-bœuf coloured glazes. The development of railways in China had involved the discovery and destruction of tombs when cuttings were dug for the lines. These had revealed enormous quantities of ceramics of a much earlier date than hitherto generally known in Europe. These pieces, of Tang and Song dynasties (7th – 13th century), were of a different character: bold and vigorously made earthenwares, and stonewares of simple harmonious shapes with quiet monochrome 'natural' coloured glazes. These excited tremendous interest in Europe, as they did among collectors in Japan who were in turn stimulated by European and American publications. The Burlington Fine Arts Club held an exhibition of *Early Chinese Pottery and Porcelain* in 1910 and the Oriental Ceramic Society was formed in 1921. The wares were collected ferociously by the British Museum and the Victoria and Albert Museum, and by such influential collectors as George Eumorfopoulos.

Bernard Leach had spent his childhood in Japan, Hong Kong and Singapore.[26] He was sent back to England for schooling at the age of 10, but the East had made a deep impression on him. Though his family planned for him a career in banking, Leach managed to train in drawing and etching at the Slade and London Schools of Art and in 1910 he returned to Japan with the idea of introducing etching – a technique little known in the East at that time. He met a group of young Japanese artists and intellectuals concerned in various ways with rediscovering their artistic traditions as well as exploring the European avant-garde. Leach was introduced to the art of pottery at a raku party where bowls were decorated by the guests and immediately glazed and fired. From then on his life was devoted to exploring and mastering this new medium. He worked closely with his Japanese friends, Kenkichi Tomimoto in particular, and he met Soetsu Yanagi who was to become a dominating influence in the development of the *mingei* school in Japan. As in Europe, Japanese ceramics were not the focus of their attention. It was the wares of China, where Leach lived from 1914 to 1916, and of Korea, which he visited with Yanagi in 1918, that provided their 'classic standards'.

In 1920, Leach, accompanied by the young Shoji Hamada (1894–1978), returned to England to set up a pottery and practise his newly learnt art. He settled in St Ives, in Cornwall,

PL. 7 Bernard Leach, panel of nine tiles, stoneware, 1938 (cat. 334)

partly by the inducement of a substantial grant from a local lady who wished to encourage the crafts in the area to help with local unemployment, partly in the need of distancing himself from industry and finding the natural roots of his craft in his native land. Leach and Hamada built a kiln and set about finding suitable clays and other materials for their products. They together developed two kinds of ware: slip-decorated earthenwares following the old English traditions (cat. 313–316) and Chinese stonewares of the mediaeval period (cat. 317–328). He attracted numbers of students who underwent a practical training in all aspects of pottery production, from finding, digging and preparing the clay to preparation of glazes and firing of the kiln. At that time, the Leach Pottery was the only place where students from middle-class families with an artistic bent could obtain such practical training. The only alternative would have been an apprenticeship at one of the surviving country potteries such as Brannam's in Devon, or in Staffordshire with one of the industrial firms. There, aspiring potters would have had to work as apprentices alongside working-class potters for whom pottery was just a means of earning a living. There would have been no element of self-expression allowed and little experimentation, and the social and intellectual life would have been restricted.[27]

Leach's first student after Hamada was Michael Cardew (1901–83)[28] who developed a passion for English earthenwares. He stayed at St Ives for three years before setting up his own pottery at Winchcombe in Gloucestershire. Winchcombe Pottery had been in production from the early 19th century until shortage of coal had forced its closure early in the 20th century. It had mainly made farmhouse ware – bread-crocks, milk-pans, washing-pans and flowerpots. Cardew reopened the pottery and continued the tradition of making domestic slip-decorated earthenwares (cat. 78–94). He re-employed Elijah Comfort, then in his 60s, who had previously been employed as the potter's chief thrower. Cardew was the only one of the pre-war studio potters who tried and succeeded in re-establishing a traditional pottery for the production of cheap domestic ware, but he did it at great personal cost. He and his family lived in considerable penury and survived by dint of enormous hard work and self-deprivation. The original market for such traditional wares had all but disappeared and the interest in re-creations such as Cardew's was only just beginning. Cardew managed to survive, and just before the Second World War planned a return to Cornwall, the county that he loved above all. In the event, the war intervened, and gave Cardew the chance of working in Africa, which absorbed most of his energies until the mid-1960s.

Leach's other main students could not have differed more from Cardew. Katharine Pleydell-Bouverie (1895–1985) spent a year at St Ives in 1924 before setting up her pottery on the family estate at Coleshill in Buckinghamshire. She was joined in 1928 by Norah Braden (b. 1901) who had spent three years at St Ives with Leach. They together developed and explored ash-glazed stonewares using cuttings from the estate's numerous and exotic bushes and trees. Their work with quiet simple shapes and soft natural colours found a ready audience. Not having to live by their sales, they were under less pressure than Leach. Braden, considered by some, including Leach, to be the best of his students, ceased potting after the war. Pleydell-Bouverie moved to Kilmington Manor in Wiltshire after the family home was sold in 1946, and continued to pot in a similar style until her death in 1985.

In the 1920s Leach gained a considerable reputation with other potters and among a small band of collector *cognoscenti*, but though he was often reviewed well in the press, he was not assured of success. For example, he was refused membership of the Arts and Crafts Exhibition Society in 1922 as his work was not considered to be up to standard;[29] he was not one of the potters singled out in the official British report of the 1925 Paris exhibition, but was merely listed among other contributing potters 'who showed good work'.[30] Gwendolen Parnell and William Staite Murray were the biggest names through the 1920s.[31] Leach was considered for the post of tutor in pottery at the Royal College of Art in 1925, but the job went, after some rather acrimonious wrangling, to William Staite Murray.

PL. 8 Michael Cardew, dish, earthenware, 1938 (cat. 85)

PL. 9 Katharine Pleydell-Bouverie, vase, stoneware, 1932 (cat. 483)

both in teaching and participating in the life of the community, but also to produce wares for everyday use. Leach moved to Dartington in 1932 to set up a workshop, and serious discussions soon began about moving the St Ives Pottery *in toto* to Dartington. The advantages for Leach were better access to materials, to customers and to money. In the end, because of the uncertain conditions before the war, the St Ives Pottery did not move. However, Dartington invested some £3000, a very considerable amount of money,[33] for the modernisation of the St Ives Pottery and to help with the development of the standard range of domestic ware. They had also financed a trip to Japan for Bernard in 1935, and a course at Stoke-on-Trent for his son while he was away.

Bernard's son, David Leach (b. 1910), had joined the pottery as an apprentice in 1930, and had realised what grave difficulties it faced in trying to develop a production pottery for useful wares. His father's pottery had been set up as an artist's studio, and his father was prepared for the sake of his art to suffer kiln losses, unpredictability of results and inefficient production techniques; he was simply not interested in improving his technical control, and certainly not through contact with industry.[34] This would not do for a production pottery for tableware which demanded a certain degree of standardisation of product and control over the budget. David took advantage of his father's absence to attend a pottery managers' course at the Technical College in Stoke-on-Trent – the home of industrial pottery. Bernard Leach was horrified. He feared that his son's taste and sensitivity would be ruined by the 'industrial devils' and their ways, and recommended that he should visit Japan, or at least Scandinavia, instead. However, David Leach persisted and, having completed the course, modernised the Leach Pottery by introducing oil-firing and installing various machines to help in the preparation of the clay, until then all done by hand. There was an immediate improvement in quality, control and success-rate and David recounts that his father's feelings were considerably mollified when he saw the results coming from the kiln. Dartington and David Leach together saved the Leach Pottery from bankruptcy and ensured its future success in St Ives, which was to come after the war.

Staite Murray, however, was the towering figure in the 1920s and 1930s. Much has been made of the differences between him and Bernard Leach, but the personal antagonism that certainly existed should not blind us to the many similarities between the men and their work. Both were deeply religious, and both were intensely interested in oriental religions. Both believed in ceramics as a medium for high artistic expression, both revered the Chinese 'classics' of the Tang and Song period, both worked primarily in thrown stonewares with reduced glaze effects or

It is clear that Leach's distance from London, and his reluctance to leave St Ives, helped tip the scales in Murray's favour. Indeed, a major disadvantage of St Ives was its isolation. Leach depended on selling his pots to make a living. Local and tourist sales were meagre: St Ives, one of the remotest parts of England, 280 miles from London, enjoyed a six-week summer tourist season, but this did not generate enough sales, nor the right kind of interest to support Leach. Leach's London shows were expensive to organise and did not provide much income. Batches of work were sent regularly to Japan, where he still enjoyed a considerable esteem, and these provided both some income and, more important, a sense of recognition so lacking in England.

In fact, during the 1920s Leach was steadily going bankrupt. He was only saved by his involvement with the Elmhirsts at Dartington Hall, near Totnes in Devon. Leonard Elmhirst had married Dorothy Whitney Straight, daughter of the wealthy American, William C. Whitney, and together they had embarked on 'an experiment in rural reconstruction': the forming of a community which aimed to integrate education, art and crafts with the agricultural and forestry work on which the estate was based.[32] They wanted a potter to join other craftsmen and artists,

painted decoration. They differed in other ways – Staite Murray wanted to claim his place as a contemporary artist: he lived in London, showed only in fine-art galleries with painters and sculptors, never made 'functional' ware (though a very large part of his output was in the form of teabowls – but these were an accepted form of Japanese artistic expression). He was concerned that the artist-potter should engage in the contemporary world and should not be confused with the jobbing tableware potter. Leach's romantic yearning for a purer pre-industrial society and his talk of the artist-craftsman's role in improving standards in industry must have left him completely unmoved.

Staite Murray was an influential teacher, though according to one student (Vera Moss) he claimed: 'I don't teach, I create an atmosphere'. This appears to be true, for while the atmosphere he created was certainly an artistic stimulus, most of his students had to resort to Dora Billington's evening classes at the Central School of Art to learn the technical basis of their subject. Indeed, Murray only turned up at the College on one day a week; he would occasionally demonstrate throwing, but the students were rarely seen individually or given criticisms of their work. On one occasion Murray agreed, after long delay, to comment on Sam Haile's work but only by pointing with his stick, without saying a word, at those pieces he thought Haile should not consign to the dustbin. Staite Murray's aesthetic, however, was readily adopted by his students – in almost all of their work one can see the influence of his forceful shapes, his pronounced footrings and necks, and his approach to decoration.

Staite Murray came from an engineering family, and was technically very competent, however little he wished to give away to his students. His skill in throwing was prodigious, achieving pots of a size few other studio potters have ever managed. He designed and built his own gas-fired kiln, and the control he achieved is clearly reflected in the quality of his pots. This is in sharp contrast to Bernard Leach's early technical struggles.

Though at the present time it is the relationship of studio pottery to the fine arts that excites most discussion, in the pre-war period the main issue revolved round the relationship with industry. Few then doubted its status as art: it was exhibited in the fine-art galleries in Bond Street and reviewed in the art press. But, following ideas of the Arts and Crafts movement, a key importance was attached to the role of crafts in setting the standards for industry. For example, an exhibition of studio pottery was reviewed in *The Times* in 1927: 'The true relation, we believe, should be that of pure to applied science, or pure

PL. 10 William Staite Murray, vase, stoneware, 1926 (cat. 592)

to applied scholarship, the benefit to the industry being that of a high standard of quality, produced regardless of cost. It leaves us unmoved that the wares of potters such as Mr. W. Staite Murray and Mr. Bernard Leach – with Mr. R. F. Wells, Miss Constance Wade, and, at her best, Miss Dora E. Lunn, in the second rank – have to be produced at prices prohibitive to most of us; they serve their purpose as "Museum Pieces" and the pottery trade will ultimately benefit by their example – as the world benefits by "cloistered virtues." '[35]

The comment about 'Museum Pieces' raises another issue – that of price. The accepted wisdom is that William Staite Murray was an artist who charged artist's prices, while Bernard Leach, the craftsman, wished to charge modest prices affordable by ordinary people. In the pre-war period, this is not born out by the facts. In an exhibition at the Beaux Arts Gallery in 1928, Leach offered for sale 123 pieces of stoneware for a total price of $925\frac{1}{2}$ guineas, an average of $7\frac{1}{2}$ gns a pot. Sixty-two cost 5 gns or less, thirty-three were between 5 and 10 gns and the highest prices were 20 gns (four pieces), 25 gns (two pieces) and 30 gns (one piece). William Staite Murray, at a sale in Patterson's Gallery in 1927, offered 289 pieces for sale for a total price of 2,289 gns, an average of 7.9 gns a pot. He had a larger number of the more expensive pieces: ten at 20 gns, seven at 25 gns, one at 27 gns and two at 30 gns; but also four at 35 gns, one at 37 gns, one at 55 gns and one at 100 gns. However, he also had a large number of cheap pots: one hundred and sixty-one at 5 gns or less, sixty-eight between 5 and 10 gns, and forty-three between 10 and 20 gns. In other words, he had proportionally roughly the same number of pieces at 10 gns or under as Bernard Leach. In spite of the high prices for some pots, including one at the emotive 100 gns mark, he evidently earned the bulk of his money in roughly the same price range as Bernard Leach.[36] None of these wares was particularly cheap, and they were certainly not for 'ordinary' people.

To put these sums in context, we know that Muriel Rose in 1928 paid herself £3 per week as the manager of the Little Gallery, and paid her assistants 27/6d (£1.37p). A skilled worker's wage might be around £5 per week, the earnings Bernard Leach aspired to in the early 1930s in his negotiations with Dartington Hall. In her correspondence, Rose calls pots of £8 to £10 'very expensive', and pots at 10/6d (52p) 'cheap', though in her gallery she also sold modern Chinese celadon bowls for 1/6d (7p) which she herself had purchased at 4d (less than 2p).[37]

Unlike Staite Murray, Leach made domestic wares which were less expensive; in 1929 Harry Trethowan wrote about him: 'We know Bernard Leach and his years of research work in Japan; we know his pieces of individual work, at prices only within reach of the collector of rare gems of the potter's craft.

We have watched the development of his work, and now we have from him those things that fulfil all his ideals, but that are within reasonable reach of the person of taste.'[38] He illustrates a breakfast set with jugs, plates and cups-and-saucers. We can presume that the 'person of taste' is a fairly well-to-do member of the middle classes, and that 'within reasonable reach' actually means 'not unreasonably expensive', though he does not quote the price.

The Post-War Period[39]

The war caused considerable disruption to potters. William Staite Murray was stranded in Rhodesia (now Zimbabwe). By then in his late 50s, he settled in Africa and gave up potting altogether. Cardew abandoned attempts to establish his new pottery at Wenford Bridge in Cornwall and in 1942 went to Africa to run the pottery at Achimota College in the Gold Coast (now Ghana), and from 1945 to 1948 he ran a pottery at Vumé on the River Volta. Most men of eligible age were conscripted into the armed forces, and women potters interrupted their potting to work for the war effort; Norah Braden and Margaret Rey never resumed potting. A few potteries struggled on, but had great difficulty in obtaining the relevant permission from various Government Ministries to allow them to keep labour and be supplied with fuel and materials. Bernard Leach managed to keep the St Ives Pottery going, though both William Marshall and David Leach were absent in the army. Leach's friendship with the Japanese is said to have roused the suspicion of some locals; though a German land-mine damaged the pottery in 1941, there was apparently even a rumour that he signalled to enemy aircraft with his kiln fires! A large craft exhibition was organised by the British Council which toured the USA and Canada for three years from 1942, justified in part by a desire to show the traditions of the 'old country' that was under threat from fascism.[40] A small number of refugees from Europe were to have an important impact on later events – Ruth Duckworth, Lucie Rie and Hans Coper.

In the years immediately after the war, the situation for the crafts changed completely. The art colleges filled with keen ex-soldiers; more emphasis was placed on the teaching of art and crafts in schools, and training courses were organised to produce the teachers. Many more Colleges and Schools of Art began to teach pottery as a craft-based subject rather than as a training for industrial design and the number of practising potters grew enormously. The post-war period is often seen as the interplay of two rival strands, the 'orientalist (or ethical) school' personified by Bernard Leach on one side, and 'modernism' represented by Lucie Rie and Hans Coper on the other. This is somewhat simplistic, but the careers of these potters do provide a continuity for the history of the post-war decades. Their different perspectives still provoke discussion and disagreement.

It was only after the war that Leach finally achieved great popular success. He now had a secure technical base thanks to David Leach's training in Stoke-on-Trent which allowed him to produce efficiently and relatively cheaply a range of domestic wares as well as produce individual work on a scale rarely reached before. He managed to continue to keep the pottery working through the war and was thus able to supply the sudden upswing in demand for wares that had individuality, colour and warmth, qualities that were completely lacking in the undecorated war-time industrial utility wares. Greater income and longer holidays brought more visitors to St Ives. Improved transport helped him distribute his wares, and the Leach Pottery pioneered a system of mail-ordering. Growth in interest in the crafts brought a greater number of outlets as new galleries were opened. Exhibitions of his work abounded, as Leach took on the role of the grand old man of British studio pottery. He travelled a great deal, particularly to the USA and Japan, lecturing and giving demonstrations.

The greater part of the Leach Pottery's output was standard ware (cat. 352–371) produced with the aid of a series of students who clamoured to be able to work at St Ives. The commercial success of the standard ware allowed Leach to develop his own work, best exemplified by the series of large vases (cat. 341–351). Even though over 60 years old in 1950, his inventiveness in form and decoration continued for two more decades in a wide range of types and styles; he would design the larger pieces on paper and the basic forms were thrown by William Marshall before being finished and decorated by Leach himself. *A Potter's Book*, published in 1940, was the most forcible and fully developed exposition of Leach's philosophy. It was the first truly practical do-it-yourself book for the self-sufficient potter, and his passionate claim for the validity of pottery as an ethical craft in the contemporary world has influenced generations of potters. The book has never been out of print and has to date sold some 130,000 copies. Leach fully articulates the ideas that he had been developing since his return from Japan in conjunction with his Japanese friends.

The re-emergence of local potters producing domestic ware is a phenomenon of the post-war period that can be directly attributed to Bernard Leach.[41] He trained dozens of potters in St Ives, as did also, among others, Cardew at Wenford Bridge and Finch at Winchcombe. Farnham and Harrow Colleges of Art in particular directed courses in practical workshop potting, and the Dartington Pottery Training Workshop, later renamed Dart Pottery, was set up specifically to train potters to run their own production potteries. Small, individual potteries producing domestic ware were set up all over the country; most were directly inspired by Leach's message. The classic 'brown-mug' potters of the Leach school would, ideally, dig their own clay, fire with wood, and produce work for a local community. Most survive by providing for urban visitors, selling reminders of the country-side and a natural life for those trapped in the suburbs. The best of these domestic potters produce pots of great quality: Richard Batterham, for example, is an outstanding potter by any criteria. His work is of great integrity: his shapes have an unforced and inevitable look, and are thoroughly practical; his craftsmanship is outstanding.[42]

Domestic work is now largely done in stoneware using an anglicised 'oriental' style and predominantly with celadon, oatmeal or tenmoku glazes. This was not always the case.

Earthenware had the advantage of being easier and cheaper to produce, requiring lower temperatures and less fuel. It was used by many potters in the immediate post-war period: John Bew at Odney, Sam Haile and Marianne de Trey at Dartington, Margaret Leach and George Cook. Some worked in slip-decorated earthenwares, others also developed painted decoration on opaque white tin-glazes. Few potters continued to work in earthenware after the 1950s. Alan Caiger-Smith has continued to pursue the decorative possibilities of tin-glazed earthenwares, exploiting both the bright colours possible in this technique and the difficult but spectacular lustre decoration. Recently there has been a revival of interest in earthenware by potters wishing to take advantage of its particular qualities. David Garland uses a crisp bright blue painting on a white slip ground; Clive Bowen

PL. 11 Richard Batterham, table ware, stoneware, 1984 (cat. 35–38)

decorates in painted and trailed slip with a verve and energy reminiscent of Cardew's early work and the early English wares to which they both refer. Geoffrey Fuller develops a softer, more endearing charm.

Cardew worked in earthenware before the war, but during his time in Africa changed to stoneware for practical reasons – it was stronger, non-porous and didn't chip so easily. Similar considerations prompted the change by Ray Finch at Winchcombe in the early 1960s. Harry Davis, who had worked in earthenware at St Ives, spent much energy in developing a practical, strong, non-chip material. The technical quality of this British-oriental stoneware tradition can be very high. Richard Batterham, Jim Malone and Mike Dodd have developed distinctive and robust oriental-based styles, while highly refined technical control is seen in the work of Harry Davis, Geoffrey Whiting and David Frith. Some potters break away from the East: A. & J. Youngs' work has overtones of Victorian stonewares, Robin Welch developed modern shapes and colours using industrial methods of production.

Saltglazing, a technique which came to Britain from Germany in the 17th century, has been used on occasion by a number of potters and a few have adopted it as their main technique. Jane Hamlyn, Sarah Walton, Micky Schloessingk and Walter Keeler have developed very individual expression with an impressive range of colouristic and decorative effects with neither their forms nor decoration beholden to the Orient.

Not all domestic potters work in the country, though full-scale urban domestic potteries are not common. In the 1950s and 1960s in particular, the production of useful ware was seen as a means of producing a regular income to support more individual work. This method of supplementing income was replaced to a certain extent by teaching during the great growth of pottery in schools and colleges in the 1960s and 1970s. Emmanuel Cooper, Janice Tchalenko and Lucie Rie have all made production ware in London workshops.

Lucie Rie's domestic ware, which she developed in co-operation with Hans Coper, shows that not all tableware need be based on oriental stonewares or on old English traditions. Their work together is made in a contemporary style, reminiscent of industrial and studio ware from Scandinavia, with thinly thrown, elegant forms, black and white glazes and fine incised decoration. While largely 'modernist' in feel, Rie and Coper demonstrate an awareness of and sensitivity to ceramic history world-wide. The jug (cat. 531) ultimately stems from a British mediaeval form, and Rie's bowl shapes have echos of mediaeval Chinese and Persian forms.

For the greater part, domestic tableware potters have been content to continue in styles developed several decades ago. A few potters have challenged such traditionalism and developed wares of a new character manifest in complexity of form, interest in pattern and an enjoyment of colour. Walter Keeler's inventive talent for form, with shapes based on tin oil-cans and the like, is matched by skilled use of saltglazes with subtle textures of grey and brown combined with intense blues and greens. Tchalenko shocked the craft world in her change from orthodox brown glazes to a range of intense colours – reds, pinks, blues, yellows and blacks in exuberant designs on bold forms. Other potters, such as Jane Hamlyn and A. & J. Young, have similarly extended the repertoire of shapes and decorative techniques.

Together with Bernard Leach, Lucie Rie and Hans Coper are the most important post-war studio potters. Their work is significantly different though they are often considered together. Rie brought to this country a continental approach to design, based not on the orientalism of Leach and Staite Murray, but on the aesthetics of the modern movement. She has developed over the years a refined approach to form coupled with a daring use of colour and texture. Coper has shown the possibilities of using the thrown vessel as the basis for a formal exploration of form. They are important, not just for the quality of their work, but for the continuity they provide. They had already gained a considerable reputation in the 1950s, and were leading figures among potters through the following decades; Coper until his illness make him cease potting in the late 1970s, Rie continues to this day. Only recently have they become known to a wider public, though neither is as yet the 'household name' that Leach became in the 1960s. This is in part due to the fact that neither was interested in articulating artistic theory, neither has published anything of substance and neither has been drawn into partisan debate.[43] Both Rie and Coper believed that the essential qualities of integrity and commitment are revealed in the pots themselves and need no elaboration in words.

Rie is a potter in the profoundest sense. She has for most of her life made only the most basic ceramic forms – vases and bowls. At the end of the war, Rie found an unusual opportunity of making a living as a potter: the austerity measures of the war years had caused a drastic shortage in coloured or interestingly shaped buttons for dress-making. She employed some helpers, Hans Coper among them, and went into production, taking the opportunity to develop her skills with glaze colours and textures (cat. 524) which she later exploited on her vessels. Her subsequent production of domestic pottery, again with Hans Coper, helped her to perfect a sensitivity to the subtleties of shape in simple forms. In later years she has returned to the vase and the bowl. Simplicity is one of the keys to her power as a potter.

PL. 12 Lucie Rie, two bottles, porcelain, 1959 (cat. 535–536)

Nothing is overdone, but everything is deeply considered. Her pots are precisely thrown and are beautifully balanced in the hand. Her work has no easily recognisable historical echoes, but is conversant with the full breadth of world ceramic traditions, Chinese, Islamic and European.

Coper was an artist who claimed not to have liked clay. He described it as the most intractable and unresponsive of all materials, but no other gave him the results he wanted. Few potters, however, have been able to manipulate clay to their needs with as much conviction – he was a thrower of prodigious skill. He started off with the intention of becoming a sculptor, spent a time as a potter making domestic ware with Lucie Rie, and ended by transforming the pot into sculpture of the highest order. All his work in some way 'contains' and to this extent he accepted the limitations of ceramic tradition. He used virtually only two colours – a light and a dark glaze, almost completely matt and appearing more like slips. He took a small number of shapes, all formed on the wheel and often assembled from two or more sections, and, in great depth and with great subtlety, explored their variation in proportion and scale, with the different surface textures and his two colours; he compared this approach, in a lecture to students at the Harrow College of Art, to the improvisations found as the basic musical development in jazz. Earlier work tended to formal geometric shapes – the interlockings of cylinder, sphere and disc, while his small-scale work, towards the end of his life, with references to cycladic figures, took on bud- and flower-like organic qualities. Coper has a great reputation as a teacher; David Queensbury claims that recruiting Coper was his single most important achievement in his years as Head of Ceramics at the Royal College of Art. Coper was not dogmatic in matters of style or technique, but was quietly insistent on the students exploring why they were doing whatever they did. This could be terrifying for a student, but those who benefited show an impressive determination and single-mindedness. Liz Fritsch, Alison Britton, Jacqui Poncelet, Jill Crowley, Carol McNicoll and Glenys Barton were all students of Coper and all graduated from the Royal College of Art in the early 1970s. The fact that their work is so different in look and in intention from each other and from Coper pays testimony to Coper's ability to draw out innate qualities rather than imposing external standards.

The 1950s is usually regarded as Bernard Leach's decade. The immensely successful conference of potters and weavers held at Dartington in 1952, and his subsequent lecturing and demonstrating tour of the USA and Japan in the company of Yanagi and Hamada, proclaimed the triumph of the folkcraft philosophy and the ethical pot. However, critical voices were already raised: a review of the exhibition of craftwork which came from Dartington to London says: '... the general effect is of an ethnographical exhibition of the remains of a lost civilisation, of a village and market town community of highly aesthetic peasants.... Only the stoneware of Hans Coper and the porcelain of Lucie Rie remains outside the atmosphere of rural quietism. They alone make the point that the whole exhibition was intended to make. They show that the artist craftsman is not necessarily an anachronism in our time, that it is not impossible for him or her, so to speak, to be with us.'[44]

In addition to the success of pots in the Leach school, there was a considerable demand for wares in contemporary styles suitable for the modern interior. Industry, particularly in Scandinavia, catered for this market, but this was an opening which craft ceramics could exploit. Sam Haile had already started to introduce modern styles of painting into the decoration of pottery, and would have played a major role had he not died so tragically young. Picasso's ceramics, exhibited in London in 1950, showed what could be done – the blending of art and craft in a thoroughly modern style. It was a revelation to a group of trainee art-teachers who studied ceramics as the craft part of their Diploma with William Newland at the Institute of Education.[45] They started to work in tin-glazed earthenwares,

PL. 13 *Left* Hans Coper, two vases, stoneware, 1968 (cat. 142–143)

PL. 14 Sam Haile, dish, earthenware, *c.* 1947 (cat. 244)

encouraged by Dora Billington at the Central School to whom they went for additional technical training in evening classes (just as the students of William Staite Murray had done in the 1930s). Newland, Vergette, Hine and Tower made dishes with contemporary designs in stark contrasts of dark and light. They made figures of cats, bulls and birds, all from thrown elements.[46] Vergette cut up thrown vases to produce abstract human figures. Anne Wyne Reeves, Christopher Russel and the Chelsea Pottery adopted highly coloured versions of this modern style, Paul Brown introduced a handbuilt organic quality. The use of tin-glaze was not fortuitous: under the name maiolica or faience, this technique is traditional to the country wares of Spain, Italy and France. London of the 1950s was quite aware of these associations, and its use formed part of the post-war discovery and celebration of the Mediterranean. Elizabeth David published *A Book of Mediterranean Food* in 1950, followed a year later by *French Country Cooking* and in 1954 by *Italian Food*. Soho, with its Italian and French groceries and restaurants, became a fashionable quarter of London. Coffee bars with expresso machines proliferated, and Newland and Hine became involved in making tile panels and decorative models for them.

Figural work was a characteristic vogue of the 1950s, whether as small sculpture or as decoration on dishes and tiles. The Institute of Education group produced animal and human figures, as did William Gordon, the Parkinsons, Stephen Sykes and Rosemary Wren. Stephen Sykes decorated plates with raised figures, and became involved with large-scale murals, winning commissions for a Pavilion at the Festival of Britain and for Coventry Cathedral.

Scandinavian ceramics, both functional and 'artistic', were very fashionable in the 1950s.[47] Potters followed their example in producing finely thrown bowls of elegant form, often 'soft' shapes made by gently distorting the walls after throwing, glazed in simple bright colours. Lucie Rie adopted some of these forms in her tableware, and lesser known potters such as Estella Campavias and Eleanor Whittal followed such influences more closely.

The work of James Tower, who showed exclusively at Gimpel Fils, a London fine-art gallery, is particularly interesting in view of developments in the 1970s and 1980s. His work presents the vessel as an autonomous object, with no need for functional justification; he anticipates the interest in flattening form to play with perspective, suggesting volume the vase does not actually occupy. These were approaches taken up by Liz Fritsch and others in the 1970s.

The magazine *Pottery Quarterly* was started by the potter Murray Fieldhouse in 1954. Several galleries which sold potters' work in the 1920s and 1930s had closed during the war; the large stores such as Liberty's and Heal's were only of importance in the immediate post-war years. Primavera was opened by Henry Rothschild in 1945 and became of increasing importance as an outlet for new potters through the 1950s; the Craft Centre of Great Britain, supported by the Board of Trade, opened in Hay Hill in 1950 and promoted the ethical craft tradition.[48] The imposition of a 'punitive' purchase tax in 1955 brought together a group of potters to discuss marketing methods, from which meetings the Craftsmen Potters Association was born.

In the 1960s, the most characteristic fashions were not ones which readily allowed of interpretations in pottery. Prime Minister Harold Wilson's society basking in the 'white heat of technology' looked to high-tech design in modern materials such as plastic and polished metal. The 'Swinging London' of the Beatles and psychedelic rock-music later in the decade needed swirling neo-Art-Nouveau day-glo pastel colours and inflatable plastic furniture. In ceramics, the new Diploma in Art and Design in the art schools stressed individual creativity rather than craft practice, but at the same time cut pottery off from the departments of fine art. A new trend was seen in the work of Ruth Duckworth, Dan Arbeid, Louis Hanssen and Alan Wallwork who built large, rugged, sculptural pots by hand, concentrating on the elemental qualities of the materials, and on recording the processes of making. In this they show similar interests to the 'abstract-expressionist' work of Voulkos and his associates in California in the 1950s.[49] The work of Gordon Baldwin and pieces by Gillian Lowndes were more purely sculptural. There is no reference to 'the vessel'; the pieces are investigations of form, material and captured movement. A different sculptural style is seen in the work of Tony Hepburn. He employed more explicit subject matter, casts of real-life objects being incorporated on occasion; parallels can be drawn with the beginning of the 'funk' movement in the USA. In 1960 the Craftsmen Potters Association shop was opened in London; in 1964 the Crafts Council of Great Britain, a rival to the Craft Centre, opened a gallery in Waterloo Place, London.

It is tempting to relate the characteristic images of pottery in the 1970s to the contemporary 'alternative' cultures: magical worlds of a mythical past, hallucinogenic 'magic' mushrooms, the universal spiritual forces captured in ley lines, centring on King Arthur's seat at Glastonbury. More important, perhaps, are the new attitudes to nature seen in the post-1960s and post-Vietnam generations. The 1970s is the period of the back-to-the-land movement and aspirations to self-sufficiency, of Schumacher's 'small is beautiful', the decade when organic vegetables displace gladioli in urban gardens.

The most characteristic pots of the 1970s are the somewhat enigmatic objects by Ian Godfrey and Peter Simpson. Godfrey evokes a surreal and magical world. Pieces, seeming found rather than made, are like strange ritual objects from a far distant civilisation. His covered boxes, populated with small dwellings and animals, evoke a similar mysterious archaeological atmosphere. Simpson uses more organic imagery reminiscent of fossils and fungi, but with science-fiction overtones, and equally mysterious. Simpson's work is also an exploration of the material –

revelling in the fine translucent qualities of porcelain. Similar interests are evident in the work of other potters. Mary Rogers pinches paper-thin porcelain bowls, Swindell turns his pots to similar fragility from a thickly thrown pot; Jacqui Poncelet achieves a breathtaking delicacy in her cast bone-china bowls.

The 1970s also see the beginning of the 'new ceramics', as they are termed,[50] with the graduation of the group of students

PL. 15 Gordon Baldwin, sculpture, earthenware, 1969 (cat. 13)

of Hans Coper from the Royal College of Art, and their promotion by the recently formed Crafts Council: Liz Fritsch, Alison Britton, Jill Crowley, Carol McNicoll, Glenys Barton and Jacqui Poncelet. Their work marks the beginnings of a number of interests that are to dominate the pottery world in the late 1970s and 1980s: games with perspective, the 'vessel' and colour-and-decoration.

Decoration, beyond the brief oriental brush-stroke of the Leach school, had been a dangerous area for the studio potter in the 1960s. In the 1970s, Glenys Barton and Liz Fritsch entered it boldly. Barton produced bright silk-screened op-art patterns on precise geometrical shapes in bone-china. Fritsch took inspiration from her musical interests to make patterns reflecting the interactions and syncopations of rhythm and melody. Fritsch is also a key figure in developing an interest in 'the vessel'. 'The vessel' is an analysis of the vessel-form done in clay: rather than being a pot, it interprets a pot and explores how it behaves. The pot has become the subject matter of the work – a still-life done in clay. Fritsch's work shows this most clearly; she explores

and plays with perspective by flattening forms and providing in the decoration an illusory and sometimes contradictory sense of volume. Its relation to two-dimensional work (she says her work operates in two-and-a-half dimensions) is emphasised by the single view-point that her pots seem to demand. Alison Britton similarly explores jug forms and their personalities. However, 'the vessel' is not sculpture; it never abandons an interest in the vessel as a container.

In the 1970s, studio pottery sees a great increase in popular interest and institutional support. In 1970, the magazine *Ceramic Review* was started by the Craftsmen Potters Association. In 1971, the Crafts Advisory Committee (upgraded into the Crafts Council in 1979) was set up, with money now provided, significantly, from the Ministry of Arts rather than the Department of Trade. Its first achievement was to combine the Crafts Centre of Great Britain with the Crafts Council of Great Britain into

PL. 16 *Above* Peter Simpson, *Open Spinner*, porcelain, 1975 (cat. 566)

PL. 17 *Right* Liz Fritsch, *Saxophone and Piano Duo*, stoneware, 1978 (cat. 215)

the British Crafts Centre, a gallery space in Earlham Street, London[51]; in 1973 it started the magazine *Crafts*. In 1977 the Crafts Study Centre, an independent venture, opened in Bath with the aim of collecting both work and archival papers.

The diversity of interests in the 1970s multiplied in the 1980s when, in spite of the economic hardships and Government retrenchment, more potters were doing more different things than ever before. The 1980s show a complete range of contrasts: from the domestic potters of the Leach school, such as Richard Batterham, Svend Bayer and Clive Bowen, to sculptors with no functional associations such as Mo Jupp and Gillian Lowndes; from Peter Smith's delight in messing with clay to the highly crafted work of Walter Keeler, from the intellectual wit and caprice of Richard Slee to the serious painterly and sculptural concerns of Gordon Baldwin; from the concentrated precision of Martin Smith to Ewen Henderson's rugged grandeur.

'The vessel' is probably the most pervasive theme of the 1980s, and many potters have developed individual means of re-interpreting basic forms – the bowl, the vase, the teapot. This work is all essentially non-functional, the only aim is to represent, but they all deal with the themes of containing and of function. Ewen Henderson, Liz Fritsch, Alison Britton, Carol McNicoll, Jacqui Poncelet and Martin Smith are the leading figures; Henry Pim, Angus Suttie and Sarah Radstone are of a younger generation.

Brighter colour and a more painterly approach to pattern have emerged. Janice Tchalenko has uninhibitedly and unashamedly led the way to bolder and brighter pots. David Garland and Sandy Brown develop a particularly painterly approach to decoration, and brilliant colour is seen in many other potters' work.

Interest in sculptural ceramics has greatly increased. The work of Gillian Lowndes was finally given official recognition with a Crafts Council exhibition in 1987, and a retrospective exhibition of Gordon Baldwin toured in 1983. These two represent a polarity: Lowndes dealing with ceramic materials and processes, but with no reference to the vessel; Baldwin pushing the vessel towards both painting and sculpture. A new feature is the growth of interest in figural sculpture, Mo Jupp using the figure symbolically, Jill Crowley starting with caricature and developing an analytical vision, and Christie Brown operating in the space between graphic representation and sculpture in the round.

Other noticeable themes of the decade include the use of humour, such as in the work of Richard Slee, the Barrett-Danes, Jill Crowley and Ruth Franklin; and an awareness of pottery

PL. 18 *Left* Jill Crowley, *Hand*, stoneware, 1988 (cat. 150)

PL. 19 Janice Tchalenko, teapot, stoneware, 1983 (cat. 624)

from Africa or South America, for example in the work of Angus Suttie, Magdalene Odundo and Fiona Salazar.

Domestic potting reached a particularly healthy state: Richard Batterham, John Leach and Jim Malone represent the 'traditional' Leach school, Takeshi Yasuda brought new life from Japan, Clive Bowen resurrected slip-decorated earthenwares and Sarah Walton and Micky Schloessingk developed saltglaze into a rich and satisfying medium. The work of Janice Tchalenko, Walter Keeler, A. & J. Young, Jane Hamlyn, and Carol McNicoll show that there is enormous potential for the development of new ideas in the making of practical tableware, while the co-operation of Janice Tchalenko and the Dart Pottery show what benefits may come from studio-based small-scale industry.

In retrospect, the last seventy years have seen the establishment of the studio pottery movement as a permanent feature of the British cultural landscape. It is perhaps not surprising that the issues that fuelled debate within the movement as it took its first faltering steps in the decade after the end of the First World War are still those that fire discussion today: Is it art or is it craft? Is it useful or is it not? What exactly is craft and what is its role in contemporary society? Today the debate carries on within a movement much larger and much more diverse than before; the very diversity adding fresh fuel to embers of old debates that many had expected to die out. The passion with which this debate is pursued by makers, buyers and critics, and the abundance of material for their arguments supplied by continually emerging new generations of potters with new ideas and new pots, amply demonstrate that the studio pottery movement is still full of life and vigour. Whatever position one takes in arguments over craft versus industry, craft versus art, or the ethical versus the expressive pot, it is clear that studio pottery fulfils a real need and plays a significant role in contemporary society – not just for the potters but more importantly for their public who buy, use and enjoy their work. I would wager that when a second volume of the V&A's collection of studio pottery is produced, sometime in the 21st century, it will be filled with an even richer and more diverse body of work which will be as stimulating, pleasing and challenging as any found here; we may feel sure, however, that the questions and issues that are raised will be the same as they have always been.

Growth of the Collection

In a Museum catalogue such as this, pragmatic decisions must be made about exactly what to include, and some boundaries have of necessity had to be somewhat arbitrarily drawn. Consideration has been given not only to whether individuals could fairly be described as studio potters, but to whether their work as a whole might be better considered in some other context. On this basis, potters often proposed as the forefathers of studio pottery, such as the Martin Brothers and Sir Edmond Elton, are not included. Their work would more sensibly receive discussion along with other late Victorian and Edwardian art-potteries which are certainly beyond the scope of this book. The products of Dora Lunn's Ravenscourt Pottery have been included, though she could be seen as a somewhat amateurish art-pottery manufacturer: it is her amateurism and her own involvement in the practical processes of making which gives her work relevance in the present context. Also omitted is the work of Roger Fry and the Omega workshops, and the later ceramic work of Duncan Grant, Vanessa Bell and their associates. Their pots would be better treated in a discussion with their non-ceramic work. More difficult was the decision to leave out the work of Gwendolen Parnell and other figure-makers of the 1920s and 1930s. These interesting artists, including Harry Parr, Phoebe Stabler, Stella Crofts and others, were mostly classified by their contemporaries as studio potters. However, their work has been little researched, and their connections with industry and work in other material makes them more suitable for separate treatment.[52] This decision has meant that Charles Vyse's figures, the work for which he is perhaps best known, are also omitted, though his vessels are included.

The earliest potter to be included is Reginald Wells, a studio potter by any definition. His interest in English slipwares and Chinese stonewares make his work particularly relevant to the later development of studio pottery. Other early potters have a similar historical interest: Dora Lunn (1881–*c*.1955), Frances E. Richards and Denise Wren represent the development of the genteel amateur into the true potter; Alfred Hopkins (dates unknown, working *c*. 1915–40) represents a move from the opposite direction – from the craft-based professional tradesman into the individual artist potter.

Tilework has only been included by potters known primarily for their vessels. The work of traditional country potteries is omitted, though they may often bear a great resemblance, in product and organisation, to studio potteries.[53]

The collection contains a number of pieces by indisputable 'fine-artists' who work as painters or sculptors but have turned their hand briefly to clay, and these are catalogued separately (cat. 733–741). The Museum does not collect large-scale sculpture or installation art, these being in institutional terms the proper domain of the Tate Gallery in London and other museums devoted to contemporary fine art.

It is pertinent to ask in what sense these studio pots form a 'collection'. A 'collection' suggests a group of objects brought together by a 'collector', a single individual who brings a consistent taste and a consistent purpose to collecting. It presupposes some underlying cohesion – an organic unity which gives the whole a greater meaning. In this sense, the studio pottery acquired by the very Rev. Milner White (now in the City Museum and Art Gallery in York) is a true 'collection', as is that in the Paisley Museum, Strathclyde.[54] Milner White confined his interests to work in stoneware and an aesthetic based on the work of Leach and Staite Murray; the collection reveals a distinct 'taste'. That at Paisley, formed in isolation from other collections of ceramics, presents a less personal but nevertheless as distinct a taste. On this basis the Victoria and Albert Museum's 'collection' barely qualifies for the title. The pots serve amply to illustrate the development of studio pottery over the last seventy years or so, but they were collected over a long period of time by two separate Departments, and have been chosen by different individuals and for different purposes. It is more a series of collections than a single collection.

The Circulation Department was responsible for collecting all 20th-century work until it was abolished, a victim of Government cuts, over the years 1976–8. Its primary aim was to provide small travelling exhibitions which went to local museums and art colleges all over the country. These exhibitions – for example, ceramic figures, tableware, the product of specific factories or groups of studio potters – contained perhaps 30 or 40 pieces and were hired out as complete packages, with cases, labels and accompanying pamphlets. Notable curators such as Peter Floud, Hugh Wakefield, Carol Hogben and David Coachworth were all involved in selection at various times, though in the pre-war era in particular, opinion was asked of the curators in the Ceramics Department. Bernard Rackham, Keeper of the Ceramics Department until 1938, took an active interest in contemporary work, as did W. B. Honey, Keeper over the war years, and Arthur Lane, Keeper from 1950 to his death in 1963.

After the abolition of the Circulation Department, its objects and its responsibilities for 20th-century collecting were passed to the various material-based or cultural Departments.[55] Some 7,000 pieces of pottery and glass, including almost 400 studio pots, were received from Circulation Department by the Ceramics Department whose holdings already numbered over 60,000 pieces. In the Ceramics Department the uses of the collection are quite different; the contemporary work is considered against a background, numerically much larger, of historic pots illustrating the whole history of luxury pottery in Europe and Asia. The Department shows objects in two types of Gallery: the Art and Design Galleries, where work in all materials is brought together to show a rounded picture of the styles of a period, and the Material and Technique Galleries, where the history of a single material is shown. About 100 pieces of studio pottery had previously been acquired by the Ceramics Department but almost entirely as gifts, and mostly by historic 'great names'. The Ceramics Department actively took up the aim of developing a broad 'representative' collection of studio pottery and the number of objects has grown by some 250 pieces in the last ten years.

The reasons for the acquisition of a particular object can vary enormously.[56] Most objects are acquired because they are considered to be good examples of the work of significant figures. However, there are people who are significant figures historically, perhaps as teachers, who are but mediocre potters, yet their pots can still be of interest (Frances E. Richards and W. B. Dalton, for example). Equally, a 'bad' pot by a 'good' potter can be historically very enlightening[57] and ordinary pots by ordinary figures have their place in illustrating the range of standards and interests which at any one time make up a period style.

Pots have not always been acquired for aesthetic reasons: in 1954 the Department of Ceramics purchased its first studio pots (earlier acquisitions were all gifts). They were by James Walford (nos. 653 & 655), their interest being that they were of 'porcelaneous stoneware'. In recommending these pots for purchase, Arthur Lane wrote : '... Mr Walford very successfully repro-duced the effect of the glazes on one of the earliest classes of Chinese glazed stoneware ... as unsound theories have been put forward about their technique, Mr Walford's experiments provide a useful material piece of evidence'. It was not the aesthetic merit of the piece that had interested him. Likewise the pots by Stephanie Kalan were acquired primarily to demonstrate their use of crystalline glazes. The Museum accepted a gift from Bernard Leach who was particularly pleased with a glaze effect (no. 340): in a letter to the Museum he says: 'There is also a tiny bottle with the most beautiful combination of Tenmoku and Kaki in spots which I would be very glad to give to the Museum if you would care to have it'.

Some pots were acquired for less orthodox reasons. Bernard Rackham notes in his recommendation for acquisition of work by A. G. Hopkins (cat. 286): 'He is not one of our best potters and much of his work is in my opinion bad, but the white pot ... is interesting as a revival of white saltglaze ware and the little pot which I picked out ... may serve to show Mr Hopkins the direction he should take if he is to improve his output.' We do not know whether this pious wish had any effect on the potter's work.

The Museum has avoided disposing of work once acquired, sometimes to a potter's dismay. We generally decline offers to swap pieces with potters who would like a 'better' piece to represent them in the collections. We are never averse to obtaining something better in addition, and may at times oblige a very embarrassed potter by agreeing to remove temporarily a particular object from display. However, the collection documents what was thought interesting to acquire in a particular period as much as it tries to represent fairly the work of an individual potter.

Most acquisition has been to a certain extent planned — the acquisitions for Circulation Department exhibitions were carefully considered, and a notional 'wanted' list of potters is kept in Ceramics Department. Some chances for acquisition, however, are inevitably unanticipated, in particular gifts and bequests. The entire collection of the British Institute for Industrial Art was acquired by gift, for example, in 1934. Gifts accounted for almost half of all acquisitions before the war, and a significant, though diminishing, percentage afterwards. The planning of acquisitions may well be directed towards an individual project, rather than to shaping the collections as a whole; for example, the inordinate number of tablewares purchased in the early 1950s were acquired for a particular circulating exhibition.

It is clear that this acquisition history conspires against the forming of a homogeneous collection. The representation of potters and their pots is irregularly distributed across the years.

Luckily, the Museum has been well served in the past by its curators. The collection is not the rag-bag it may have threatened to be. It is not weakened by major gaps in any area, it has a large number of 'great masterpieces' and a high percentage of first-rate work. Its great strength is its diversity — a strength which no other collection possesses. It represents a great range of potters from the leading figures to now-forgotten 'one pot' potters; it has a great range of styles from classic stonewares to unglazed coilpots, it shows a wide range of functions from tableware to funky sculpture.

The number of pots we hold by any potter does not directly equate to a judgement of a potter's brilliance or importance. Because we have many more pots by Reginald Wells than by James Tower does not mean that he is, in the Museum's view, many times the greater potter. Indeed representation is not seen by the Museum as an act of validation, a sign that a certain level of excellence has been achieved. Even less is the converse true: exclusion is by no means a sign of rejection or disapproval. We are acutely aware of the many potters who are worthy of a place in the Museum but who are not represented.

The collection numbers some 753 objects by almost 200 potters.[58] These are roughly equally divided between Ceramics Department acquisitions and those of the now defunct Circulation Department. 538 (71 per cent) are purchases, the remainder coming as gift or bequest. The total sum spent on the collection is £50,135.03, of which the vast bulk (£42,672.45 or 85 per cent) has been spent in the 1980s. This both reflects the high rate of acquisition in the last decade, and the much higher prices for studio pottery.

Sixteen objects of the fledgling studio pottery movement were acquired before 1920, fifteen by Reginald Wells and one by Dora Lunn. All were gifts. Wells's interest was as a reviver of ancient techniques, whether English slip-wares or Chinese stonewares, and all but three of Wells's pieces went into the Ceramics Department rather than into the Circulation Department.

Thirty-five pieces were acquired between 1920 and 1929, of which thirty-one were gifts, including nine from Lt-Col. Dingwall, a noted collector. Ten of the pieces were by Staite Murray, ten by Reginald Wells and seven by Leach, with three by Shoji Hamada and one each by A.G. Hopkins, Dora Lunn, F. E. Richards, Henry Bergen and Matsubayashi. Twenty-four of the pieces went to the Ceramics Department and eleven to the Circulation Department. Only six pieces were purchased — 8 gns and 7 gns were paid for two Staite Murray's, £5 and £4 for two Leach's, £7.85 for a piece by Wells and £2.75 for a bowl by Hamada. Many of these acquisitions are due to Bernard Rackham, keeper of the Ceramics Department from 1914 to 1938, who was particularly interested in the work of Staite Murray and Bernard Leach. He was also adept at soliciting gifts — Museum funds were extremely restricted, and not thought by some worthy of spending on such modern items. In a letter to the wealthy collector, Eumorfopoulos, in 1924, Rackham solicited a gift from an exhibition of work by William Staite Murray: 'There are several pieces in the Exhibition which are, in my opinion, up to the standard of a permanent place in the national collections; but there are difficulties of policy in connection with the purchase of modern pottery out of the Museum Grant. It is difficult to spend public funds on the work of one craftsman without exciting jealousy among others.'

It is clear from other comments by Rackham that much of the interest of studio pottery, even that of William Staite Murray, was as revivals of old techniques. There are indications in the Museum records that there was a demand from the Circulation Department for contemporary studio pottery, then described as 'modern'. A curator, recommending acceptance of a gift, wrote in 1924: 'In view of the requests received from time to time for a case of good modern pottery, we began to form a collection for one case last year. But for reasons which will be readily understood, it was difficult to find suitable specimens, and the case remains rather thin. Mr Winkworth ... kindly offered us a piece by Hamada and another by Wells ... these two will be useful additions and will strengthen the case.'

Museum collecting accelerated in the 1930s. Eighty-nine pots were acquired: forty-two were purchased at an average price of about £4.70, for a total cost of £197.23. Forty-nine of the acquisitions were gifts, twenty-one from the BIIA when its collections were handed over to the Victoria and Albert Museum in 1934; many of these were pieces dating from the 1920s. Eleven pieces were given through the CAS. Twenty-six potters were represented: seventeen pieces by Michael Cardew, eleven by William Staite Murray and ten by Bernard Leach. Circulation Department took the bulk of the pieces, Ceramics Department acquiring thirty-six. Seventeen potters are represented by only one or two pieces; these include the otherwise unknown Mrs Uusman and Pamela Tacon, and a number of potters who worked for only a short while — James Dring, Gwilym Thomas, Charlotte Epton, Margaret Rey and Sylvia Fox-Strangways. Twenty-five of the pieces cost £5 or less, and thirteen cost between £5 and £10. Of the four that cost over £10, two were by William Staite Murray and two by Bernard Leach. Leach's pieces both came from a famous firing in 1931 and cost £15.75 and £21 (cat. 330 and 329); those by Staite Murray cost £12.12 and £25.20 (cat. 598 & 600). The purchases were made almost entirely through London galleries — the Brygos Gallery in particular. This short-lived venture closed in 1939. Other pieces were bought from Patterson's, the Beaux Arts and Lefèvre Galleries in the West End. Pieces were bought directly from Katharine Pleydell-Bouverie and Philip Wadsworth, while work from Helen Pincombe, Pamela Tacon and Gwilym Thomas was purchased from their diploma show at the Royal College of Art.

Only 11 pieces were acquired during the 1940s; six were purchases for a total cost of £3.22. Until the end of the war in 1945, four pieces were acquired: a vase of about 1935 by Norah Braden given by the CAS (cat. 55); two Leach Pottery standard ware jugs (one for 23p, the other for 93p, cat. 360 & 361) and a jug by Ray Finch (17p, cat. 199). These jugs were all purchased from Heal's which had set up a section of the store specifically to sell British craft work in order to help craftsmen who were suffering from the closure of many of their normal outlets. In 1946 Bernard Leach gave three tile panels that had been lent for a planned exhibition of tiles in 1939, Dora Billington similarly gave a tile panel she had lent for the same exhibition; three pieces by Spindler were purchased from the Odney Pottery. The tile panels and the Norah Braden vase were taken by Ceramics Department, the remainder by Circulation Department.

Between 1950 and 1959 there is a tremendous increase in the numbers of pots acquired and potters represented: 168 pieces by 54 potters, of which 146 are purchases for a total of £975.91; the average price was just over £6.50. Eighty-six of the purchases were for £5 or less, twenty-eight were between £5 and £10, twenty-eight between £10 and £20. Only five were above £20: a vase by James Tower for £22.48, two Leach's for £30 each (cat. 345 & 346) and a Hans Coper for £36.75. The most expensive studio pot so far purchased by the Museum, by a factor of almost three, was the *Wheel of Life*, a vase by William Staite Murray, purchased for £94.50 from the exhibition of pre-war work cleared from his studio in 1958 (cat. 607). The most numerous wares were among the cheapest: fourteen pieces by Cardew head the list, purchased for a total of £69.72; twelve by Marianne De Trey for £8.85 and ten pieces of standard ware from the Leach Pottery for £11.57. These were the core of an exhibition of domestic functional pottery planned by the Circulation Department, and other work was acquired with the same intention: Barron, Hammond, Bew, Billington, Cook, Davis, Finch, Kemp, Mills, Sharp, Shelly, Spindler and Whiting. An exhibition of ceramic figures was also being organised, and work by Newland, Hine, Sykes, Gordon, Parkinson and Rosemary Wren was acquired. Almost two-thirds of the acquisitions (some 92 pieces) came directly from the potters; over thirty-five pieces were bought from galleries (eighteen from the Berkeley Galleries, twelve from the newly opened Primavera). The Circulation Department acquired all but five of the pots;

the Ceramic Department took three pieces by James Walford (acquired for technical reasons, see cat. 653–655) and two pieces by the Chelsea Pottery (cat. 122 & 125).

The 1960s saw a decline in the number of pieces acquired (to 82) and in the number of potters represented (to 29); this was accompanied by an increase in the money spent to £1388.13. The average price was now just over £20. Only ten of the purchases cost £5 or less, thirteen cost between £5 and £10, twenty-two between £10 and £20, thirteen between £20 and £30 and eleven between £30 and £50. Only two pieces cost more than this: a piece by Coper for £84 (cat. 140) and a vase by Bernard Leach for £85 (cat. 350). This piece, made before the war, was one of 12 pieces more than ten years old acquired in this decade. No piece was more expensive than the William Staite Murray vase purchased for over £90 in the previous decade. Direct purchasing from the potters was still the commonest form of acquisition, accounting for twenty-nine objects from the total. Primavera, with fourteen purchases, was by far the most important gallery, others contributing less than ten acquisitions. The Craft Centre of Great Britain, which eventually became the British Crafts Centre and later Contemporary Applied Arts, supplied 10 objects. The Craftsmen Potters Association shop, surprisingly, supplied only one object during the decade, though it had opened its shop in 1960. A touring exhibition *Five Studio Potters* was organised in 1968, consisting of the work of Lucie Rie, Dan Arbeid, Alan Caiger-Smith, Anthony Hepburn and Gillian Lowndes. Eight pieces by Dan Arbeid entered the Museum; Lucie Rie and Leach standard ware each contributed seven pieces to the total, followed by Bernard Leach and Hans Coper with six each, and Gillian Lowndes and Alan Caiger-Smith with five. Only one piece was acquired in this decade by the Ceramics Department: the gift of a Bernard Leach vase (cat. 344).

In the 1970s roughly the same number of acquisitions was made as in the 1960s, but for over three times the cost. Eighty-eight pieces were acquired, of which seventy-five were purchased for £4667.70. The average price was just over £62. No pot cost less than £5, and only three cost £10 or less. Twenty-nine pieces cost between £10 and £30; fifteen between £30 and £50, and nineteen between £50 and £100. Nine pieces cost more than £100: two pieces by Bernard Leach cost £200 and £220 (cat. 313 and 333) and a piece by Lucie Rie cost £200 (cat. 548). The *Madonna* vase by William Staite Murray (cat. 599) cost £312, and a work by Liz Fritsch was purchased for £420. It is interesting to note that both pieces by Bernard Leach and the vase by William Staite Murray are pre-war works — historical pieces are now being collected in greater number and for high prices. In all, twenty-three pieces were acquired which were more than ten years old; of these 17 were purchases costing a total of £1694.50 or more than a third of the total expenditure of the decade. Seven pieces by both Bernard Leach and Charles Vyse were acquired, the second highest number for any potter for the decade. All Vyse's pieces were made before the war, as were four of those by Leach. Only one of the pieces by Leach was contemporary. Circulation Department acquired 46 pieces, the Ceramics Department 42, of which 38 came after the closure of the Circulation Department. An exhibition entitled *Six Studio Potters* toured the country in 1977; the potters included in this show account for the remaining highest scoring potters in terms of numbers: Poncelet (nine pieces), Godfrey (six pieces), Simpson (five pieces), Casson (five pieces) and Baldwin (four pieces). Only Hans Coper was relatively neglected with only two pieces acquired. Direct purchasing from the potter (thirty pieces) was being matched by purchases from galleries (twenty-seven pieces).

The 1970s were a somewhat disturbed decade for acquisitions. Museum policy dictated by the Director, Sir John Pope Hennessy, in the early part of the decade curtailed Circulation Department's activities in the collecting of contemporary work. The new director, Roy Strong, in the face of severe financial cutbacks imposed by the Government, chose to close the Circulation Department and transferred the responsibility for the collecting of studio pottery to the Ceramics Department. He enthusiastically encouraged, however, collecting in the 20th-century field, and the Ceramics Department actively took over this role.

The 1980s saw the greatest expansion in the studio pottery collections in the Victoria and Albert Museum. Two hundred and fifty-two pieces were acquired, of which 185 were purchased for £42,672.45. This represents 85 per cent of the total money spent over seven decades by the Museum on studio pottery, but it represents less than one half of one per cent of the Museum's purchase budget for the decade. The average price was just over £230; sixty-seven pieces cost £10 or less, forty-six cost between £10 and £50, thirty-one between £50 and £100; fifty-eight between £100 and £200; twenty-four between £200 and £300 and the same number between £300 and £500. Eleven cost more than £500, and six more than £1000; no piece reached £2000. The top prices, £1800 and over, were for work by Andrew Lord, Bruce McLean and Liz Fritsch. Gordon Baldwin and Mo Jupp were purchased for just over £1600, the Barry Flanagan for just under £1500. The work of some 107 potters was added to the collections: Lucie Rie leads the field with 22 pieces, Denise Wren, Heber Mathews and Richard Batterham follow with eight pieces each, Wally Keeler with seven, Dart Pottery with six, and Tchalenko, Slee, Pleydell-Bouverie, Ponce-

let, Henderson and Haile with five each. There is little significance in this jumble of potters; it is caused by major acquisitions of leading figures (Rie), a complete spectrum of 'useful' potters (Batterham, Keeler, Tchalenko, Dart), and retrospective acquisition of earlier potters (Wren, Mathews and Haile). Acquisitions directly from the potters (thirty-four) are overtaken by purchases from galleries (one hundred and forty); twenty-three are acquired from private individuals and dealers. Gifts and bequests are an important source, accounting for fifty-five acquisitions. The CPA, the BCC/CAA and the V&A Craft Shop account for the bulk of the purchases from galleries, with almost twenty other galleries furnishing pieces. The exhibition of Lucie Rie's work, held in the Museum in 1982, prompted a most generous gift by the potter of her early work, and the purchase by the Museum of her latest work. The Friends of the V&A purchased and donated to the Museum 15 pieces from the Craftsmen Potters Association's 25th anniversary exhibition, held in the Museum in 1983.

The great part of the collection over the years has been of 'new' objects. Only one hundred and thirty-two pieces (17 per cent) were more than 10 years old when acquired. Forty-six of these were purchases totalling £7932.87. Over half this total entered the Museum in the 1980s and cost £6100, or 77 per cent of the total spent on historic pots.

Notes

1   In exactly which country 'studio pottery' started is a matter of debate. It is customary to cite as pioneers a number of French potters, such as Deck and Delaherche, in the late 19th century. They influenced the British art pottery manufacturers, but appear to have had no noticeable effect on the development of British studio pottery. For contemporary studio pottery world-wide, see Tamara Préaud and Serge Gautier, *Ceramics of the 20th Century*, Rizzoli, NY, 1982.

2   'Michael Cardew, in conversation with Patrick Heron', *Crafts*, May/June, 1981.

3   Rachael Gotlieb, *The Critical Language and Aesthetic Criteria of Art-Pottery Manufacturers and Studio-Potters 1914–1934*, MA Thesis, V&A/RCA Course in the History of Design and Decorative Art, 1987. This study formed the basis for a much briefer discussion in ' "Vitality" in British Art-Pottery and Studio-Pottery', *Apollo*, March, 1988.

4   See, for example, Malcolm Haslam, *English Art Pottery, 1865–1915*, Antique Collectors Club, 1975, and E. Lloyd Thomas, *Victorian Art Pottery*, London, 1974.

5   To a lesser extent also Staite Murray, Pleydell-Bouverie, Denise Wren, Britton, Fritsch, Caiger-Smith and Baldwin; see their individual bibliographies.

6   Casson (1967), Birks (1967), (1976), Cameron and Lewis (1976), Eileen Lewenstein and Emmanuel Cooper, *New Ceramics*, London, 1974 and Peter Lane, *Studio Porcelain, Contemporary Design and Techniques*, London, 1980, and *Studio Ceramics*, London, 1983, and Peter Dormer (1986).

7 Bernard Leach had major exhibitions in 1961 and 1977, Lucie Rie in 1967, Cardew in 1976, but the majority of retrospective exhibitions have taken place in the 1980s: Leach, Cardew, William Staite Murray, Rie, Coper, Pleydell-Bouverie, Baldwin, Caiger-Smith. There is an increasing tendency for major exhibitions of contemporary work to include sections of earlier pieces. In 1988–89, the Craft Council organised the exhibition *Craft Classics since the 1940s*, with accompanying seminar and publication. The 1950s have started to be resurrected, see Harrod (1989), and the work of Art Colleges reviewed, see Sunderland (1989) and Frayling (1987). In 1988, seminars were held on the Society of Designer Craftsmen, see *Craft History One*, 1988, and on the Applied Arts in 20th Century Britain (in the Institute of Contemporary Art, London).

8 This is the approach, for example, of the latest historical account by Paul Rice (1989).

9 A brief story of the Craftsmen Potters Association is given in London, CPA (1983), and by Rosemarie Pitts, 'A Bush Telegraph Come Alive', *Crafts*, September/October, 1983. The story of the Royal College of Art has been told by Christopher Frayling (1987), and an exhibition of the Harrow School of Art is accompanied by a publication including an important essay by Tanya Harrod, 'From "A Potter's Book" to "The Maker's Eye"; British Studio Ceramics 1940–1982', Sunderland (1989). The V&A/RCA MA Degree course on the History of Design has produced two relevant theses: Rachel Gotlieb (1987) compares studio pottery and art pottery by contrasting contemporary critical language, and Woodhead (1989) gives a history of Muriel Rose's Little Gallery in the pre-war years. Most of the discussion on the relations of crafts to art and industry is polemic rather than analytic in nature, see e.g. the writings of Peter Dormer, 'The Ideal World of Vermeer's Little Lace Maker', in *Design After Modernism*, ed. John Thackara, London, 1988, or 'Familiar Forms' in London, ICA (1985).

10 A cartoon in the very first issue of *Crafts* magazine in March, 1973, depicts a stall selling garden gnomes; the stall holder persuades a customer: 'There's only a few craftsmen left who know how to use the old fashioned plastic injection moulder'.

11 They had not vanished. A surprising number of local 'country' potteries survived making bread-crocks, salting pans, jugs and other rough functional wares. They became less and less relevant to even local economies, though some survived to this day, generally by redirecting their production at the tourist trade: see Peter C. D. Brears, *The English Country Pottery; Its History and Techniques*, Newton Abbot, 1971, pp. 79–81, and *The Collector's Book of English Country Pottery*, Newton Abbot, 1974. It is surprising that Bernard Leach and Cardew did not try to seek out more thoroughly the remnants of the tradition whose passing they so deplored.

12 Sir Edmond Elton, working from the 1880s, is the only 'gentleman potter' from that period who was involved with all the stages of making, from preparation of the clay onwards. A contemporary discussion of his work was, however, at pains to point out that he was a gentleman of independent means with no need to work at all, and praises the fact that he was (almost) entirely self-taught. It is evidently important that this gentleman had needed no recourse to learning skills from ordinary working potters who, of course, were plentiful at that time. See Cosmo Monkhouse, 'Elton Ware', *Magazine of Art*, VI, 1882, reproduced in Malcolm Haslam, *English Art Pottery, 1865–1915*, Antique Collectors Club, 1975.

13 Floud (1953) argues that the 'identity of designer and craftsman' is what distinguishes crafts from 'Arts and Crafts'. See Peter Dormer, 'The Appearance of Craft', *Craft History One*, 1988, for an elaboration of some of these ideas.

14 Is it a coincidence that two years previously an article appeared in the same magazine on an 'art installation' using rope as the basic expressive material?

15 See 'The Original Print Versus the Reproduction' in Susan Lambert, *The Image Multiplied*, Victoria and Albert Museum, 1987, pp. 31–3. Only wood-block engraving seems to have retained a strong 'craft' overtone, see John Farleigh, *Fifteen Craftsmen on their Crafts*, London, 1945.

16 Bernard Leach represents the moral 'Arts and Crafts' approach to pottery, see 'Towards a Standard' in his *A Potter's Book*, London, 1940. William Staite Murray represents the fine-art potter, see his 'Pottery from the Artist's Point of View', *Artwork*, 1/4, 1925.

17 Brian Moeran, 'Morris, Yanagi and the Japanese Folkcraft Movement', *CR*, 66/1980. The potter Kenkichi Tomimoto, a close friend and colleague of Bernard Leach during his stay in Japan, had studied stained-glass at the Central School of Art from 1908 to 1911. He discovered William Morris at an exhibition at the Victoria and Albert Museum in 1909, and on his return to Japan published a series of articles on him and his ideas.

18 Similar associations are continually used in advertising to promote such 'traditional' products as sliced bread, canned soup and cars. This argument is persuasively developed by Christopher Frayling and Helen Snowdon, 'The Myth of the Happy Artisan', *Crafts*, January/February, 1982, reprinted in *Craft Classics Since the 1940s*, ed. John Houston, Crafts Council, London, 1988.

19 For a detailed discussion of the relationship between pottery and metal in China, Greece and the Islamic world, see *Pots and Pans*, Studies in Islamic Art, vol. III, Oxford University Press, 1987. Similar comparisons are easily made in European production from the Roman period onwards.

20 The term 'expressive', used in contrast to 'ethical', is perhaps slightly misleading; it is not at all intended to imply that 'ethical' potters do not make pots which are also expressive.

21 Greenhalgh (1989).

22 For a general overview of this period, see Fiona MacCarthy, 'The Inheritance of Diffidence: Crafts in Britain between the Wars', *Craft History One*, 1988.

23 See London, Tate Gallery (1985) for a development of some of these ideas.

24 Gotlieb (1987), p. 42.

25 London, VAM (1935); see also Geoffrey Grigson, 'In Search of English Pottery', *The Studio*, 110, 1935, pp. 256 ff.

26 For Leach's life see in particular his autobiography, *Beyond East and West*, London, 1978.

27 The class barriers worked in both directions: Bernard Leach took on local men as apprentices to help make his standard ware just before the war; of such employees he writes: 'Local lads with a half-education grow up with a normal expectation of pleasure after work which tends to prevent them from really entering a craftsman's life'; see 'Pottery', in John Farleigh, *Fifteen Craftsmen on their Crafts*, London, 1945.

28   For details of Cardew's life see his autobiography: *A Pioneer Potter*, London, 1988.

29   He was eventually given membership without having to submit work in 1935, along with Eric Gill, Marion Dorn, Ethel Mairet and Sydney Cockerell, by an embarrassed Society anxious, by then, to make amends; see Meg Sweet, 'From Combined Arts to Designer Craftsmen; the Archives of the ACES', *Craft History One*, 1988.

30   Gordon Forsyth, 'Pottery', in *Report on the Present Position and Tendencies of the Industrial Arts as Indicated at the International Exhibition*, Department of Overseas Trade, London, 1927.

31   For Gwendolen Parnell see Mrs Stuart Erskine, 'Gwendolen Parnell and her Chelsea Cheyne Figures', *Apollo*, February, 1929.

32   Michael Young, *The Elmhirsts of Dartington*, London, 1982.

33   The equivalent to more than ten years' salary for Bernard Leach.

34   The truth is that Leach had not received an extensive technical training while in Japan; most of his pre-war work in England shows some blemish or fault. See, as an illustration of his difficulties, the letters written to him by Katharine Pleydell-Bouverie in 1928 commiserating with a disastrous firing, and chiding him for not preparing sufficient fuel: *Katharine Pleydell-Bouverie: A Potter's Life*, Crafts Council, 1986.

35   *The Times*, 30/9/1927.

36   A thorough analysis of prices remains to be done. The prices given here are listed in the respective exhibition catalogues, but the real significance depends, of course, on how many at each price were actually sold. On the assumption that the less-expensive pieces sold better than the more-expensive, the difference between William Staite Murray and Bernard Leach was even less marked. We know that Staite Murray sold at least one pot at 100 gns (see Haslam, *William Staite Murray*, London, 1984), though A. G. Hopkins is reputed to have been the first potter to ask for and receive this sum. Prices were usually quoted in guineas, a notional unit which equalled £1.05p.

37   Information taken from Woodhead (1989). Wealth was extremely polarised in the interwar years; in 1924 the official statistics indicate that 2.5 per cent of the population owned two-thirds of the total wealth of the country.

38   Harry Trethowan, 'Pottery and Glassware', *The Studio Yearbook of Decorative Art*, 1929.

39   For an excellent survey of the post-war years, see Harrod (1989a), and Pamela Johnson, 'One Hundred Years of Grumbling', *Craft History Two*, 1989, a report on the Craft Council discussion held in November 1988: *Personalities, Priorities and Changes in the Crafts since the 1940s*.

40   James Noel White, 'The Unexpected Phoenix I', *Craft History One*, 1988.

41   For domestic pottery see the *Studio Yearbook of Decorative Art* annually from 1906 to 1980, and Casson (1967), London, CC (1977) and (1984), and I. Anscombe 'Put it on the Table', *Crafts*, May/June, 1982.

42   Alas, 'brown-mug' horrors, of a standard of design and craftsmanship which would appal and sadden Bernard Leach, have also been made and sold in enormous numbers to an uncritical audience, and the market for country-style wares is exploited by industrial firms in Staffordshire, with mass-produced, faked 'hand-made' mugs and with transfer-printed decoration of rural scenes.

43   Hans Coper is known for only one brief statement about his work, see London, VAM (1977). He was not particularly happy about even this short passage and, in a letter to the exhibition organiser, said that he would be glad to see it omitted from the catalogue.

44   Robert Melville, exhibition review, *Architectural Review*, 112, November, 1952, quoted in Harrod (1989a).

45   Tanya Harrod (1989); see also Billington (1953) and (1955), and Floud (1953).

46   It is interesting that they stress the use of the wheel in their sculptural work — resonances of the ethical pot, perhaps, even here.

47   *The Studio Yearbook of Decorative Art* illustrates more Scandinavian than any other industrial ceramics during the 1950s. Many of the ideas of the 'modern' British studio potters of this period appear to have been suggested from this source. For a general survey, see Jennifer Opie, *Scandinavian Ceramics of the 20th Century*, Victoria and Albert Museum, London, 1989.

48   John Farleigh, 'The Craft Centre of Great Britain', *The Studio*, August, 1950.

49   The impact of American studio pottery begins to be felt in this decade though virtually no pieces were to be seen in Europe; *Pottery Quarterly* devotes an issue to work from the USA in 1961 (vol. 25/7).

50   Dormer (1986).

51   The BCC changed its name to Contemporary Applied Arts in 1987.

52   Blunt (1973); J. Opie, 'Art and Deco: the Problems of British Ceramics in the International Exhibition, Paris, 1925', *V&A Album*, 4, 1985.

53   Peter C. D. Brears, *The English Country Pottery; Its History and Techniques*, Newton Abbot, 1971, pp. 79–81, and *The Collector's Book of English Country Pottery*, Newton Abbot, 1974.

54   Milner-White (1971) and Melissa Dalziel, 'The Dean's Taste', *Crafts*, March/April, 1985; Paisley(1984).

55   Japanese studio pots, for example, are held by the Far Eastern Department.

56   For a brief exposition of the Victoria and Albert Museum's collecting policy see Oliver Watson, 'The Victoria and Albert Museum and Studio Ceramics' in London, CPA (1983) and J.V.G. Mallet, 'Collecting for the Victoria and Albert Museum', *CR*, 70/1981.

57   John Leach once remarked to the author how encouraging for him it was to see the early work of Bernard Leach, for it made him realise that even his grandfather was a potter who had struggled and whose work started off far from perfect; improvement over time was a possibility!

58   Discrepancy between the numbers given here, and, for example, the catalogue numbers is caused by different means of identifying 'an object'. Gillian Lowndes's *Three Standing Pipes*, for example, is here catalogued as one piece, but counted for the purposes of the statistics as three separate objects.

PL. 20 Reginald Wells, vases, earthenware, *c.* 1910–1914 (cat. 676–679)

Colour Plates

PL. 21 Reginald Wells, bowl and vase, stoneware, *c.* 1924–1925 (cat. 698–699)

PL. 22 *Right* Dora Lunn, two vases, stoneware, 1916–1928 (cat. 410–411)

PL. 23 *Left* Alfred Hopkins, bowl and two vases, stoneware and porcelain, 1927–1931 (cat. 285–287)

PL. 24 Bernard Leach, dish, earthenware, 1923 (cat. 315)

PL. 25 *Left* Michael Cardew, large jar, earthenware, 1938 (cat. 86)

PL. 26 Michael Cardew, jug, earthenware, 1938 (cat. 89)

PL. 27 Bernard Leach, vase, stoneware, 1926–1927 (cat. 322)

PL. 28 *Right* Bernard Leach, vase, stoneware, 1931 (cat. 329)

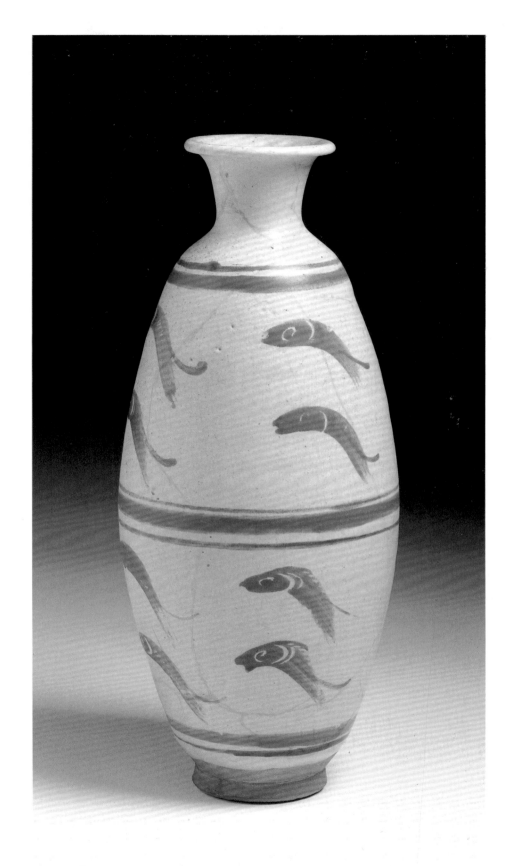

PL. 29 Shoji Hamada, vase, stoneware, 1923 (cat. 252)

PL. 30 *Right* Katharine Pleydell-Bouverie, vase, *Roc's Egg*, stoneware, 1929–1930 (cat. 476)

PL. 31 *Left* Norah Braden, two vases, stoneware, *c.* 1930–1935 (cat. 51–52)

PL. 32 Norah Braden, bowl, stoneware, 1938 (cat. 56)

PL. 33 William Staite Murray, bowl, stoneware, *c.* 1930 (cat. 601)

PL. 34 *Right* William Staite Murray, vase, *Wheel of Life*, stoneware, *c.* 1939 (cat. 607)

PL. 35 *Left* R. J. Washington, two vases, stoneware, 1938 (cat. 664–665)

PL. 36 Henry Hammond, vase, stoneware, 1939 (cat. 258)

PL. 37 Charles Vyse, jug and mug, stoneware, 1934–1936 (cat. 635–636)

PL. 38 *Right* Sybil Finnemore, vase, stoneware, 1926 (cat. 207)

PL. 39 *Left* Denise Wren, vase, earthenware, *c.* 1930–1935 (cat. 717)

PL. 40 Lucie Rie, pot with lid, earthenware, 1936–1937 (cat. 516)

PL. 41 *Left* Bernard Leach, vase, stoneware, *c.* 1955 (cat. 344)

PL. 42 Michael Cardew, tureen, stoneware, 1950 (cat. 96)

PL. 43 *Left* Michael Cardew, dish, *Pheasant and Palm*, stoneware, 1950 (cat. 98)

PL. 44 Leach Pottery, three jugs, stoneware, 1940–1949 (cat. 360–362)

PL. 45 *Left* Harry and May Davis, tableware, stoneware, 1950–1951 (cat. 160–162)

PL. 46 Marianne De Trey, tableware, earthenware, 1950 (cat. 167–169)

PL. 47 *Left* Lucie Rie and Hans Coper, jug and two beakers, stoneware 1950–55 (cat. 531)

PL. 48 Sam Haile, jug, earthenware, *c.* 1947 (cat. 245)

PL. 49 *Left* Heber Mathews, vase, stoneware, 1958 (cat. 436)

PL. 50 William Newland, figure of a bull, earthenware, 1954 (cat. 451)

74

PL. 51 *Left* William Gordon, *Clown*, porcelain, 1950 (cat. 229)

PL. 52 Richard and Sue Parkinson, *Cockerel and Hen*, porcelain, 1954 (cat. 460)

PL. 53 Steven Sykes, *Trumpeting Angel*, earthenware, 1950 (cat. 614)

PL. 54 *Right* Nicholas Vergette, bowl, earthenware, 1954 (cat. 632)

PL. 55 James Tower, vase, earthenware, 1957 (cat. 628)

PL. 56 *Right* Paul Brown, vase, *Noctulid*, earthenware, 1958 (cat. 63)

PL. 57 Hans Coper, handled pot, stoneware, 1951 (cat. 136)

PL. 58 *Right* Hans Coper, vase, stoneware, 1958 (cat. 138)

PL. 59 *Left* Lucie Rie, bottle, stoneware, 1959 (cat. 534)

PL. 60 Helen Pincombe, vase, stoneware, 1958 (cat. 471)

PL. 61 *Left* Dan Arbeid, vase, stoneware, 1959 (cat. 1)

PL. 62 Ruth Duckworth, dish, stoneware, 1959 (cat. 183)

PL. 63 Bernard Leach, vase, porcelain, 1967 (cat. 350)

PL. 64 *Right* Hans Coper, pot, stoneware, 1968 (cat. 140)

PL. 65 Lucie Rie, two vases, stoneware, 1967 (cat. 539–540)

PL. 66 *Right* Lucie Rie, vase, stoneware, 1967 (cat. 541)

PL. 67 Alan Caiger Smith, bowl, earthenware, 1968 (cat. 68)

PL. 68 *Right* Alan Caiger Smith, pot-pourri jar, earthenware, 1968 (cat. 69)

PL. 69 *Left* Dan Arbeid, pin pots, stoneware, 1968 (cat. 6–9)

PL. 70 Ian Auld, vase, stoneware, 1965 (cat. 11)

PL. 71 Janet Leach, pot, stoneware, 1965 (cat. 381)

PL. 72 *Right* Louis Hanssen, vase, stoneware, 1965 (cat. 266)

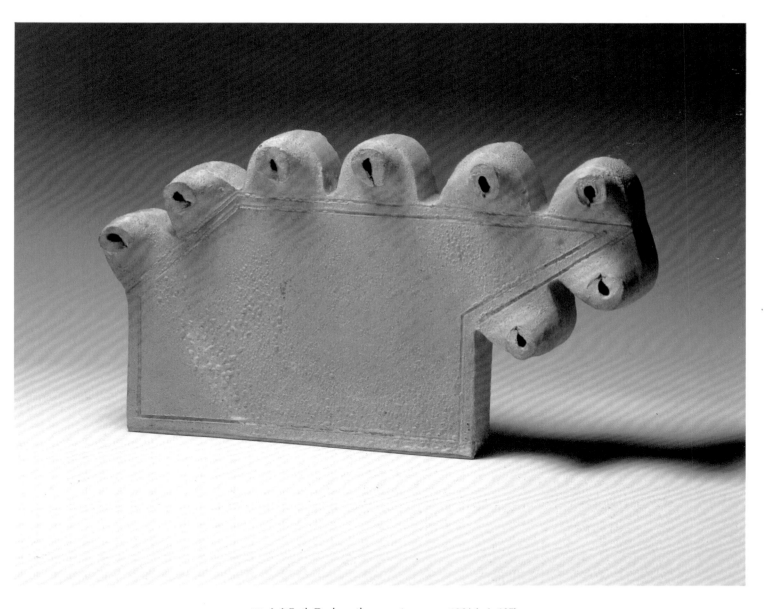

PL. 73 *Left* Ruth Duckworth, vase, stoneware, 1966 (cat. 187)

PL. 74 Gillian Lowndes, sculptural form, stoneware, 1968 (cat. 407)

PL. 75 *Left* Anthony Hepburn, *Large White Double Box*, stoneware, 1967 (cat. 274)

PL. 76 Ian Godfrey, *Large White Chest of Drawers*, stoneware, 1969–70 (cat. 222)

PL. 77 *Left* Ian Godfrey, *Grey Fox Box*, stoneware, 1974 (cat. 225)

PL. 78 Michael Casson, footed bowl, stoneware, 1975 (cat. 116)

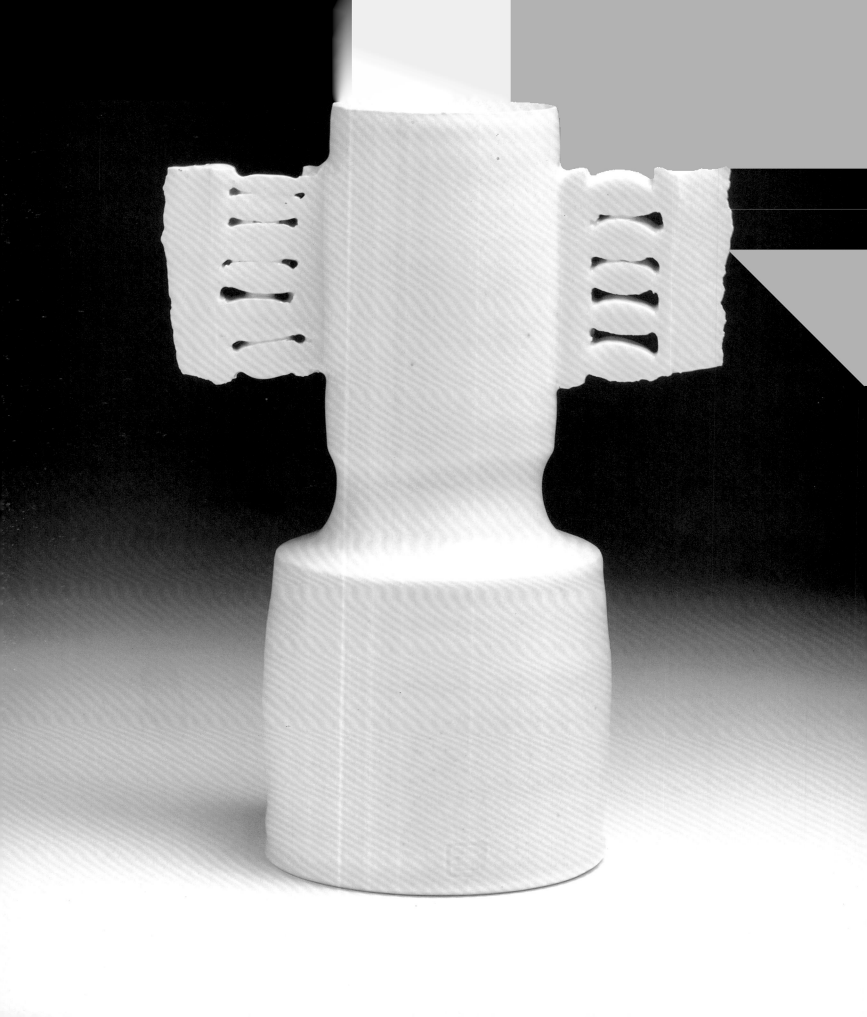

PL. 79 *Left* Colin Pearson, winged pot, porcelain, 1971 (cat. 461)

PL. 80 Jacqueline Poncelet, bowl, *Double Circle Form*, and pot, bone china, 1974 (cat. 489–490)

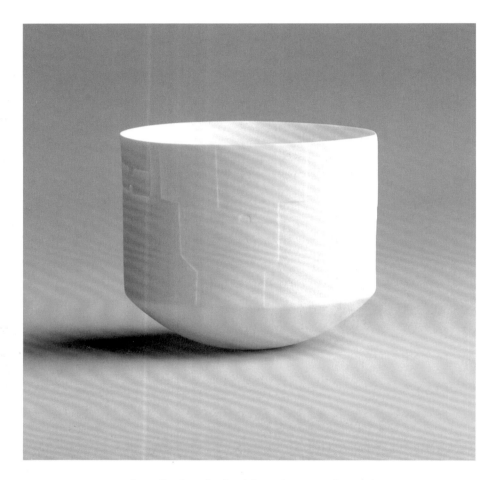

PL. 81 Jacqueline Poncelet, bowl, bone china, 1974 (cat. 491)

PL. 82 *Right* Gordon Baldwin, *Painting in the Form of a Dish*, stoneware, 1976 (cat. 15)

PL. 83 *Left* Hans Coper, black form, stoneware, 1975 (cat. 147)

PL. 84 Lucie Rie, bowl, porcelain, *c.* 1976 (cat. 545)

PL. 85 *Left* Lucie Rie, bottle, stoneware, *c.* 1979 (cat. 544)

PL. 86 Ewen Henderson, vase, stoneware and porcelain, 1979 (cat. 268)

PL. 87 *Left* Mo Jupp, helmet, stoneware, 1972 (cat. 293)

PL. 88 Andrew Lord, box, earthenware, 1972 (cat. 403)

PL. 89 *Left* Glenys Barton, *Monte Alban II*, bone china, 1977 (cat. 29)

PL. 90 Alison Britton, two jugs, earthenware, 1978 (cat. 57–58)

PL. 91 Martin Smith, bowl, earthenware, 1978 (cat. 572)

PL. 92 *Right* Jacqueline Poncelet, vase, earthenware, 1978 (cat. 497)

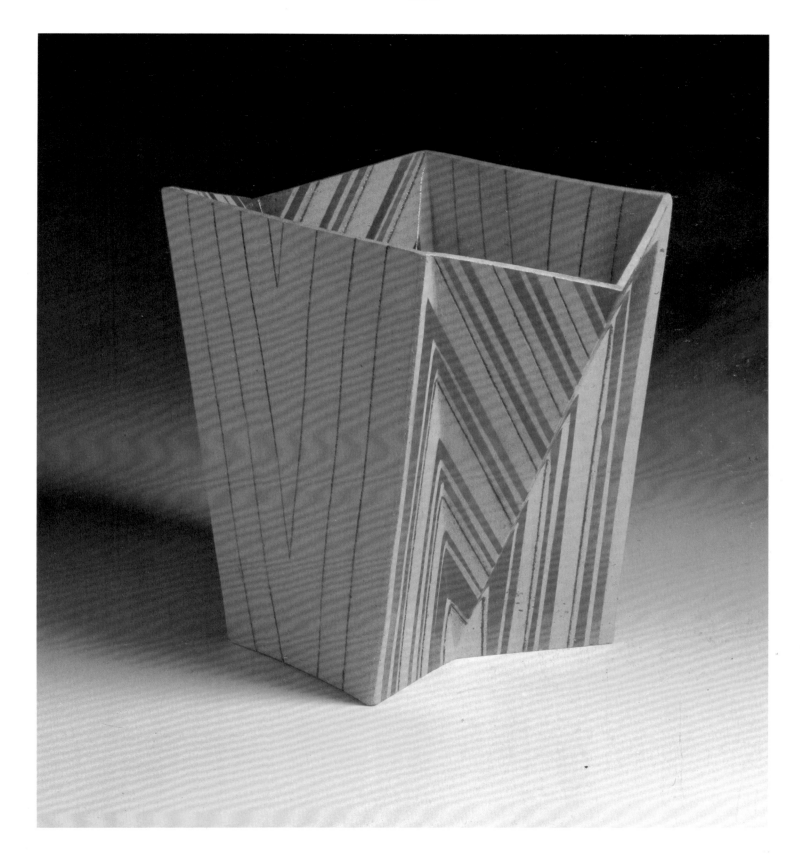

PL. 93 *Left* Liz Fritsch, *Optical Pot*, stoneware, 1980 (cat. 216)

PL. 94 Alison Britton, vase, *Yellow Friangle*, stoneware, 1981 (cat. 59)

PL. 95 *Left* Alison Britton, *Big White Jug*, earthenware, 1987 (cat. 61)

PL. 96 Jacqueline Poncelet, form, stoneware, 1981 (cat. 499)

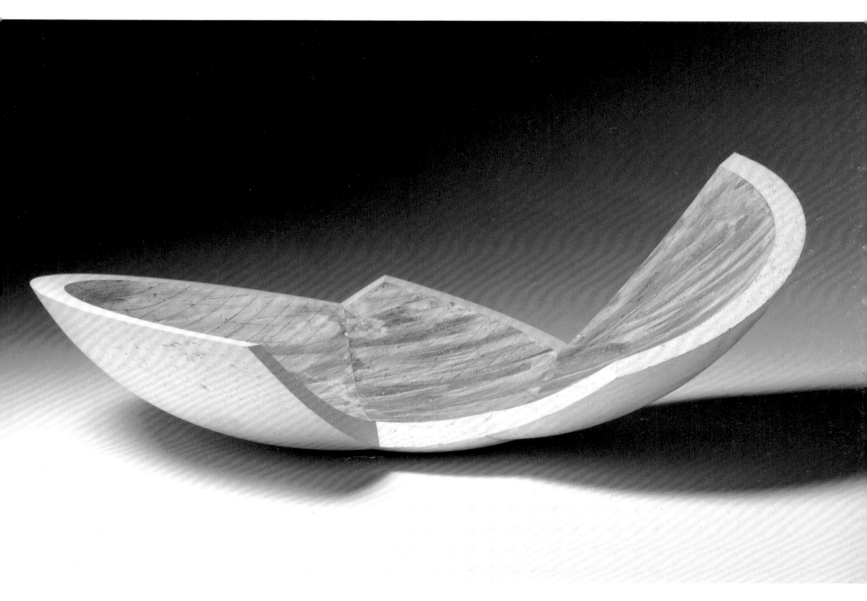

PL. 97 *Left* Carol McNicoll, bowl, earthenware, 1985 (cat. 439)

PL. 98 Martin Smith, form, stoneware, 1986 (cat. 574)

PL. 99 Richard Slee, vase, earthenware, *c.* 1981 (cat. 568)

PL. 100 *Right* Ewen Henderson, vase, stoneware, 1986 (cat. 271)

PL. 101 *Left* Ewen Henderson, form, from the series *Skull Mountain*, laminated porcelain and stoneware, 1988 (cat. 273)

PL. 102 Sara Radstone, vase, stoneware, 1983 (cat. 503)

PL. 103 Henry Pim, form, stoneware, 1988 (cat. 467)

PL. 104 *Right* Bruce McLean, jug, earthenware, 1987 (cat. 738)

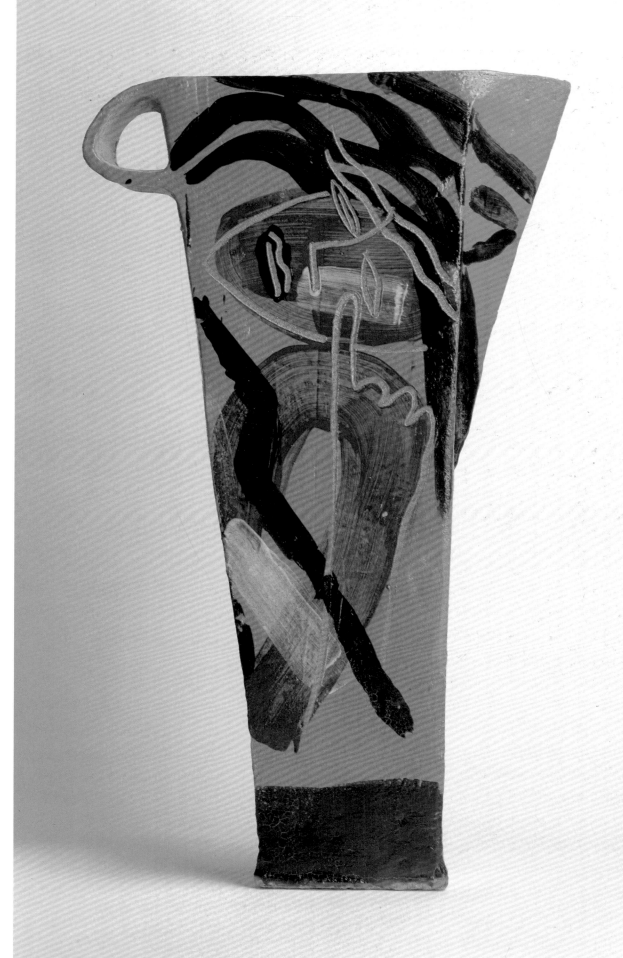

PL. 105 *Left* Gordon Baldwin, *Avis II, No. 4*, stoneware, 1984 (cat. 17)

PL. 106 Gillian Lowndes, sculpture, *Cup on Base*, stoneware, 1986 (cat. 408)

PL. 107 *Left* Ruth Barrett-Danes, *Sacrificial Sheep*, porcelain, 1988 (cat. 22)

PL. 108 Jill Crowley, *Portrait of a Darts Player*, stoneware, 1981 (cat. 149)

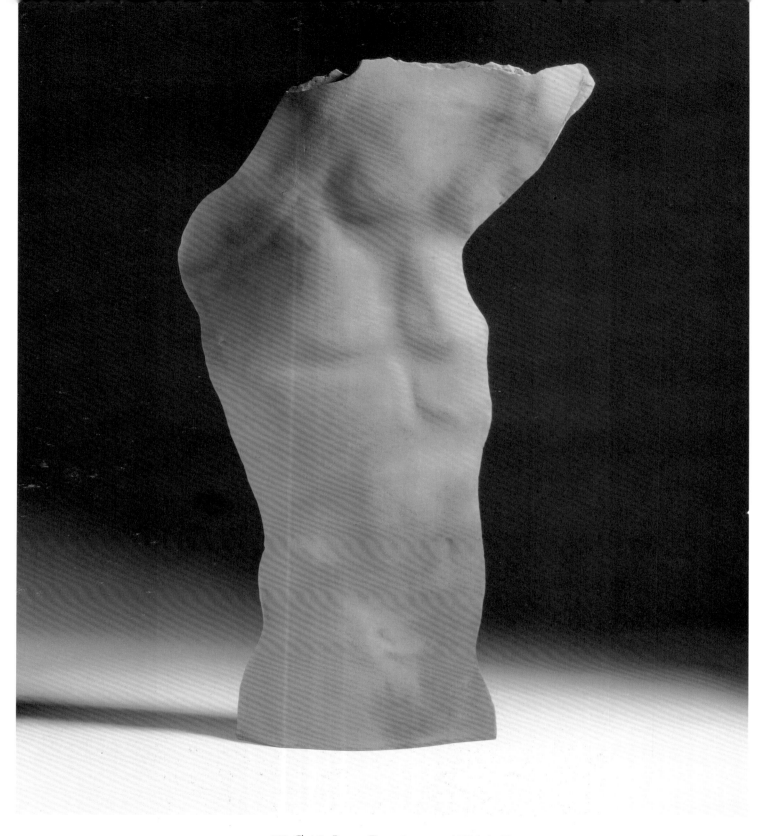

PL. 109 Christie Brown, *Torso,* stoneware, 1988 (cat. 62)

PL. 110 *Right* Mo Jupp, figure, low-fired porcelain, 1987–88 (cat. 294)

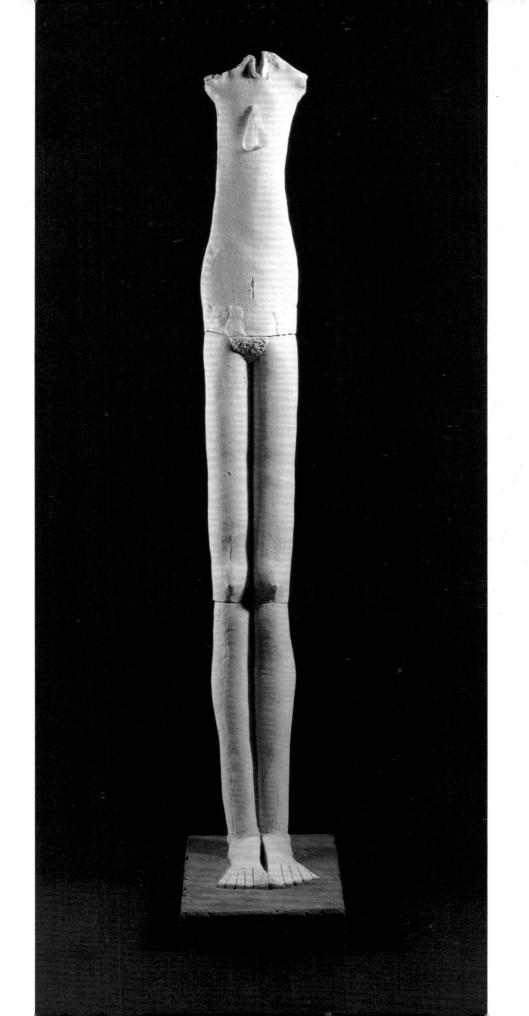

133

PL. 111 Richard Batterham, bowl, stoneware, 1984 (cat. 33)

PL. 112 *Right* John Leach, cider jar, stoneware, 1981 (cat. 385)

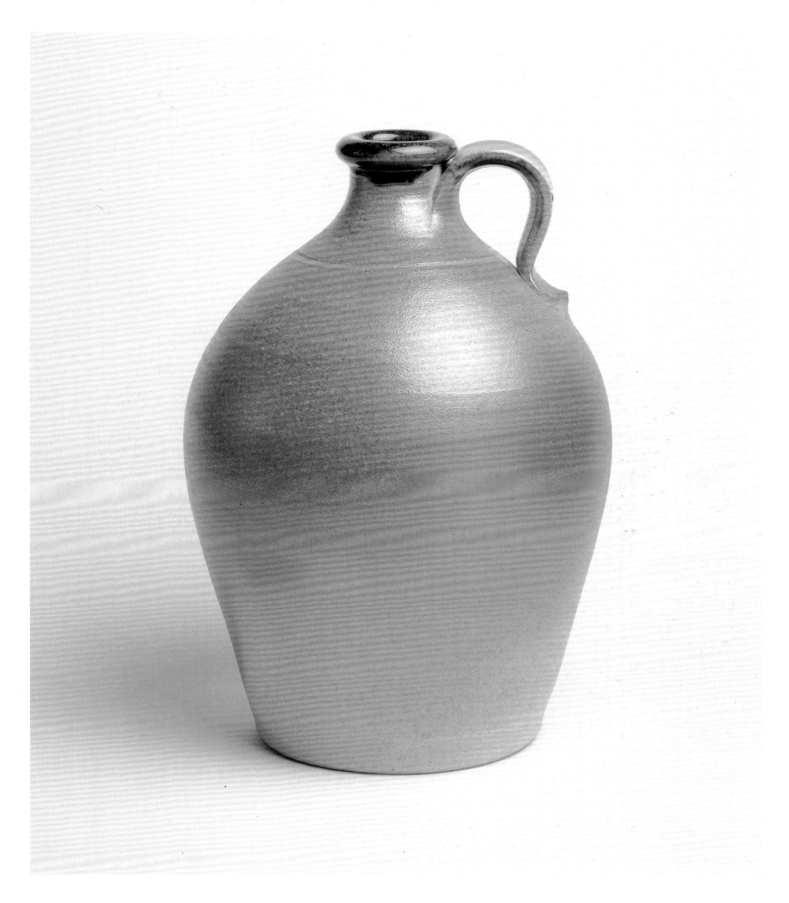

PL. 113 *Left* Mike Dodd, vase, stoneware, 1989 (cat. 179)

PL. 114 Sarah Walton, tea caddy, stoneware, 1981 (cat. 660)

PL. 115 *Left* David Frith, dish, stoneware, 1982 (cat. 213)

PL. 116 Clive Bowen, dish, earthenware, 1982 (cat. 47)

PL. 117 *Left* Peter Smith, dish and jug, earthenware, 1981 (cat. 575–576)

PL. 118 Walter Keeler, dish, stoneware, 1982 (cat. 301)

PL. 119 Walter Keeler, two teapots, stoneware, 1982–1984 (cat. 302–303)

PL. 120 *Right* Janice Tchalenko, bowl, stoneware, 1983 (cat. 623)

PL. 121 William Newland, four bottles, earthenware, 1958–1959 (cat. 453)

The Catalogue

This catalogue is ordered alphabetically by name of potter, with the exception of the work a small group of fine-artists which is placed, again alphabetically, at the end of the main sequence. The entries follow a standard format. A brief biography is given in tabulated form (unless too few datable facts are known) followed by brief comment. Exhibition history is not given, apart from major or key shows included in the biographies. The bibliography for each potter consists first of work written by the potter, if such exists, followed by work written about the potter. Abbreviated references are to works where more than one potter is discussed, and these titles may be found in full in the general bibliography at the end of the book.

The catalogue entries for the pots follow the sequence of the illustrations and are almost invariably in chronological order, though for some group shots this was not possible and the chronology is disrupted. The entry gives a simple technical description, a description of the mark (illustration of a typical mark by most potters is to be found at the end of the book), the size (including handles and spouts), the Museum accession number (which gives the year of acquisition), the source from which the pot was obtained and the price.

Abbreviations:

BCC	British Contemporary Crafts (CAA after 1987)
BIIA	British Institute of Industrial Art
CAA	Contemporary Applied Art (BCC before 1987)
CAS	Contemporary Art Society
CC	Crafts Council
CPA	Craftsmen Potters Association
CR	Ceramic Review
PQ	Pottery Quarterly
V&A	Victoria and Albert Museum

Arbeid, Dan 1928–

1942–55	works as a tailor
1955	travels to Israel, works on a kibbutz
1956–57	works in ceramics factory at Beersheba
1957	returns to England, appointed technical assistant at the Central School of Art, London; sets up studio in New Barnet, Herts
1959	solo show, Primavera, London
1963–83	new studio at Wendens Ambo, Essex
1966–	lecturer at Central School of Art, London
1970–	senior lecturer, time increasingly taken by teaching rather than making
1983–	studio in Brighton, Sussex
1988	retires

Dan Arbeid is an important post-war pioneer in exploring handbuilding and surface-textures in a style strongly opposed to the oriental-style wheel-thrown orthodoxy of the Leach or Staite Murray schools. In the 1960s he was regarded as working on the extremes of pottery making. He shows an imaginative and inventive approach to form, a willingness to experiment and a delight in extremes of texture. It is a shame that his considerable talent was not developed in later years, perhaps hindered by teaching commitments.

Birks (1967), (1976)
PQ, 8/29, 1963–64, p.33
Crafts, May/June, 1982, illustration p. 56

1 Vase, 1959 (pl. 61)
Stoneware, coil built, unglazed exterior, grey glazed interior; marks: 'Arbeid', painted; h. 21.4 cm, d. 21 cm
Circ.157–1959. Source: Primavera, London, £8.40
Arbeid commented of this piece (Birks 1976): 'I remember it looked beautiful with cornflowers in it, but I wish I had it back now to alter that terrible rim'.

2 Bottle, 1961
Stoneware, pale grey glaze; marks: 'Arbeid', painted; h. 42 cm, d. 7.2 cm
Circ.297–1961. Source: Bristol Guild of Applied Art, £10.50

3 Pot, 1968
Stoneware, coil built, with thick pitted grey-green ash glaze; h. 38.4 cm, d. 38.5 cm
Circ.837–1968. Source: the potter, £45

4 Pot, 1968
Stoneware, coil built, with thick pitted grey-green ash glaze; marks: 'DA', impressed; h. 33.9 cm, d. 19.5 cm
Circ.836–1968. Source: the potter, £25

5 Bowl, 1968
Stoneware, coil built, with thick pitted grey glaze; marks: 'DA', impressed; h. 10 cm, d. 23.6 cm
Circ.838–1968. Source: the potter, £15

3

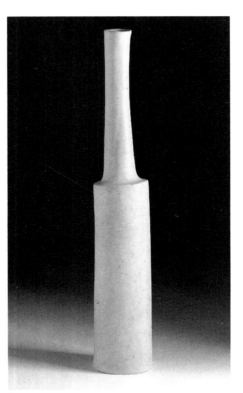

2

5 4

6 Pin pot, 1968 (pl. 69)
Stoneware, handbuilt, with thick pitted grey glaze;
marks: 'DA', impressed; h. 35.2 cm, d. 8.5 cm
Circ.839–1968. Source: the potter, £15
The pin pot is so called because it is initially formed
round a rolling-pin.

7 Pin pot, 1968 (pl. 69)
Stoneware, handbuilt, with thick pitted grey glaze;
marks: 'DA' in a circular monogram, impressed;
h. 32.4 cm, d. 7.4 cm
Circ.840–1968. Source: the potter, £12

8 Pin pot, 1968 (pl. 69)
Stoneware, handbuilt, with thick pitted grey glaze;
marks: 'DA', impressed; h. 33.3 cm, d. 8.2 cm
Circ.841–1968. Source: the potter, £12

9 Pin pot, 1968 (pl. 69)
Stoneware, handbuilt, with thick pitted grey glaze;
marks: 'DA', impressed; h. 25.6 cm, d. 8.5 cm
Circ.842–1968. Source: the potter, £10

Auld, Ian 1926–

1947–48 Brighton College of Art
1948–51 Slade School of Art, London, studying
painting and print-making
1951–52 teacher training at Institute of Education,
University of London, studies pottery with
William Newland (qv); spends six months at
Odney Pottery with John Bew (qv) in
Berkshire
1952–54 technical assistant at the Central School of
Art, London
1954–57 three years teaching in Baghdad, Iraq, much
travel in the Middle East
1957– returns to England, teaching at the Central
and Camberwell Schools of Art
1957–66 studio at Saffron Walden, Essex
1959 first exhibition, at Primavera, London
1965 appointed senior lecturer at Bath Academy
of Art in succession to James Tower (qv);
later moved to Bristol Polytechnic
1966–74 shares studio with his wife Gillian Lowndes
(qv) at Chippenham, Wilts
1970–72 Research Fellow at Ife University, Nigeria,
with Gillian Lowndes
1974–85 Head of Ceramics at Camberwell School,
teaching takes over from making
1979 last major show, at BCC, London

Ian Auld's earliest work, like that of William Newland
(qv) and others from the Institute of Education group,
is in earthenware with tin glazes and a prime interest
in surface decoration. After his return from the Middle
East he started to work in stoneware; his pots become
concerned with form – mostly simple press-moulded
or slab built rectangular shapes with dry glazes and
more restrained, integrated decoration. African
sculpture and decoration, and Roman glass are
important influences. Since the 1970s, Auld has had a
shop dealing in African art in Camden Passage Market,
Islington, London.

PQ, 7/27, 1961–2 (illustrations pp. 10–11)
Birks (1967), (1976)
Rose (1970; pl. 80)
Sue Harley, 'Ian Auld and Gillian Lowndes', *CR*, 44/1977
Rosemary Hill, 'Dealer in African Art: Ian Auld discusses
his Passion', *Crafts*, January/February, 1988

10 Vase, 1959
Stoneware, slab built, with raised ornament under
a yellow-brown glaze; marks: 'IA' in square
monogram, impressed; h. 41.8 cm, d. 12.5 cm
Circ.240–1960. Source: the potter, £8

11 Vase, 1965 (pl. 70)
Stoneware, slab built, with matt yellow-brown
glaze; marks: 'IA' in rectangular seal, impressed;
h. 33.9 cm, d. 22 cm
Circ.351–1965. Source: The Craft Centre of Great
Britain, £12.60

Baldwin, Gordon 1932–

1932 born in Lincoln
1949 Lincoln Art School
1950–54 studies ceramics at Central School of Art,
London, under Dora Billington (qv), first as
student, then technical assistant
1955 part-time teaching at Goldsmith's, London
1956 visiting lecturer at Central School of Art
1957– full-time teaching at Eton College; associate
lecturer, Camberwell School of Art
1983 *Gordon Baldwin, a Retrospective View*,
retrospective touring exhibition, organised
by Cleveland County Museum,
Middlesborough
1989 solo exhibition at the BCC, London

Baldwin's work has developed, in the opposite direction
to that of potters such as Poncelet (qv) or Barry (qv),
from 'pure' sculpture into an integrated 'sculptural-
pottery'. Starting as a sculptor, he has become a potter,
albeit a 'fine-art' potter. He has become progressively
more interested in the vessel as a form and a concept,
and in the crucial relationships between form and surface
and between form and decoration. As influences
Baldwin lists, amongst other things, surrealist art and
contemporary music, especially John Cage. He works
in series, and each piece may be subjected to repeated
firings with added layers of slip and decoration.

Gordon Baldwin, 'Sculptors in Limbo?', *Crafts*,
July/August, 1978
Charles S. Spencer, 'The Experimental Work of Gordon
Baldwin', *The Painter and Sculptor*, 2/3, Autumn, 1959
Birks (1967), (1976)
Exhibition reviews, *CR*, 2/1970; 6/1970; 22/1973
David Reeves, 'Gordon Baldwin/Peter Simpson',
exhibition review, *Crafts*, July/August, 1974
London, CC (1974)
Jeannie Lowe, 'Gordon Baldwin', *CR*, 31/1975
London, VAM (1977)
Tony Birks, 'Upstart Forms', *Crafts*, July/August, 1981
Gordon Baldwin, a Retrospective View, Cleveland County
Museum Service, 1983 (detailed illustrated catalogue)
Tanya Harrod, 'Sources of Inspiration', *Crafts*,
January/February, 1989
Gordon Baldwin, CAA exhibition pamphlet by Alison
Britton, London, 1989

12 *Reptilian Black*, 1969–1970
Earthenware, handbuilt, with a black shiny glaze;
marks: 'GB 69', incised; h. 33.5 cm, d. 48.8 cm
Circ.461–1970. Source: Crafts Centre of Great
Britain (solo exhibition *Objects from an Inscape*),
£24.75

10

12

13 Sculpture: *Seascape*, 1969 (pl. 15)
Earthenware, handbuilt, with a black shiny glaze;
h. (standing form) 64.3 cm, l. (laying form) 60.3 cm
Circ.466&a–1970. Source: given by the potter

14 Bowl on a base, 1974
Porcelain, thrown, turned and assembled, blue
colouring in a white matt glaze; marks: 'GB 74',
painted; h. 19.8 cm, d. 19 cm
Circ.486–1974. Source: BCC, London (exhibition
with Peter Simpson, 1974), £22.50

15 *Painting in the Form of a Dish*, 1976 (pl. 82)
Stoneware, press-moulded, pink, blue, yellow and
green painting in a white glaze; marks: 'GB 76',
painted; h. 9.7 cm, d. 46.5 cm
Circ.530–1976. Source: the potter, £25

16 Extended dish: *Seferis Series No. 1*, 1980
Earthenware, white glaze with incised and painted
decoration; marks: 'GB 80', painted; h. 35.9 cm,
d. 40.7 cm
C.25–1980. Source: CPA, £250
From a series of pieces inspired by a poem of the
Greek poet George Seferis about boats on the Nile.

17 Pot: *Avis II No. 4*, 1984 (pl. 105)
Stoneware, hand built, with mottled blue matt
surface; marks: 'GB 3/84', incised; h. 58.8 cm,
d. 53.8 cm
C.155–1984. Source: BCC, £862

18 *Vessel from an Inscape*, 1988–1989
Stoneware, coiled, black glaze inside with green
patches outside; marks: 'GB 88', incised; h. 58.4 cm,
d. 48.4 cm
C.40–1989. Source: CAA, London, £1620

Ballantyne, David 1913–1990

1913	born in London
1919	family moves to Liverpool
1932–35	studies painting at Liverpool School of Art
1936	teacher training at the University of London, attends classes in ceramics at Central School of Art with Dora Billington (qv)
1946–51	teaching at a boys school, Bridgnorth, West Midlands
1951–78	teaching at Bournemouth School of Art, retires as senior lecturer in Ceramics and Environmental Design
c.1955–67	workshop at home, produces standard ware and individual work in saltglaze
1968–	moves house and workshop, abandons saltglaze; produces wider range of stoneware and porcelain

From the late 1960s Ballantyne became increasingly
interested in environmental ceramics, eventually
ceasing to make standard ware and turning his attention
to a wide range of things from door furniture,
architectural lettering and ceramic calligraphy and
replicas of architectural elements for the restoration of
historic buildings to wine-tasting spitoons for châteaux
in the Médoc, France. His interest in environmental
design led him to the use of other materials such
as concrete and wood.

David Ballantyne, 'Some Techniques Associated with
Handbuilt Pottery', *PQ*, 2/1955
– 'The anatomy of Kick-Wheels', *PQ*, 4/1957

14

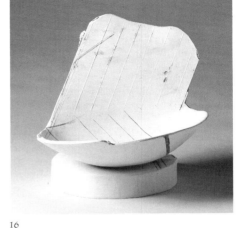

16

18

—'Decorative Ventilator Bricks', *CR*, 82/1983
'David Ballantyne', exhibition review, *Crafts*,
  January/February, 1975, p. 50
London, CC (1981; p. 80)
Richard Grasby, 'Retrospect and Prospect', exhibition
  review, *Newsletter of the Dorset Craft Guild*,
  January/February, 1989, pp. 12–13

19 Vase: *Meteorite*, 1962
  Saltglazed stoneware, oval section, with non-
  vitreous black and brown slip; h. 58 cm, d. 17.4 cm
  Circ.487–1962. Source: the potter, £21

20 Pot-pourri jar and lid: *Seabird*, 1962
  Stoneware, saltglaze; h. 12.5 cm, d. 12.2 cm
  Circ.488&a–1962. Source: *see* Circ.487–1962,
  £3.50

19

20

Barrett-Danes, Ruth and Alan

Alan: 1935–
Ruth (née Long): 1940–

Alan:
1951–55 Medway College of Design
1955–57 design course at Stoke College of Art, before
         working in the Design Department of the
         Paragon Bone China Company
1962–68 workshop in Slough, Berks
1963–70 part-time teaching at Stoke College of Art

Ruth:
1956–61 Plymouth and Brighton Colleges of Art
1961–68 various teaching posts and design work
1968   together they set up a workshop near Cardiff
1970   Alan breaks with industry; appointed lecturer
         at Cardiff College of Art, Wales
1974   they move to new workshop in
         Abergavenny, Wales
1982   Ruth sets up a workshop to work on her own;
         Alan reverts to wheel-made tableware and
         individual work

Alan Barrett-Danes comes from a long line of country
potters responsible for the Hoo Pottery, Upchurch
Pottery and Rainham Pottery. Initially Ruth and Alan
worked together making the figurative models, but
from 1982 Ruth has continued modelling alone, while
Alan has returned to making domestic and one-off
wheel-thrown ware.
  The small-scale figural modelling, usually of animals,
is far from the twee elf-and-pixie souvenir-shop world
that the subject matter may at first suggest. An initial
fascination with mushrooms and their decay led on to
study of toads and snails, to cabbage sculptures, then
to fantastic human and animal metamorphoses, or
furniture absorbing the people sitting on them. The
work, initially charming, has on closer inspection an
unsettling vision, with fantastic, almost sinister,
nightmarish qualities.

Birks (1976)
Tony Birks, 'Alan Barrett-Danes – Narrative Potter',
  CR, 36/1975
Cameron and Lewis (1976)
Craig Raine, 'Ruth and Alan Barrett-Danes: Ceramic
  Sculptures', exhibition review, *Crafts*,
  January/February, 1978
'Ruth and Alan Barrett-Danes: Ceramic Sculptures',
  exhibition review, *Crafts*, January/February, 1978
Malcolm Cook, 'Ruth Barrett-Danes – Ambiguities of
  Identity', *CR*, 113/1988

21 *Frog-pot*, 1980
  Porcelain, modelled, with matt glaze, with painting
  in pale brown; h. 9 cm, d. 10.5 cm
  C.24&a–1980. Source: CPA, £140
  Made in partnership by Alan and Ruth Barrett-
  Danes. One of a series of frogs grappling with
  spheres.

22 Figure of sheep and frogs: *Sacrificial Sheep*, 1988 (pl.
  107)
  Porcelain, coiled and modelled, body stains with
  terra sigillata and vitreous slip; marks: 'RBD',
  incised; h. 16.2 cm, d. 19.1 cm
  C.14–1989. Source: CAA, London, £624
  Made by Ruth Barrett-Danes alone.

Barron, Paul 1917–1983

1937–39 Brighton School of Art under Norah Braden
         (qv)
1940–46 National Service during the war
1946–49 Royal College of Art, under Helen Pincombe
         (qv)
1949–54 studio at Runnick House, Hants
1954–83 studio in Bentley, Hants, shared with Henry
         Hammond (qv)
1949–82 teaching at Farnham College of Art with
         Henry Hammond

Paul Barron, a colleague and friend of Henry Hammond
(qv) over many years, is most remembered for his role
as a teacher at West Surrey College of Art and Design,
Farnham.

Paul Barron, 'A Glaze Spectrum', *PQ*, 10/38,1971–73,
  p.45
—'Glazes', *CR*, 20 & 21/1973
Wingfield Digby (1952, p. 82)
Rose (1955), (1970)
Henry Hammond, 'Paul Barron 1917–1983, Obituary',
  CR, 85/1984

23 Jug, 1949–1950
  Earthenware, 'wiped' decoration in white and dark
  slips; marks: 'B', in a square, impressed; h. 31.7 cm,
  d. 20.4 cm
  Circ.277–1950. Source: Arts and Crafts Society
  (exhibition in V&A, 1950), £3.67

21

24 23

24 Jug, 1949–1950
Earthenware, 'wiped' decoration in dark over light slip under an amber glaze; marks: 'B', in a square, impressed; h. 28 cm, d. 15.3 cm
Circ.276–1950. Source: *see* Circ.277–1950, £2.62

25 Pot, *c.*1965
Stoneware, incised decoration through a dark slip under a bluish glaze; h. 28 cm, d. 28 cm
C.37–1989. Source: bequest of Kathleen Stickland

Barry, Val (now working as Valerie Fox) 1937–

1937 born in Barnsley, Yorkshire
1967–70 office work and nursing followed by training at Sir John Cass School of Art, London and evening classes at the Royal College of Art
1969– studio in North London
1969–72 teaching in the Pottery Department, South Lambeth Institute, London
1975 Gold medal, Faenza International Ceramics Competition
mid-1980s abandons clay to work as a sculptor in metal

Barry's work takes its main influence from the orient – at first from ceramics, but later from objects such as jade and bronzes, or the shapes of the sails of Chinese junks. In the mid-1980s Val Barry abandoned clay and took to bronze, making sculptures which follow her same interests in form, but in new materials and on a larger scale.

Exhibition review, *CR*, 13/1972
'CPA New Members', *CR*, 31/1975
Emmanuel Cooper, 'The Pots of Val Barry', *CR*, 57/1979
Jon Catleugh, 'Ceramic Sculptured Forms by Val Barry', exhibition review, *Crafts*, July/August, 1979
Feeling Through Form, exhibition catalogue, Windhorse Trust, Barbican Centre, 1986 (illustrating her work as a sculptor)

26 *Sword Form*, 1981
Porcelain, slab built; marks: 'VaB', impressed; h. 23 cm, d. 14.8 cm
C.44–1981. Source: CPA, £115.20

27 *Abstract Form*, 1981
Stoneware, slab built; marks: 'VaB', impressed; h. 35.2 cm, d. 25.1 cm
C.45–1981. Source: CPA, £212.50

Barton, Glenys 1944–

1944 born in Stoke-on-Trent
1968–71 Royal College of Art, London
1971–75 shares a studio with Jacqui Poncelet
1975–84 new studio in Wandsworth, London
1976 artist in residence at Wedgwood & Co., Staffordshire
1977 *Glenys Barton at Wedgwood*, Crafts Council exhibition, London
1977– teaching at Camberwell School of Art
1984– new studio at Burnham-on-Crouch, Essex

Glenys Barton is associated with the group of women who emerged from the RCA in the 1970s and who form the core of the 'new ceramics' group – Fritsch, Crowley, Britton, Poncelet and McNicoll. Barton is the most purely sculptural of them, though while a student at the Royal College of Art she won an award for a range of stacking tableware that was retailed through

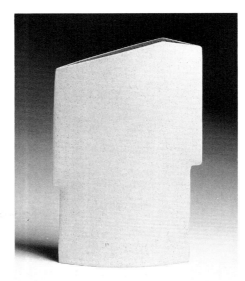

26

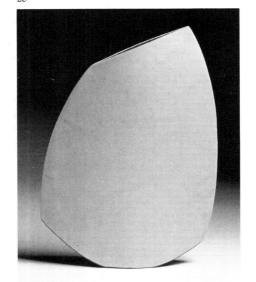

27

Habitat. Her early work consisted of cubes and pyramids of bone china with screen printed geometric decoration in bright colours. Later came sculptures with small figures set on plaques of bone china, or large cast heads, again with screen printed decoration. These were followed by work, still in bone china, but raku fired to add colour and random effect. She was one of the first potters to be represented by a fine-art gallery alone.

Glenys Barton, 'A Search for Order', *CR*, 34/1975
F. Adamceski, 'Outside Tradition', *Crafts*, May/June, 1973
Belfast (1974)
London, CC (1974)
E. Fritsch, 'Glenys Barton', review, *Crafts*, January/February, 1975
Glenys Barton at Wedgwood, London, CC (1977)
'Outstanding Teamwork in Design and Craftsmanship', *Wedgwood Review*, Summer, 1977
'Glenys Barton at Wedgwood', review, *Crafts*, July/August, 1977
'Sculptors in Limbo', *Crafts*, July/August, 1978
London, Christopher Wood Gallery (1980)
'Glenys Barton', *CR*, 69/1981
Emmanuel Cooper, 'Glenys Barton – Sculptures and Reliefs', *CR*, 85/1984
'Glenys Barton – Heads', *CR*, 102/1986

28 Twelve cubes, 1971
Bone china, slip-cast, with silk-screened decoration; each 5.3 cm square
Circ.277 to 279–1973. Source: the potter, London, £40
These cubes, which were made in sets of four, were exhibited in the International Ceramics exhibition in 1972 at the V&A where they were awarded a Diploma of Merit by the International Jury. They are cast in bone china and are ground to the required degree of accuracy after the biscuit firing.

25

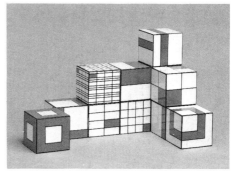

28

29 Figure group: *Monte Alban II*, 1977 (pl. 89)
Bone china, made from cast elements; marks:
'WEDGWOOD/Made in England/MONTE
ALBAN II/Glenys Barton', printed; h. 33.4 cm,
d. 43.5 cm
C.115–1979. Source: given by J. Wedgwood & Sons

30 Plaque: *Fragments of Him*, 1981
Bone china, cast, with raku-fired glaze; marks:
'Glenys Barton 1981', incised; h. 22.8 cm, w. 31.5
cm, d. 3.5 cm
C.79–1981. Source: Angela Flowers Gallery,
London, £200

Batterham, Richard 1936–

1949–54	introduced to pottery by Donald Potter while at school at Bryanston
1957–58	two-year apprenticeship at the Leach Pottery, St Ives
1959	establishes own pottery at Durweston, near Blanford, Dorset
1966–67	builds new pottery and larger four-chambered oil and wood-fired climbing kiln, fired about five times a year
1972	solo exhibition at the BCC
1978	builds small saltglaze kiln
1984	solo exhibition at the BCC

Richard Batterham is the most gifted and dedicated of the domestic potters following in the tradition of Bernard Leach. He has slowly developed over the years a limited range of shapes and glazes; his work is the most satisfying of its kind for its easy and natural forms and generous glazes. His pots are for use though the monumental scale of some pieces tends to the sculptural. Only a few of his early works are marked with 'RB' in an oval.

R. Batterham, 'Richard Batterham', *Crafts*, November/December, 1981

Rose (1955), (1970; pls. 76–77)
PQ, 7/1961–2 (illustrations of standard ware, p. 138, pls. 8–9)
Casson (1967)
Tarby Davenport, 'Prolific Potter', *Design*, August, 1968
F. Adamczewski, 'Richard Batterham – a Potter's Potter', *CR*, 17/1972
London, Christopher Wood Gallery (1980)
Richard Batterham, BCC exhibition pamphlet, 1984
Tony Birks, 'Richard Batterham', *Revue de la Céramique et du Verre*, January, 1985
Ceramic Series, no. 28, Aberystwyth Arts Centre, 1989
Reviews: *Crafts*, March/April, 1977; *Crafts*, January/February, 1979; *CR*, 6/1970, 17/1972, 60/1979; *PQ*, 8/32, 1963–64

31 Bottle-vase, 1981
Stoneware, green glaze with incised decoration;
h. 62 cm, d. 27.5 cm
C.46–1981. Source: V&A Craft Shop, £162

32 Teapot, 1984
Stoneware, celadon ash glaze; h. 23.6 cm,
d. 37.1 cm
C.45–1985. Source: BCC (solo exhibition, 1984),
£112

30

32

31

33 Bowl, 1984 (pl. 111)
Stoneware, poplar-ash celadon glaze inside, dark
iron glaze outside; h. 22.2 cm, d. 37.5 cm
C.46–1985. Source: BCC (solo exhibition, 1984),
£350

34 Dish, 1984
Porcelain, incised decoration under a pale green
glaze; h. 7.6 cm, d. 29.5 cm
C.47–1985. Source: BCC (solo exhibition, 1984),
£112

35 Teapot and cover, 1988 (pl. 11)
Stoneware, saltglazed; h. 12.2 cm, d. 19.5 cm
C.28&a–1989. Source: V&A Craft Shop, £50.60

36 Jug, 1988 (pl. 11)
Stoneware, brown glaze outside, green ash glaze
inside and lip; h. 18.4 cm, d. 15.2 cm
C.29–1989. Source: see C.28–1989, £18.65

37 Bowl, 1988 (pl. 11)
Stoneware, brown glaze outside, green ash glaze
inside and incised decoration; h. 8 cm, d. 16.2 cm
C.30–1989. Source: see C.28–1989, £46

38 Supper dish, 1988 (pl. 11)
Stoneware, green ash glaze and incised decoration;
h. 5 cm, d. 23 cm
C.31–1989. Source: see C.28–1989, £23

Bayer, Svend 1946–

1946   born in Uganda of Danish parents, lives in
Africa until the age of 16 when comes to
England
1965–68   studies Geography and Economics at Exeter
University
1969   starts working with Michael Cardew (qv) at
Wenford Bridge
1972–73   leaves Wenford Bridge, works at Brannam's
Pottery in North Devon as a thrower
1973   travels in Far East and South East Asia
1974–75   sets up workshop in USA
1975–   workshop in Sheepwash, Devon

Bayer is regarded by many as the best of Cardew's
students. He makes a range of strong domestic ware,
large bowls with boldly painted decoration, often birds
in a Cardew-esque manner, and is particularly known
for enormous garden pots.

Svend Bayer, 'Garden and Kitchen Pots', *Crafts*,
January/February, 1983
Cameron and Lewis (1976)
York City Art Gallery (1983)

39 Covered jar, 1988
Stoneware, ash flashings outside, speckled pale
brown glaze interior and lid; h. 27.3 cm, d. 27.5 cm
C.20&a–1989. Source: David Mellor, Kitchen
Shop, London, £30.48

Bergen, Henry
see Catalogue no. 352, under Leach Pottery
Standard Ware

Bergne, Suzanne 1939–

1939   born Upper Silesia, Germany
1958–63   Vienna University
1963   marries a British diplomat
1964–77   residence in various Middle Eastern countries
1971–72   studies at Gulbenkian College for Women,
Beirut
1972–75   works at Fisher Pottery, Abu Dhabi
1975–77   own workshop in Cairo
1977–80   studies ceramics at Croyden College of Art
1980–85   works in Athens
1984–88   workshop in London
1985–87   works in Hong Kong
1988–   workshop in Upper Slaughter,
Gloucestershire

Suzanne Bergne, 'Colour and Light', *CR*, 86/1984
Jane Norrie, exhibition review, *Arts Review*, 21/10/1988

40 Dish, 1984
Porcelain, poured green and blue glazes with
silkscreen enamel decoration; marks: 'SB' in
monogram, impressed; made in Athens; h. 9.1 cm,
d. 28.8 cm
C.107–1986. Source: the potter, £160

41 Footed dish, 1986
Porcelain, poured blue glaze; marks: 'SB' in
monogram, impressed; made in Hong Kong;
h. 12.2 cm, d. 20.6 cm
C.108–1986. Source: the potter, £75

34

39

40 41

42

43

Bew, John 1897–1954
(Odney Pottery)

*c.*1922   studies ceramics at Camberwell School of Art under Hopkins (qv)

1930–36   workshop in Farleigh, Surrey; works in porcelain with an interest in coloured glazes

1936   moves to a Quaker settlement in the Rhondda Valley, Wales, set up to help unemployment in the depression; establishes a pottery which employs local workers

1942   invited by the John Lewis Partnership to establish a pottery at Odney, Cookham, Berks, to undertake training of disabled people; after conversion of a derelict farm, 6 potters are taken on; A. F. Spindler (qv) works with him

1948   Odney Pottery granted a Government licence to produce domestic pottery

1954   November, Bew dies; Odney Pottery continues for one further year

John Bew, 'Slip Methods at Odney', *PQ*, 1/1, 1954
—Letter in *PQ*, 1/2, 1954
Cooper (1947; pls. 34–5)
Obituary, *PQ*, 5/1955
Godden (1964)

For the 'standard' work of the Odney Pottery *see* under A. F. Spindler

42 Vase, *c.* 1950
Earthenware, dark splash under an amber glaze; marks: 'J' painted, 'ODNEY' impressed; made at Odney Pottery, Cookham; h. 23.3 cm, d. 17.7 cm
Circ.335–1955. Source: bequest of the potter

Billington, Dora 1890–1968

1890   born in Stoke-on-Trent; studies in Hanley School of Art and works as a decorator for Bernard Moore

1915   takes over teaching at Royal College of Art, London, from Richard Lunn, father of Dora Lunn (qv), after his death, while she is a student there

1916   takes diploma at Royal College of Art, continues to teach

1924–*c.*55   takes over pottery classes at the Central School of Art, London, eventually becomes Head of Department

1925   on appointment of new Principal, William Rothenstein, ceases teaching at Royal College of Art where she is succeeded by Staite Murray (qv); continues to teach at the Central School of Art

mid-1950s   retires, ceases to pot

Dora Billington was born in the Potteries and had a continuous connection with industry for which she worked as a designer. She played an important part in the history of studio pottery, though, as she was more a teacher than a maker, she is now rather forgotten. At the Central School of Art, before the war, she gave technical instruction to Staite Murray's pupils who could not get much from him; in the 1950s she encouraged handbuilding, tin-glaze and colourful painted decoration and supported potters such as Newland (qv), Hine (qv), Tower (qv) and Sykes (qv) in opposition to the oriental stoneware aesthetic of Leach and Staite Murray.

Billington *The Art of the Potter*, London, 1937
— (1953), (1955)
—*The Technique of Pottery*, London, 1962
Farleigh (1950; chapter 12)
Wingfield Digby (1952; p. 80, pl. 53)
Rose (1955), (1970)
G. Harding-Green, 'Dora Billington, 1890–1968', obituary, *PQ*, 9/35, 1969
Aileen Dawson, *Bernard Moore Master Potter 1850–1935*, Richard Dennis, London, 1982

The Museum possesses a number of factory-made pieces designed or decorated by Dora Billington: wares by J. and G. Meakin of 1927 and 1937 (C.503 to 505–1934 and Circ.341 to 345–1954) and a 'rouge flambé' vase by Bernard Moore of 1905 (C.177–1984).

43 Panel of six tiles, *c.*1937
Earthenware, painting in brown and blue in a pinkish grey glaze; h. 38 cm, d. 25.4 cm
C.19–1946. Source: given by the potter

44 Coffee pot and cover, *c.*1950
Stoneware, tenmoku glaze; marks: 'DB' in monogram, impressed; h. 23.2 cm, d. 13.8 cm
Circ.434&a–1950. Source: Arts and Crafts Society (exhibition in the V&A, 1950), £8.40 (for the whole set)
The Museum possesses a second identical coffee pot: Circ.435&a–1950.

45 Sugar basin, *c.*1950
Stoneware, tenmoku glaze; marks: 'DB' in monogram, impressed; h. 10.2 cm, d. 12.7 cm
Circ.436–1950. Source: *see* Circ.434–1950

46 Two coffee cups and saucers, *c.*1950
Stoneware, tenmoku glaze; marks: 'DB' in monogram, impressed; h. 7.9 cm, d. 13.5 cm
Circ.437&a/438&a–1950. Source: *see* Circ.434–1950

William Newland (qv) suggests that he may have made this coffee set to Billington's design when he trained with Billington in evening classes at the Central School of Art. She was by then 60 years old and she enlisted the help of talented students in making her own wares.

Bowen, Clive 1943–

1959–63   studies painting at Cardiff College of Art

1965–70   apprentice to Michael Leach (qv) at Yelland Pottery, then works as a production thrower at Brannam's Pottery, Barnstaple, Devon

1970   helps Cardew (qv) at Wenford Bridge at weekends; builds kiln in garden and experiments with slipware

1971–   pottery at Shebbear, N. Devon

Clive Bowen is the true inheritor of Cardew's role as the defender of old English slipware traditions. Using simple materials, techniques, forms and decoration, his work is full of confident energy – he has the expansive gesture that this ware demands, not the timid attention to detail that it often receives.

York City Art Gallery (1983)
Stephen Course, 'Clive Bowen – Slip Decorated Earthenware', *CR*, 91, 1985

46 44 46 45

47 Dish, 1982 (pl. 116)
Earthenware, slip trailed decoration in white on a dark ground; marks: 'CB' in a circle, impressed; h. 7.3 cm, d. 55 cm
C.68–1984. Source: given by the Friends of the V&A
Purchased at the CPA 25th Anniversary exhibition, *Studio Ceramics Today*, held at the V&A in 1983.

48 Jug, 1988
Earthenware, incised decoration with dark slip under an amber glaze; h. 28.2 cm, d. 18.9 cm
C.7–1989. Source: CAA, London, £54

Braden, Norah (D.K.N.) 1901–

1919–21	studies book illustration at Central School of Art, London
1921–25	diploma in painting at Royal College of Art, London
1925	joins Leach Pottery, St Ives, as a pupil
1928	joins Katharine Pleydell-Bouverie (qv) at Coleshill
1936–	leaves Coleshill, teaches at Brighton School of Art
1939–	virtually ceases to pot
post-war	some teaching at Brighton and Central Schools of Art

Norah Braden was considered by Bernard Leach to have the best eye of any of his pupils. His respect for her was in no small part due to the fact that she was not in awe of him, and was able to criticise him and his work. She is thought by many to have the greatest sensitivity to shape of any of Leach's followers.

Thorpe (1930)
Marsh (1943)
Cooper (1947)
Rose (1955), (1970)
Wingfield Digby (1952)
London, Hayward Gallery (1979)
see also under **Katharine Pleydell-Bouverie**

49 Bowl, c.1925
Stoneware, green-brown ash-glaze; marks: 'NB' and 'SI' in monogram, impressed; made at the Leach Pottery, St Ives; h. 5.3 cm, d. 9 cm
C.59–1973. Source: given by Dr Mildred Creak and Mrs Falchikov

50 Pot and cover, 1931
Stoneware, painting in brown in a grey-green glaze; marks: 'NB' in monogram, painted; made at Coleshill; h. 7.5 cm, d. 11 cm
Circ.765&a–1931. Source: the potter (shown at the Arts and Crafts Society, Burlington House, London), £0.75

51 Vase, c.1930 (pl. 31)
Stoneware, mottled green-brown glaze with painted decoration in green; marks: 'NB' in monogram painted; made at Coleshill; h. 17.5 cm, d. 15.6 cm
C.959–1935. Source: given by the CAS through Ernest Marsh. A paper label on the base gives the price £2/2/- (= £2.10).

52 Vase, c.1935 (pl. 31)
Stoneware, green-grey ash-glaze streaked with rust; marks: 'NB' in monogram, painted; made at Coleshill; h. 14.8 cm, d. 12.7 cm
C.960–1935. Source: given by the CAS

53 Covered jar, c. 1932
Stoneware, unglazed with brushed decoration in brown on a speckled body; marks: 'Made by N. Braden for Bendicks, Kensington', painted: made at Coleshill; h. 19.3 cm, d. 16.2 cm
C.247&a–1976. Source: Sotheby's Belgravia, £77
One of a set of about 12 commissioned by the London firm of chocolate manufacturers, Benedicks, as chocolate boxes.

54 Vase, 1935
Stoneware, unglazed, with ash-flashing and painting in brown; marks: 'NB' in monogram, impressed; made at Coleshill; h. 19.8 cm, d. 20 cm
Circ.333–1935. Source: The Little Gallery, London, £3.15

55 Vase, c.1935
Stoneware, dark ash-glaze with rust splashes; marks: 'NB' in monogram, painted; made at Coleshill; h. 20.4 cm, d. 19.3 cm
C.31–1943. Source: given by Ernest Marsh through the CAS

56 Bowl, 1938 (pl. 32)
Stoneware, ash-glazed with iron splashes; made at Coleshill; h. 14.8 cm, d. 23.4 cm
Circ.304–1938. Source: Arts and Crafts Society, Burlington House, £7.35

53

54

48

50 49

55

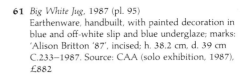

Britton, Alison 1948–

1948   born in Harrow, Middlesex
1966–67 foundation course at Leeds College of Art
1967–70 studies ceramics at Central School of Art, London; trains in traditional skills, including throwing; contemporaries Andrew Lord (qv) and Richard Slee (qv)
1970–73 Royal College of Art, London; turns to photography after getting stuck in pottery; eventually to tilework; tutor Hans Coper
1973–75 shares studio with Carol McNicoll (qv) in 401 1/2 workshops; works on tiles with commissions for bathrooms and a swimming pool; makes a few pots between commissions
1975–87 new workshop at Kings Cross, London, shared with Jacqui Poncelet (qv) until 1977
1979   solo exhibition at Crafts Council
1981   selector and writer for Crafts Council exhibition *The Maker's Eye*
1984–   part-time tutor in ceramics at the Royal College of Art
1985   solo exhibition at Miharudo Gallery, Tokyo, Japan
1986–   new studio in Hackney
1987   solo exhibition at CAA, London

Alison Britton is one of the 'RCA group' – women who emerged in the 1970s – along with Fritsch, Crowley, Poncelet, Barton and McNicoll (qv). Her early work has a strong decorative and narrative appeal. Over the last years she has become progressively more interested in form and her decoration has become abstract and bold. The initial appearance is of spontaneity; closer acquaintance reveals a deeply considered and deliberate approach both to form and decoration. This is confirmed by her manner of working – the painting is largely done on sheets of clay which are subsequently cut and constructed into vessels – not decorating a pot, but turning decoration into a pot. She does not produce functional work (her jugs are not intended for use other than, perhaps, as containers for flowers) but she holds to vestiges of functional form – the functional pot is the subject matter which she addresses; she has described her work as 'a still-life of a pot done in clay'.

Alison Britton is an articulate critic of the craft scene, and has produced much for various magazines and from 1984 has written with increasing frequency many of the CAA exhibition pamphlets.

Alison Britton, Selector for London, CC (1981)
—'Sèvres with Krazy Kat', *Crafts*, March/April, 1983
—'Hans Coper 1920–1981', *American Craft*, April/May, 1984
—'The Modern Pot', in London, ICA (1985)
—'Introduction' to Dormer (1986)
M. Coleman, 'Public and Private', *Crafts*, November/December, 1976
Fritsch, Liz, 'Juggling into Jugs', *Crafts*, November/December, 1979
J. Russel Taylor, 'Playing with Clay', *CR*, 60/1979
London, CC (1979)
Peter Dormer, *Alison Britton in Studio*, London, 1985
Alison Britton, exhibition pamphlet by Oliver Watson, CAA, London, (1987)
Angus Suttie, 'Alison Britton', *CR*, 107/1987

57 *Jug*, 1978 (pl. 90)
Earthenware, high fired, slab built with underglaze crayon and painted decoration; marks: 'Alison Britton 78', incised; h. 24.5 cm, d. 21.4 cm
C.99–1979. Source: the potter, £80

58 *Jug*, 1978 (pl. 90)
Earthenware, high fired, slab built with underglaze crayon and painted decoration; marks: 'Alison Britton 78', incised; h. 27.5 cm, d. 28.3 cm
C.100–1979. Source: the potter, £90

59 *Vase: Yellow triangle*, 1981 (pl. 94)
Earthenware, slab built with painted slip and underglaze decoration; marks: 'Alison Britton 1981', incised; h. 27.8 cm, d. 21.5 cm
C.87–1981. Source: Prescote Gallery, Banbury, Oxon (solo exhibition, 1981), £315

60 *Green Vessels Set*, 1983
Earthenware, slab built, painted decoration in green, brown, blue, yellow and white; marks: 'Alison Britton 83', incised (on both pieces); h. (of angular pot) 17.5 cm, d. (of dish) 37.6 cm
C.322&a–1983. Source: Aspects Gallery (exhibition *Pots and Tables*, with Floris Van de Broecke), London, £630

61 *Big White Jug*, 1987 (pl. 95)
Earthenware, handbuilt, with painted decoration in blue and off-white slip and blue underglaze; marks: 'Alison Britton '87', incised; h. 38.2 cm, d. 39 cm
C.233–1987. Source: CAA (solo exhibition, 1987), £882

Brown, Christie 1946–

1966–69 BA Degree at Manchester University
1970–75 television researcher for ITV
1975–77 freelance propmaker; toured with community theatre; begins life-drawing and pottery classes at Sir John Cass School of Art, London
1978–79 domestic ware thrower at Elephant Pottery, London
1979–80 sets up production pottery at Kingsgate Workshops, London, making domestic ware
1980–82 ceramics course at Harrow School of Art
1988   solo exhibition at Michaelson and Orient, London
1989   moves workshop to Hebden Bridge, Yorkshire

Christie Brown forms part of a new interest in figural sculptural ceramics that has grown during the 1980s: 'As a woman artist I am interested in women observing men and observing themselves. Often I use idealized portraits of the human figure, classical sculpture, the glossy magazine imagery, to explore the gap between fantasy and reality' (*Ceramics Monthly*).

'British Figurative Expression', *Ceramics Monthly*, June–August 1987

62 *Form: Torso*, 1988 (pl. 109)
Stoneware, handbuilt, from slabs and modelled, painted vitreous slip and smoked; marks: 'CB', incised; h. 77.4 cm, d. 46.3 cm
C.3–1989. Source: Michaelson and Orient, London, (solo exhibition, December 1988), £472.50

Brown, Paul 1921–

Paul Brown worked in Yorkshire from the mid-1950s, and later in Scotland and in France before returning to North Yorkshire. He is a potter who is committed to modern art and technology and to many if not all aspects of modern life, and is a man of outspoken opinions: '... I am happy ... to be living in this 20th century Western Society. I positively like plastics, fast cars and motorways, Brazilia and Chandigarh.... I am sure that one channel of a more complete education should be through work in new materials with new techniques (aluminium alloys, plastics, synthetic fibres and so on), but ... I also cherish the threatened values of quietness and privacy, contact with nature, working with natural materials ... and the preservation of those things which are the product of the passage of time ... or the loving hand of men long dead.... although I know that not everybody can live two miles off the roads as we do, or ... build their own dry walls or cut their own firewood from their own woods....' (*CPA Newsletter*, 10, September, 1962, p. 33).

Paul Brown, 'Towards a New Standard', *PQ*, 6/21, 1959 (with a reply from Bernard Leach)
Crafts Review, 6, 1960, p. 81 (illustration)
Michael Casson, 'Ceramics by Paul and Yvette Brown', exhibition review, *PQ*, 8/29, 1963

60

63 Vase: *Noctulid*, 1958 (pl. 56)
Earthenware, with white, yellow, blue and black
glazes; h. 54 cm, d. 13.8 cm
Circ.1–1959. Source: the potter, £18.90

Brown, Sandy 1946–

1968	to Japan, works teaching English and as a beauty consultant
1970–73	discovers pottery, works at Daisei kiln, Mashiko, Japan
1973	returns to England
1981	to Devon, South Molton, where she works with her husband Takeshi Yasuda (qv) whom she married in 1977

Sandy Brown is an exuberant potter whose dramatic
'gestural' decoration in startlingly fresh colours has
made a considerable impact on the British domestic
pottery scene.

Sandy Brown, 'Takeshi Yasuda: a Sensual Approach to
Clay', *CR*, 93/1985
—'A Potter in Japan', *CR*, 96/1985
—'A Theatre of Colour', *CR*, 99/1986
—'Sandy Brown: Bold, Wild and Dangerous', *CR*,
116/1989
Sandy Brown: the Complete Picture, exhibition catalogue,
Welsh Arts Council, Oriel 31 Welshpool, 1987
(reviews *Crafts*, November/ December, 1987, *Arts
Review*, July, 1987)
Tanya Fields, 'Leading Questions: Sandy Brown',
ArtsWest, June, 1987
Ceramic Series, no. 16, Aberystwyth Arts Centre
Hedley Potts, 'British Artist in residence at Gippsland
Institute', *Craft Arts* (*Australia*), September/
November, 1988

64 Platter, 1987
Stoneware, painted decoration and slip in blue,
brown and red; h. 2.9 cm, d. 47.9 cm
C.60–1988. Source: CAA, £242.10

Buck, Steve 1949–

1979–81	studies ceramics at Harrow School of Art
1981	first workshop in London
1982	moves to Kingsgate Workshops, London
1984	Crafts Council grant to visit galleries in the USA
1989	solo exhibition at Michaelson and Orient, London; awarded Unilever Prize, Portobello Arts Festival; 3-month scholarship to work in Japan

Steve Buck's work has changed over the last years from
small-scale finely worked sculptures in bright colours
and metallic finishes that look somewhat like models
for vast sci-fi alien creatures, to larger softer textured
sculptures with more organic allusions.

Tanya Harrod, 'Rococo Buck', *Crafts*, July/August, 1988

65 Sculpture, 1987
Earthenware, handbuilt, matt glazes and
underglaze colours in pale blue, pinks and oranges;
h. 39.6 cm, d. 33 cm
C.83–1987. Source: Anatol Orient, London, £360

64

65

Burnett, Deirdre 1939–

1939   born in Simla, India
1962–63   studies painting at St Martin's School of Art, London
1964–67   studies ceramics at Camberwell School of Art, London
1967   sets up her first workshop in East Dulwich, individual work at first supported by production of table ware

Burnett was known in the 1970s for her fine, finger-built bowls in porcelain which recalled fungus, pod and fossil forms. Murray Fieldhouse, a stalwart of Leachian 'traditional' work, commented in a review that her work would best be judged in the pages of *Studio International*, for it fell in the category of 'fine art'.

Exhibition review, *CR*, 13/1972
'CPA New Members', *CR*, 29/1974
Exhibition review, *Crafts*, September/October, 1976

66   Bowl, 1980
Porcelain, carved decoration with a matt glaze; marks: 'DB', in an applied seal; h. 7.9 cm, d. 11.9 cm
C.40–1981. Source: V&A Craft Shop, £153.70

66

Caiger-Smith, Alan 1930–

1930   born in Buenos Aires, Argentina
1947   studies painting and drawing at Camberwell School of Art, London
1949–52   reads history at King's College, Cambridge University
1954–55   evening classes in ceramics at Central School of Art, London, with Dora Billington (qv)
1955–   pottery at Aldermaston, Berkshire
1956–63   studio in Homer Street, London, run concurrently with that in Aldermaston
1958   solo exhibition at Heal's, London
1963   begins experiments with reduced lustre decoration
1973–78   Chairman of the British Crafts Centre
1985   retrospective touring exhibition, Stoke-on-Trent
1988   awarded MBE

The Aldermaston Pottery has been for many years the main centre of decorated production pottery. Caiger-Smith concentrates on tin-glazed wares with painted decoration in colours or reduced lustre. Some painted porcelain is also produced. Aldermaston is run as a production pottery where the potters, around 6 or 7 in number, all partake of all the tasks; time is also left for individual work. Caiger-Smith is a historian of his chosen area – tin glaze and lustre decoration – on which he has written extensively.

Alan Caiger-Smith, 'Notes on Tin-Glaze Earthenware', *PQ*, 9/35, 1969
—'Workshop/Aldermaston Pottery', *CR*, 5/1970
—*Tin-glaze Pottery in Europe and the Islamic World*, London, 1973
—*Three Books of the Potter's Art*, by Cipriano Picolpasso, with R. Lightbown, London, 1980
—'Why Decorate Pottery?', *Crafts*, September/October, 1981
—*Lustre Pottery*, London, 1985

—'A Potter's Day', *CR*, 118/1989
Casson (1967)
Exhibition review, *CR*, 25/1974
Belfast (1974)
Cameron and Lewis (1976)
Neal French, 'Lustre and Light', *CR*, 90/1984
Tin Glaze and Smoked Lustre . . . Pottery by Alan Caiger-Smith and Aldermaston Pottery, 1955–1985, exhibition catalogue, Stoke-on-Trent City Museum and Art Gallery, 1985 (detailed history, with full lists of marks, assistants, exhibitions and publications)

67   Bowl, 1959
Earthenware, tin-glaze with painted decoration in green and red; marks: 'ACS' in monogram, painted; made at Homer Street, London; h. 13 cm, d. 40.9 cm
Circ.59–1959. Source: the pottery, £7.35

68   Bowl, 1968 (pl. 67)
Earthenware, tin-glaze with painting blue and gold lustre decoration; marks: 'ACS' in monogram, painted; made at Aldermaston Pottery; h. 12.8 cm, d. 44.3 cm
Circ.592–1968. Source: Primavera, Cambridge, £18

69   Pot-pourri jar, 1968 (pl. 68)
Earthenware, tin-glaze with lustre decoration; marks: 'ACS' in monogram, painted; made at Aldermaston Pottery; h. 34 cm, d. 31.5 cm
Circ.820&a-1968. Source: the potter, £18

70   Onion form, 1968
Earthenware, tin-glaze with lustre decoration in golden-orange; made at Aldermaston Pottery; h. 25.8 cm, d. 21.2 cm
Circ.821–1968. Source: *see* Circ.820–1968, £10

67

70

71

71 Tea-pot, 1968
Earthenware, tin-glaze with painted decoration in blue and grey; marks: 'ACS' in monogram, painted; made at Aldermaston Pottery; h. 16.3 cm, d. 20.8 cm
Circ.822&a-1968. Source: *see* Circ.820–1968, £8

72 Pebble bottle, 1968
Earthenware, tin-glaze with painted decoration in blue and green; marks: 'ACS' in monogram, painted; made at Aldermaston Pottery; h. 9.8 cm, d. 14.8 cm
Circ.823–1968. Source: *see* Circ.820–1968, £5

73 Dish, 1976
Earthenware, tin-glaze with lustre decoration; marks: 'ACS' in monogram, painted; made at Aldermaston Pottery; h. 18.3 cm, d. 49.5 cm
C.79–1976. Source: given by Morley College Ceramic Circle in memory of their Chairman, James Cross
Purchased by Morley College Ceramic Circle at the British Crafts Centre (solo exhibition, May 1976, no. 60) for £194.40

74 Bowl, 1987
Earthenware, lustre painting over a dark blue slip and transparent glaze; marks: 'ACS' in monogram, painted; made at Aldermaston Pottery; h. 9.1 cm, d. 28.6 cm
C.2–1989. Source: given by the CAS

72

73

74

Campavias, Estella *c.*1918

*c.*1918 born in Istanbul, Turkey
1947 leaves for Europe, settles in London
1954 starts ceramic courses at Chelsea Pottery (q.v.)
1961 ceases to make pottery
1974 takes up sculpture

Campavias worked in London and produced earthenwares between 1954–1956, and stonewares from 1957 onwards. These bowls show a contemporary interest in altered forms and in bright colours which characterised many industrial products at the time.

Godden (1964)
G. & P. Couteau, *Estella Campavias*, Paris, 1981
Paisley (1984)

75 Bowl, 1957
Stoneware, pale blue glaze; marks: indistinct seal; h. 10.4 cm, d. 21.8 cm
Circ.131–1958. Source: the potter, £15.75

76 Bowl, 1958
Stoneware, bright yellow-green glaze; h. 13 cm, d. 14.2 cm
Circ.6–1959. Source: the potter, £16.80

Cardew, Michael 1901–1983

1901 born in Wimbledon, London
1919–23 reads Humanities at Exeter College, Oxford
1921–22 learns pottery in summer vacations at Braunton Pottery, run by W. Fishley Holland; hears of St Ives Pottery
1923 1 January, visits St Ives; takes up apprenticeship in November
1923–26 works at St Ives with Bernard Leach (qv)

1926 in June, sets up own pottery at the old Greet Pottery near Winchcombe which had closed in 1915 after about 100 years of operation; help from Elijah Comfort (then in his sixties)
1927 Sidney Tustin joins the pottery
1933 marries Mariel Russel
1934 Seth (qv) born
1935 Charlie Tustin joins pottery
1936 Ray Finch (qv) joins pottery
1938 exhibition at Berkeley Galleries, Cardew works for 6 weeks at Copelands making tea-sets in 'fine earthenware' as prototypes for mass production which were never made
1939 leaves Winchcombe now run by Ray Finch, sets up new pottery at Wenford Bridge, produces small amount of slipware
1941 Wenford Bridge closed because of the war, Cardew returns to Winchcombe
1942–45 appointed pottery instructor at Achimota College in Ghana, Africa, which had originally been set up by Meyerowitz, helped by Harry Davis (qv) in 1937; it had collapsed on Meyerowitz's death
1945 Cardew sells the Winchcombe business to Ray Finch
1946–48 sets up pottery at Vumé, on the Volta river
1948 forced through ill-health to return to England; works briefly at Kingwood, Whitely, Surrey and at Winchcombe
1949 Wenford Bridge looked after by the Australian Ivan McMeekin; Cardew builds downdraft kiln for the firing of stoneware; McMeekin becomes partner
1950 returns to Africa (Nigeria) when invited by authorities to become Pottery Officer with a brief to improve the quality of 'native' pottery

1950s–65 works 10 months a year in Nigeria and 2 in Wenford Bridge which is looked after by Ivor McMeekin
1951 sets up Pottery Training Centre at Abuja, Nigeria
1958 exhibition in London of Abuja pottery
1959 runs 'Geology for Potters' courses at Wenford Bridge
1960 exhibition of Abuja pottery in Lagos
1964 awarded MBE
1965 'retires' and returns to Wenford Bridge, awarded CBE
1967 visits USA, University of Winsconsin
1968 visits New Zealand and Australia where he helps McMeekin to start a pottery for Aborigines in the Northern Territory; later visits Abuja
1971 Seth joins Wenford Bridge Pottery
1973 visits Vumé and Abuja
1976 retrospective exhibition organised by the Crafts Council
1981 selector and writer for Crafts Council exhibition *The Makers Eye*; awarded OBE
1983 dies 11 February

Students of Michael Cardew represented in the Museum collections:
Ray Finch 1936–
Svend Bayer 1969–72
Clive Bowen 1970
Seth Cardew 1971–

Michael Cardew, 'Industry and the Studio Potter', *Crafts*, Quarterly of the Red Rose Guild, 2/1, 1942, pp. 9–12
—'Raw Materials for Pottery', *Athene*, 7/1&2, 1955, 19–21
—*Pioneer Pottery*, London, 1969
—'Potters and Amateur Potters', *PQ*, 10/38, 1971–73
—'What Pots Mean to Me', *CR*, 32/1975
—'Slipware and Stoneware', in London, CC (1976)
—'Michael Cardew at 75', compiled by Len Dutton, *CR*, 40/1976
—'The Fatal Impact', *CR*, 55/1979
—Selector for London, CC (1981)
—'Michael Cardew in conversation with Patrick Heron', *Crafts*, May/June, 1981
—'Book review – a History of World Pottery, by Emmanuel Cooper', *CR*, 69/1981
—*A Pioneer Potter*, London, 1988
Ernest Marsh, 'Michael Cardew, Potter of Winchcombe, Gloucestershire', *Apollo*, May, 1943
Wingfield Digby (1952)
Rose (1955), (1970)
Katharine Pleydell-Bouverie, 'Michael Cardew, a personal account', *CR*, 20/1973
Cameron and Lewis (1976)
London, CC (1976)
Garth Clark, *Michael Cardew*, London, 1976
London, CC (1976a)
Ray Finch, 'Cardew at Winchcombe', *Crafts*, November/December, 1976
Ian Bennett, 'An Ironic Look at One Man's Ceramics', *The Times Saturday Review*, 7/8/1976
Ronn Hartviksen, 'A Day in the Field with Michael Cardew', *CR*, 45/1977
London, Hayward Gallery (1979)
York City Art Gallery (1983): a detailed account with bibliography
Peter Dick, 'Michael Cardew and Pupils', *CR*, 80/1983

75 76

W. A. Ismay, 'Kindred Pots', *Crafts*, July/August, 1983
'Michael Cardew – Pioneer Potter', tributes by seven
potters, *CR*, 81/1983
'Michael Cardew – a Pioneer Potter', including a book
review by W. A. Ismay, *CR*, 111/1988

Winchcombe Pottery, Gloucestershire

Cardew's Winchcombe Pottery was originally the Greet
Pottery, owned and worked by the Beckett family from
the early 19th century until shortage of coal had forced
its closure early in the 20th century. It had in the main
made farmhouse ware – bread-crocks, milk-pans,
washing-pans and flowerpots. Cardew reopened the
pottery under the name 'Winchcombe Pottery' to
continue the tradition of making domestic
earthenwares. He re-employed Elijah Comfort, then in
his sixties, who had been chief thrower to the Beckett
family and who was still living in Winchcombe. With
him came a young local lad – Sidney Tustin, who also
after a few years became a good thrower. Six or more
kiln loads were made each year, each of upward of
2,000 pieces though mostly of smaller household use
than the larger Beckett types. In 1935 Charlie Tustin,
Sidney's younger brother, joined the pottery, and Ray
Finch applied to join. Cardew advised him to get more
experience, and Ray Finch returned to London where
he worked for a year in the Pottery Department of the
Central School with Dora Billington. He joined the
Winchcombe Pottery in 1936. Cardew by the late
1930s was feeling dissatisfaction with the Winchcombe
product – the earthenwares were proving
temperamental to make, and were often technically of
poor quality. Cardew chose to move to another
pottery – Wenford Bridge in Cornwall – in order to
accommodate his growing family and to try new
ceramic types. Ray Finch, by then his partner, was to
remain as manager of the Winchcombe Pottery, and
the two were to maintain a relationship. In 1940 the
Tustin brothers were conscripted, and Cardew was
forced to return to Winchcombe. Ray Finch joined the
National Fire Service in 1943, a year after Cardew left
for Africa, Elijah Comfort continued on his own until
his death in 1945. At the end of the war, Cardew
decided to stay on in Africa, and sold the pottery to
Ray Finch. In 1946 Ray Finch and Sidney Tustin began
to work the pottery again, later that year joined by
Charlie Tustin. *See also* **Ray Finch**.

77 Dish, *c.*1923–1924
Earthenware, incised decoration through a white
slip under an amber glaze with green splashes;
marks: 'MC' and 'SI' in monogram, impressed;
made at the Leach Pottery, St Ives; h. 4.7 cm,
d. 17.3 cm
C.60–1985. Source: Paul Rice Gallery, London,
£270
The seal is an early one in a rectangular frame.

78 Tobacco jar, 1929
Earthenware, slip painted decoration under an
amber glaze; marks: 'WP' in monogram,
impressed; made at Winchcombe Pottery;
h. 17.5 cm, d. 12 cm
C.424&a-1934. Source: given by the BIIA (gift of
the potter in 1929)

79 Dish, *c.*1929
Earthenware, slip with 'finger-wipe' decoration
under an amber glaze; marks: 'MC' and 'WP' in
monogram, impressed; made at Winchcombe
Pottery; h. 8.3 cm, d. 24.5 cm
C.957–1935. Source: given by the CAS
The dating was suggested by the potter on a visit
to the Museum on 24/7/1981.

77

78

79

80 Water jar, *c.*1934
Earthenware, decoration in brown on a cream slip under an amber glaze; marks: 'MC' and 'WP' in monogram, impressed; made at Winchcombe; h. 25.5 cm, d. 18.3 cm
Misc.2(153)-1934. Source: Margaret Bulley Gift
Paper label on base gives the price: '8/6' (=£0.42).

81 Quart bottle, 1938
Earthenware, black slip with incised decoration under the glaze; marks: 'MC' and 'Wp' in monogram, impressed; made at Winchcombe Pottery; h. 20.4 cm, d. 13.6 cm
Circ.317–1938. Source: Brygos Galleries, London, £1.50

82 Vase with handles, *c.*1935
Earthenware, slip-painted decoration in brown under a green glaze; marks: 'MC'(in a rectangle) and 'WP' in monogram, impressed; made at Winchcombe Pottery; h. 19.5 cm, d. 16.6 cm
C.956–1935. Source: given by the CAS, London

83 Bowl, *c.*1936 (pl. 1)
Earthenware, white and dark slip-painted decoration under an amber glaze; marks: 'MC' and 'WP' in monogram, impressed; made at Winchcombe Pottery; h. 13.5 cm, d. 35 cm
Circ.37–1938. Source: given by Henry Bergen (shown in the UK Pavilion at the Paris International Exhibition in 1937)
Published: London, Hayward Gallery (1979; no. 2.55)

84 Cider jar, 1938
Earthenware, black slip with incised decoration through the glaze; marks: 'MC' and 'Wp' in monogram, impressed; made at Winchcombe Pottery; h. 45 cm, d. 27.5 cm
Circ.319–1938. Source: Brygos Galleries, London, £5.25

85 Dish, 1938 (pl. 8)
Earthenware, with 'finger-wiped' slip decoration in white under an amber glaze; made at Winchcombe Pottery; h. 6.3 cm, d. 43 cm
Circ.312–1938. Source: Brygos Galleries, London, £1.25

86 Large jar, 1938 (pl. 25)
Earthenware, slip-painted decoration in white under an amber glaze; marks: 'MC' and 'WP' in monogram, impressed; made at Winchcombe Pottery; h. 35.8 cm, d. 32.7 cm
Circ.313–1938. Source: Brygos Galleries, London, £3.15

82

80 81

84

87 Jug, 1938
Earthenware, with slip-trailed decoration in white on black; marks: 'MC' and 'WP' in monogram, impressed; made at Winchcombe Pottery; h. 28.5 cm, d. 22.7 cm
Circ.310–1938. Source: Brygos Galleries, London, £1.57
Published: London, Hayward Gallery (1979; no. 2.56)

88 Jug, 1938
Earthenware, with slip-trailed decoration on a dark ground under an amber glaze; marks: 'MC' and 'WP' in monogram, impressed; made at Winchcombe Pottery; h. 24 cm, d. 21.2 cm
Circ.311–1938. Source: Brygos Galleries, London, £0.75

89 Jug, 1938 (pl. 26)
Earthenware, slip decoration in white on black under an amber glaze; marks: 'MC' and 'Wp' in monogram, impressed; made at Winchcombe Pottery; h. 29.5 cm, d. 23.2 cm
Circ.318–1938. Source: Brygos Galleries, London, £1.05
'£1.1s' (one guinea) is written in pencil on the base.

90 Breakfast dish and cover, 1938
Earthenware, slip in white on black under a transparent glaze; marks: 'WP' in monogram, impressed; made at Winchcombe Pottery; h. 11.4 cm, d. 25.4 cm
Circ.314&a–1938. Source: Brygos Galleries, London, £0.52
In 1981 Michael Cardew suggested that the base was thrown by himself and the lid by Elijah Comfort. This was revealed by the thick profile of the lid's flange – 'lazy throwing' which was according to Cardew the 'sign of a true professional'

91 Plate, 1938
Earthenware, with white slip decoration on a red clay body under an amber glaze; marks: 'MC' and 'WP' in monogram, impressed; made at Winchcombe Pottery; h. 6.5 cm, d. 35.5 cm
Circ.315–1938. Source: Brygos Galleries, London, £1.57

92 Plate, 1938
Earthenware, white slip decoration on black; made at Winchcombe Pottery; h. 2.8 cm, d. 24.4 cm
Circ.316–1938. Source: Brygos Galleries, London, £0.32

90

91

88 87

92

93 Vase, 1939
Earthenware, slip decoration in white on black
under an amber glaze; marks: 'MC' and 'WP' in
monogram, impressed; made at Winchcombe
Pottery; h. 32 cm, d. 20.2 cm
Circ.346–1939. Source: given by the CAS through
Ernest Marsh

94 Bowl, 1939
Earthenware, white slip decoration on black under
an amber glaze; marks: 'MC' and 'WP' in
monogram, impressed; made at Winchcombe
Pottery; h. 7 cm, d. 31.8 cm
Circ.347–1939. Source: *see* Circ.346–1939

95 Covered bowl, 1947–1948
Stoneware, painted decoration in iron-brown in a
deep blue-grey glaze; marks: 'MC' in monogram,
seal of the Volta pottery, impressed & 'MC'
painted; made at Volta Pottery, Vumé, Gold
Coast, Africa; h. 12.5 cm, d. 17.5 cm
Circ.33&a-1950. Source: the potter, £3.15

96 Soup tureen, 1950 (pl. 42)
Stoneware, painted decoration in blue and brown
on a grey glaze; marks: 'MC' in monogram and
Wenford Bridge seal, impressed; made at Wenford
Bridge Pottery; h. 18.6 cm, d. 26.9 cm
Circ.423&a-1950. Source: Berkeley Galleries,
London, £5.25

97 Casserole, 1950
Stoneware, painted decoration in brown on a grey
glaze; marks: 'MC' in monogram and Wenford
Bridge seal, impressed; made at Wenford Bridge
Pottery; h. 24.5 cm, d. 23.2 cm
Circ.424&a-1950. Source: *see* Circ.423–1950,
£5.25

98 Dish: *Pheasant and Palm*, 1950 (pl. 43)
Stoneware, painting in dark grey on a light grey
glaze; marks: 'MC' in monogram and Wenford
Bridge seal, impressed; made at Wenford Bridge
Pottery; h. 4.3 cm, d. 27.2 cm
Circ.425–1950. Source: *see* Circ.423–1950, £3.15

95

94 93

97

99 Cider jar, 1950
Stoneware, painted decoration in brown on a grey glaze; marks: 'MC' in monogram and Wenford Bridge seal, impressed; made at Wenford Bridge Pottery; h. 31.5 cm, d. 20.4 cm
Circ.426–1950. Source: *see* Circ.423–1950, £6.30

100 Jug, 1950
Stoneware, painted decoration in iron on a pale greenish-grey glaze; marks: 'MC' in monogram and Wenford Bridge seal, impressed; made at Wenford Bridge Pottery; h. 27.5 cm, d. 25 cm
Circ.427–1950. Source: *see* Circ.423–1950, £7.35

101 Bowl, 1950
Stoneware, painted decoration in iron on a grey glaze with pink blushes; marks: 'MC' in monogram and Wenford Bridge seal, impressed; made at Wenford Bridge Pottery; h. 12.5 cm, d. 26.5 cm
Circ.428–1950. Source: *see* Circ.423–1950, £4.50

102 Bowl, 1950
Stoneware, painted decoration in brown on a grey glaze; marks: 'MC' in monogram and Wenford Bridge seal, impressed; made at Wenford Bridge Pottery; h. 12.3 cm, d. 24 cm
Circ.429–1950. Source: *see* Circ.423–1950, £4.20

103 Covered bowl, 1950
Stoneware, painted decoration in brown on a grey glaze; marks: 'MC' in monogram and Wenford Bridge seal, impressed; made at Wenford Bridge Pottery; h. 12.9 cm, d. 19.7 cm
Circ.430&a-1950. Source: *see* Circ.423–1950, £2.10

104 Soup bowl, 1950
Stoneware, painted decoration in brown on a grey glaze; marks: 'MC' in monogram and Wenford Bridge seal, impressed; made at Wenford Bridge Pottery; h. 6 cm, d. 16.4 cm
Circ.431–1950. Source: *see* Circ.423–1950, £0.87

105 Tea-pot, 1950
Stoneware, painted decoration in iron on an unglazed surface; marks: 'MC' in monogram and Wenford Bridge seal, impressed; made at Wenford Bridge Pottery; h. 22.8 cm, d. 21.5 cm
Circ.432&a-1950. Source: *see* Circ.423–1950, £4.50

101 102

103 104

100 99

105

106 Vase, 1950
Stoneware, incised decoration; marks: 'MC' in monogram and Wenford Bridge seal, impressed; made at Wenford Bridge Pottery; h. 24.3 cm, d. 19.4 cm
Circ.433–1950. Source: *see* Circ.423–1950, £5.25

107 Water jar with screw top, *c*.1957
Stoneware, painted decoration in a dark glaze; marks: 'MC' in monogram and 'ABUJA' seal, impressed; made at Abuja Pottery, Nigeria; h. 31.9 cm, d. 24.7 cm
Circ.112&a-1958. Source: Berkeley Galleries, London, £12.60
The form is taken from an African earthenware shape.

108 Dish, *c*.1957
Stoneware, 'finger-wiped' decoration in a milky glaze over black slip; marks: 'ABUJA' seal, impressed; made at Abuja Pottery, Nigeria; h. 5.5 cm, d. 39.8 cm
Circ.113–1958. Source: *see* Circ.112–1958, £5.25

109 Dish, 1967
Stoneware, incised decoration through a greenish-brown glaze; marks: 'MC' in monogram and Wenford Bridge seal, impressed; made at Wenford Bridge Pottery; h. 17 cm, d. 41 cm
Circ.474–1969. Source: British Potters '69 (exhibition at Qantas Gallery, London, 1969), £18

110 Bowl, *c*.1982
Stoneware, painting in brown and blue in a grey glaze; marks: 'MC' in monogram and Wenford Bridge seal,impressed; made at Wenford Bridge; h. 12 cm, d. 24 cm
C.57–1985. Source: Wenford Bridge Pottery, £250

106

107

108

109

110

Cardew, Seth 1934–

1934	born in Gloucestershire, son to Michael Cardew (qv)
1952–4	studies painting at Chelsea School of Art, London
1955–57	national military service in the RAF
1957–59	studies sculpture at Camberwell School of Art, London
1960–70	working as a model-maker for Pinewood, Elstree and Shepperton film studios
1972	joins father's pottery at Wenford Bridge as an assistant
1983	takes over Wenford Bridge Pottery on death of father

Seth Cardew has carried on the tradition established by his father at Wenford Bridge of making good tablewares in stoneware, primarily decorated in blue and brown painting on a grey glaze. Seth Cardew's characteristic 'bird' pattern is developed from a design of his father's. Seth's children have started to pot at Wenford Bridge – the third generation of Cardews to do so.

York City Art Gallery (1983)

111 Dish, 1981
Stoneware, painting in blue and brown in a grey glaze; marks: 'SC' in monogram and Wenford Bridge seal, impressed; made at Wenford Bridge; h. 47 cm, d. 26.5 cm
C.152–1981. Source: O'Casey's Craft Gallery, London, £24

Cass, Barbara (later Wolstencroft) 1921–

1921	born in Germany, studies sculpture in Berlin
1950	comes to UK
1952–61	studio in York
1956	starts working in stoneware
1962–	moves workshop to Henley-in-Arden, Warwickshire, also runs a workshop in Frankfurt
1966–88	workshop in Stratford-upon-Avon, Warwickshire
1988	retires to Chipping Campden, Gloucestershire

This potter is also known under her married name, Barbara Wolstencroft.

Casson (1967)
London, CPA (1980)

112 Bowl, 1961
Stoneware, black decoration in a pale brown glaze; marks: 'BW YORK 1961', incised; h. 9.7 cm, d. 43.7 cm
Circ.263–1961. Source: Primavera, London, £12.60

Casson, Michael 1925–

1925	born in London
1945	evening classes in pottery at Hornsey College of Art, London
1948–51	studies pottery at Hornsey College of Art
1952	first workshop in Russell Square, London
1955	marries potter Sheila Casson
1957	founder member of the CPA
1957–73	part-time teaching
1959	first solo exhibition at Heal's, London – tin-glazed earthenware
1959	new workshop in Prestwood, Bucks.; works in stoneware
1963	sets up pottery course at Harrow School of Art with Victor Margrie (qv)
1964	film: *Michael Casson, Studio Potter*
1971–73	Head of Ceramics Department, Harrow
1973	gives up full-time teaching for full-time potting
1975–76	produces *The Craft of the Potter*, 5 programmes and accompanying book for BBC TV
1975	ceases to make repetition domestic ware in favour of individual pieces
1977	moves to Wobage Farm, Herefordshire, a pottery he shares with his wife and the potter Andrew McGarva
1977–	regular teaching visits to USA and Canada
1983	awarded OBE
1983–	teaching history of ceramics at South Glamorgan College of Higher Education, Cardiff
1985–88	Vice-Chairman of the Crafts Council

Michael Casson occupies an important place in the history of British studio pottery. The Harrow course that he set up in 1963 with Victor Margrie was an important step in art education – a pottery course directed at training potters to run production ware workshops. His work as a writer, film maker and general publicist has also been very influential and he is much in demand for lectures and demonstrations. His work as a potter is distinctive – strongly thrown individual

111

112

113

114

115

shapes with decoration that veers between bold, spontaneous and abstract, to rather sweeter landscape designs. He is particularly known for his jugs, some of which reach monumental size.

Michael Casson, Casson (1967), (1977)
—'Decoration Paper Resist', *CR*, 6/1970
—'Ceramics and Education', *CR*, 21/1973
—'Potters at Wobage Farm', *CR*, 106/1987
Victor Rienacker, 'Pottery by Michael Casson', *Apollo*, December, 1961
Rose (1970; pl. 82a&b)
Tony Birks, 'Michael Casson, Man in the Middle of the Road', *CR*, 24/1973
Cameron and Lewis (1976)
Marigold Coleman, 'On being a Potter', *Crafts*, January/February, 1976
'Michael Casson Throwing', *CR*, 43/1977
W. A. Ismay, 'Michael Casson – Pots', *CR*, 58/1979
London, VAM (1977)
E. Lewenstein and E. Cooper, 'Wobage Farm Pottery', *CR*, 73/1982
Alice Bree, 'Wobage Farm Summer School', *CR*, 74/1982
W. A. Ismay, 'Michael Casson – Pots from Three Kilns', *Crafts*, November/December, 1983
Tanya Harrod, 'Michael Casson – Sources of Inspiration', *Crafts*, July/August, 1989

113 Dish, 1973
Stoneware, sponge wiped decoration in a poured red slip under a tenmoku glaze; marks: 'MC' in monogram, painted in black enamel; h. 6.7 cm, d. 40 cm
Circ.4–1974. Source: CPA, London, £20

114 Large jug, 1974
Stoneware, wiped decoration in a red slip under a tenmoku glaze; marks: impressed seal; h. 43 cm, d. 32.5 cm
Circ.517–1974. Source: the potter, £30

115 Dish, 1975
Porcelain, incised decoration under a pale blue-green glaze; marks: 'MC' in monogram, painted; h. 9.5 cm, d. 37.6 cm
Circ.8–1976. Source: Casson Gallery, London, £45
This dish is double glazed, with a barium underglaze to give an optical blue effect.

116 Footed bowl, 1975 (pl. 78)
Stoneware, inlaid decoration in porcelain, green-brown dry clay-ash glaze; marks: 'MC' in monogram, painted in black enamel; h. 16.5 cm, d. 18.7 cm
Circ.9–1976. Source: *see* Circ.8–1975, £25
This bowl, one of the potter's favourite pieces, was the first non-domestic piece Casson made and marks the moment when he decided to abandon making repetition table wares in favour of one-off individual pieces. The inspiration for this piece comes from ancient Greek and Cretan pottery.

117 Bowl, 1976
Stoneware, brushed decoration in blue and grey in a grey glaze; marks: 'MC' in monogram, painted; h. 11 cm, d. 15 cm
Circ.531–1976. Source: the potter, £6

118 Jug, 1984
Stoneware, mottled brown saltglaze; marks: 'MC' in monogram, impressed; h. 50.4 cm, d. 22.2 cm
C.151–1984. Source: BCC, £121

117   118

Chappell, John 1931–1964

1950   after six months potting as an obsessional hobbyist, studies with Murray Fieldhouse (qv) at Pendley Centre of Adult Education

1953   sets up own workshop, Coldharbour Pottery, developing saltglaze wares, after teaching in Algeria

1955   pottery moved to new premises at Wilstone

1956–59 works as a cook and English teacher in Sweden, saving money to go to Japan

1959   leaves for Japan, studies with Kunio Uchida in Kyoto; later working in Gojo kilns after visit to Australia and New Zealand

1962   sets up kilns at Do Mura Shiga-Ken, Japan

1964   killed in a motor-bike accident in Australia, on his way to New Zealand and Europe with an exhibition of his pottery

John Chappell, a conscientious objector who served terms in prison rather than do his military service, worked in Japan for some years. He was killed in 1964 in a motorbike accident in Sydney, Australia, while on route to New Zealand with the Japanese potter Takeichi Kawai and an exhibition of pottery. The pots in the V&A were selected from this exhibition.

John Chappell, 'Making Saltglaze Stoneware', *PQ*, 2/1954

—'A Visitor's Views' (on New Zealand), *PQ*, 7/1961–2

Takeichi Kawai, John Chappell, exhibition catalogue, Dominion Museum, Wellington, New Zealand, 1964

119 Bottle, *c.*1963
Stoneware, brown mottled saltglaze; marks: 'JC', impressed; h. 18.3 cm, d. 11.5 cm
Circ.47–1966. Source: Mrs Anja Chappell (the potter's widow), NZ£4

120 Wine jar, *c.*1963
Stoneware, green glaze round rim and top of handle, ash flashings on body; h. 17.4 cm, d. 21 cm
Circ.46–1966. Source: *see* Circ.47–1966, NZ£8

121 Bottle, *c.*1963
Porcelain, painting in underglaze blue; h. 14.6 cm, d. 9.3 cm
Circ.45–1966. Source: *see* Circ.47–1966, NZ£3

Chelsea Pottery 1952–

The Chelsea Pottery was established in Chelsea, London, by David and Mary Rawnsley in 1952 as an 'open studio' to allow any interested potter to come and work. It developed into a two-sided business: classes for the amateur potters and a commercial pottery. This latter produced earthenwares decorated in a distinctive technique described as 'inlay and overlay', which involved elaborate painting with coloured glazes. Daphne Corke and Joyce Morgan worked at the pottery from the beginning, and on occasion signed their work. Daphne Corke left to continue on her own at a pottery in Lexden, Colchester, Essex in 1955. Joyce Morgan still works at the Chelsea Pottery; John Drummond was only briefly associated with it.

The four pieces acquired by the Museum are marked in commemoration of the coronation of Queen Elizabeth the Second.

The Guardian, 3/6/1961, p. 4
Marita Ross, 'New Pottery in Old Chelsea', *Everybody's Weekly*, 15 October, 1955

119 120

121

Daphne Corke

122 Dish: *Fossil Fish Series*, 1953
Earthenware, decoration in coloured glazes in 'inlay and overlay technique'; marks: 'EIIR, Chelsea Pottery, 1953', incised on base; made at the Chelsea Pottery, London; h. 6.3 cm, d. 19.7 cm
C.73–1953. Source: given by David Rawnsley of the Chelsea Pottery

123 Bowl, 1953
Earthenware, decoration in coloured glazes in 'inlay and overlay technique'; marks: 'E II R, Chelsea Pottery, 1953', incised; made at the Chelsea Pottery, London; h. 7.7 cm, d. 19.4 cm
Circ.406–1953. Source: given by David Rawnsley of the Chelsea Pottery

John Drummond

124 Bowl, 1953
Earthenware, painting in coloured glazes in 'inlay and overlay' technique; marks: 'EIIR, Chelsea Pottery, 1953', incised; made at the Chelsea Pottery; h. 4.2 cm, d. 19.8 cm
Circ.407–1953. Source: given by David Rawnsley of the Chelsea Pottery
Painted with coloured glazes and incised

Joyce Morgan

125 Dish, 1953
Earthenware, decoration in coloured glazes in 'inlay and overlay technique'; marks: 'EIIR, Chelsea Pottery, 1953', incised on base and 'Jem' signed; made at the Chelsea Pottery, London; h. 3.5 cm, d. 19.5 cm
C.74–1953. Source: Given by David Rawnsley of the Chelsea Pottery

Clarkson, Derek 1928–

1944–47 Manchester School of Art
1949–61 visiting lecturer in ceramics at Stockport, Bolton and Burnley Schools of Art
1959–61 finally takes diploma at Burnley School of Art
1961–65 lecturer in charge of ceramics, Stafford College of Art
1965–79 senior lecturer, Mather College and City of Manchester College of Higher Education
1980– takes up potting full time
1982– working also in porcelain

Clarkson is particularly known for the bottle form illustrated here which accounts for the greater part of his production.

Derek Clarkson, 'Turned and Thrown Bottles', *CR*, 88/1984
—'Light Fantastic', *CR*, 107/1987
Casson (1967)
Godden (1988)

126 Bottle, 1982
Stoneware, painting in black and brown in an oatmeal glaze; marks: 'DC' in a rectangle, impressed; h. 24.3 cm, d. 16 cm
C.69–1984. Source: given by the Friends of the V&A.
Purchased at the CPA 25th Anniversary exhibition, *Studio Ceramics Today*, held at the V&A in 1983.

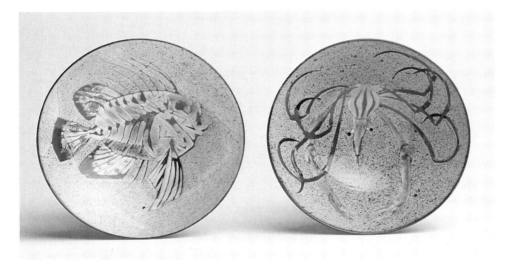

122 123

125 124

126

Clinton, Margery 1931–

1949–53 trains as a painter at Glasgow School of Art
1960s begins to work in ceramics
1969 moves to London
1973–4 research into reduction lustre glazes at Royal College of Art, London
1978 moves back to Scotland, sets up workshop at Newton Port, East Lothian
1978–81 works in partnership with Jan Williamson

Margery Clinton's work is of interest for the lustre technique she had pursued, particularly in-glaze lustres, as opposed to the on-glaze lustres developed by Alan Caiger-Smith (qv). She has used this technique recently to produce a series of replicas of mediaeval Persian tiles for the Glasgow Museums. Earlier work was in earthenware, since 1985 most work, apart from the tiles, is in porcelain or high-fired stoneware.

The Museum also possesses a number of Clinton's lustre tiles with silk-screened decoration in lustre with designs taken from Persian lustre tiles of the 13th century (C.116 to c-1979).

Margery Clinton, 'Elusive Lustres', *CR*, 103/1987
'CPA New Members', *CR*, 41/1976
Godden (1988)

127 Vase, 1979
Earthenware, matt black glaze with decoration of poured in-glaze lustre glazes; marks: 'MC JW Feb 79', painted; h. 38 cm, d. 23.6 cm
C.117–1979. Source: the potter, £18.50
The initials 'JW' stand for Jan Williamson, Margery Clinton's partner.

Cohen, David 1932–

1932 born in Milwaukee, USA
1957 Layton Art School, Milwaukee
1958–62 studies sculpture at Edinburgh College of Art
1962–63 fellowship to Scripps College, California, USA, with Paul Soldner
1963 returns to Edinburgh, sets up workshop
1964–86 teaches at Edinburgh College of Art
1988– appointed Head of Ceramics at Glasgow School of Art

Cohen, an American who has settled in the UK, specialises in raku work. The large jar with small foot and neck is a characteristic shape.

London, CPA (1989)

128 Pot, 1988
Stoneware, raku fired, unglazed body with green-gold neck and foot, gold interior; h. 46.2 cm, d. 35.4 cm
C.34–1989. Source: given by Agi Katz, Boundary Gallery, London

Cole, John 1908–1988

John Cole trained as a woodwork and metalwork teacher at Shoreditch Training College in the mid-1920s. In 1930 he spent a year at the Central School of Art studying art. In about 1936 he started to teach pottery at Camberwell School of Art and at the Beckenham School of Art where he eventually became Principal, and later was appointed Principal of the new Ravensbourne College of Art when Beckenham and Bromley Schools of Art were amalgamated. He retired in 1967. In the 1930s he shared kilns and workshops with his brother Walter Cole (qv), and with him re-opened the Rye Pottery in 1947 (see below). Though his teaching commitments prevented him playing a major part in the day to day direction of the pottery, he was involved in decisions in policy and improvements until the late 1960s.

A letter from John Cole written in 1937 in the Museum archives gives the significance of the name 'EARTH': 'It is our hope that we may yet start a small pottery with the name "Earth" stamped on each piece. The

127

128

name arose from a desire that unless more natural materials were used in the making we did not think good pottery would result.'

In the introduction to the pottery section of the 1942 British Council craft exhibition which toured the USA and Canada, Cecilia Semphill lists John Cole along with Pleydell-Bouverie, Norah Braden and Michael Cardew as following Bernard Leach and William Staite Murray in developing ceramics in new artistic and philosophic directions.

129 Beaker, 1937
Stoneware, blue grey glaze with painting in copper red; marks: 'EARTH', impressed; h. 7.7 cm, d. 6.7 cm
C.74–1937. Source: given by Lt-Col. K. Dingwall, DSO, through the NACF

Cole, Walter (Wally) Vivian 1913–

1913	born in London
1930–31	studies ceramics and drawing at Woolwich School of Art, London
1931–36	Special Talent Scholarship to the Central School of Art, London, studies ceramics, sculpture and animal drawing under John Skeaping; builds own kiln, first in Plumstead, London, then in Gravesend, Kent
1936–38	works on architectural carvings for Eric Kennington; makes and exhibits ceramics and sculpture; work purchased for the CAS
1940–45	war service, camouflage
1946–47	on staff of Council for Industrial design, teaches at Central School of Art
1947	re-opens the Rye Pottery with brother John Cole (qv) making production line pottery with a team of workers as well as individual pots and sculpture
1962	silver medallist, International Ceramics Exhibition, Prague
1966	Design Award, Design Centre, London
1978	retires from management of the Pottery
1982	awarded MBE

The initial impetus for opening the Rye Pottery came when W. B. Honey, Keeper of the Ceramics Department at the V&A, suggested to the brothers Cole at an exhibition of their work at the Brygos Gallery in 1937 that their prices were too high to enable their work to be enjoyed by ordinary people as useful ware. If they could not make things cheaper their work would remain at the level of 'Art Object'. Experiments to this end before the war were finally put into operation in 1947 when they acquired the disused Rye Pottery and set up a small team, on small-scale industrial lines, to produce modestly priced studio tableware.

Casson (1967)
Rye Pottery, 1869–1969, booklet, Rye Pottery, 1969
Colin Pearson, exhibition review, *Crafts*, January/February, 1980

130 Bowl, 1935
Stoneware, tenmoku glaze; h. 3.7 cm, d. 8 cm
C.73–1937. Source: given by Lt-Col. K. Dingwall, DSO, through the NACF

Constantinidis, Joanna 1927–

1927	born in York
1946–49	Sheffield College of Art, followed by teaching at the Chelmsford Technical College and School of Art
1950–	studio in Great Baddow, Essex
1965	solo exhibition, Craft Centre, London
1976	solo exhibition, CPA
1982	solo exhibition, Oxford Gallery

Constantanidis is a potter who has not had great exposure nor much acclaim, yet consistently produces high quality work – great sensitivity and expression in form, together with subtlety of surface colour and texture. Her work gains greatly from seeing it in groups, where the individual character of each piece can be seen contrasted against its fellows.

Joanna Constantinidis, CR, 90/1984
Casson (1967)
W. A. Ismay, 'Joanna Constantinidis – Recent Work', CR, 42/1976
A large private collection of pieces by Constantinidis was sold at auction at Bonham's, London, on 27 February 1989, lots 138–159 (illustrated catalogue).

131 Vase, 1976
Porcelain, brown glaze with irregular spiral dark lines; marks: 'C', impressed; h. 11.8 cm, d. 12.6 cm
C.292–1976. Source: CPA, London (potter's solo exhibition, September 1976), £22.56
This bowl was purchased at a period when the potter was just commencing her interest in lustred surfaces.

129

130

132 Bottle, flattened form, 1983
Stoneware, iridescent copper-gold saltglaze; marks: 'C', impressed; h. 52 cm, d. 25.5 cm
C.211–1983. Source: Henry Rothschild Associates, Ltd, Cambridge, £225
The saltglazing is done by putting the pot and glazing materials into a saggar, the flashing effects are produced by the confined local action.

131

132

171

Cook, George Frederick 1919–1982

c.1938   ceramics at Blackpool School of Art
1940s   ceramics at Central School of Art, London, with Dora Billington; interrupted by war service, course completed after the war
1948–66 works in the artistic community at Ambleside, Cumbria, sets up a pottery
1966–68 part-time teaching at Preston and Ulster Schools of Art
1968–82 full-time senior lecturer at Ulster School of Art

Cook was known for his domestic slipwares in the 1950s. His use of coloured slips – in particular, blue – led to an accusation by a more purist slipware potter of having corrupted the Old English slipware tradition.

Godden (1964)

133   Jug, 1950
Earthenware, decoration in blue and white slips on a dark ground; marks: 'COOK AMBLESIDE', incised; h. 33.7 cm, d. 22.3 cm
Circ.273–1950. Source: Arts and Crafts Society (exhibition in V&A, 1950), £5.25

Cooper, Emmanuel 1938–

1938   born in Derbyshire
1958–60 Dudley College of Education
1960–61 studies ceramics at Bournemouth School of Art under David Ballantyne (qv)
1961–62 Hornsey School of Art, London
1963   takes up potting, works with Gwyn Hanssen (qv)
1964   works with Bryan Newman (qv)
1964   sets up Fonthill Pottery in London
1970–   co-editor of *Ceramic Review* with Eileen Lewenstein (qv)
1971–   part-time teaching at Middlesex Polytechnic
1972–80 teaches at Camberwell School of Art, London
1981   selector for *The Maker's Eye*, London, CC

133

Cooper produces tablewares as well as individual bowls and vases, these latter with reference to Lucie Rie's work, both in form and in the band of metallic pigment at the rim. Cooper's work as a writer and critic is of importance – and together with Eileen Lewenstein he has had a major role in developing and maintaining the special status of the magazine *Ceramic Review* to which he also contributes a great deal.

Emmanuel Cooper, (1971), (1972), (1974), (1978), (1981)
Selector for London, Crafts Council (1981)
'Amazing Glaze', *CR*, 105/1987
Godden (1988)

134   Dish, 1970
Stoneware, decoration in black and white slips under a bone-ash glaze; made at Fonthill Pottery, London; marks: impressed device; h. 7.5 cm, d. 35 cm
Circ.490–1970. Source: Crafts Centre of Great Britain, London, £10

135   Vase, 1981
Porcelain, green glaze with a metallic glazed rim; made at Fonthill Pottery, London; h. 13.2 cm, d. 16 cm
C.51–1982. Source: the potter, £74.75
This was thought by the potter to be then one of his most successful pieces of recent years.

134

135

Coper, Hans 1920–1981

1920   born in Germany
1939   leaves for England
1940   arrested as alien, sent to Canada
1941   returns to England, enrols in Pioneer Corps
1943   discharged from army
1946–59 meets Lucie Rie (qv), starts working at Albion Mews Pottery
1954   wins Gold medal at the Milan Triennale
1958   becomes a naturalised British subject
1959   moves to Digswell, Herts to set up his own studio
1962   makes candlesticks as commission for Coventry Cathedral
1963   moves to Princedale Road, London
1963–72 teaches at the Camberwell School of Art, London
1966–75 teaches at Royal College of Art, London
1967   moves to Frome, Somerset
1975   last British Exhibition; amyotrophic lateral sclerosis diagnosed, potting with increasing difficulty
1981   June 16, dies
1983–84 retrospective exhibition, Sainsbury Centre, Norwich which travels to Düsseldorf, Rotterdam, and ends at Serpentine Gallery, London

Hans Coper, quite simply, is the most important post-war potter in the UK, if not world-wide. His importance stems both from the formidable body of work, which shows how wheel-thrown clay can be the vehicle for sculptural expression of the highest order, and from his effect as a teacher. He is quoted as the prime influence by a whole generation of potters – Liz Fritsch (qv), Alison Britton (qv) and others from the Royal College of Art in particular. Lucie Rie (qv) herself claims that she learnt far more from Coper than she ever possibly taught him. His skill as a teacher lay in drawing out the innate talents and perceptions of his students, not forcing any pre-conceived notions of aesthetic standards upon them – hence the very varied work produced by his students, quite in contrast to the work of followers, for example, of Bernard Leach or William Staite Murray. The complete lack of any school of Coper-esque work is a testimony to the high standards which he achieved.

Wingfield Digby (1952)
Melville (1952), (1954)
Fennemore (1953)
Rose (1955), (1970; pls. 104–117)
Casson (1967)
London, VAM (1969)
Birks (1967), (1976)
London, VAM (1977)
'Hans Coper', tributes, *Crafts*, January/February, 1982
Birks (1983): major work with full details and bibliography
Crafts, November/December, 1983, exhibition review article by Christopher Reid
M. Dunas and Sarah Bodine, 'In Search of Form: Hans Coper and Lucie Rie', *American Ceramics*, 3/4, 1983
Emmanuel Cooper, 'Hans Coper – Artist Potter', *CR*, 84/1983

Alison Britton, 'Hans Coper 1920–1981', *American Craft*, April/May, 1984
Warwick (1987; nos. 141–3)

See also mentions in *CR*, nos. 5,7,11,17,21,25,33,36,62,66,71,73, 76,77,78

Several of Coper's numerous exhibitions had accompanying pamphlets; *see* Birks (1983) for a detailed bibliography

136 Handled pot, 1951 (pl. 57)
Stoneware, black glaze with incised decoration showing yellow; marks: 'HC' in monogram, impressed; made at Lucie Rie's pottery, London; h. 26.6 cm, d. 19.9 cm
Circ.54–1951. Source: the potter, £6.50
The Museum register gives the maker as '... Hans Coper (an associate of Lucie Rie)'.

137 Vase, 1954
Stoneware, incised decoration with black and white matt glazes; marks: 'HC' in monogram, impressed; made at Lucie Rie's studio; h. 43 cm, d. 19 cm
Circ.337–1955. Source: the potter, £12.60

138 Vase, 1958 (pl. 58)
Stoneware, black and white matt glazes; marks: 'HC' in monogram, impressed; made at Lucie Rie's studio; h. 49.2 cm, d. 38.1 cm
Circ.154–1958. Source: Primavera, London, £36.75

139 Dish, 1958
Stoneware, white glaze with brown flecks; marks: 'HC' in monogram, impressed; made at Lucie Rie's studio; h. 10.2 cm, d. 39.1 cm
Circ.155–1958. Source: *see* Circ.154–1958, £12.60

140 Pot, 1968 (pl. 64)
Stoneware, white matt glaze, interior glazed black; marks: 'HC' in monogram, impressed; h. 54 cm, d. 42 cm
Circ.204–1969. Source: the potter (exhibition Collingwood/Coper, V&A, 1969, no.17), £84

141 Bottle, 1968
Stoneware, white and black matt glazes; marks: 'HC' in monogram, impressed; h. 19.2 cm, d. 14.9 cm
Circ.205–1969. Source: *see* Circ.204–1969 (Collingwood/Coper exhibition, V&A, 1969, no.45), £24.50

142 Vase, 1968 (pl. 13)
Stoneware, white and black matt glazes; marks: 'HC' in monogram, impressed; h. 32.8 cm, d. 19.4 cm
Circ.207–1969. Source: *see* Circ.204–1969 (Collingwood/Coper exhibition, V&A, 1969, no.39), £33.60

143 Vase, 1968 (pl. 13)
Stoneware, black matt glaze; marks: 'HC' in monogram, impressed; h. 19.4 cm, d. 12.8 cm
Circ.206–1969. Source: *see* Circ.204–1969 (Collingwood/Coper exhibition, V&A, 1969, no.38), £20.30

144 Vase, 1968 (pl. 2)
Stoneware, white and black matt glazes; marks: 'HC' in monogram, impressed; h. 30.4 cm, d. 22.2 cm
Circ.208–1969. Source: *see* Circ.204–1969 (Collingwood/Coper exhibition, V&A, 1969, no.87), £28

145 Pot, 1975
Stoneware, white matt glaze, interior with black glaze; marks: 'HC' in monogram, impressed; h. 24 cm, d. 14.3 cm
Circ.398–1976. Source: the potter, £108

146 Pot, 1968
Stoneware, white and black matt glazes; marks: 'HC' in monogram, impressed; h. 18 cm, d. 12.8 cm
Circ.767–1969. Source: given by J.M.W. Crowther (from Collingwood/Coper exhibition, V&A, 1969, no. 86)

147 Black form, 1975 (pl. 83)
Stoneware, black matt glaze; marks: 'Hc' in block script, impressed; h. 27.5 cm, d. 8.1 cm
Circ.399–1976. Source: the potter, £122

139

137

141

146 145

Crowley, Jill 1946–

1946	born in Eire
1966–69	studies ceramics at Bristol Polytechnic
1969–72	Royal College of Art, London
1972	travelling scholarship to Greece, and to USA where she attends summer school with Paul Soldner working with raku
1972	founder member of 401 1/2 workshops
1977	solo exhibition at the Crafts Council Gallery, London
1981	new workshop in Brixton, London

London, CC (1974)
Jill Crowley, exhibition catalogue, Crafts Council, London, 1977
London, Christopher Wood Gallery (1980)
Christopher Reid, 'Jill Crowley', *Crafts*, March/April, 1982
London, Sotheby's (1984)
Crafts, July/August, 1985, exhibition review by Tanya Harrod
Tanya Harrod, 'Jill Crowley', CR, 114/1988

Jill Crowley is one of the RCA group of graduates that include Fritsch, Britton, McNicoll, Poncelet and Barton (qv). She was given a solo exhibition only five years after graduation from the RCA – before any of her peers. Her work is immediate and appealing with a stimulating wit and sense of caricature. These do not however override a deeper purpose – a satire, a strong sculptural sense and a detached but tender observation. This is seen particularly in the series of hands and arms modelled after those of her baby – not gruesome or sinister severed limbs, but an intimate and fascinated concentration.

148 *Cat Portrait*, 1980
Earthenware, handbuilt, raku fired, with areas of white glaze; marks: 'J Crowley', incised; h. 35.4 cm, d. 10.9 cm
C.116–1980. Source: BCC, London, £230
The series of cat portraits based on Crowley's own Burmese cat 'Ollie' and on a neighbour's tom that used to pester him. The plinth developed as a major feature because Crowley felt that craft shops at that time only displayed pots on shelves, whereas she felt that her work needed the special focus of a plinth.

149 *Portrait of a Darts Player*, 1981 (pl. 108)
Stoneware, handbuilt, with low-fired coloured glazes; h. 23.5 cm, d. 30.8 cm
C.84–1982. Source: Oxford Gallery, Oxford, £508.10
Inspired from professional darts players seen on television, '. . . with nylon jackets and overfed and drunk, bloated features'.

150 *Hand*, 1988 (pl. 18)
Stoneware, handbuilt, pink, yellow, green and cream matt glazes; marks: 'J. Crowley', incised; h. 38.4 cm, d. 36.6 cm
C.4–1989. Source: Michaelson and Orient, London, £715.50
Here the plinth acts to focus the onlooker's attention to the piece in a particular way – not as a comment on the lack of proper display as had been originally intended in the cat portraits (*see* Catalogue no. 148). By this date, craft galleries had developed more sophisticated and appropriate means of display than rows of shelves.

Dalton, William Bower 1868–1965

1888–92	Manchester School of Art
1892–96	Royal College of Art, London
1896–98	lecturer in art at a technical college in Yorkshire for 18 months
1898–1919	appointed Principal of the newly established Camberwell School of Arts and Crafts, London
1909–41	establishes his own workshop in Longfield, Kent
1919–	Curator of the Passmore Edwards South London Art Gallery
1941	retires to USA, establishes a pottery at Stamford, Connecticut; returns to England shortly before his death

W. B. Dalton, *Craftsmanship and Design in Pottery*, London, 1957
—*Notes from a Potter's Diary*, London, 1960
—*Just Clay*, Bristol, 1962
London, Hayward Gallery (1979)

151 Bowl, 1933
Stoneware, brown and green-grey mottled glaze; marks: 'WBD' in monogram, incised; h. 6.4 cm, d. 17.2 cm
C.412–1934. Source: given by the BIIA (gift of the potter in 1933)

152 Bowl, 1933
Stoneware, brown and grey mottled glaze; marks: 'WBD' in monogram, impressed; h. 11.2 cm, d. 16.9 cm
C.413–1934. Source: given by the BIIA (gift of the potter in 1933)

148

151 152

Dart Pottery 1975–

The Dart Pottery started life as the Dartington Pottery Training Workshop, and it still has an important training function. The original idea for a 'community workshop' to train students to a high standard in workshop production came in 1972 from David Leach (qv) and David Canter. The proposal was eventually taken up by Dartington Hall Ltd, and in 1975 Peter Starkey was appointed director. The workshop was set up at the Shinner's Bridge Pottery where Bernard Leach (qv) had worked in the 1930s and where Marianne de Trey (qv) had worked since the war. In 1976 the first students arrived for a one- or two-year period, in which they learnt not just potting skills but the necessary business skills to run a small workshop. Production consisted of a range of domestic pottery designed to be a good commercial product but easy to make by relatively inexperienced students. The first range of products was designed by Peter Starkey and Peter Cook. In 1984, the pottery was bought out by the management – Peter Cook, Steven Course and Peter Hazell, who continued to run it as a training workshop, but with a renewed commercial emphasis. Janice Tchalenko (qv) was asked to develop a new range of shapes and designs, and others based on these have been developed in-house. These new wares have been extremely successful.

Murray Fieldhouse, 'The Dartington Pottery Training Workshop', *CR*, 58/1979

Stephen Course, 'Dart Pottery – Colour from the Quarry', *CR*, 116/1989

153 Teapot and cover, *Black Rose* pattern, 1989
Stoneware, painted with coloured glazes; made at Dart Pottery; h. 16.2 cm, d. 21.3 cm
C.22&a–1989. Source: CPA, London, £46.55
Designed by Janice Tchalenko

154 Mug, *Black Rose* pattern, 1989
Stoneware, painted with coloured glazes; marks: 'DP' in monogram, impressed; made at Dart Pottery; h. 7.7 cm, d. 11.6 cm
C.23–1989. Source: CPA, London, £6.20
Designed by Janice Tchalenko

155 Jug, *Poppy* pattern, 1989
Stoneware, painted with coloured glazes; marks: 'DP' in monogram, impressed; made at Dart Pottery; h. 15.8 cm, d. 14.7 cm
C.24–1989. Source: CPA, London, £11
Designed by Janice Tchalenko

156 Plate, *Poppy* pattern, 1989
Stoneware, painted with coloured glazes; made at Dart Pottery; h. 3.4 cm, d. 27 cm
C.25–1989. Source: CPA, London, £13.15
Designed by Janice Tchalenko

157 Vase, *Leopard* pattern, 1989
Stoneware, painted with coloured glazes; made at Dart Pottery; h. 19.8 cm, d. 14.2 cm
C.26–1989. Source: CPA, London, £11.40
Designed by Janice Tchalenko

158 Plate, *Peacock* pattern, 1989
Stoneware, painted with coloured glazes; made at Dart Pottery; h. 3 cm, d. 22.2 cm
C.27–1989. Source: CPA, London, £24.20
Designed by Claire Woodhall, Dart Pottery

Davis, Derek 1926–

1945–49   studies painting at Central School of Art, London, self-taught potter
1953–   workshop in Essex producing press-moulded and slip-decorated earthenwares
1955–   new workshop in Arundel, Sussex; production includes handbuilt stonewares and porcelains as well as wheel-made wares
1967   Artist-in-residence, University of Sussex

Derek Davis is a very varied potter, producing until recently both vessels and more expressive handbuilt works. His recent work is intended as commentary on contemporary social issues.

159 Dish, 1982
Stoneware, painting in brown and black in a grey glaze; marks: 'Davis', painted in black; h. 5.5 cm, d. 34 cm
C.70–1984. Source: given by the Friends of the V&A
Purchased at the CPA 25th Anniversary exhibition, *Studio Ceramics Today*, held at the V&A in 1983.

Davis, Harry 1910–1986

Harry Davis worked in partnership with his wife, May.

Harry Davis trained at Bournemouth Art School before working as a thrower in a small tourist pottery at Broadstone, near Poole

c.1932   works for Bernard Leach (qv) at Dartington
1933–37   runs the Leach Pottery, St Ives, with Laurie Cookes during absence of Bernard and David Leach (qv) in the mid-1930s
1937–42   teaches at Achimota College, Ghana; taken over by Cardew (qv) in 1942
c.1943–6   works in Patagonia and South America
1946–62   sets up Crowan Pottery, Praze, Cornwall
1962–72   emigrates to New Zealand and sets up the Crewenna Pottery
1972–79   joins aid project at Izcuchaca in the Peruvian Andes, where he sets up a pottery
1979–   returns to Crewenna Pottery, New Zealand

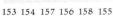
153 154 157 156 158 155

159

Harry Davis is a major figure as a domestic ware potter. He believed passionately in the importance of crafts in redressing the ills found in modern industrial society, but nevertheless took what could be usefully employed in the way of machinery from the industrialised world. He was exasperated by what he saw as a middle-class fear of the machines that infected Leach and Cardew, and he strove to make his product as efficient and practical as possible – any other view he would have seen as romantic amateurism. He made great efforts to develop a strong clay body that would not chip in normal use – and would demonstrate that his plates could be stood upon without breaking.

Harry Davis, 'Some Thoughts on Attitudes', CR, 13/1972
—'An Assessment of the Craft Movement', CR, 67/1981
—'Handcraft Pottery – Whence and Whither', CR, 93/1985
—*The Potter's Alternative, Methuen*, Australia, 1987
Cooper (1947)
Wingfield Digby (1952)
Rose (1955), (1970)
Exhibition review, CR, 13/1972
Michael Buckley, 'The Handworked Machine', CR, 67/1981
'Harry Davis – the Complete Potter', tributes, CR, 109/1988
Harry Horlock-Stringer, 'Harry and May Davis – Pots from Crewenna', CR, 115/1989

160 Bowl, 1950 (pl. 45)
Stoneware, incised decoration in a tenmoku glaze; marks: 'CP' in monogram, impressed; made at Crowan Pottery, Cornwall; h. 6.8 cm, d. 15.5 cm
Circ.61–1951. Source: Primavera, London, £0.30

161 Coffee pot and cover, 1950 (pl. 45)
Stoneware, iron painting in a grey-green glaze; marks: 'CP' in monogram, impressed; made at Crowan Pottery, Cornwall; h. 15.7 cm, d. 18.2 cm
Circ.62&a-1951. Source: *see* Circ.61–1951, £0.60

162 Tea-pot, 1951 (pl. 45)
Stoneware, tenmoku glaze; marks: 'CP' in monogram, impressed; made at Crowan Pottery, Cornwall; h. 16.6 cm, d. 19.8 cm
Circ.19&a–1952. Source: Primavera, London, £1.08

163 Dish, 1958
Stoneware, painting in a tenmoku glaze; marks: obscured seal; made at Crowan Pottery, Cornwall; h. 3.8 cm, d. 34.6 cm
Circ.42–1959. Source: the pottery, £4

164 Crock and cover, 1958
Stoneware, wax-resist painting in tenmoku over an oatmeal glaze; marks: 'CP' in monogram, impressed; made at Crowan Pottery, Cornwall; h. 32.6 cm, d. 34.7 cm
Circ.18&a-1959. Source: Primavera, London, £16.50. Published: London, Tate Gallery (1985, C27)
A paper label on base says 'Restricted sale. See Mr Rothschild'; another says 'Museum only. £16/10/-'.
This piece is remarkably well made with very thin walls and base, and shows the considerable skill of Davis as a thrower.

de Trey, Marianne 1913–

1913   born in London of Swiss parents
1932–36   studies textile design at the Royal College of Art
1938   marries Sam Haile (qv) with whom she learns pottery
1939   travels with Haile to USA
1945–47   returns to UK, becomes a full-time potter with Haile at Bulmers Brickyard, Sudbury, Suffolk
1947   takes over, with Haile, Shinner's Bridge Pottery, Dartington
1948   Haile killed in car accident, de Trey carries on pottery alone
1985   moves to a smaller workshop nearby

De Trey's earliest productions were domestic ware in slip-decorated or tin-glazed earthenware. These were made in a production pottery which employed several people and established a regular apprentice scheme. In the mid-1950s she started to produce oxidised stoneware, and finally a small wood-fired kiln allowed her to develop more personal work, in particular small pieces for flower arranging. De Trey has carried out several commissions for domestic and architectural tiles.

She has recently phased out the domestic ware, and works mostly in porcelain. Earlier domestic work, mostly made by her assistants, is marked with a shell alone; her personal work is marked with a device containing the letters 'dTe'.

Marianne de Trey, '35 Years a Potter', CR, 83/1983
The Studio Yearbook of Decorative Art, 1950, 1951, 1954, 1956 and 1967
Wingfield Digby (1952)
Casson (1967)
'Workshop', CR, 10/1971

165 Bowl, 1949–1950
Earthenware, tin glaze with decoration incised through a dark pigment; marks: 'de T' in a rectangular seal; h. 8.3 cm, d. 29 cm
Circ.278–1950. Source: Arts and Crafts Society (exhibition in V&A, 1950), £2.10

166 Dish, 1950
Earthenware, painting in colours in a white tin glaze; marks: scallop shell seal, impressed; made at Shinner's Bridge Pottery, Dartington; h. 5 cm, d. 28 cm
Circ.14–1951. Source: the potter, £1.50

165

163

166

167 Mug, 1950 (pl. 46)
Earthenware, painting in black, pink and yellow
in a white glaze; marks: scallop shell seal
impressed; made at Shinner's Bridge Pottery,
Dartington; h. 11.7 cm, d. 12.9 cm
Circ.11–1951. Source: the potter, £0.52

168 Jug, 1950 (pl. 46)
Earthenware, painting in blue, brown, green and
purple on a white tin glaze; marks: scallop shell
seal, impressed; made at Shinner's Bridge Pottery,
Dartington; h. 10 cm, d. 11.5 cm
Circ.6–1951. Source: the potter, £0.37

169 Butter dish, 1950 (pl. 46)
Earthenware, painting in blue on a white tin glaze;
marks: scallop shell seal, impressed; made at
Shinner's Bridge Pottery, Dartington; h. 2 cm,
d. 12.6 cm
Circ.5–1951. Source: the potter, £0.25

170 Jam pot, 1950
Earthenware, painting in brown, yellow and green
in a white tin glaze; marks: scallop shell seal
impressed; made at Shinner's Bridge Pottery,
Dartington; h. 8.2 cm, d. 9.5 cm
Circ.10&a–1951. Source: the potter, £0.62

171 Mug, 1950
Earthenware, slip decoration in white on a dark
ground; marks: scallop shell seal, impressed; made
at Shinner's Bridge Pottery, Dartington; h. 9.6 cm,
d. 11.2 cm
Circ.9–1951. Source: the potter, £0.37

172 Dish, 1950
Earthenware, slip decoration in green and white
on a black ground; marks: scallop shell seal,
impressed; made at Shinner's Bridge Pottery,
Dartington; h. 3.2 cm, d. 24.6 cm
Circ.8–1951. Source: the potter, £0.12

173 Dish, 1950
Earthenware, slip decoration in white and green
on a black ground; made at Shinner's Bridge
Pottery, Dartington; h. 2.4 cm, d. 16.2 cm
Circ.7–1951. Source: the potter, £0.25

174 Jug, 1950
Earthenware, decoration in white and green slip
on a red clay body; marks: scallop shell seal,
impressed; made at Shinner's Bridge Pottery,
Dartington; h. 12.4 cm, d. 12.8 cm
Circ.15–1951. Source: the potter, £0.52

175 Jug, 1950
Earthenware, incised decoration through a dark
slip; marks: scallop shell seal impressed; made at
Shinner's Bridge Pottery, Dartington; h. 17.6 cm,
d. 27.8 cm
Circ.12–1951. Source: the potter, £1.25

176 Bowl, 1950
Stoneware, applied decoration under a saltglaze;
made at Shinner's Bridge Pottery, Dartington;
h. 10.5 cm, d. 15 cm
Circ.13–1951. Source: the potter, £1.50

177 Bowl, 1961
Stoneware, cut decoration with a white glaze;
marks: scallop shell seal, impressed; made at
Shinner's Bridge Pottery, Dartington; h. 11 cm,
d. 18.5 cm
Circ.256–1961. Source: Craft Centre of Great
Britain, £2.10

178 Set of three bowls, 1961
Stoneware, cut decoration through an oatmeal
glaze; marks: scallop shell seal, impressed; made
at Shinner's Bridge Pottery, Dartington; largest
bowl: h. 9.9 cm, d. 12.6 cm
Circ.255 to b-1961. Source: *see* Circ.256–1961,
£2.63

170

174 175

177

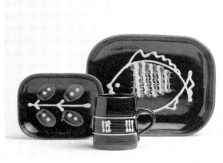

173 171 172

176

178

Dodd, Mike 1943–

1957–	inspired to make pottery by lessons from Donald Potter at Bryanston School
1962–65	takes a Natural Science degree at Cambridge University
1966–67	Hammersmith School of Art, London, where he finds the 'design orientation' unsympathetic
1967–71	first workshop in Edburton, Sussex
1971–75	new workshop near Battle, Sussex
1975–79	new workshop near Hayle, Cornwall
1979	spends six months with Indians in Peru helping set up large wood fired kiln at Amuesha project started by Harry Davis (qv)
1981–	moves to Cumbria, appointed Head of Ceramics at Carlisle College of Art
1986–	new workshop near Wigton, Carlisle

It is interesting to note that Donald Potter at Bryanston School inspired both Batterham (qv) and Dodd to make a career in pottery – both potters whose work follows the oriental stoneware tradition. Dodd's work is similar to that of Batterham, but rather freer and somewhat rougher in decoration and finish. He has developed an interest in textured glazes.

Mike Dodd, 'In Defence of Tradition', *PQ*, 11/43
—, 'Studio Pottery, Cumbria College of Art and Design', *Real Pottery*, 14/56
'CPA New Members', *CR*, 5/1970
Tim Proud, 'Mike Dodd – Unambiguous Potter', *CR*, 107/1987
Godden (1988)

179 Vase, 1989 (pl. 113)
Stoneware, incised decoration through a rough-textured green brown ash glaze; marks: 'MD' in a square monogram, impressed; h. 25.7 cm, d. 21.5 cm
C.38–1989. Source: CAA, London, £135

Dring, James *c*.1910–1985

1927–30	enters the Royal College of Art, London, as a painter, but attends pottery courses with William Staite Murray
1932–	own workshop in London, producing decorated tiles, plates and dishes
1947	ceases to pot, continues to work as a painter

Dishes similar to those catalogued here are illustrated in *The Studio Yearbook of Decorative Art*, 1950, pp. 84–5. *See* Catalogue no. 239 for a loving cup made by his friend Sam Haile to commemorate his marriage.

180

180 Plate, 1947
Earthenware, industrial blank, painted decoration in yellow, green, brown and blue; marks: 'J. DRING' and device, painted; h. 2.3 cm, d. 25.6 cm
C.83–1986. Source: bequest of the potter

181 Cup and saucer, dated 1947
Earthenware, industrial blank, painted decoration in green, yellow and black under a clear glaze; marks: 'JAMES DRING, 47' and mark, painted; h. 6 cm, d. 14.7 cm
C.81&a–1986. Source: bequest of the potter

182 Plate, 1947
Earthenware, industrial blank, painted decoration in blue, yellow, green, pink and brown; h. 4.3 cm, d. 25.6 cm
C.82–1986. Source: bequest of the potter

182 181

Duckworth, Ruth 1919–

1919	born in Hamburg, Germany
1936	emigrates to England
1936–40	studies sculpture and painting at Liverpool School of Art
1944	sets up sculpture workshop at Mortlake, Surrey
1956	consults Lucie Rie (qv) about glazes for small sculptures
1956–58	takes pottery course at Central School of Art, London
1959–64	teaches at Central School of Art, London
1964	receives invitation to teach in Chicago, USA; eventually emigrates permanently

184

185

Ruth Duckworth and Alice Westphal, *Ruth Duckworth*, Gallery of American Studies, Evanston, Illinois, 1977
Rose (1955),(1970; pls. 83–84)
Birks (1967), (1976)
Casson (1967)
Emmanuel Cooper, 'Ruth Duckworth – A Great Original', *CR*, 25/1974
Ruth Duckworth, exhibition at Boymans Museum, Rotterdam, with catalogue, 1979
Emmanuel Cooper, 'Ruth Duckworth – Artist Potter', *CR*, 68/1981
Garth Clark and Oliver Watson, *American Potters Today*, VAM, London, 1986
'Ruth Duckworth', *CR*, 102/1986
Tanya Harrod, 'Free Spirit', *Crafts*, March/April, 1987

Ruth Duckworth was much admired for her strongly designed tableware, but in retrospect it is her rough-textured, sculptural hand built work that seems the most innovative and influential.
The Museum possesses later work by Ruth Duckworth made in the USA catalogued in Clark and Watson cited above. The pieces catalogued here are all made in the UK, either before she went to the USA, or on her early trips back before she emigrated permanently.

183 Dish, 1959 (pl. 62)
Stoneware, painting in thick black pigment on a greenish glaze; marks: 'RWD', impressed; h. 9.2 cm, d. 40 cm
Circ.241–1959. Source: the potter, £7

184 Vase, 1959
Stoneware, coil made, unglazed with pale green glaze at the lip; h. 24.5 cm, d. 23.8 cm
Circ.242–1959. Source: the potter, £6

185 Form: *Tile Mask*, 1962
Stoneware, matt black mask on a mottled green glazed tile; h. 15 cm, d. 15 cm
Circ.617–1962. Source: Primavera, London, £4

186 Form, 1966
Porcelain, greenish glaze with black; h. 11.8 cm, d. 12.6 cm
Circ.763–1967. Source: Primavera, London, £8

187 Vase, 1966 (pl. 73)
Stoneware, handbuilt with spattered black and green glaze; h. 31.4 cm, d. 34 cm
Circ.764–1967. Source: *see* Circ.763–1967, £20

Dunn, Constance E. (née **Wade**)

1921–24 Cambridge School of Art
1924–27 studies pottery at Royal College of Art under Dora Billington (qv)
1927–30 studies ceramics at Royal College of Art under Staite Murray (qv)
1930–32 teaches at Constantine College, Middlesborough
c.1933 sets up own workshop at Billingham, Durham, working until the war on high-fired wares
1946 builds new oil kiln to her own design

Wingfield Digby (1952; p. 80, pl. 54)

188 Bowl, 1931
Stoneware, incised decoration in mottled brown and grey glaze; marks: 'W' in a triangle, impressed; h. 7 cm, d. 12.3 cm
C.415–1934. Source: given by the BIIA (acquired in 1931)
This piece was accessioned in the Museum under the potter's maiden name 'Wade'.

189 Bowl, 1954
Stoneware, brown painting in a mottled grey glaze; marks: impressed seal; h. 12 cm, d. 15.2 cm
Circ.338–1955. Source: the potter, £4.20

190 Bowl, 1947
Stoneware, black-green mottled glaze, brown rim; marks: 'W' in triangular seal, impressed; h. 7.8 cm, d. 17.2 cm
Circ.339–1955. Source: the potter, £6.30

El Nigoumi, Siddig 1931–

1931 born in the Sudan
1952–55 Khartoum Art School; calligrapher for Publications Bureau, Khartoum
1957–60 Central School of Art, London
1960–67 teaches in Khartoum
1967 returns to England
1968– teaches at West Surrey College of Art and Design, Farnham

El Nigoumi employs a traditional African technique – burnished handbuilt earthenware with incised decoration. His training as a calligrapher has given him a lively sense of form and line, and he achieves a

186

188

189 190

particularly satisfying colour and quality of surface for this most basic of all ceramic techniques.

Siddig El Nigoumi, 'Press Moulded Dishes', CR, 33/1975
'CPA New Members', CR, 24/1973
Paul Barron, 'Ceramics by Siddig El Nigoumi', exhibition review, *Crafts*, July/August, 1979

191 Drinking Vessel: *Ibreeq*, 1980
Earthenware, unglazed burnished clay with incised decoration; marks: 'Nigoumi 80' and a scorpion, incised; h. 22.4 cm, d. 20.5 cm
C.56–1980. Source: CPA, London (*Jugs* exhibition, 1980) £26
Ibreeq is the Arabic for jug.

192 Dish: *The Great Royal Wedding*, 1981
Earthenware, unglazed burnished clay with incised decoration; marks: a scorpion, incised; h. 6.4 cm, d. 38 cm
C.77–1984. Source: given by the Friends of the V&A
Purchased at the CPA 25th Anniversary exhibition, *Studio Ceramics Today*, held at the V&A in 1983.
The inscription (in Arabic) reads: al-zawwaj al-maliki al-kabir 1981 (= 'The Great Royal Wedding 1981'). On the reverse is incised: 'THE GREAT ROYAL WEDDING 1981 "ARABIC"' and 'Nigoumi 1981'.

Epton, Charlotte 1902–1970

c.1920–23	studies design at the Royal College of Art, London
1924–26	teaches art at Cheltenham Ladies College
1927–c.1930	works at the Leach Pottery, St Ives; allowed to do own work in the evenings; leaves distressed after firemen destroy her work by flooding a hot kiln while extinguishing a fire in the pottery
c.1931	comes to London, works as sales assistant in the Little Gallery
1932	marries the artist Edward Bawden, after which she ceased potting

Charlotte Epton was one of a number of people before the war who came for periods or on an occasional basis to work with Bernard Leach at St Ives. These pieces show her to have developed an individual style, and to have been a potter of subtlety and sensitivity.

London, Tate Gallery (1985)

193 Jar and cover, *c.1930*
Stoneware, pale grey crackled glaze; marks: 'EP' and 'SI' in monogram, impressed; made at Leach Pottery, St Ives; h. 17.7 cm, d. 10.4 cm
Circ.766&a-1931. Source: the potter (shown at the Arts and Crafts Society, Burlington House, London), £3.15
A note by B. Rackham, then Keeper of the Ceramic Department, in favour of acquisition says: 'I am satisfied that we were right in selecting for purchase for its admirable form and good glaze qualities this jar by Miss Epton for one of the exhibits of contemporary pottery'.

194 Bowl, 1931
Stoneware, a pale grey glaze and a green flush; marks: 'EP' and 'SI' in monogram, impressed; made at Leach Pottery, St Ives; h. 14 cm, d. 16 cm
C.417–1934. Source: given by the BIIA (purchased through the Spielmann Fund)

Feibleman, Dorothy 1951–

1951	born in Indiana, USA
1969–73	studies ceramics at Rochester Institute of Technology, New York, USA
1973	moves to England,
1973–75	workshop in Retford, Nottinghamshire
1975–	workshop in London

Feibleman is known for her fine agate work in porcelain, a technique she was inspired to develop by the desire to copy African glass beads. Different coloured clays are laminated and formed into small 'mille-fiore' bowls or elements for jewellery. Recently, jewellery has predominated in her work.

The Museum also possesses a necklace of gold and porcelain beads by this artist (M.127–1984).

'CPA New Members', CR, 35/1975
Fiona Adamczewski, 'Ceramics ... by Dorothy Feibleman', exhibition review, *Crafts*, September/October, 1979
John Catleugh, 'Dorothy Feibleman's Agate Porcelain', CR, 68/1981

195 Bowl: *Lunar II*, 1981
Porcelain, yellow, black, red and green clays in 'mille-fiore' technique; h. 7.1 cm, d. 11.5 cm
C.43–1981. Source: CPA, London, £288

196 Bowl, 1983
Porcelain, blue, yellow, green and white clays in 'mille-fiore' technique; h. 8 cm, d. 9.8 cm
C.161–1984. Source: the potter, £575

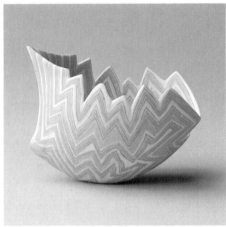
195

192

196

193 194

Fieldhouse, Murray 1925–

1945   decides to become a craftsman when demobbed from the RAF
1946–7   works with Harry Davis (qv) in Cornwall
1947–8   works at Kingwood Design and Craftsmanship, a craft workshop at Wormley, Surrey
1948–62   joins Pendley Centre for Adult Education, a pioneering Adult Education Centre, where amongst other other activities he sets up and teaches pottery courses
1949   produces first catalogue of 21 tableware shapes
1954–   produces, edits and publishes the journal *Pottery Quarterly* (from vol. 14, no. 56 renamed *Real Pottery*)
1959–60   produces journal *Crafts Review*, nos. 1–6

Murray Fieldhouse is a potter whose energies were progressively taken up by teaching, lecturing and publishing. He has been of great importance through his indefatigable and challenging editorship of *Pottery Quarterly* and the regrettably short-lived *Crafts Review*. These have provided an important and pioneering forum for lively, often pointed debate on issues of all kinds facing potters of all persuasions.

Murray Fieldhouse, *PQ* (throughout)
—*Crafts Review* (throughout)
—*Pottery*, London, 1952
E. E. Gilbert, 'Pendley Pottery', *Studio*, 141, 1951, pp. 86–7
The Studio Yearbook of Decorative Art, 1952, 1953, 1954, 1960 & 1961

197   Bowl, 1958
Stoneware, white glazed interior, unglazed exterior; marks: 'mf' in monogram, impressed; h. 8.4 cm, d. 15.4 cm
Circ.40–1959. Source: the potter, £2.36

198   Bowl, 1958
Stoneware, white glazed interior, unglazed exterior; marks: 'mf' in monogram, impressed; h. 6.4 cm, d. 12.4 cm
Circ.41–1959. Source: *see* Circ.40–1959, £2.36

Finch, Ray 1914–

c.1934   asks to join Michael Cardew's (qv) workshop after seeing some of his pots; Cardew advises him to get some experience
1935   spends year at the Central School of Art, London, under Dora Billington (qv)
1936   joins Cardew at Winchcombe
1939   Cardew moves to Wenford Bridge, Finch takes over Winchcombe as partner
1941   Cardew returns for a year before going to Africa
1943   Finch joins National Fire Service
1946   purchases business from Cardew, continues to rent premises
1952   small kiln experiments with stoneware; purchases workshops from owners
1959   earthenware production much reduced (discontinued in 1964), new oil-fired stoneware kiln
1960   Winchcombe Pottery is first exhibition at the new CPA shop
1961   Winchcombe supplies first Cranks vegetarian restaurant in London
1970–71   Finch spends six months in Lesotho running Kolonyama Pottery
1974   new large (130 cubic feet) wood-fired kiln built
1979   'officially' retires and hands pottery over to son Michael, but continues to work
1980   awarded MBE

Finch has kept the Winchcombe Pottery running for nearly 40 years. Its basic product has remained much the same – well-designed, well-crafted tableware. Finch was responsible for developing Cardew's wood-fired earthenware into a more practical stoneware product which has gained much popular success. His tableware, together with that of St Ives, set the standards for standard-ware potters round the country.

Raymond Finch, 'Winchcombe Pottery' *CR*, 3/1970
—'Making Teapots', *CR*, 99/1986
Wingfield Digby (1952)
Casson (1967)
Rose (1970)

Marigold Coleman, 'Ray Finch's Workshop', *Crafts*, September/October, 1974
London, CPA (1979): detailed booklet
Michael Cardew, 'Ray Finch', *CR*, 59/1979
York City Art Gallery (1983)
See also under **Michael Cardew**

199   Jug, 1941
Earthenware, dipped in white slip, green glaze; marks: 'RF' and 'WP' in monogram, impressed; made at Winchcombe Pottery; h. 15.8 cm, d. 14 cm
Circ.11–1941. Source: Heal and Son Ltd, London, £0.17

200   Jug, c.1950
Earthenware, white slip and brownish glaze; marks: 'WP' in monogram, impressed; made at Winchcombe Pottery; h. 20.4 cm, d. 18.2 cm
Circ.419–1950. Source: the potter, £1.05

201   Bowl, c.1950
Earthenware, white slip painting over a dark greenish slip; marks: 'WP' in monogram, impressed; made at Winchcombe Pottery; h. 7.4 cm, d. 12.6 cm
Circ.420–1950. Source: the potter, £0.37

202   Bowl, c.1950
Earthenware, decoration incised through a dark slip; marks: 'WP' in monogram, impressed; made at Winchcombe Pottery; h. 8 cm, d. 12.7 cm
Circ.421–1950. Source: the potter, £0.37

199 200

203 201 202

197 198

203 Baking dish, 1950
Earthenware, trailed white slip on black under an amber glaze; marks: 'WP' in monogram, impressed; made at Winchcombe Pottery; h. 3.5 cm, d. 19 cm
Circ.422–1950. Source: the potter, £0.37

204 Teapot, 1982
Stoneware, tenmoku glaze with decoration incised through glaze; made at Winchcombe Pottery; h. 17.7 cm, d. 20.6 cm
C.71&a–1984. Source: given by the Friends of the V&A
Purchased at the CPA 25th Anniversary exhibition, *Studio Ceramics Today*, held at the V&A in 1983

Winchcombe Standard Ware:

205 Handled pot and cover, 1988
Stoneware, wood fired with ash flashings; marks: seal, impressed; made at Winchcombe Pottery; h. 9.8 cm, d. 20.9 cm
C.21&a–1989. Source: David Mellor, Kitchen Shop, London, £8.66

206 Handled pot and cover, 1988
Stoneware, ash flashings; marks: seal, impressed; made at Winchcombe Pottery; h. 11.6 cm, d. 15 cm
C.18–1989. Source: David Mellor, Kitchen Shop, London, £5.27

Finnemore, Sybil dates not known

Sybil Finnemore attended classes at the Central School of Art, London, in the mid-1920s; she was commended for her work in a review of an exhibition of students' work in the *Pottery Gazette*, 1/8/1925. With her husband T. R. Parsons she ran the Yellowsands Pottery on the Isle of Wight from 1927–1932, and the Bembridge Pottery on the Isle of Wight from 1949–1961.

The Studio Yearbook of Decorative Art, 1928, 1930 & 1931
Godden (1964)

207 Vase, dated 1926 (pl. 38)
Stoneware, painting in black on a grey slip; marks: 'S. FINNEMORE 1926', incised; h. 21.8 cm, d. 16.2 cm
C.416–1934. Source: given by the BIIA (acquired in 1926)

Fournier, Sheila 1930–

1949–50 Teacher Training at Goldsmiths College, London
1961 marries potter Robert Fournier, from whom she learns pottery
1961–65 workshop in Greenwich, London
1965–71 workshop in Kent
1971–87 workshop in Lacock, Wiltshire
1987 retires from potting

Sheila and Robert Fournier formed a potting team which produced interesting work, both repetition table wares and individual pieces, over a long period of time. Sheila Fournier is known for the bold sweeping bowls as represented here, and for more delicate work in inlaid porcelain that she developed later.

Sheila Fournier, 'Built-in Decoration', *CR*, 9/1970

208 Bowl, 1969
Stoneware, handbuilt, with blue glaze of varying thickness; marks: 'SF' in a circle, impressed; h. 16 cm, d. 35.5 cm
Circ.661–1969. Source: Primavera, London, £16

205 206

204

208

Fox-Strangways, Sylvia *c.1900–c.1975*

c.1920–25 attends classes at the Central and Camberwell Schools of Art, and at the Royal College of Art, London

1926 works at the Leach Pottery, St Ives

1926–29 works as resident artist on the Dartington Estate, having been recommended by Bernard Leach (qv); teaches drawing and painting, and builds a small pottery workshop and kiln

1929 retires through ill-health from active participation in the Dartington Community; remains a friend of Dorothy Elmhirst at Dartington, and occasionally recommends paintings to her from the London galleries

The Studio, January, 1926, p. 34

Sylvia Fox-Strangways exhibited with the BIIA and ACES in the 1920s. She was highly active in her three years at Dartington Hall, the progressive, artistic and agricultural estate developed by the Elmhirsts from the 1920s. Fox-Strangways, to the eventual detriment of her health, committed herself wholeheartedly to introducing art into the life of the entire community, including the agricultural and forestry workers. She made both tiles and vessels in her workshop – tiles similar to those catalogued here decorate many of the fire-surrounds at Dartington Hall where a number of her pots are also still preserved.

209 Tile, 1926
Stoneware, painting in red, yellow and black in a cream glaze; made at the Leach Pottery, St Ives; h. 10.5 cm, d. 10.3 cm
C.418–1934. Source: given by the BIIA (gift of Bernard Leach in 1926)

210 Tile, 1926
Stoneware, painting in red, green and black; marks: 'S.F.S.' in monogram, and '1926', painted; made at the Leach Pottery, St Ives; h. 10.5 cm, d. 10.2 cm
C.419–1934. Source: given by the BIIA (gift of Bernard Leach in 1926)

Franklin, Ruth 1948–

1965–6 foundation course at Hornsey School of Art, London

1966–72 works in advertising as designer and art director

1971 lives for five months in Kibbutz in Israel, then travels in Iran and Afghanistan

1972 studies ceramics at Croyden School of Art, London

1973–75 takes ceramics course at Harrow School of Art, London

1975–84 workshop with the Barbican Arts Group, London

1977 nine months' travel in West Africa

1984– teaching on foundation course at Camberwell School of Art, London

c. 1982 gives up clay to move into sculpture and eventually into painting

1984–89 new workshop at Faroe Rd Studios, London

1989– new workshop in North London

'CPA New Members', *CR*, 60/1979
Exhibition review, *Arts Review*, 30 September 1983
Ruth Franklin, Ladies and Chairs, exhibition pamphlet, Sunderland Arts Centre, n.d.

In early 1980s, Franklin stopped making the vessels and concentrated on making figures built from clay slabs painted with acrylic paints. Frustrated by the technical limitations of clay and the small scale it imposed, she abandoned ceramics to work in wood and other materials, before taking up painting.

211 Vase: *Arsenal, c.* 1980
Porcelain, painted in underglaze colours; marks: 'R. Franklin', painted; h. 14.3 cm, d. 12.5 cm
C.69–1980. Source: V&A Craft Shop, £31

Frith, David 1943–

1960s studies industrial ceramics at Wimbledon Art School, London, followed by pottery course at Stoke-on-Trent School of Art

1963 sets up workshop in North Wales with wife, Margaret, making slip-decorated earthenware

1968– produces stonewares

1976– produces porcelain

Frith is very much a 'workshop' potter – earning his living almost entirely from sales of his work. He exemplifies the very high levels of technical achievement by the stoneware potters of the Leach school.

Exhibition review, *Crafts*, November/December, 1981
Emmanuel Cooper, 'David Frith – Potter', with section on workshop practice by David Frith, *CR*, 97/1986

212 Covered jar, *c.* 1982
Stoneware, tenmoku glaze, green glazed interior; marks: 'df' in monogram and a device, impressed; h. 19 cm, d. 15.8 cm
C.14&a–1982. Source: CPA, London (solo exhibition, 1982), £27

213 Dish, square,on four feet, 1982 (pl. 115)
Stoneware, tenmoku glaze with wax resist decoration and painting in iron; marks: 'df' in monogram and a device, impressed; h. 8.6 cm, d. 38.8 cm
C.72–1984. Source: given by the Friends of the V&A
Purchased at the CPA 25th Anniversary exhibition, *Studio Ceramics Today*, held at the V&A in 1983

211

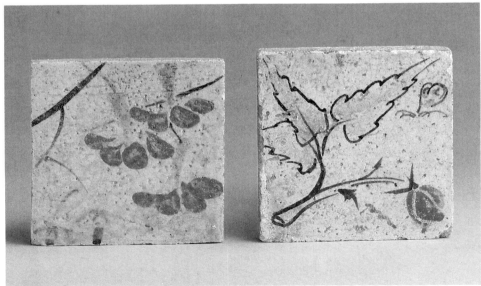

209 210

212

Fritsch, Elizabeth 1940–

1940	born in Wales
1958–64	studies harp and piano at the Royal Academy of Music, London
1968–71	studies ceramics at Royal College of Art, London, awarded Silver medal and Herbert Read Memorial Prize
1972–73	works at Bing and Grondahl factory, Copenhagen, Denmark; wins major prize in Royal Copenhagen Porcelain Jubilee Competition
1973–76	studio at Gestingthorpe, Suffolk
1974	solo exhibition at the Crafts Advisory Council gallery, London
1976–85	studio at Digswell, Herts
1978–79	*Pots about Music*, touring solo exhibition, Leeds Art Galleries
*c.*1980–84	little work done
1984	*Pots From Nowhere*, solo exhibition, Royal College of Art, organised by Queensbury Hunt
1985–	studio in East London

Fritsch has been perhaps the most influential potter of recent decades. The first of the 'new ceramics' group to emerge from the Royal College of Art in the 1970s, she anticipated many of the themes that were to be widely taken up in the 1970s and 1980s: handbuilding, concentration on the 'vessel', games with perspective and flattened forms, new attention to decoration and colour. Her pots are almost to be treated as still lifes, viewed from a single standpoint. The subject matter of her vessels is twofold: the self-referential theme of the space that the vessel both occupies and contains, both in reality and in the onlooker's perceptions; and the nature of the decoration, both in its relationship to the form of the vessel, and in its relationship to music, a major inspiration behind the work. Fritsch has developed a formidable technical skill with which to realise her ideas; her pots are beautifully balanced, the textures and colours developed with great subtlety, and the patterns applied with great clarity but without deadening precision. Few potters can 'work' their pots so much and still retain such real ceramic quality.

Elizabeth Fritsch, 'Juggling into Jugs', *Crafts*, November/December, 1979
—'Pots from Nowhere', *Crafts*, November/December, 1984
—'Notes on Time in Relation to the Making and Painting of Pots', *Crafts*, March/April, 1989
London, CC (1974)
Cameron and Lewis (1976)
Ian Bennet, 'Elizabeth Fritsch', exhibition review, *Crafts*, March/April, 1977
J. Catleugh, 'Recent Pots by Elizabeth Fritsch', exhibition review, *CR*, 44/1977
Elizabeth Fritsch, Pots about Music, exhibition catalogue, Leeds Art Galleries, Temple Newsam House, 1978
Peter Inch, 'Pots about Music', exhibition review, *Crafts*, November/December, 1978
John Russel Taylor, 'Elizabeth Fritsch – Pots about Music', *Crafts*, July/August, 1979
'News', *Crafts*, July/August, 1980
Pots from Nowhere, exhibition leaflet, Royal College of Art, 1984
Philip Rawson, 'Pots from Nowhere', exhibition review, *Crafts*, March/April, 1985
Peter Dormer, *Elizabeth Fritsch in Studio*, London, 1985

214 Vase, 1975
Stoneware, mottled white matt glaze on the exterior, yellow glaze inside, coloured blue and red on rim; marks: 'R' in a circle, impressed; h. 22.8 cm, d. 11.6 cm
Circ.408–1975. Source: Primavera, Cambridge (exhibition: Ceramic Form, Kettles Yard, Cambridge, 1975), £72

215 Vase: *Saxophone and Piano Duo*, 1978 (pl. 17)
Stoneware, pale green, black, pink, brown, mauve and white matt glazes; h. 26 cm, d. 10.3 cm
C.160&a-1979. Source: Leeds City Art Galleries (from the exhibition: *Pots About Music*, 1978), £420

216 Vase: *Optical Pot*, 1980 (pl. 93)
Stoneware, coloured matt glazes; h. 31.1 cm, d. 23.2 cm
C.13–1981
Given in memory of Robert Kenedy, Assistant Keeper of the National Art Library, by a group of colleagues and friends.

217 Vase: *Funeral Urn: Windblown*, 1984
Stoneware, matt glazes in pale blue, white and black; h. 31.3 cm, d. 22.1 cm
C.51–1985. Source: Queensbury Hunt, London (*Pots from Nowhere*, RCA exhibition, 1984), £1800

Fuller, Geoffrey 1936–

1936	born in Chesterfield, Derbyshire
1953–65	librarian in Sheffield
1965–66	foundation course at Chesterfield College of Art
1966–70	studies ceramics at West Surrey College of Art and Design, Farnham, followed by 18 months as technical assistant
1971–88	workshop in Chesterfield, North Derbyshire
1972–73	works with young female offenders in an assessment centre, Sheffield
1973–75	course tutor, Adult Education Centre, Chesterfield
1975–87	part-time and later full-time lecturer on the ceramics course at Chesterfield College of
1987	gives up teaching to pot full-time
1988–	purchases and takes on licence to run 17th century farmhouse/pub at Tideswell, Derbyshire

Fuller is a potter who produces curiously folksy mediaeval pots: they charm by strong, rather wobbly forms enhanced by positive applied decoration and generously warm colour of glaze. Fuller also makes figure-models with the same innocent quality of his vessels.

Occasionally Fuller's name is inscribed on the base of the slab figures. Earlier pieces of salt-glazed stoneware may be marked with initials or with a stamp of a bearded face.

'CPA New Members', *CR*, 10/1971
Ceramics Monthly, October, 1985
'Geoffrey Fuller – Folk Potter', *CR*, 110/1988

218 Pot and cover, 1988
Earthenware, green slip under a clear glaze; h. 15.1 cm, d. 14.3 cm
C.8&a–1989. Source: CAA, London, £86

214

217

Garland, David 1941–

1941   born in Kettering, Northamptonshire
1946–61   lives in New Zealand
1961–64   London College of Printing and Graphic Design
early 1970s teaches himself pottery, living in Oxford
1972–75   workshop in Oxford
1975–   moves workshop to Chedworth, Gloucestershire
1987   *David Garland: Ceramics*, Crafts Council touring exhibition

David Garland, a painter and graphic artist, turned to pottery while working as a designer for the Oxford University Press. Making a range of domestic shapes, he has been much acclaimed for his painting talent, done in blue or brown on a white slip ground.

Pamela Johnson, 'Singing the Blues', *Crafts*, September/October, 1984
Henry Pim, 'Finding a Voice', *CR*, 105/1987
Tanya Harrod, 'David Garland: Ceramics', exhibition review, *Crafts*, September/October, 1987

219 Bowl, 1984
Earthenware, painting in blue on a white slip under a transparent glaze; marks: 'Garland', incised and 'Garland 84', painted; h. 11.3 cm, d. 36 cm
C.187–1984. Source: Amalgam Gallery, London, £128

Gaunce, Marion 1945–

1969–70 foundation course at Worthing School of Art
1970–71 one year at West Surrey College of Art and Design, Farnham
1978–81 ceramics at Croydon College of Art, London, winning the Marlow Award in her last year
1980–   sets up a workshop at home in South Croydon, London

Gaunce uses a painstaking process to achieve laminated colours in porcelain. Her output is small as the work is very slow to make and difficult to fire.

Kenneth Clark, 'Marian Gaunce – Colour in Clay', *CR*, 91/1985

220 Vase, 1982
Porcelain, press-moulded, laminated pink, grey, black and white clays, unglazed; h. 18.6 cm, d. 18.6 cm
C.148–1982. Source: Christopher Wood Gallery, London, £500

221 Dish, 1984
Porcelain, laminated white and blue-grey clays, unglazed; marks: 'MG', impressed; h. 5.9 cm, d. 27.9 cm
C.186–1984. Source: Queensbury Hunt, London, £250

Godfrey, Ian 1942–

1942   born in London
1957–62 Camberwell School of Art, London, studying first painting, then pottery with Dick Kendall
1962–67 first workshop in City Road, London
1967–68 uses the facilities at the Royal College of Art, London
        workshop in Goswell Road, Islington, London
1976–80 sets up and runs domestic pottery workshop for Hans Jorgen Grum in Copenhagen, Denmark
1980–   returns to Britain and sets up a new workshop in Highgate, London

Ian Godfrey enjoyed great success in the 1970s with his private world created in landscape boxes populated with miniature animals and houses (though never with people). His work, hand-carved by penknife and covered with dry, matt glazes, is imbued with archaeological and ritual references and decorated with symbols from distant civilisations, in particular the ancient Near East. It is illuminating to contrast his imagery and humour with the more robust, urban and cynical humour of the potters of the 1980s: Godfrey appears, true to the spirit of the time, otherworldly, mystical and magical.

Rosemary Wren and Peter Crotty, 'The Secret Life of Ian Godfrey', *CR*, 16/1972
Tony Hepburn, 'Ian Godfrey', exhibition review, *Crafts*, July/August, 1974
Cameron and Lewis (1976)
Birks (1976)
London, VAM (1977)
Ian Godfrey, exhibition pamphlet, Besson Gallery, London, 1989

218

220 221

219

222 *Large White Chest of Drawers*, 1969–1970 (pl. 76)
Stoneware, handbuilt with a matt off-white glaze;
h. 31 cm, d. 23.8 cm
Circ.57 to dd-1970. Source: Primavera, London,
£20

223 Dish, 1972
Stoneware, cut and incised decoration under a
matt black glaze; h. 6.8 cm, d. 25.7 cm
Circ.423–1972. Source: *see* Circ.422–1972, £12.15

224 Lidded pot, 1972
Stoneware, matt white and yellow-brown glaze;
h. 20.2 cm, d. 14.5 cm
Circ.422&a-1972. Source: Crafts Centre of Great
Britain, £16.20

225 *Grey Fox Box*, 1974 (pl. 77)
Stoneware, applied modelled elements under a
grey matt glaze; h. 27 cm, d. 28.5 cm
Circ.491&a-1974. Source: BCC, London, £55.12

226 *Anxiety Bowl*, 1976
Stoneware, carved elements assembled, with a
matt black glaze; h. 8.8 cm, l. 35.9 cm
Circ.532–1976. Source: BCC, London, £21.27

227 *Barrel Pot*, 1976
Stoneware, hand modelled, with thick pitted grey-
green glaze; h. 13.5 cm, d. 25 cm
Circ.533–1976. Source: the potter, £42.50
The piece contains pellets of clay to rattle when
it is moved.

Gordon, William dates not known

1930s sculptor and designer of decorative ironwork
1939 begins experimenting in a small salt-glaze
factory at Brampton in Chesterfield, work is
interrupted by the war
1946– sets up his own saltglaze workshop, continuing
to develop saltglazes and cast forms

William Gordon forms part of a vogue for animal figures
which occurred in the 1950s. He had, however,
developed both his technique and some of his models
already by the beginning of the war. His work in the
1950s is to be seen in association with the figurative
model work of William Newland (qv), Margaret Hine
(qv), the Parkinsons (qv), Stephen Sykes (qv) and others.
His work is in fact very different in technique – it is all
slip-cast in porcelain or white stoneware and saltglazed
over coloured slips. Gordon was seen by Wingfield
Digby as a bridge between the artist and industry – a
workshop using industrial techniques, producing in
some quantity, while small enough to be under the
direct control of the artist-designer who is personally
responsible for all the moulds.

London, British Council (1942)
Hugh Wakefield, 'William Gordon's Saltglaze', *The
Studio*, 141/1951, p. 114
Wingfield Digby (1952; p. 84–5, pl. 63)

228 Bowl, 1950
Porcelain, cast, with incised decoration, brown
painting and saltglazed; made at the Walton
Pottery Co., Chesterfield; h. 6.3 cm, d. 13 cm
Circ.189–1950. Source: the pottery, £1.50

229 *Clown*, 1950 (pl. 51)
Porcelain, cast with a grey slip, salt-glazed; made
at the Walton Pottery Co., Chesterfield; h. 36 cm,
d. 7 cm
Circ.186–1950. Source: the pottery, £2.50
A version of this model was designed and made
before the war, and was included in the exhibition
which toured the USA and Canada during the
war, *see* London, British Council (1942)

230 *Seagull*, 1950
Porcelain, cast, with a black slip and saltglazed;
made at the Walton Pottery Co., Chesterfield;
h. 16.2 cm, d. 20.8 cm
Circ.187–1950. Source: the pottery, £1.50

231 *Quail*, 1951
Porcelain, covered with a cream slip and
saltglazed; marks: 'O' with stroke through in black
enamel and 'Made in England', printed; made at
the Walton Pottery Co., Chesterfield; h. 17 cm,
d. 20.3 cm
Circ.76–1952. Source: Story & Co., London, £2.10

223

224

226

227

228

232 231 230

232 *Duck*, 1955
Porcelain, cast, with a black slip and saltglazed;
made at the Walton Pottery Co., Chesterfield;
h. 16.6 cm, d. 16.7 cm
Circ.116–1956. Source: given by the pottery

233 Lamp base, 1950
Porcelain, cast, with blue-black slip and saltglazed;
marks: 'O' with a stroke through, incised; made at
the Walton Pottery Co., Chesterfield; h. 41 cm,
d. 11.6 cm
Circ.188–1950. Source: the pottery, £2.20

234 Lamp base, 1955
Porcelain, cast, saltglaze over a grey slip; marks:
'O' with a stroke through, painted and 'MADE
IN ENGLAND', printed; made at the Walton
Pottery Co., Chesterfield; h. 21.2 cm, d. 13.4 cm
Circ.117–1956. Source: *see* Circ.116–1956

Gregory, Ian 1942–

1968– returns to large-scale sculpture having worked
as an actor in films, TV and the theatre for 10
years

1972 sets up a workshop to make wood-fired
earthenware; self-taught potter; starts by
making terracotta flowerpots 'to learn to throw
efficiently'

1976 begins to develop the saltglaze technique for
his sculpture

1977 publishes book on *Kiln Building*, visiting lecturer
at Bath, Cardiff, Corsham and Medway Schools
of Art

1978 interest develops in watercolours, while
continuing to produce sculpture in clay and
bronze

1980 moves to Suffolk; starts to paint in oils; later
returns to Dorset

In the ceramic world, Gregory is particularly known for
his 'portraits of old buildings' and other small-scale
modelling which he initially developed as a break from
his larger scale sculptural work.

Ian Gregory, *Kiln Building*, London, 1977
'CPA New Members', *CR*, 36/1976

235 Model: *Chest of Drawers*, 1980
Stoneware, brown saltglaze; h. 13.8 cm, d. 7 cm
C.180–1980. Source: Casson Gallery, London,
£11.50

Groves, Lewis A. dates not known

Lewis Groves is recorded as working with Margaret
Leach (qv) at the Barnhouse Pottery from 1946–47,
and at the Taena Community, Upton St Leonards,
Gloucestershire, from 1948, where he was joined by
Margaret Leach in 1951.

Godden (1964)

236 Dish, 1950
Earthenware, black slip trailed on white under an
amber glaze; marks: cross in a double circle,
impressed; made at the Taena Community,
Aylburton; h. 3.8 cm, d. 28.5 cm
Circ.156–1950. Source: the potter, £1.25

237 Jug, 1950
Earthenware, amber glaze; marks: cross in a double
circle, impressed; made at the Taena Community,
Aylburton; h. 10.5 cm, d. 12 cm
Circ.157–1950. Source: the potter, £0.33

Gunn-Russel, Linda 1953–

1953 born in London
1971–75 ceramics at Camberwell School of Art
1975–78 studio in 401 1/2 Workshops
1978–82 studio in Clapham, London
1982–88 studio in East Dulwich, London
1988– studio in Swiss Cottage, London

Gunn-Russel's work elaborates on visual tricks of
perspective, following on from the pots with flattened
form first made by James Tower (qv) and later
developed by Liz Fritsch (qv). This early piece is in
raku. Later pots are technical *tours de force* of
construction and decoration, often tall sinuous vases
or jugs in flattened perspective.

Abigail Frost, exhibition review, *Crafts*,
January/February, 1985

238 Jug, 1980
Stoneware, raku fired with a trailed white glaze
over unglazed black; h. 26 cm, d. 26.8 cm
C.117–1980. Source: BCC, London, £47.90

233 234

235

236 237

238

187

Haile, Thomas Sam 1909–1948

1909 born in London; leaves school at 15, works in a shipping firm, attending evening classes at Clapham School of Art, London

1931–34 scholarship to Royal College of Art, London; sees that he will fail his diploma if he continues to paint in a contemporary idiom, so transfers to pottery school under William Staite Murray

1935 appointed pottery instructor in the Department of Industrial Design, Leicester College of Art

1936– moves to London, teaching Kingston and Hammersmith Schools of Art, shares workshop with Margaret Rey (qv) at Raynes Park

1937 first solo show, Brygos Gallery, London

1938 marries Marianne de Trey (qv); joins Surrealist Group and Artists International Association

1939 moves to USA

1940–41 various 'bum jobs' including teaching kids on the Lower East Side, eventually teaching at New York State College of Ceramics

1942 appointed pottery instructor in the College of Architecture, University of Michigan

1943 September, enlisted in army

1944 transferred to British Army and sent to Britain, sergeant-instructor in the Army Educational Corps

1945 concussed in motorcycle accident, discharged from army; works at Bulmer Brickyard and workshop at Sudbury, Suffolk; confidence much shaken by interruption of Army life and turns to 'traditional' form of slipware as a means of rebuilding confidence

1946 appointed pottery consultant to the Rural Industries Bureau

1947 moves to Shinners' Bridge, Dartington

1948 March, killed in motor accident at Poole, Dorset; memorial exhibitions at Southampton Art Gallery and Institute of Contemporary Arts, Washington, USA

Sam Haile is a tantalising figure in British studio pottery. His tragically early death prevented him having a major influence on the British scene, though he is given an important role in the development of pottery in the USA. Obviously a man of great talent, his life was constantly disrupted, forcing him to start from scratch on more than one occasion. From the work that does survive, we can see a genuinely inventive mind, able to reinterpret old forms and techniques in a thoroughly 'modern' manner. He has an individual view of pottery form, a mastery in integrating decoration with a pot's form and of revealing depths of space. He trained as a painter, becoming involved with the surrealist movement.

Cooper (1947; pls. 9-14)
Tributes in *Craft Horizons*, Summer, 1949
Wingfield Digby (1952; pls. 36–40)
Rose (1955), (1970)
The Surrealist Paintings and Drawings of Sam Haile, Manchester Institute of Contemporary Arts, touring show catalogue, with introduction and chronology by A.C. Sewter, 1967–8 (with good bibliography)
Garth Clark and Marianne de Trey, 'Sam Haile', *Studio Potter*, 1977
London, Hayward Gallery (1979)
London, Christopher Wood Gallery (1980)
Sam Haile, exhibition pamphlet, Birch and Conran, London, 1987
Marianne de Trey, 'Sam Haile – Painter and Potter', *CR*, 107/1987

239 Loving cup, 1947
Earthenware, white slip decoration under an amber glaze; marks: 'HS' in monogram, impressed; h. 21.1 cm, d. 20.6 cm: the inscription reads: 'Olive & James Dring/29 March/1947/Drink Be Merry & Marry'
C.80–1986. Source: bequest of James Dring
Made to commemorate the marriage of his friend James Dring (qv).

240 Jug, *c*.1947
Earthenware, white on dark slip with dragged decoration under an amber glaze; marks: seal, impressed; h. 24 cm, d. 19.5 cm
C.78–1986. Source: bequest of James Dring

241 Mug, *c*.1947
Earthenware, white over dark slip with dragged decoration under an amber glaze; marks: seal, impressed; h. 10 cm, d. 12.4 cm
C.79–1986. Source: bequest of James Dring

242 Jug, *c*.1947
Earthenware, dark and white slip and finger-wipe decoration under an amber glaze; marks: 'HS' in monogram, impressed; h. 24.7 cm, d. 19.4 cm
C.77–1986. Source: bequest of James Dring

243 Jug, *c*.1946
Earthenware, white and dark slip with incised decoration under an amber glaze; marks: 'Bulmer', incised and 'HS' in monogram, impressed; made at Bulmer Brickyard, Suffolk; h. 24.4 cm, d. 16.9 cm
C.76–1986. Source: bequest of James Dring

239

240 241

243 242

244 Dish, *c*.1947 (pl. 14)
Earthenware, decoration in coloured slips; marks: 'SH' in monogram, impressed; made at Bulmer Brickyard, Suffolk; h. 9.5 cm, d. 34.6 cm
Circ.286–1951. Source: Marianne de Trey (Haile memorial exhibition, Craft Centre, London, August 1951), £9.80

245 Jug, *c*.1947 (pl. 48)
Earthenware, decoration in brown and white slips under an amber glaze; marks: impressed device; made at Shinner's Bridge Pottery, Dartington; h. 32.7 cm, d. 16.5 cm
Circ.287–1951. Source: *see* Circ.286–1951, £5.25
This jug exemplifies Haile's creative use of old traditions – the shape here is clearly based on a mediaeval form, and the slip trailed technique dates back many centuries, yet he has produced a totally contemporary object, with no nostalgic overtones.

246 Jug, 1948
Earthenware, painting in blue and yellow in a white tin glaze; marks: 'HS' in monogram and a 'acorn' seal, impressed; made at Shinner's Bridge Pottery, Dartington; h. 19.7 cm, d. 17.5 cm
Circ.288–1951. Source: *see* Circ.286–1951, £4.20

Hall, William R. 1945–

1941	born in Jerusalem
1959–61	Lowestoft School of Art
1962–65	Central School of Art, London
1966–74	teaches at School of Design and Furniture, High Wycombe
1974–	lecturer, then senior lecturer in charge of ceramics, Sir John Cass School of Art, London

Hall's early work consisted of slip-cast models of cars and aeroplanes. Later work shows an interest in the integration of art and design, using techniques from printing, painting and sculpture in his tile-plaques.

William Hall, *Slip Casting*, CR, 9/1971
Marigold Coleman, 'Painting on Clay', *Crafts*, November/December, 1978
Geoffrey Weston, '3 in Ceramics', exhibition review, *Crafts*, March/April, 1980

247 Wall plaque: *Future Man, c*.1978
Porcelain, inlaid with coloured stoneware clays; h. 22.5 cm, d. 11.3 cm
C.111–1978. Source: the potter, £60

Hamada Shoji 1894–1978

1894	born in Tokyo, Japan
1913	studies ceramics at Tokyo Technical College
1915	visits Japan's traditional pottery sites
1918	meets Bernard Leach (qv)
1919	works with Leach at Abiko
1920	accompanies Leach to England, helps build climbing kiln at St Ives
1923	two shows at Paterson's Gallery, London
1923–24	tours Europe, returns to Japan
1929	visits England with Yanagi, exhibition at Paterson's Gallery, London
1930–	pottery at Mashiko
1931	exhibition at Patterson's Gallery, London
1952	to Dartington with Yanagi for conference, followed by trip to USA with Leach and Yanagi
1950s-60s	frequent trips to the USA
1955	declared a National Living Treasure

Hamada is an enormously influential potter in the story of British studio pottery. He helped Leach establish his pottery in St Ives and gave Leach help and support at critical moments in his career. He is regarded by many potters and critics as the ultimate potter and has been a source of inspiration to a wide range of potters far beyond the 'St Ives school'. There is a very relaxed quality about the process of Hamada's throwing and decorating, but, paradoxically, the finished results are highly charged. His work stands in marked contrast to that of his life-long friend Bernard Leach (qv) who tends to tighter forms and more graphic decoration. Hamada's qualities are already apparent in these early works from St Ives, though they reveal some of the difficulties in materials and firing that characterise all the earliest products from St Ives.

The Museum also possesses a number of later works of Hamada made in Japan, and not catalogued here.

'Hamada', in conversation with Bernard Leach, Victor Margrie and Michael Casson, *Crafts*, September/October, 1973
Bernard Leach, *Hamada, Potter*, Tokyo and New York, 1975
Bernard and Janet Leach, 'Shoji Hamada', CR, 50/1978

248 Bowl, 1922–1923
Earthenware, incised decoration through a white slip, brown glaze and painting; marks: Hamada's seal and 'SI' in monogram, impressed; made at Leach Pottery, St Ives; h. 6.5 cm, d. 18.2 cm
Circ.542–1923. Source: Paterson's Gallery, £2.75

246

247

248

249 Bowl, 1923
Stoneware, wax resist decoration in a tenmoku
glaze; marks: Hamada's seal and 'SI' in monogram,
impressed; made at the Leach Pottery, St Ives;
h. 7 cm, d. 19.7 cm
C.106–1924. Source: given by S. K. Greenslade

250 Bowl, *c*.1923
Stoneware, tenmoku glaze with black splashes;
marks: 'SI' in monogram and Hamada's seal,
impressed; made at the Leach Pottery, St Ives;
h. 5.4 cm, d. 17 cm
Circ.992–1924. Source: given by W. Winkworth,
London
Willie Winkworth recounts in a letter : 'Murray,
the potter [William Staite Murray qv], admired it
enormously at Hamada's first show and told
Hamada to raise the price; which he was about
to do when he found I had been there the day
before and bought it.'

251 Bowl, 1923
Stoneware, iron painting in a tenmoku glaze;
marks: Hamada's seal and 'SI' in monogram,
impressed; made at the Leach Pottery, St Ives;
h. 8.6 cm, d. 22.8 cm
C.407–1934. Source: given by the BIIA (gift of
Bernard Leach in 1927)

252 Vase, 1923 (pl. 29)
Stoneware, painting in brown under a milky grey
glaze; marks: Hamada's seal and 'SI' in monogram,
impressed; made at the Leach Pottery, St Ives;
h. 19.5 cm, d. 12.4 cm
C.411–1934. Source: given by the BIIA (gift of
Bernard Leach in 1927)

249

250 251

Hamlyn, Jane 1940–

1961–	trains as State Registered Nurse, University College Hospital, London
1968	pottery classes at Putney Adult Education Centre, London
1972–74	Harrow School of Art, London
1975–	Millfield Pottery in Nottinghamshire

Jane Hamlyn is one of the most creative potters making
functional wares. She has developed a very satisfying
range of saltglaze textures and colours on an inventive
range of forms which tend now to be highly decorated.
Her work, unlike that of Keeler (qv) to which it is often
compared, is robust and eminently usable.

Jane Hamlyn, 'Paper resist Decoration', *CR*, 55/1979
—'Salt Glaze and Something Else', *Ceramics Monthly*,
April, 1989, pp. 32–36
Rosemary Wren and Peter Crotty, exhibition review,
'Jane Hamlyn: Salt-Glazed Pottery', *Crafts*, May/June,
1976
'CPA New Members', *CR*, 43/1977

253

254

Anne Leon, 'Jane Hamlyn at Millfield Pottery', *CR*,
74/1982
Peter Starkey, 'Jane Hamlyn – Potter', *CR*, 101/1986
'Jane Hamlyn', *Ceramic Series*, no.19, Aberystwyth Arts
Centre, 1987
For Use and Ornament –Jane Hamlyn, Saltglaze, with an
appreciation by Peter Dormer, Craft Centre and
Design Gallery, Leeds, 1988
Peter Dormer, 'Jane Hamlyn's Current Work', *Ceramics
Monthly*, April, 1989, pp. 30–32

253 Jug, *c*.1980
Stoneware, brown saltglaze with decoration in
green and blue; marks: 'JH' in monogram,
impressed; h. 20.1 cm, d. 14.2 cm
C.44–1980. Source: CPA, London, 'Jugs'
exhibition, 1980, £10

254 Oval dish, 1988
Stoneware, saltglazed with blue and green-brown
glazes and incised decoration; marks: 'JH'in
mongram, impressed; h. 10.5 cm, d. 53.7 cm
C.16–1989. Source: CAA, London, £162

Hammond, Henry 1914–1989

1929–34	Croydon School of Art, London, first as a junior student from age 15–17, then in night school; taught among others by Reginald Marlow (qv)
1934–8	awarded Royal Exhibition Scholarship to Royal College of Art, London, having studied mural painting; design courses under Eric Ravillious and Edward Bawden, joins pottery classes under William Staite Murray (qv)
1939	appointed to West Surrey College of Art and Design as pottery instructor, war prevents him taking up the post
1940–46	war service, followed by 2 weeks at St Ives with Bernard Leach (qv)
1946–80	teaches at West Surrey College of Art and Design
1946–51	working in slipware only
1947–48	studio at Runnick House, Hants
1948–	studio at Bently, Hants, shared from 1954 with Paul Barron (qv)
1980	retires; awarded MBE

Henry Hammond, 'Tradition', *Athene*, 7/1&2, 1955
—Contribution to: 'Bernard Leach – a Living Tradition',
CR, 108/1987
—'A Magnetic Teacher', *Crafts*, May/June, 1975
—'Bernard Leach', in *Great Masters of Pottery and Ceramics*, Oxford, 1984
—'A Visit to Kilmington Manor', in *Katharine Pleydell-Bouverie – A Potter's Life*, Crafts Council, London, 1986
Wingfield Digby (1952)
Melville (1954)
Rose (1955), (1970)
Casson (1967)
David Hamilton, 'Henry Hammond and David Leach', exhibition review, *Crafts*, January/February, 1978
London, Hayward Gallery (1979)
London, Christopher Wood Gallery (1980)

255 Bowl, 1938
Stoneware, painted decoration in a mustard-coloured glaze; marks: 'HH' in monogram, painted; h. 10.5 cm, d. 26.8 cm
Circ.93–1939. Source: Brygos Gallery, London, £4.20

256 Vase, 1938
Stoneware, painted decoration in brown on a pinky-cream glaze; h. 30 cm, d. 26.3 cm
Circ.94–1939. Source: *see* Circ.93–1939, £7.35

257 Bowl, 1938
Stoneware, painted decoration in brown on a yellow-brown glaze; h. 14 cm, d. 33.5 cm
Circ.95–1939. Source: *see* Circ.93–1939, £6.30

258 Vase, 1939 (pl. 36)
Stoneware, painted decoration in brown on an oatmeal glaze; marks: 'HH' in square monogram, impressed; h. 28.2 cm, d. 26 cm
Circ.478–1939. Source: the potter, from a diploma show at the Royal College of Art, £5.25

259 Jug, 1949–1950
Earthenware, painted decoration in white slip on a dark ground under a honey-coloured glaze; marks: 'HH' in monogram, impressed; h. 27.3 cm, d. 21 cm
Circ.274–1950. Source: Arts and Crafts Society (exhibition in V&A, 1950), £3.15
On seeing this jug in 1989, Hammond commented that he had never really felt happy as an earthenware potter, unlike his colleague Paul Barron (qv), but they had no stoneware kiln at Farnham at that date.

260 Jug, 1949–1950
Earthenware, white slip on a dark ground under a greenish glaze; marks: 'HH' in monogram, impressed; h. 29.7 cm, d. 20 cm
Circ.275–1950. Source: *see* Circ.274–1950, £3.15

261 Vase, *c.* 1959
Stoneware, painted decoration in brown on an oatmeal-coloured glaze; marks: 'HH' in monogram, impressed; h. 38.1 cm, d. 14.8 cm
Circ.129–1959. Source: Primavera, London, £8.40

262 Bowl, *c.* 1977
Stoneware, painted decoration in brown on a grey glaze; marks: 'HH' in monogram, impressed; h. 11.3 cm, d. 22.3 cm
C.152–1980. Source: Paul Rice Gallery, London (from a solo exhibition, Casson Gallery, London, 1977), £155.20

255

257

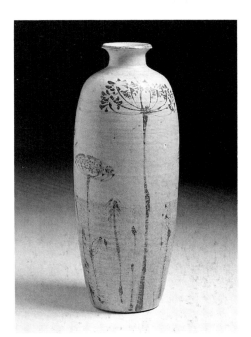

261

256

259 260

262

263 Dish: *Morning*, 1982–1983
Stoneware, painted decoration in black and brown on an oatmeal glaze; marks: 'HH' in monogram, impressed; h. 5.8 cm, d. 22.7 cm
C.82–1984. Source: given by the Friends of the V&A
Purchased at the CPA 25th Anniversary exhibition, *Studio Ceramics Today*, held at the V&A in 1983. This piece was ex-catalogue.

Hanssen, Gwyn (née John, later Hanssen Pigott) 1935–

1935	born in Ballarat, Australia
1958	comes to England from Australia after working with Ivan McMeekin
c.1958–60	works with Bernard Leach (qv) at St Ives also with Cardew (qv) and Finch (qv) and Caiger-Smith (qv)
1960	sets up workshop in Portobello Road, London with husband Louis Hanssen (qv)
1964	developing interest in French traditional earthenwares, buys house in France and begins to set up pottery
1964–65	runs Wenford Bridge while Cardew is away in Africa, revisits Australia
1966–73	moves to Achères, France, making wood-fired pots
1969–71	Tutor at Harrow School of Art
1973	moves back to Australia
1974–80	pottery with John Pigott in Tasmania
1981–	pottery at Kelvin Grove, Queensland, Australia
1988–	Workshop at Netherdale, Central Queensland

Gwyn Hanssen has been an important and influental potter even after she moved abroad. The Museum has only a single piece by her, made in France, and no work from the period she was in England.

Casson (1967)
Exhibition review, *PQ*, 7/1961–62 (illustrations p. 138, pls. 5-6)
Emmanuel Cooper and Eileen Lewenstein, 'Gwyn Hanssen Talking', *CR*, 11/1971
Margaret Tuckson, 'Gwyn Hanssen Pigott – Seeking Perfection', *CR*, 89/1984

264 Bowl, 1970
Stoneware, exterior with thin pinky-cream glaze, interior white flecked glaze; marks: 'GH' in monogram, impressed; made at Achères, France; h. 15.5 cm, d. 46.8 cm
Circ.237–1971. Source: Crafts Centre of Great Britain, £35

263

Hanssen, Louis 1934–1968

1958–	a Canadian poet living in London, learns pottery from his wife, Gwyn Hanssen (qv)
1960–	sets up studio in London, shared with wife until 1963
1963	New workshop in Hampstead, London

Louis Hanssen was a very talented artist, whose career was cut short by a tragically early death.

Exhibition review, *PQ*, 7/1961–62 (illustrations p. 138, pl. 6)

265 Bowl, c.1961
Stoneware, incised decoration under a yellow-brown glaze; marks: illegible square seal; h. 19.5 cm, d. 27 cm
Circ.454–1962. Source: Primavera, London, £6.50

266 Vase, 1965 (pl. 72)
Stoneware, handbuilt with dark brown, blue and orange-brown glazes; h. 67 cm, d. 49.5 cm
Circ.304–1965. Source: Primavera, London, £31.50
This piece was illustrated in *The Studio Yearbook of Decorative Art*, 1966–67

264

265

Harding, Deborah N. dates not known

Deborah Harding is recorded as having made studio pottery in Letchworth, Hartfordshire, in the 1920s and 1930s. In 1935 she was invited by the Museum to take part in an exhibition 'English Pottery, Old and New'; she was given prominent exposure in the subsequent publication.

London, VAM (1936; pls. 42–43)
Godden (1964)

267 Vase, c.1937
Stoneware, green streak in a creamish glaze; marks: 'D.N.H.', incised; h. 18.6 cm, d. 10.7 cm
Circ.311–1954. Source: given by the Council for Art and Industry, Department of Overseas Trade

267

Henderson, Ewen 1934–

1934   born in Staffordshire
1964   foundation course at Goldsmith's College, London, after seven years as manager of a timber preservation company in South Wales
1965–68 Camberwell School of Art, London
1968–73 first studio in Camberwell, London
1973–   new studio in Camden Town, London
1986   *A Retrospective View*, solo exhibition, BCC, London

Ewen Henderson is a very individual potter, and has pursued his interests singlemindedly. His work has developed consistently: the forms have become more organic, his textures rougher and his colours more muted. His latest work breaks away from pure vessel forms to explore jagged cratered shapes reminiscent of skulls.

Fiona Adamcewski, 'Ewen Henderson and his coiled pots', *CR*, 35/1975
Ewen Henderson at Amalgam, exhibition booklet, Amalgam Gallery, London, 1979
London, Christopher Wood Gallery (1980)
Christopher Reid, 'Henderson Country', *Crafts*, January/February, 1981
Angus Suttie, 'Radstone and Henderson', in *Six Ways*, exhibition catalogue, Anatol Orient Gallery, London, 1988
Henry Pim, 'Creative Games', *CR*, 98/1986
Ewen Henderson; A Retrospective View 1970–1986, BCC exhibition pamphlet by Christopher Reid, London, 1986
Tanya Harrod, 'Ewen Henderson', exhibition review, *Crafts*, July/August, 1986
Tanya Harrod, 'Ewen Henderson' *Ceramic Series*, no. 33, Aberystwyth Arts Centre, 1989

268 Vase, 1979 (pl. 86)
Stoneware and porcelain, handbuilt from coloured clays, with thin feldspathic glaze; h. 24.7 cm, d. 22 cm
C.139–1979. Source: Amalgam Gallery, London, £50

269 Vase, 1982
Stoneware and porcelain, handbuilt, with orange, cream, grey and bluey glazes; h. 59 cm, d. 35 cm
C.82–1982. Source: V&A Craft Shop, £283.50
Henderson thought that this was one of his best pieces to date.

270 Vase, 1984
Bone-china and porcelain laminated to stoneware, handbuilt, with green, brown and white surface; h. 44 cm, d. 22 cm
C.152–1984. Source: BCC, London, £285
The distinctly human form is unusual in Henderson's work.

271 Vase, 1986 (pl. 100)
Bone-china and porcelain laminated to stoneware, handbuilt, with bubbled cratered surface; h. 71 cm, d. 30 cm
C.176–1986. Source: BCC, London, £675

272 Teabowl, 1987
Bone-china and porcelain laminated to stoneware, handbuilt, with bubbled cratered brown glaze and red flashings; h. 9.8 cm, d. 10 cm
C.102–1987. Source: Paul Rice Gallery, London, £110

273 Form, from the series *Skull Mountain*, 1988 (pl. 101)
Bone-china and porcelain laminated to stoneware, handbuilt, with body-stains and glazes; h. 45 cm, d. 35.8 cm
C.39–1989. Source: given by Ed Wolfe, London

Hepburn, Anthony 1942–

1942   born in Stockport, near Manchester; school at the Manchester High School of Art, which aimed to teach all subjects through art
1959–63 Camberwell School of Art, London
1963–65 teacher training at the University of London
1965–68 shares a studio with Ian Godfrey (qv) and Mo Jupp (qv), and works at Digwell, Hertfordshire, in Hans Coper's (qv) old studio
1968   working in Lemington Spa, visits USA
1969   visits USA, and Japan with Bernard and Janet Leach (qv)
1969–76 increasing teaching commitments in USA
1976–   appointed Professor of Ceramic Art, Alfred University, New York

Hepburn was a pioneer among British potters for his cast sculptural forms which stand in distinct contrast to the abstract work of sculptural potters such as Duckworth and Badwin (qv). His work has more association with the 'funk' pottery movement in the USA where he eventually settled. He abandoned representational sculpture for abstract work in about 1970. He is a vigorous commentator and critic of the contemporary scene.

Tony Hepburn, 'Issues for American Ceramics in 1975', *CR*, 1975
—'The Battle of Dreams: American Ceramics Today', *CR*, 1986
London, VAM (1968)
The Studio Yearbook of Decorative Art, 1968–9, p. 131
Exhibition reviews, *CR*, 9/1971, 13/1972
Birks (1976)

274 *Large White Double Box*, 1967 (pl. 75)
Stoneware, slab formed, white glaze with enamel colouring; h. 56.2 cm, d. 41.3 cm
Circ.1206&a-1967. Source: Crafts Centre of Great Britain, £25
Made as 'one of a series dealing with the suggested pressure of box forms'.

269

270

272

275 *Box with Telephone and Table Leg*, 1968
Stoneware, handbuilt, with brown dolomite glaze
and red enamel; h. 29.5 cm, d. 55 cm
Circ.831–1968. Source: the potter, £45

276 *Box with Tubes*, 1968
Stoneware, slab formed with creamy-white glaze
and enamel colours; h. 46.5 cm, d. 43.2 cm
Circ.832–1968. Source: *see* Circ.831–1968, £30

Hine, Margaret 1927–1987

1948–   after the Derby College of Art, studies at
Central School of Art, London, with Dora
Billington (qv), and the Institute of Education
of London University with William Newland
(qv)
1949–54   studio in Bayswater, London, with William
Newland and Nicholas Vergette (qv)
1950   marries William Newland
1954–   new workshop with Newland in Prestwood,
Buckinghamshire

Hine was known in the 1950s for her animal figures,
but also produced painted dishes and ceramic murals.

The Studio Yearbook of Decorative Art, 1953–4
Billington (1953), (1955)
Exhibition review, *PQ*, 1/1954
Craft Review, 5/1960, pp. 11,15
Paisley (1984)

277 *Pair of Doves*, 1954
Earthenware, incised decoration through purple-
brown pigment to a white glaze; marks: 'Margi
Hine', painted; h. 21 cm, d. 24.7 cm
Circ.58&a–1954. Source: the potter, £10.50

275

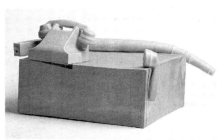

276

194

Homoky, Nicholas 1950–

1950   born in Hungary
1956   emigrates to England
1970–73 Bristol Polytechnic
1973–76 Royal College of Art, London
1975   travels in Hungary on Royal College of Art
scholarship
1976–79 studio in Cardiff
1979–   new studio in Bristol; teaches at Bristol
Polytechnic

Homoky was much acclaimed on his graduation from
the Royal College for his elegantly shaped bowls and
beakers in polished unglazed porcelain with inlaid black
decoration. He has also explored perspective and the
deconstruction of images which gave rise to slab-built
forms. He has recently started using a red clay.

Nicolas Homoky, 'Mixing Metaphores', *Crafts*,
September/October, 1981
'CPA New Members', *CR*, 58/1979
London, Christopher Wood Gallery (1980)

278 *Jar*, 1979
Porcelain, unglazed, with inlaid decoration in
black; marks: 'NH' in monogram, impressed;
h. 9.8 cm, d. 15.8 cm
C.120–1979. Source: Casson Gallery, London,
£76

279 *Spouted bowl*, 1979
Porcelain, unglazed, with inlaid decoration in
black; marks: 'NH' in monogram, impressed;
h. 13.1 cm, d. 8.9 cm
C.119–1979. Source: Casson Gallery, London,
£72

280 *Coffee pot*, *c.*1980
Porcelain, unglazed, with inlaid decoration in
black; h. 13.5 cm, d. 12.1 cm
C.26&a–1980. Source: CPA, London, £80

277

279 278

Hopkins, Alfred G. dates not known

?–1915   working for Doulton's Lambeth, possibly
helping Richard Lunn at Camberwell School
of Art, London
*c.*1915–40 teaches in Camberwell School of Art on
death of Lunn
*c.*1916–   own pottery studio in Lambeth Road,
London
1932   plans to transfer workshop to Stone Pottery,
St Peter's, Thanet

Alfred Hopkins, in the 1920s and early 1930s, was a
potter of some note; he was reputed to be the first
potter to ask for £100 for a pot – the 'first red saltglaze porcelain ever produced' shown at a Fine Art
Society exhibition in 1927. He specialised in saltglazes
and produced, as well as vases of the type illustrated
here, bellamines and birds after the model of the Martin
Brothers. He worked with his brother Henry 'Harry'
Hopkins who also taught with him at Camberwell. They
were both potters from a professional trade
background. Helen Pincombe recounts that they were
dogmatic in matters such as throwing technique, and
discouraged experimentation: '... if you want green,
miss, you go to the bottle of copper, miss – if you
want brown, miss, you go to the bottle of manganese
...' The firm run by the Hopkins Brothers in Lambeth
Road, London, before the war, supplied ceramic
materials and machinery, undertook commissions and
offered to fire work by other potters, presumably
amateurs or artists.

Ernest Marsh, *The Revival of Salt-glaze Stoneware Pottery*,
 pamphlet for the Fine Art Society, November, 1927
Exhibition review, *Manchester Guardian*, 3/12/1932
Aberystwyth (1979)
London, Christopher Wood Gallery (1980)
Haslam (1984, pp. 8,30)

280

281 Dish, 1916
Earthenware, white body under a transparent
glaze, painted in black, green and crimson enamel;
marks: 'A. & H. Hopkins/203 Lambeth
Rd/London SE', impressed, 1916 incised;
d. 30.5 cm
C.61–1972. Source: T. Stainton, Beaconsfield,
Bucks, £16.50
Made by Alfred Hopkins in partnership with his
brother Harry

282 Bowl, 1927
Stoneware, saltglaze over a yellow-brown glaze;
marks: 'A G Hopkins Lambeth 1927', incised;
h. 6.4 cm, d. 16.7 cm
Circ.355–1958

283 Vase, 1927
Stoneware, saltglazed over a yellow-brown
mottled glaze; marks: 'A G Hopkins/
Lambeth/1927/3', incised; h. 11 cm, d. 13.2 cm
Circ.354–1958. Source: George Wingfield-Digby,
London, £1.75 (for both Circ.354 and 355–1958)

284 Jug, 1927
Stoneware, rich brown saltglaze; marks: '1927/
A G Hopkins', incised and 'A G Hopkins
LAMBETH', impressed; h. 12 cm, d. 16.9 cm
C.488–1934. Source: given by the BIIA (gift of
the potter)

285 Bowl, 1927 (pl. 23)
Stoneware, saltglazed over bubbled muddy green
glaze; marks: '1927 [probably '7'] A G Hopkins',
incised; h. 11.7 cm, d. 18.6 cm
C.474–1927. Source: given by a group who
attended lectures on modern pottery given in the
Museum
Bernard Rackham, Keeper of the Ceramic
Department, notes: 'This jar is an important piece
of the stoneware being made by Alfred G.
Hopkins at Lambeth and illustrates his limitations
as an artist (apart from his skill in technique) as
compared with such masters of present day
pottery as W.S. Murray and B. Leach.... The vase
will be useful as a record specimen.'

286 Vase, 1931 (pl. 23)
Stoneware, mottled brown glaze; marks: 'A G
Hopkins/Lambeth', incised; h. 11.5 cm, d. 12 cm
C.2–1933. Source: given by Miss A. J. Tufnell,
London
Bought by the donor at Fine Art Society Ltd. in
December 1932. Described by the maker: 'Sea
warm shell quality; madripore form; softened
latitudinal ribs.' B. Rackham notes: 'He is not one
of our best potters and much of his work is in my
opinion bad, but the white pot ... is interesting
as a revival of white saltglaze ware and the little
pot which I picked out ... may serve to show Mr
Hopkins the direction he should take if he is to
improve his output.'

287 Vase, 1931 (pl. 23)
Porcelain, saltglazed in white; marks: 'A G
Hopkins/Lambeth', incised and '1931', painted;
h. 26.5 cm, d. 11.2 cm
C.3–1933. Source: *see* C.2–1933
Described by the maker: 'White saltglaze porcelain
vase, translucent. Lily form; pitted.'

283 282

Hoy, Anita (Agnete) 1914–

1933–36   Copenhagen College of Arts and Crafts
1937–39   works with Gerhard Nielsen at Holbaek and
         with Nathalie Krebs at Saxbo, Herlev
1939   to UK for holiday, outbreak of war prevents
         return
1940–52   heads studio department at Bullers Ltd., Stoke
1952–56   works with Royal Doulton, Lambeth as
         designer for saltglazed ware
1952–   own studio for porcelain and stoneware in
         Acton, London; teaching at West Surrey
         College of Art and Design, Farnham

Anita Hoy forms a bridge between industry and the
studio potter. After her work with the Buller's studio,
she continued to be involved with industry as a designer
while also making individual work and teaching.
The Museum also possesses a number of pieces made
by Anita Hoy in her factory studio at Buller's (C.255
to 263–1983) and three pieces designed by her for
Doulton's (Circ.842 to 844–1956).

Anita Hoy, 'Art Among the Insulators', *CR*, 69/1981
(on the Buller's studio)
'An Adventure in Porcelain', *Pottery and Glass*, August,
1947
'New Stoneware from Lambeth', *Royal Doulton
Magazine*, June, 1953
Casson (1967)
Art Among the Insulators; the Bullers Studio 1932–52,
exhibition catalogue, Gladstone Pottery Museum,
1977
Godden (1988)

288 Bowl, 1960
Porcelain, 'wet on wet' slip decoration in green
and pink; marks: 'Agnete Hoy' in script,
impressed; h. 4.7 cm, d. 13.5 cm
C.262–1983. Source: the potter, £50

281

284

285

Ions, Neil 1949–

1949 born Newcastle, Staffordshire
1968–9 foundation course, Newcastle School of Art, Staffs.
1969–72 sculpture at Newport College of Art
1972–75 ceramics at Royal College of Art, London
1975–81 founder member of Fosseway House Workshops, Stow-on-the-Wold, Gloucestershire
1981– sets up Kitebrook Workshop

Ions is particularly known for his clay wind-instruments. He trained as a sculptor which he also still practises. His imagery is drawn from the natural world, and especially from American Indian ceramics.

Neil Ions, 'Playing with Clay', *CR*, 90/1984
'CPA New Members', *CR*, 66/1980

289 Pair of bird ocarinas, 1980
Earthenware, painted decoration in coloured slips and burnished; marks: 'Neil Ions', incised; h. 10.3 cm, d. 19 cm
C.42&a–1980. Source: CPA, London, £28

290 Vase, 1982
Earthenware, painted in matt grey, green, brown, white and black slips and burnished; marks: 'Neil Ions 1982', painted; h. 43.2 cm, d. 18.7 cm
C.73–1984. Source: given by the Friends of the V&A
Purchased at the CPA 25th Anniversary exhibition, *Studio Ceramics Today*, held at the V&A in 1983.

Jupp, Mo 1938–

1959–64 Camberwell School of Art, London
1964–67 Royal College of Art, London
1967–72 workshop at Brands Hatch, Kent
1970s teaches at Harrow, Farnham and Hornsey Schools of Art
1972–77 workshop in English Bicknor, Gloucestershire
1977–85 workshop near Lydney, Gloucestershire
1980s teaching five days a week, including the Central School of Art
1985–87 workshop at Symonds Yat, Herefordshire
1987– workshop in Bermondsey, London

Jupp's work, consistently challenging and interesting, has come in batches, as much of his time has been devoted to teaching and house renovation. His themes usually contain some social or political comment. His helmets were much acclaimed in the early 1970s, not so his temples with human genitalia later in the decade, or the female busts in the early 1980s. These had bird-heads (sparked off from the expression 'bird' for a girl) or the head covered with a paper bag (from an adolescent saying about girls considered to be less than adequately attractive). His latest work of tall female figures shows him to be a sculptor of considerable sensitivity. The glass breasts make allusion to the vulnerability of women in western culture.

Cameron and Lewis (1976)
Fiona Adamczewski, 'Mo Jupp – Maverick Potter', *CR*, 28/1974
Tanya Harrod, 'Mo Jupp: New Work', *Crafts*, March/April, 1988
CAA exhibition leaflet, 1988

291 Pot on pedestal, 1969
Stoneware, thrown sections joined, white glaze with silver enamel; h. 20.2 cm, d. 11.5 cm
Circ.540–1969. Source: Primavera, London, £9.45

292 Pot on pedestal, 1969
Stoneware, thrown sections joined, white glaze with silver enamel; h. 24.6 cm, d. 11.6 cm
Circ.541–1969. Source: *see* Circ.540–1969, £9.45

293 Helmet, 1972 (pl. 87)
Stoneware, press-moulded, with black and white and green surface; h. 23.9 cm, d. 29 cm
Circ.290–1973. Source: the potter, £25

294 Figure, 1987–1988 (pl. 110)
Low-fired porcelain, handbuilt, constructed from sections; h. 108.6 cm
C.41–1989. Source: CAA, London, £1620

289

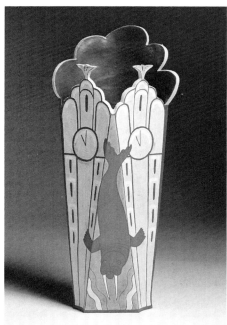

290

291 292

Kalan, Stephanie ?–1978

Stephanie Kalan's two pieces were accepted for the Museum as interesting experiments in crystalline glazes – a difficult technique usually associated with industrial production. She produced work from the early 1950s.

Stephanie Kalan, 'Chrome Tin Pink and Red Glazes–', *CR*, 47/1977

295 Bowl, 1966
Stoneware, crystalline glaze, blue crystals in yellow glaze; marks: 'S KALAN', incised; h. 8.6 cm, d. 16.5 cm
Circ.1219–1967. Source: given by the potter

296 Vase, 1966
Stoneware, crystalline glaze; marks: 'S KALAN', incised; h. 11.4 cm, d. 10.9 cm
Circ.1220–1967. Source: *see* Circ.1219–1967

Kalindjian, Sona 1934–

1969–73 Hornsey College of Art, London
1973–80 teaches at Loughton College of Further Education
1974– sets up Chiswick Ceramics, London

Chiswick Ceramics specialises in tile murals, sculptural tableware and commemorative wares, mostly slip-cast with screen-print decoration. The Museum also possesses a slip-cast box in the form of Chiswick House made for sale in the shop, C.4–1979.

297 Tea set, 1979
Earthenware, cast with enamel decoration screen printed in blue and red; marks: 'SK 79', painted and 'Sona Kalindjian', incised; made at Chiswick Ceramics, London; h. 26.6 cm, d. 22.7 cm (teapot)
C.3 to d-1980. Source: the potter, £49

296 295

Keeler, Walter 1942–

1958–63 Harrow School of Art, London
1965 first studio at Bledlow Ridge, Buckinghamshire
1976 new studio at Penallt near Monmouth, Dyfed, Wales
1964–68 teaching Sutton and Cheam School of Art
1964–78 teaching Harrow School of Art, London
1974–76 teaching Central School of Art, London
1976– teaching Bristol Polytechnic

Walter Keeler is the most inventive and explorative of the 'new' domestic-ware potters. He now makes only functional forms, shaped basically on the wheel and, surprising though the shapes may seem, they all do function. However, he has developed the teapot, the dish and the jug into sculptures which explore, as much as do any of the non-functional new potters, matters of the organisation of volumes, relationship of exterior and interior, the space and stance taken by the pot. He is perhaps one of the most important and influential potters of the 1980s in showing that domestic potting need not just be a continued replaying of Leachian themes, but, through manipulation of form and the effects of a single simple technique (here saltglazing), a completely new, stimulating aesthetic can be created.

298 299

297

Keeler describes his history thus:
'I was trained at Harrow School of Art by Victor Margrie and Michael Casson. My first workshop was established at Bledlow Ridge in Buckinghamshire, in 1965. I made oxidised stoneware functional pots, and an assortment of non-functional pieces which reflect the plastic pleasures of thrown pottery. During the '70s I concentrated on functional pots in reduced stoneware and saltglaze. In 1976 I moved to Penallt in Gwent, but within a couple of years the profit and the joy went out of my down to earth domestic ware. To stimulate my interest I recalled my early non-functional pieces (rejected as an indulgence ten years before) and brought some of their tactile qualities and a more sculptural attitude to my functional pots. A whole range of possibilities revealed themselves, which combined with a return to saltglaze regenerated, and sustain, my enthusiasm.

Throwing is my primary technique, and the inspiration for my pots. They all begin on the wheel, though most are altered in some way, or assembled from various components. Pots released from their bases no longer remain circular. Rims are cut away to leave raised pouring lips, or a vessel is set back on its base, as if affronted by something in its path. Handles may be pulled and sensuous, growing from a rim, or extruded with metallic accuracy, appearing to just rest on the pot. Spouts, whether thrown and altered or pressed in a mould, contribute their peculiarities to the assembled pot. The goal in this complex process is the finished pot performing its function; a surprising object doing a commonplace job.'

Keeler confesses to a wide range of influences, Greek pottery, Roman glass, 18th century Staffordshire wares and tin oil-cans.

Walter Keeler, 'Young Potters Reply', *PQ*, 9/33, 1967–70
—'Raku', *CR*, 1/1970
Rosemary Wren and Peter Crotty, 'Walter Keeler', *CR*, 18/1972
W. A. Ismay, 'Saltglazed Stoneware by Walter Keeler', exhibition review, *Crafts*, March/April, 1981
Michael Casson, 'Walter Keeler – Creative Potter', *CR*, 77/1982
Colin Voake, 'Salt of the Earth', *Crafts*, July/August, 1986
David Briers, 'Walter Keeler – Serious but not Solemn', *CR*, 112/1988
'Walter Keeler – Making a Lidded Jar', *CR*, 113/1988

298 Mug, 1982
Stoneware, blue-brown mottled saltglaze; marks: circular device, impressed; h. 9.6 cm, d. 12.3 cm
C.108–1982. Source: CPA, London, £6.45

299 Jug, 1982
Stoneware, brown and blue mottled saltglaze; marks: circular device, impressed; h. 21 cm, d. 16.5 cm
C.109–1982. Source: CPA, London, £19.35

300 Jug, 1982
Stoneware, blue saltglaze; marks: circular device, impressed; h. 24.8 cm, d. 13.6 cm
C.74–1984. Source: given by the Friends of the V&A
Purchased at the CPA 25th Anniversary exhibition, *Studio Ceramics Today*, held at the V&A in 1983.

301 Dish, 1982 (pl. 118)
Stoneware, brown saltglaze with blue-grey glaze interior; marks: 'WK' and a circular device, impressed; h. 8.3 cm, d. 41 cm
C.111–1982. Source: CPA, London, £64.50

302 Teapot, 1982 (pl. 119)
Stoneware, brown mottled saltglaze; marks: circular device, impressed; h. 19.5 cm, d. 20 cm
C.110&a–1982. Source: CPA, London, £103.2

303 Teapot, 1984 (pl. 119)
Stoneware, grey-brown saltglaze; marks: circular device, impressed; h. 10.7 cm, d. 26 cm
C.153–1984. Source: BCC, London, £70

304 Cache pot, 1984
Stoneware, blue-grey saltglaze, blue glazed interior; marks: circular device, impressed; h. 19.6 cm, d. 22.6 cm
C.154–1984. Source: BCC, London, £40.25

Kemp, Dorothy 1905–?

Kemp made slipware with Bernard Leach (qv) at Shinner's Bridge in the early 1930s. During and after the war she worked at St Ives in summer vacations. In the 1940s, she is recorded as making stoneware in Cornwall and also working with Margaret Leach (qv) at the Barnhouse Pottery. She is later recorded in Felixstow, Suffolk, and teaching at a girl's school in Ipswich.

Dorothy Kemp, *English Slipware: How to Make It*, 1954
Cooper (1947; pl. 18a)
Wingfield Digby (1952)

305 Tankard, 1949
Stoneware, tenmoku glaze; marks: 'DK' and 'SI' in monogram impressed; made at the Leach Pottery, St Ives; h. 13.2 cm, d. 10.6 cm
Circ.167–1950. Source: the potter, £0.37

306 Jug, 1949
Stoneware, tenmoku glaze; marks: 'DK' and 'SI' in monogram, impressed; made at the Leach Pottery, St Ives; h. 28 cm, d. 15.2 cm
Circ.166–1950. Source: the potter, £2.10

307 Tankard, 1949
Stoneware, tenmoku glaze; marks: 'DK'and 'SI' in monogram, impressed; made at the Leach Pottery, St Ives; h. 13.2 cm, d. 10.6 cm
Circ.168–1950. Source: the potter, £0.37

308 Bowl, 1949
Earthenware, decoration in black under an amber glaze; marks: 'DK' in monogram, impressed; made at the Barnhouse Pottery, Chepstow (run by Margaret Leach qv); h. 10.5 cm, d. 27.9 cm
Circ.169–1950. Source: the potter, £1.50

309 Jug, 1949
Stoneware, wax resist in brown glaze on a grey glaze; marks: 'DK' in monogram, impressed; made at the Leach Pottery, St Ives; h. 22.2 cm, d. 18 cm
Circ.165–1950. Source: the potter, £2.10

304

308

300

305 306

309

King, Ruth 1955–

1955   born in Enfield, Middlesex
1974–77   Camberwell School of Art, London
1978–79   workshop in Brixton, London
1979–81   workshop in Charlton, London
1981–   workshop in York

'CPA New Members', *CR*, 68/1981

310 Vase, 1981
Stoneware, slab built, mottled green matt glaze;
marks: 'RK', applied; h. 41.7 cm, d. 38.2 cm
C.75–1984. Source: given by the Friends of the
V&A
Purchased at the CPA 25th Anniversary
exhibition, *Studio Ceramics Today*, held at the
V&A in 1983.

La Salle, Vivian Neil 1911–

1928–33   student at the Architectural Association,
           London
1935   elected associate member of the RIBA
1946–47   student at the Central School of Art,
and   London, with Dora Billington (qv)
1949–51
1947–   joins teaching order of De La Salle Brothers,
           with the name Brother Damian, St Joseph's
           Academy, Blackheath; teaches at boys'
           schools in Manchester
1972   retires

This dish was made by Brother Damian, who joined a
teaching order, while still a student at the Central
School.

311 Dish, 1950
Earthenware, tin-glazed with painted decoration
in green, yellow and blue; marks: 'Bro D', incised;
made at the Central School of Arts and Crafts;
h. 7.8 cm, d. 40.2 cm
Circ.46–1951. Source: the potter (Arts and Crafts
Society exhibition, V&A, 1950), £7.35

Leach, Bernard Howell 1897–1979

1887   5 January, born in Kong Kong; mother dies,
        taken by grandparents to Japan
1890   returns to Hong Kong with father and his
        new wife
1894   moves to Singapore where his father is
        appointed a High Court judge
1897   to Beaumont Jesuit College, Windsor,
        England
1903   to Slade School of Art under Henry Tonks,
        where he is the youngest student
1905   studies in Manchester for Bank exams
1906   enters Hong Kong and Shanghai Bank as clerk
1907   leaves Bank; to London School of Art under
        Frank Brangwyn to learn etching
1909   leaves for Japan; builds house in Tokyo;
        marries cousin Muriel Hoyle
1910   meets Tomimoto
1911   discovers pottery at Raku tea party; meets
        Yanagi, and Ogata Kenzan 6th
1913   Kenzan builds kiln in Leach's workshop; Leach
        and Tomimoto inherit title of 7th Kenzan
1914   first one-man show; moves to Peking to visit
        a scholar of Confucius, Dr Westharp
1915   family joins him in China
1916   returns to Japan
1916   with encouragement from Yanagi rebuilds
        Kenzan's kiln with his help on Yanagi's land
        at Abiko
1918   visits Korea with Yanagi
1919   pottery burns down; exhibition in Tokyo;
        meets Hamada
1920   returns to England with Hamada and
        establishes pottery at St Ives, arriving there
        in August; twin daughters born
1921   discovery of method of slip-combing
1922–24 Matsubayashi joins pottery and re-builds kiln
1923   exhibition of work with Hamada in London;
        Hamada returns to Japan
1926   exhibition in Japan (with William Staite
        Murray and Ethel Mairet)
1929   Yanagi and Hamada visit St Ives
1930   David Leach joins pottery as apprentice
1932   Bernard starts teaching at Dartington Hall
        part-time; builds pottery at Shinner's Bridge;
        becomes interested in Baha'i faith during
        friendship with Mark Tovey

1933   David takes over at Dartington
1934–35 Bernard visits Japan invited by National Craft
        Society; travels making pots in a number of
        different kilns; visits Korea returning to
        Britain in July
1934–36 David Leach to College in Stoke; pottery left
        in charge of Laurie Cookes and Harry Davis;
        Bernard Forrester takes over teaching at
        Dartington Hall
1935   Bernard purchases caravan; living with Laurie
        Cookes in various parts of the countryside
1936   Bernard resumes teaching at Dartington;
        Dartington funds St Ives Pottery, where
        David Leach is in charge – £3,000 over next
        three years; Bernard and Laurie Cookes visit
        Ditchling and later in year stay with Cardew
        at Winchcombe
1937   builds 'cabin' at Shinner's Bridge; David
        becomes manager at St Ives and installs oil-
        fired kiln, earthenware production abandoned
1939   Bernard living at Dartington with Laurie
        Cookes, writing *A Potters' Book*
1940   becomes Baha'i; *A Potters' Book* is published
1941   returns to St Ives when David Leach is
        conscripted; German landmine damages
        pottery
1944   marries Laurie Cookes
1945   David Leach returns from army
1946   David taken into partnership
1949   Spring, visits Sweden, Norway and Denmark
1950   travels in USA for 4 months at invitation of
        Institute of Contemporary Art, Washington
1952   International Crafts Conference, Dartington
        Hall; Yanagi and Hamada attend
1952–54 tour in USA and Japan
1955   David and Michael Leach leave St Ives to set
        up own potteries
1956   Janet Darnell (*see* Janet Leach) arrives and
        marries Bernard
1960   lecture tour in USA; visit to Scandanavia
1961   *Fifty Years a Potter*, retrospective, Arts
        Council Gallery, London, and retrospective
        in Japan; awarded Hon. D.Litt. at Exeter
        University together with Agatha Christie;
        visits USA and Japan, where he is shown a
        group of Kenzan pots and diaries
1962   returns to England via Australia and New
        Zealand. Awarded CBE
1963   exhibition and visit to Paris
1964   visits Japan, attending Japanese Folk Crafts
        meeting in Okinawa
1966   visits Colombia, Venezuela returns via USA
        and Japan, where awarded Order of the
        Sacred Treasure, second class
1968   awarded Freedom of the Borough of St Ives
        with Barbara Hepworth
1969   visits Japan with Janet Leach
1970   visits Denmark
1971   visits Japan
1972   sight failing, virtually ceases to pot
1973   visits Japan; made Companion of Honour in
        Queen's Birthday Honours List
1974   visits Japan, Japan Foundation cultural award
1977   *The Art of Bernard Leach*, retrospective
        exhibition, Victoria and Albert Museum,
        London
1979   6 May dies

310

311

312

314

313

Bernard is often called the father of studio pottery in Britain. He is certainly the most dominant figure – a forceful presence for almost sixty years after his return from Japan in 1920, the date that more than any other marks the birth of the history of studio pottery. Leach's story is not one of unmitigated success, however. His struggles in the 1920s and 1930s to achieve a consistently good product, to achieve critical success and to make however modest a living serve more than anything to underline how strong was his commitment and his belief in the face of adversity. His success came in the post-war period when his writings, his pots and his Pottery all combined to illustrate his philosophy of life and work to a generation that was by then ready to receive it.

Bernard Leach is said to have made about 100,000 pots, perhaps 10 per cent of the St Ives Pottery's total. *A Potter's Book* had sold over 100,000 copies in English editions by 1987 – 92,000 in hardback and 27,000 in softback.

Workers and students at St Ives represented in the Catalogue:

Hamada Shoji 1920–1923
Katharine Pleydell-Bouverie 1923
Michael Cardew 1923–1926
Norah Braden 1925–1928
Charlotte Epton *c.*1927–30
Sylvia Fox Strangways 1920s
David Leach 1930–1955
Harry and May Davis 1933–1937
William Marshall 1938–1977
Michael Leach 1939–1955
Dorothy Kemp 1940s
Margaret Leach 1941–1946
Kenneth Quick 1945–1963
Richard Batterham mid-1950s
John Leach 1961–1962

Bernard Leach, *A Review, 1909–1914*, Tokyo, 1914
—*An English Artist in Japan*, 1920
—*The Leach Pottery*, St Ives, 1928
—*A Potter's Outlook*, London, 1928
—*A Potter's Book*, London (+ later editions), 1940
—'Pottery', *Fifteen Craftsmen on their Crafts*, ed. John Farleigh, London, 1945
—*The Leach Pottery, 1920–1946*, Berkeley Galleries, London, 1946
—*A Potter's Portfolio*, London, 1951
—'The Contemporary Studio Potter', *PQ*, 5/1958
—'In Reply to Paul Brown', *PQ*, 6/1959–60
—*A Potter in Japan*, London, 1960
—*Kenzan and his Tradition*, London, 1966
—*A Potter's Work*, London, 1967
—'Students and Hand-Made Standard Ware', *CR*, 9/1971
—*The Unknown Craftsman*, translated and adapted from the work by Soetsu Yanagi, Tokyo, 1972
—*Drawings, Verse and Belief*, London, 1973
—*Hamada, Potter*, Tokyo, New York, San Francisco, 1975
—*A Potter's Challenge*, London, 1976
—*Beyond East and West*, London, 1978
—'Shoji Hamada: a tribute', *CR*, 50/1978
Michael Cardew, 'The Pottery of Mr Bernard Leach', *The Studio*, 1925, pp. 298–301
John Gould Fletcher, 'The Pottery and Tiles of Bernard Leach', *Artwork*, VII, Summer, 1931, pp. 117–119
'Leach and Tomimoto', *The Studio*, 1931, pp. 346–349

Ernest Marsh, 'Bernard Leach, Potter', *Apollo*, January, 1943

Patrick Heron, exhibition review, *New English Weekly*, Summer, 1946

J.P. Hodin, 'Bernard Leach and his Thirty Years in the Service of Ceramic Art', *The Studio*, 1947, pp. 89–92

John Farleigh (1950; chapter 4)

David Lewis, 'Leach and Hamada', *The Studio*, 144/1952, p. 114

Wingfield Digby (1952)

Murray Fieldhouse, 'Workshop Visit: the Leach Pottery', *PQ*, 1/1954

Rose (1955),(1970)

Bernard Leach, Fifty Years a Potter, exhibition catalogue, Arts Council, London, 1961

George Wingfield Digby, 'Bernard Leach: Fifty Years a Potter', exhibition review, *The Museums Journal*, January, 1961

Casson (1967)

Janet Leach, 'Letter from Japan', *PQ*, 9/36, 1967–70

Janet Leach, 'Fifty One Years of the Leach Pottery', *CR*, 14/1972

Hugh Wakefield, 'The Leach Tradition', *Crafts*, January/February, 1974

'The Art of Bernard Leach', exhibition reviews by Gordon Baldwin and Murray Fieldhouse, *Crafts*, May/June, 1977

Geoffrey Whiting, 'Bernard Leach Retrospective Exhibition and Seminar March 1977', *PQ*, 12/48, 1976–77

Carol Hogben, 'Towards a Standard; the Bernard Leach Seminar at the Royal Geographical Society', review, *Crafts*, May/June, 1977

'Bernard Leach Potter', by various authors, *CR*, 50/1978

Michael Cardew, 'Bernard Leach', address given at Leach's memorial service, *Crafts*, July/August, 1979

'Tribute to Bernard Leach', by various authors, *CR*, 58/1979

Obituaries: *Burlington Magazine*, July, 1979; *The Times*, 19/11/79; the *Telegraph*, 7/5/87

London, Hayward Gallery (1979)

Carol Hogben, *The Art of Bernard Leach*, London, 1980

London, Christopher Wood Gallery (1980)

Barley Roscoe, 'Pots of Inspiration', *CR*, 77/1982

Paisley (1984)

London, Tate Gallery (1985)

Barley Roscoe, 'Bernard Leach; the Sources of his Influence', in London, ICA (1985)

Christopher Reid, 'Something in the Air', *Crafts*, March/April, 1985

John Maltby, 'The Leach Tradition', *Crafts*, May/June, 1986

'Bernard Leach', supplement on the 100th anniversary of Leach's birth, by W. A. Ismay and other authors, *CR*, 108/1987

'Bernard Leach Pottery and Drawings', exhibition review, *Crafts*, July/August, 1987

Breon O'Casey, 'Towards a Standard', *CR*, 114/1988

St Ives, exhibition catalogue, Setagaya Art Museum, Tokyo, Japan, 1989, with section on the Leach Pottery by Oliver Watson

312 Cup on three legs, *c.*1919
Porcelain, painted in underglaze blue; marks: 'BL' in monogram, painted in blue; made in Japan; h. 8.6 cm, d. 6.8 cm
C.742–1921. Source: given by Lt-Col. K. Dingwall, DSO, through the NACF

313 Drug jar, *c.*1923
Earthenware, white slip with incised decoration under an amber glaze; marks: 'BL' and 'SI' in monogram, impressed; made at the Leach Pottery, St Ives; h. 15.9 cm, d. 11.5 cm
C.67–1976. Source: A. London, London, £200

314 Cup and saucer, 1920–1924
Earthenware, slip-trailed decoration in white under an amber glaze; marks: On saucer 'BL' and 'SI', on cup 'SI' in monogram, impressed; made at the Leach Pottery, St Ives; h. 6.7 cm, d. 13.2 cm
C.84&a–1972. Source: given by Dr Mildred Creak and Mrs Falchikov
Acquired from Bernard Leach by an aunt of Dr Creak who was a fairly well established artist in St Ives when Leach started his pottery, and they were friends until her death in 1934.

315 Large dish, 1923 (pl. 24)
Earthenware, slip decoration in light and dark brown under an amber glaze; marks: 'BL 1923', in coloured slips; made at the Leach Pottery, St Ives; h. 11.9 cm, d. 42 cm
Circ.1278–1923. Source: the potter, £5
This dish was seen at a BIIA exhibition and selected for purchase by the Museum as '... a suitable addition to the case of modern pottery being formed in Circ.' Bernard Rackham comments on the file: '... a very interesting revival of an old technique'. Leach reduced the price from £7.50 to £5. The design is taken from a stone carving on a Han tomb that Leach may have seen on his trip to China in 1917. The 'Tree of Life' is a theme that Leach returned to frequently during his life; in his book *A Potter's Portfolio* he comments that the motifs – tree, horse, fish, deer, the plough constellation and snails – '... may be seen as symbolic', but is not specific as to their exact meaning.

316 Pot and cover, 1923
Earthenware, decoration cut through a white slip under an amber glaze; marks: 'BL' and 'SI' in monogram, impressed; made at the Leach Pottery, St Ives; h. 13.8 cm, d. 14.7 cm
C.405&a-1934. Source: given by the BIIA (gift of the potter in 1923)

317 Vase, *c.*1922
Stoneware, kaki on a dark brown glaze; marks: 'BL' and 'SI' in monogram, impressed; made at the Leach Pottery, St Ives; h. 13.8 cm, d. 10 cm
C.1040–1922. Source: given by Lt-Col. K. Dingwall, DSO, through the NACF
Purchased by the donor for £2 at an exhibition of Leach's work held in November 1922 at Cotswold Gallery, Frith Street, London.

318 Vase, 1923–1924
Stoneware, mottled greenish-brown glaze with painting in brown; marks: 'BL' and 'SI', impressed; made at the Leach Pottery, St Ives; h. 17.2 cm, d. 19.3 cm
Circ.993–1924. Source: given by W. Winkworth, London

316

317

318

319 Vase, 1923
Stoneware, dark decoration in a pale green glaze; marks: 'BL' and 'SI' in monogram, impressed; made at the Leach Pottery, St Ives; h. 15.7 cm, d. 13.6 cm
C.406–1934. Source: given by the BIIA (gift of the potter in 1923)
The jar copies a Korean type of celadon in which the decoration is formed by inlaying different coloured clays into the body.

320 Vase, 1923
Stoneware, mottled yellow-brown glaze; marks: 'SI', impressed; made at the Leach Pottery, St Ives; h. 15 cm, d. 16.5 cm
C.408–1934. Source: given by the BIIA (gift of the potter in 1923)
A paper exhibition label gives the price: '£3'.

321 Bowl, *c*.1925
Stoneware, saltglaze over a brown glaze; marks: 'BL' and 'SI' in monogram, impressed; made at the Leach Pottery, St Ives; h. 9.8 cm, d. 13.8 cm
C.148–1926. Source: given by Lt-Col. K. Dingwall, DSO, through the NACF
This piece was unintentionally saltglazed. Leach recounts that he had purchased a number of old railway sleepers as kiln fuel without realising that they were impregnated with salts to prevent rot. The salts volatilised in the firing and added a saltglaze to the stoneware glaze. Leach nevertheless found the outcome a success and was particularly pleased with this piece, which he illustrated in a number of his writings.
An exhibition label gives the price: '£12'.

322 Vase, 1926–1927 (pl. 27)
Stoneware, pale blue glaze; marks: 'BL' and 'SI', impressed; made at the Leach Pottery, St Ives; h. 16 cm, d. 17 cm
Circ.646–1927. Source: the potter, £4
This is a particularly successful piece from the 1920s, with a generous form and rich glaze, described as 'Yuan glazed'. It was shown at a BIIA exhibition in London. In recommending it for purchase, Bernard Rackham, Keeper of the

Ceramics Department, comments: 'I consider this pot to be in every way a good piece of craftsmanship and well worth taking its place in the Circulation collections as a representative of modern English pottery.'

323 Bowl, *c*.1926
Stoneware, painting in kaki on a tenmoku glaze; marks: 'BL' and 'SI' in monogram, impressed; made at the Leach Pottery, St Ives; h. 8.5 cm, d. 12.9 cm
C.149–1926. Source: given by Lt-Col. K. Dingwall, DSO, through the NACF
A small paper label gives the price '£5'. A thin saltglaze on the foot suggests that it comes from same firing as C.148–1926.

324 Bowl, *c*.1930
Stoneware, light and dark brown glazes; marks: 'BL' and 'SI' in monogram, impressed; made at the Leach Pottery, St Ives; h. 10.7 cm, d. 13.2 cm
C.963–1935. Source: given by the CAS, London

325 Bowl, 1927
Stoneware, grey glaze with painting in black; marks: 'BL' and 'SI' in monogram, impressed; made at the Leach Pottery, St Ives; h. 9.8 cm, d. 22.2 cm
C.410–1934. Source: given by the BIIA (gift of the potter in 1927)

326 Panel of nine tiles, 1927
Stoneware, painted and incised decoration in blue and brown in an oatmeal glaze; made at the Leach Pottery, St Ives; h. (each tile) 9 cm, d. 9 cm
C.403–1934. Source: given by the BIIA (gift of the potter in 1927)

327 Three tiles, 1926
Stoneware, painted decoration in brown and blue in an oatmeal glaze; marks: 'BL' and 'SI' in monogram, painted; made at the Leach Pottery, St Ives; h. 9.5 cm, d. 9.5 cm
C.402,404 & 409–1934. Source: given by the BIIA (gift of the potter in 1927)

328 Bowl, 1925–1934
Stoneware, white slip with incised decoration and painting in blue and brown; marks: 'BL' and 'SI' in monogram, impressed; made at the Leach Pottery, St Ives; h. 7.3 cm, d. 18.4 cm
C.58–1973. Source: given by Dr Mildred Creak and Mrs Falchikov

320

323 324

319

321

325

329 Vase, 1931 (pl. 28)

Stoneware, white glaze with painting in brown; marks: 'BL' and 'SI' in monogram, impressed and 'PK', incised; made at the Leach Pottery, St Ives; h. 34.3 cm, d. 14 cm

Circ.144–1931. Source: Beaux Arts Gallery, London, £21

This jar comes from one of the most famous of all the St Ives firings. Leach recounts the laborious preparation of bracken ash, which gives the glaze its particularly subtle lustrous surface – a quality of glaze that he was never to recapture in later years of oil-firing and less labour-intensive glaze preparation. From the same firing, and with the same quality of glaze and painting, comes the *Leaping Salmon* vase in the Milner-White Collection now in the York City Art Gallery (*see* Hogben, *The Art of Bernard Leach*, 1978, p. 31 and pl. 56) – probably the most famous of all of Bernard Leach's pots. The V&A vase is the original from which a whole series of leaping fish vases were derived by Leach in the post-war period.

This vase was purchased for 20 gns from a joint exhibition by Bernard Leach and Tomimoto Kenkichi at the Beaux Arts Gallery in May 1931, together with Circ.145 to Circ.147–1931; the *Leaping Salmon* vase bought by the very Rev. Milner-White was priced at 30 gns (= £31.50).

330 Vase, 1931

Stoneware, decoration incised through a grey slip under a clear glaze; marks: 'BL' and 'SI' in monogram, impressed; made at the Leach Pottery, St Ives; h. 26.3 cm, d. 21 cm

Circ.147–1931. Source: *see* Circ.144–1931, £15.75

328

331 Tray, 1931

Porcelain, painting in underglaze blue and yellow; marks: 'SI' in monogram, impressed and 'BL', in script on the interior; made at the Leach Pottery, St Ives; h. 2.5 cm, d. 16.7 cm

Circ.145–1931. Source: Beaux Arts Gallery, London, £5.25.

The risks associated with the high temperatures needed to fire porcelain restricted Leach's use of this material in the pre-war period. This piece has warped, and cracks between the base and the walls are mended with an imitation gold lacquer. However, this piece shows how well porcelain suited the delicate qualities of Leach's painterly decorative style.

332 Dish, *c.*1932

Earthenware, slip-trailed decoration in white under an amber glaze; marks: 'BL' and 'SI' in monogram, impressed; made at the Leach Pottery, St Ives; h. 5.4 cm, d. 30.2 cm

Circ.587–1968. Source: The Artist Potters Shop, Eastbourne, £40

331

326

330

327

332

333 Vase, *c*.1935
Stoneware, dark green glaze breaking to yellow over cut-fluted body; marks: 'BL' and 'SI' in monogram, impressed; made at the Leach Pottery, St Ives; h. 20.1 cm, d. 16.1 cm
C.68–1976. Source: A. London, £220

334 Panel of nine tiles, 1938 (pl. 7)
Stoneware, painted and incised decoration in brown on an oatmeal glaze; marks: 'BL' and 'SI' in monogram, painted; made at the Leach Pottery, St Ives; h. (each tile) 15 cm, d. 15 cm
C.47–1946. Source: given by the potter
This and the following two panels were chosen for an exhibition of tiles planned to be held at the Museum in 1939. Arthur Lane, Keeper of the Ceramics Department, recommending acceptance of the gift, says: 'They are of good artistic & technical quality, and Mr Leach himself considers them worthy examples of his work. He recently called here to see whether he could offer anything superior to replace them, and decided not.'

335 Panel of nine tiles, *c*.1939
Stoneware, painted decoration in blue and brown on an oatmeal glaze; marks: 'SI' interlaced and 'BL' monogram in lower corners, painted; made at the Leach Pottery, St Ives; h. (each tile) 10 cm, d. 10 cm
C.48–1946. Source: given by the potter, *see* C.47–1946

336 Panel of nine tiles, *c*.1939
Stoneware, painted decoration in brown; marks: 'SI' and 'BL' in monogram in lower corners, painted; made at the Leach Pottery, St Ives; h. (each tile) 10 cm, d. 10 cm
C.49–1946. Source: given by the potter, *see* C.47–1946

337 Bowl, 1940
Porcelain, cream, beige and black glazes; marks: monograms 'BL', incised and 'SI', painted; made at the Leach Pottery, St Ives; h. 12.9 cm, d. 34 cm
Circ.22–1961. Source: given by Miss Madeleine Whyte
In a letter to the donor April 1961, Leach says of the bowl: 'Yes I still like it: I only did one of that sort'. The design is of a Korean washerwoman; the Museum possesses a later ink-wash drawing of the same subject, E.1203–1978.

338 Bowl, 1947
Stoneware, incised decoration through a wash of iron pigment over an oatmeal glaze; marks: 'BL', impressed; made at the Leach Pottery, St Ives; h. 12.1 cm, d. 22.5 cm
Circ.280–1950. Source: Arts & Crafts Society (exhibition in the V&A, 1950), £7

339 Vase, 1949–1950
Stoneware, tenmoku glaze with brushwork in brown; marks: 'DL' and 'SI' in monogram, impressed; made at the Leach Pottery, St Ives; h. 40 cm, d. 20 cm
Circ.281–1950. Source: Arts & Crafts Society (exhibition in the V&A, 1950), £20
Bernard Leach was not very enthusiastic about this piece: in a letter to Hugh Wakefield he says: 'I cannot help feeling rather sorry that you have got the big pot from the Arts and Crafts Society Exhibition. The history of it is that David made the shape at this end, got stuck on the decoration and handed it over to me at that stage. Then it fired very nicely, but I still don't think the shape is a good one'.

333

338

336

335

339

337

340

341

342

343

345

347

340 Small pot, 1950
Porcelain, tenmoku glaze with kaki spots; made at the Leach Pottery, St Ives; h. 5.9 cm, d. 6 cm
Circ.84–1951. Source: given by the potter
Bernard Leach gave this small vase to the Museum as he was particularly pleased with the glaze effect. He says in a letter: 'There is also a tiny bottle with the most beautiful combination of Tenmoku and Kaki in spots which I would be very glad to give to the Museum if you would care to have it.' The Museum did care to have it.

341 Vase, 1951
Stoneware, green-brown mottled glaze with resist decoration; marks: 'BL' and 'SI' in monogram, impressed; made at the Leach Pottery, St Ives; h. 24.5 cm, d. 24 cm
Circ.136–1952. Source: the pottery, £12

342 Jar, 1951
Stoneware, decoration incised through brown to a grey-green glaze; marks: 'BL' and 'SI' in monogram, impressed; made at the Leach Pottery, St Ives; h. 24.2 cm, d. 24.4 cm
Circ.137–1952. Source: the pottery, £12

343 Vase with flattened sides, c.1952
Stoneware, painted decoration in blue-black and brown on an oatmeal glaze; marks: 'BL' and 'SI' in monogram, impressed; made at the Leach Pottery, St Ives; h. 26.9 cm, d. 24.5 cm
C.66--1976. Source: A. London, London, £150

344 Vase, c.1955 (pl. 41)
Stoneware, yellow-brown mottled ash glaze; marks: 'BL' and 'SI' in monogram and 'England', impressed; made at the Leach Pottery, St Ives; h. 35.6 cm, d. 30 cm
C.29–1968. Source: given by Mr Paul Bester in memory of his son, Mr Gerald Bester

345 Pilgrim bottle, c.1956
Stoneware, tenmoku glaze and incised decoration; made at the Leach Pottery, St Ives; h. 28 cm, d. 23 cm
Circ.498–1956. Source: Liberty & Co., London, £30

346 Vase, c.1957 (Frontispiece)
Stoneware, tenmoku glaze with incised decoration; marks: 'BL' and 'SI' in monogram, impressed; made at the Leach Pottery, St Ives; h. 34 cm, d. 26.9 cm
Circ.115–1958. Source: Primavera, London, £30

347 Vase, c.1959
Stoneware, tenmoku glaze with vertical ribbing; marks: 'BL' and 'SI' in monogram and 'England', impressed; made at the Leach Pottery, St Ives; h. 36.3 cm, d. 29.7 cm
Circ.129–1960. Source: Primavera, London, £30
A note in the Museum files records: 'Leach felt at the exhibition that the piece was spoiled by the small cap which accompanied it, & the latter has therefore been excluded from the purchase.' This explains the small lugs as being intended to tie on the cap.

348 Vase, 1961–1962
Stoneware, incised decoration through an iron
pigment, under an oatmeal glaze,; marks: 'BL' and
'SI' in monogram and 'ENGLAND', impressed;
made at the Leach Pottery, St Ives; h. 40 cm,
d. 16.7 cm
C.157–1979. Source: given by George and
Cornelia Wingfield Digby in memory of Bernard
Leach
Purchased by the donor from Bernard Leach in St
Ives in 1963.

349 Jar and cover, 1963
Stoneware, tenmoku glaze; marks: 'BL' and 'SI' in
monogram, impressed; made at the Leach Pottery,
St Ives; h. 25.2 cm, d. 22.8 cm
Circ.551–1963. Source: Primavera, London, £35

350 Vase, 1967 (pl. 63)
Porcelain, white glaze, vertical cut fluting; made
at the Leach Pottery, St Ives; h. 28.7 cm,
d. 19 cm
Circ.1192–1967. Source: Crane Kalman Gallery,
London, £85

351 Vase, 1972
Stoneware, dark green glaze, brown at rim; marks:
'BL' and 'SI' in monogram, impressed; made at
the Leach Pottery, St Ives; h. 28.9 cm, d. 25 cm
Circ.332–1973. Source: the potter, £100

Leach Pottery Standard Ware

One of the great triumphs of the Leach Pottery was
the 'Standard Ware' range. This was not developed
until just before the war, when the first mail-order
catalogue was issued, and it grew into a considerable
undertaking in the 1950s and 1960s. Bernard Leach,
rather against his natural instincts, had resorted to
making cheap earthenwares for everyday use in the
1920s and early 1930s (e.g. Catalogue nos. 314 and
332). However, it was the needs of the Dartington
Community, where Leach became involved in 1932,
which pushed him to plan seriously for a production
pottery of useful wares. He found support for this
activity in the ideas of the *mingei* movement in Japan
which had over the 1920s developed the belief that
the anonymous craftsman producing repetition ware
unselfconsciously for a community market was the
basis of all that was beautiful and noble in art. His
friends Yanagi and Hamada (qv) encouraged him to
join the Dartington community. It was Bernard's son
David who realised that the Leach Pottery had not
sufficient technical or managerial skill to produce a
consistent quality product at an economic price. While
his father was in Japan, Dartington sent him to the
Stoke-on-Trent Technical College. David developed
the new stoneware body, the oil-fired kiln and arranged
for local apprentices to be taken on for the work –
William Marshall (qv) was the first. David and Bernard
together developed prototypes for the catalogue of
forms – bowls, plates, jugs, mugs, coffee-pots, but not
teapots, except as special orders, for they were too
complicated for large-scale production. Three basic
glazes were used – a dark tenmoku, a celadon and an
oatmeal with simple painting in blue and brown. This
range, modified over the years, has become the prime
standard by which all domestic ware potters are now
judged; it combined the hand-made feel with good
looks, practicality, and ease of production. The ware
was made by a team of potters, with David Leach as
manager, William Marshall as foreman, and Bernard
Leach as chief quality controller. Everyone would take
their share of decorating, and Bernard Leach's distinctive
hand may be recognised on some pieces.

352 Bowl, 1924
Earthenware, raku fired, handbuilt with a crackled
clear glaze; marks: 'SI' in monogram and 'B',
impressed; made by Henry Bergen at the Leach
Pottery, St Ives; h. 8 cm, d. 12.8 cm
C.63–1924. Source: given by Lt-Col. K. Dingwall,
DSO, through the NACF
This is not strictly a piece of standard ware, but
represents the raku ware made at St Ives in the
early days of the pottery. Leach never used the
raku technique seriously after he left Japan in
1920. However, he set up a raku demonstration
every Thursday during the summer season in
order to attract tourists to his pottery. For a small
sum, visitors could purchase and decorate a small
pot which was then glazed and fired on the spot.
This bowl was made by Henry Bergen, an
American professor of Middle-English and a
friend and patron of Leach and other studio
potters in the pre-war period. His collection,
including pieces of his own, and work by Leach,
Hamada, Cardew and other potters, was left to
the City Museum and Art Gallery, Stoke-on-
Trent.

349

348

351

352

353 Cup and saucer, *c.*1941
Porcelain, celadon glaze with cut fluted sides; marks: 'SI' in monogram, impressed; made at the Leach Pottery, St Ives; h. 7.8 cm, d. 14 cm
Circ.93&a-1964. Source: given by the pottery

354 Cup and saucer, *c.*1941
Porcelain, celadon glaze with cut fluted sides; marks: 'SI' in monogram, impressed; h. 7.3 cm, d. 14.3 cm
Circ.94–1964. Source: given by the pottery

355 Teapot, *c.*1941
Porcelain, celadon glaze, cut decoration; h. 14.7 cm, d. 23.2 cm
Circ.88–1964. Source: given by the pottery
Teapots are not strictly part of the 'standard' range. They were not listed in the mail-order catalogues, but were available by special order. They were expensive, as they were complicated to make (the spouts, for example, are much more time consuming than the lips on the coffee pots).

356 Sugar bowl, about 1941
Porcelain, celadon glaze with cut fluted sides; marks: 'SI' in monogram, impressed; h. 5.7 cm, d. 10 cm
Circ.90–1964. Source: the pottery

357 Sugar bowl, *c.*1941
Porcelain, celadon glaze; marks: 'SI' in monogram, impressed; h. 6.2 cm, d. 11.4 cm
Circ.89–1964. Source: the pottery

358 Cream jug, *c.*1941
Porcelain, celadon glaze; marks: 'SI' in monogram, impressed; h. 9 cm, d. 11.5 cm
Circ.91–1964. Source: the pottery

359 Plate, *c.*1941
Porcelain, celadon glaze; marks: 'SI' in monogram, impressed; h. 2.5 cm, d. 14.9 cm
Circ.92–1964. Source: the pottery

360 Jug, 1940 (pl. 44)
Stoneware, oatmeal glaze and brown rim and handle; h. 8.4 cm, d. 12 cm
Circ.31–1940. Source: Heal & Sons Ltd., London, £0.23

361 Jug, 1940 (pl. 44)
Stoneware, tenmoku glaze; marks: 'SI' in monogram, impressed; h. 17.3 cm, d. 18 cm
Circ.30–1940. Source: Heal & Sons Ltd., London, £0.94

362 Jug, 1949 (pl. 44)
Stoneware, green and brown mottled glaze; marks: 'SI' in monogram, impressed; h. 11 cm, d. 14 cm
Circ.179–1950. Source: the pottery, £0.35

363 Fruit bowl, 1949
Stoneware, painting in blue and brown in an oatmeal glaze, outside brown glaze; marks: 'SI' in monogram, impressed, 'BL', painted; h. 12 cm, d. 30.3 cm
Circ.171–1950. Source: the pottery, £3
A paper label on the base gives the price £3. This is a standard ware bowl decorated by Bernard Leach himself.

364 Ashtray, 1949
Stoneware, tenmoku glaze with incised decoration through to a white glaze; marks: 'SI' in monogram, impressed; h. 2.5 cm, d. 11 cm
Circ.177–1950. Source: the pottery, £0.50
The drawing was almost certainly done by Bernard Leach himself.

365 Ashtray, 1949
Stoneware, oatmeal glaze with painted decoration in blue and brown; marks: 'SI' in monogram, impressed; h. 2.8 cm, d. 11.3 cm
Circ.178–1950. Source: the pottery, £0.50

354 353 355 356

357 358 359

363

364 365

366 Bowl, 1949
Stoneware, celadon glaze interior; marks: 'SI' in monogram, impressed; h. 6.7 cm, d. 14.5 cm
Circ.173–1950. Source: the pottery, £0.20

367 Porringer (bowl), 1949
Stoneware, oatmeal glaze with painted decoration in blue-brown; marks: 'SI' in monogram, impressed; h. 7 cm, d. 12.9 cm
Circ.174–1950. Source: the pottery, £0.30
The fluency of the brushwork suggests this may have been decorated by Bernard Leach himself.

368 Teapot, 1949
Porcelain, celadon glaze with incised decoration; marks: 'SI' in monogram' impressed; h. 15.9 cm, d. 27.2 cm
Circ.170&a-1950. Source: the pottery, £1.75

369 Jam-pot and lid, 1949
Porcelain, celadon glaze with incised decoration; marks: 'SI' in monogram, impressed; h. 8 cm, d. 9 cm
Circ.175&a-1950. Source: the pottery, £0.43

370 Tankard, 1949
Stoneware, tenmoku glaze; marks: 'SI' in monogram, impressed; h. 12 cm, d. 13 cm
Circ.176–1950. Source: the pottery, £0.37

371 Jug, 1949
Stoneware, tenmoku glaze; marks: 'SI' in monogram, impressed; h. 26.4 cm, d. 16.6 cm
Circ.172–1950. Source: the pottery, £3

367 366

369 368

370 371

Leach, David 1911– (son of Bernard Leach qv)

1911	born in Tokyo, Japan
1930	decides against going to university, joins St Ives pottery as an apprentice
1933–34	works at Dartington teaching and working on experiments for the projected pottery
1934–36	attends Pottery Managers course at North Staffordshire Technical College, Stoke-on-Trent
1936–37	scheme for a production pottery at Dartington Hall is shelved; David returns to St Ives and installs oil-fired kiln; earthenware is discontinued and standard ware is developed in stoneware
1939	son John (qv) born
1941	conscripted into army, service with the DCLI
1945	demobilised, returns to St Ives
1946	forms partnership with Bernard to run St Ives and train apprentices
1949	three-month teaching job at Camberwell School of Art, London
1950	starts pottery classes started at Penzance School of Art for evening students, later taken over by Michael Leach (qv)
1951	to Sandefjord, Norway, to help start pottery
1951	begins to experiment with porcelain with the help of Edward Burke, chief chemist with the Portland Cement Company; slowly develops a low-firing porcelain which is eventually marketed successfully as 'David Leach Porcelain'
1953	invited to take over Pottery Department at Loughborough College of Art for one year, and develops a range of stoneware glazes for Podmores, Stoke-on-Trent
1954	starts pottery for Carmelite Friars at Aylesford, Kent, taken over by Colin Pearson (qv) the following year
1956	leaves St Ives and establishes own pottery at Lowerdown, Bovey Tracey
1961	builds oil-fired stoneware kiln, abandons slipware; John Maltby (qv) as student; David is appointed assessor at Harrow School of Art
1966	first one-man show at the CPA
1967	Chairman of the CPA; Gold medallist at the Istanbul International exhibition

David Leach played a crucial part in the survival of his father's Leach Pottery, for it is likely that without his technical training at Stoke, the Leach Pottery would have collapsed before the war. He is responsible for modernising the workshop and setting it up as a production pottery for tablewares. He introduced the first machinery – a pug-mill, for example, previously all clay preparation had been done by hand. He converted the kiln to oil-firing, introduced a new stoneware body, and helped his father to design the first range of standard ware shapes. Bernard Leach had strongly disapproved of his son's mixing with 'the industrial devils of Stoke', but, as David Leach recounts, he was 'considerably mollified' when he saw the results coming out of the kiln. David did not develop a real individuality as a potter until he left St Ives and set up on his own in Devon in 1955. He has produced a distinctive body of ware, but is also important for his technical interests – the development of a porcelain suitable for the studio potter, for example – and for his involvement in education.

David Leach, 'Lowerdown Pottery', *CR*, 21/1973
—'Elegance and Strength', *Crafts*, May/June, 1979
Rose (1955), (1970)
Casson (1967)
Cameron and Lewis (1976)
London, CPA (1977)
Robert Fournier (ed.), *David Leach, a Monograph Edited from Tapes made by Bernard & David Leach*, Lacock, Fournier Pottery, 1977
London, Christopher Wood Gallery (1980)
London, Tate Gallery (1985)

372 Jar, 1951
Stoneware, tenmoku glaze with brush decoration; marks: obscured seals; made at the Leach Pottery, St Ives; h. 16.8 cm, d. 22.5 cm
Circ.138–1952. Source: the pottery, £10

373 Footed bowl, 1966
Stoneware, tenmoku and mottled greenish glaze; marks: 'DL' and 'L +' in monogram, impressed; made at Lowerdown Pottery, Bovey Tracey; h. 16.2 cm, d. 39.5 cm
Circ.880–1966. Source: CPA, London, £15.75

374 Bottle vase, 1972
Stoneware, tenmoku glaze with finger wiped decoration; marks: 'DL' in monogram, impressed; made at Lowerdown Pottery, Bovey Tracey; h. 60.5 cm, d. 26.5 cm
Circ.163–1973. Source: the potter, £50

375 Round pot, 1972
Porcelain, speckled pink glaze with a crackle; marks: 'DL' in monogram, impressed; made at Lowerdown Pottery, Bovey Tracey; h. 18.5 cm, d. 20 cm
Circ.293–1973. Source: the potter, £15

376 Vase, 1980
Stoneware, tenmoku glaze; marks: 'DL' in monogram, impressed; made at Lowerdown Pottery, Bovey Tracey; h. 42.1 cm, d. 31.8 cm
C.172–1980. Source: CPA, London (solo exhibition, 1980), £162

377 Dish, 1980
Stoneware, white over a tenmoku glaze; marks: 'DL' in monogram, impressed; made at Lowerdown Pottery, Bovey Tracey; h. 5.3 cm, d. 29.5 cm
C.173–1980. Source: CPA, London (solo exhibition, 1980), £60

372

375

373

376

374

377

378 Teapot, 1980
Stoneware, celadon glaze with cut sides; marks: 'DL' in monogram, impressed; made at Lowerdown Pottery, Bovey Tracey; h. 15 cm, d. 18.2 cm
C.174–1980. Source: CPA, London, (solo exhibition, 1980), £28

379 Bowl, 1980
Porcelain, blue-grey glaze; marks: 'DL' in monogram, impressed; made at Lowerdown Pottery, Bovey Tracey; h. 7.2 cm, d. 10.7 cm
C.175–1980. Source: CPA, London (solo exhibition, 1980), £10
This was a new experimental 'gun-metal' glaze.

Leach, Janet (née Darnell) 1918– (third wife of Bernard Leach qv)

1918	born in Texas, USA
1938	goes to New York, enrols in sculpture classes
1939–45	works as welder on war ships on Staten Island
1947	interest in pottery begins, works variously, including therapist pottery teacher in mental institution
1948	sets up pottery in Steiner community at Spring Valley
1949	leaves New York and starts own pottery
1952	meets Hamada (qv) and Bernard Leach on tour in USA
1954	travels to Japan, works at Mashiko and Tamba, travels with Leach during his Japanese visit
1956	comes to England to St Ives to marry Bernard Leach

Janet Leach came to the UK as Bernard Leach's third wife. Janet Leach is a powerful potter, with a very direct manner of handling clay. In this, she is not so much a follower of her husband's style as that of Hamada (qv) who advised her on her training in Japan. She is important for she is the first potter trained in Japanese country potteries, and having adopted some of their aesthetic, to work in the UK. She introduced a looser approach to ceramics at St Ives, and the impact on her own work, with free-formed and distorted shapes, and running ash glazes, can be clearly seen.

Janet Leach, 'With Hamada in Mashiko', *PQ*, 3/1956
—'Letter from Japan', *PQ*, 9/36, 1967–70
—'Fifty One Years of the Leach Pottery', *CR*, 14/1972
—'Shoji Hamada; a tribute', *CR*, 50/1978
—'Going to Pot', *CR*, 71/1981
—'Janet Leach, American Foreigner', *Studio Potter*, 11/2, 1983
—'Pots at the Tate', *CR*, 92/1985
Casson (1967)
Rose (1970)
Exhibition review, *CR*, 17/1972
Eileen Lewenstein, 'Janet Leach', exhibition review, *Crafts*, July/August, 1975
Birks (1976)
London, Christopher Wood Gallery (1980)
Jonathan Sidney, 'Janet Leach – New Pots', *CR*, 82/1983
Tony Birks, 'Janet Leach' exhibition review, *Crafts*, July/August, 1983
Paisley (1984)
Emmanuel Cooper, 'Janet Leach—Sculptural Potter', *CR*, 120/1989

380 Vase, 1963
Stoneware, ash-glaze; marks: 'JL' and 'SI' in monogram, impressed; made at the Leach Pottery, St Ives; h. 37 cm, d. 23.6 cm
Circ.375–1963. Source: Primavera, London, £18

381 Pot, 1965 (pl. 71)
Stoneware, handbuilt, ash-glaze partially over red body, tenmoku interior; marks: 'JL' and 'SI' in monogram, impressed; made at the Leach Pottery, St Ives; h. 42 cm, d. 23 cm
Circ.352–1965. Source: Primavera, London, £30

382 Vase, 1975–1976
Stoneware, greenish ash-glaze; marks: 'JL' and 'SI' in monogram, impressed; made at the Leach Pottery, St Ives; h. 25 cm, d. 15.3 cm
C.283–1976. Source: the pottery, £40

383 Vase, 1983
Stoneware, raku fired white glaze on a dark unglazed body; marks: 'JL' and 'SI' in monogram, impressed; made at the Leach Pottery, St Ives; h. 25.6 cm, d. 32.6 cm
C.251–1983. Source: CPA, London (solo exhibition, April 1984), £450

384 Vase, 1983
Porcelain, transparent glaze with painting in brown, interior brown glazed; marks: 'JL' and 'SI' in monogram, impressed; made at the Leach Pottery, St Ives; h. 21.6 cm, d. 14.6 cm
C.252–1983. Source: CPA, London (solo exhibition, April 1984), £175

379

382

378

380

383

Leach, John 1939– (son of David and grandson of Bernard Leach qv)

1939   born in St Ives
1957   leaves school, works with father at Lowerdown Pottery, also for short periods with Ray Finch (qv) and with Colin Pearson (qv) at Aylesford
1961–62   apprentice at the Leach Pottery, St Ives
1962–63   travels and teaches in USA
1963   sets up a pottery in California for seven months
1964   returns to the UK; establishes his pottery at Muchelney, Somerset, works alone producing domestic ware – 46 different shapes and sizes
1972   takes on assistant, Nick Rees
1977   converts 2-chamber climbing kiln to wood firing
1978   catalogue of standard ware produced
1982   pieces selected by the Design Centre, London
1983   begins making signed, individual work
1984   study tour of Nigeria
1985   teaching trips to Alaska and Yukon
1987   workshop tours in USA
1989   workshop tours in USA, Canada, Sweden and Ireland

John Leach has made a considerable success of his domestic wares. These are a development from the St Ives Leach standard ware, relying for their effect on the random ash-flashing which derive from the wood firing. His shapes are very simple, strong and practical. His individual work develops directly from the forms of his standard ware but a novel form of firing gives dramatic light streaks on the dark surface.

'John Leach – Country Jugs', *CR*, 67/1981
John Leach, exhibition pamphlet, London Coffee Information Centre, 1983
Amanda Hare, 'Nigerian Journey', *Crafts*, November/December, 1987
John Leach, Potter, exhibition pamphlet, Nottingham County Council Leisure Services, 1988
W. A. Ismay, 'John Leach, Potter', exhibition review, *Crafts*, July/August, 1988
Richard La Trobe-Bateman, 'John Leach – Working Potter', *CR*, 115/1989

384

The following three pieces were ordered by the Museum from the mail order catalogue, and were acquired for a total of £43.

385 Cider jar, 1981 (pl. 112)
Stoneware, interior with brown glaze, exterior unglazed with ash flashings; marks: 'Muchelney', impressed; made at Muchelney Pottery, Somerset; h. 38.3 cm, d. 26.3 cm
C.88–1981
No. 28 in the Muchelney mail-order catalogue.

386 Casserole, 1981
Stoneware, interior with green glaze, exterior unglazed with ash flashings; marks: 'MUCHELNEY', impressed; made at Muchelney Pottery, Somerset; h. 22.8 cm, d. 26 cm
C.89&a–1981
No. 2 in the Muchelney mail-order catalogue.

387 Jug, 1981
Stoneware, interior with brown glaze, exterior unglazed with ash flashings; marks: 'Muchelney', impressed; made at Muchelney Pottery, Somerset; h. 20.6 cm, d. 18.2 cm
C.90–1981
No. 24 in the Muchelney mail-order catalogue.

388 Vase, 1984
Stoneware, raku fired, unglazed; marks: 'JHL' in monogram, and 'MUCHELNEY', impressed; made at Muchelney Pottery, Somerset; h. 18.8 cm, d. 19 cm
C.36–1985. Source: Hill Gallery, London, £200
Bought at the first exhibition where special individual one-off pieces were shown, *John Leach in Black Mood*, in October 1984.

387 386

388

Leach, Margaret (no relation to Bernard Leach) dates not known

1936–40   Art School, Liverpool
1943–45   worked at the Leach Pottery, St Ives with Bernard Leach
1946–51   takes over and re-establishes the unoccupied Barnhouse Pottery, near Chepstow, Monmouthshire; Lewis Groves (qv) works with her for the first year, before joining the Taena Community; Dorothy Kemp (qv) works with her in the late 1940s
1951–56   joins Taena Community, Aylburton (later at Upton St Leonards), Gloucestershire, works with Lewis Groves who has already established a pottery there
1956   ceases potting on marriage (married name 'Heron')

The seal 'WV' stands for Wye Valley, where the Barnhouse Pottery is situated. Margaret Leach later used a version of the Taena Community mark, a cross within a circle, similar to that of Lewis Groves (qv).
The Taena Community at Aylburton included pottery as one of its activities as well as agriculture.

Wingfield Digby (1952; p. 83, pls. 59–60)
Godden (1964)

389 Dish, 1949
Earthenware, slip trailed decoration in black on white under an amber glaze; marks: 'WV' in monogram, impressed; made at the Barn Pottery, Chepstow; h. 4 cm, d. 28.2 cm
Circ.160–1950. Source: the potter, £0.82

390 Quart jug, 1949
Earthenware, black slip under an amber glaze; made at the Barn Pottery, Chepstow; h. 15.4 cm, d. 15.7 cm
Circ.161–1950. Source: the potter, £0.62

391 Soup bowl, 1949
Earthenware, black and white slips under an amber glaze; marks: 'WV' in monogram, impressed; made at the Barn Pottery, Chepstow; h. 6.2 cm, d. 13.2 cm
Circ.163–1950. Source: the potter, £0.25

391 389 390

392 Bowl, 1949
Earthenware, white slip over black slip under an amber glaze; made at the Barn Pottery, Chepstow; h. 6.8 cm, d. 14.3 cm
Circ.162–1950. Source: *see* Circ.160–1950, £0.30

393 Vase, 1949
Earthenware, painting in black slip on a white slip under a transparent glaze; marks: 'WV' in monogram, impressed; made at the Barn Pottery, Chepstow; h. 16.9 cm, d. 18.4 cm
Circ.164–1950. Source: the potter, £2.50

393 392

394

Leach, Michael 1913–1985 (son of Bernard Leach)

1913	born in Japan
1930–33	studies biology at Cambridge
1939	finishes a period of teaching, comes to work at the pottery in St Ives
1940–46	in army, where sent to East Africa and set up two potteries with local labour to make table-ware for the troops
1946–48	worked at Bullers with Anita Hoy (qv), and at Wrecclesham Pottery, Farnham
1948	returns to Leach Pottery, St Ives
early 1950s	takes over the Penzance School of Art from his brother David Leach
1955	leaves St Ives to set up Yelland Pottery at Fremington, North Devon
1984	retires and sells pottery

Michael Leach was a retiring person, who devoted himself quietly to pottery, and spent little effort in promoting himself or his work.

London, Tate Gallery (1985)

394 Vase, *c.*1961
Stoneware, mottled yellow and brown glaze; marks: 'ML' in monogram and 'Y', impressed; made at Yelland Pottery, Cornwall; h. 24 cm, d. 17 cm
Circ.440–1962. Source: the potter, £6
This pot was selected by the potter. In correspondence he says that he had made three more versions of this piece as people had wanted it – a practice he was not happy with and did not intend to repeat. This pot he describes as 'the original'.

Lee, Jennifer 1956–

1956	born in Aberdeenshire, Scotland
1975–79	Edinburgh College of Art
1979–80	travels in USA, attends workshop in Portland, Oregon, USA with Paul Soldner and Stephen de Staebler
1980–83	Royal College of Art, London
1982	travels in Egypt and Sinai
1983–87	studio in 401 1/2 Workshops, Lambeth, London
1985	solo exhibition at Rosenthal Studio-Haus, London
1986–87	part-time teaching at Harrow School of Art
1987–	studio in Brixton, London; part-time teaching at Leicester Polytechnic

Lee's work explores with great subtlety surface colour and texture on a limited range of forms which often present an asymmetric disjuncture which disturbs their classical profiles. At their best, her work has a 'floating' presence.

Jennifer Lee, 'Handbuilt Coloured Stoneware', *CR*, 95/1985
Amanda Fielding, 'Surfacing', *Crafts*, July/August, 1987
Jennifer Lee: Ceramics, booklet, Wooleydale Press, 1987
David Sexton, 'Feats of Clay', *Daily Telegraph Colour Magazine*, 25 March, 1989

Since 1988 Lee has begun to mark her pieces with painted initials 'JL' in a circle.

395 Vase, 1985
Stoneware, unglazed, pigments mixed into the clay and rubbed into the surface; h. 24.5 cm, d. 19 cm
C.230–1985. Source: the potter (shown at a solo exhibition at Rosenthal Studio-Haus Gallery, London, 1985), £135

396 Vase, 1985
Stoneware, unglazed clay, grey with darker streaks; h. 15.2 cm, d. 12.6 cm
C.231–1985. Source: the potter, £80

396 395

Lewenstein, Eileen 1925–

1925   born in London
1941–43   studies painting at West England School of Art, Bristol
1943–44   Beckenham School of Art
1944–45   teacher training at Institute of Education, University of London, taught at Derby High School for Girls, attended evening pottery classes at Derby Art School, where much enthused by R. J. Washington (qv) who taught there
1946–47   potting in partnership with Donald Mills (qv)
1948   founds Briglin Pottery in London with Brigitta Appleby producing domestic ware
1959–63   sets up own workshop in Camden, London, works alone producing individual pieces
1960–69   lecturer in ceramics, Hornsey School of Art, London
1963–75   studio in Hampstead, London
1970–   joint editor with Emmanuel Cooper of *Ceramic Review*
1976   moves from London to Hove, Sussex; sets up new workshop

Eileen Lewenstein is co-editor of *Ceramic Review* with Emmanuel Cooper and is a prolific writer, reviewer and lecturer. She has never received the critical success as a potter that she perhaps deserves. She has consistently produced varied work which follows a wide range of interests from rugged sculptural pieces to gentle forms with delicate surfaces and colouring. They have been regularly chosen for illustration in the *The Studio Yearbook of Decorative Art* from 1957 onwards.

Her mark was modified to include two lines of 'waves' after moving to the coast in 1976.

The Studio Yearbook of Decorative Art, 1957 onwards
Casson (1967)
Rose (1970)
Cooper (1974)
Sylvia Hyman, 'England's Eileen Lewenstein', *Ceramics Monthly*, May, 1979
Crafts, exhibition reviews: March/April, 1974; *Crafts*, July/August, 1978; May/June, 1980

397   Flower holder, 1971
Stoneware, handbuilt with metallic black surface; marks: 'EL' in monogram, impressed; h. 21.3 cm, d. 24.9 cm
Circ.125–1971. Source: Pace Gallery, London, £30
This piece came about from an exploration of egg shapes that the potter had carried on for several years. These started with complete egg forms, then forms cut in two – completely separated or partly rejoined. Finally, as this piece, in single half-eggs.

398   Dish, 1982
Stoneware, with decoration in pinky-brown and blues on a grey ground; marks: 'EL' in monogram, impressed; h. 4.6 cm, d. 30.6 cm
C.76–1984. Source: given by the Friends of the V&A
Purchased at the CPA 25th Anniversary exhibition, *Studio Ceramics Today*, held at the V&A in 1983.

Lloyd Jones, David 1928–

1951–52   studies fine art at Guildford School of Art, after Army service and work in father's business
1962–   learns throwing with Helen Pincombe (qv), but largely self-taught as a potter; sets up pottery in York
1989   awarded Honorary Doctorate at York University

Lloyd Jones is a consistently good potter in the oriental stoneware tradition, with an impressive technical control.

David Lloyd Jones, 'Plate Making', *CR*, 49/1978
Rosemary Wren and Peter Crotty, 'Potters: David Lloyd Jones', *CR*, 13/1972
Exhibition review, *Crafts*, July/August, 1978
'David Lloyd Jones', *CR*, 65/1980
W. A. Ismay, 'David Lloyd Jones – 20 Years a Potter', *CR*, 87/1984

399   Jug, 1980
Stoneware, speckled grey glaze; marks: 'LJ', impressed; h. 31.4 cm, d. 25 cm
C.124–1980. Source: CPA, London (solo exhibition, 1980), £40

400   Footed bowl, 1980
Stoneware, oatmeal glaze with wax resist decoration; marks: 'LJ', impressed; h. 17.2 cm, d. 20.8 cm
C.125–1980. Source: CPA, London (*see* C.124–1980), £28

401   Dish, 1980
Stoneware, white trailing in tenmoku glaze with iron-brown blobs and lines; marks: 'LJ', impressed; h. 5.2 cm, d. 44.2 cm
C.126–1980. Source: CPA, London (*see* C.124–1980), £64

400

398

401

399

397

Locke, Donald 1930–

1930	born in Guyana, South America
1954–57	British Council Scholar to Bath Academy of Art, Corsham
1959–64	University of Edinburgh and Edinburgh College of Art, degree in Fine Arts
1971	takes up residency in UK
1974–77	lecture visits to USA and Guyana
1977	gives up teaching
1979	Guggenheim Fellow in sculpture, State University of Arizona, USA
1980	returns to Guyana

London, VAM (1972)

Locke worked both as a sculptor and as a potter. He showed at various exhibitions at Amalgam Gallery, London, in the 1970s, and was included in the British section of the 1972 V&A exhibition of International Ceramics. This intriguing and enigmatic object, reminiscent of mediaeval or African leather flasks, is typical of his pots.

402 Bottle, 1976
Stoneware, handbuilt, matt black slip glaze; marks: 'TTE (?) 76 HAYSTACK'; h. 30.7 cm, d. 16.8 cm
C.68–1980. Source: Anthony Shaw, London, £125

Lord, Andrew 1950–

1950	born in Rochdale, Lancashire
1967	Rochdale School of Art
1968–71	Central School of Art, London
1972	included in the *International Ceramics 1972* exhibition at the V&A in 1972, moves to Holland, where he works in a ceramics factory
1974	travels in Mexico
1975	moves to Rotterdam, then The Hague, Holland, and later to New York, USA, where he now works

Lord started as an inventive potter who has since joined the fine-art world in the United States where he has achieved success. His exploration of perspective, space and volume in the 'cubist' series co-incided with similar interests among such potters as Fritsch (qv) and Alison Britton (qv).

London, VAM (1972)
Birks (1976)
Tony Birks, 'Andrew Lord – Pottery', exhibition review, *CR*, 53/1978
William Packer, 'Ceramics by Andrew Lord', *Crafts*, September/October, 1978

403 Box, 1972 (pl. 88)
Earthenware, hand-modelled, with coloured slips under a transparent glaze; marks: 'Andrew Lord 1972', incised; h. 23.5 cm, d. 21 cm
Circ.154&a-1973. Source: the potter, £15

404 *Cubist Vase and Tray*, 1978
Stoneware, hand formed, matt green-grey surface; marks: 'Andrew Lord 1978', incised on both pieces; h. (vase) 29.4 cm, d. (tray) 31.9 cm
C.172 & 173–1984. Source: Anthony Stokes Ltd., London, £1897

Lowndes, Gillian 1936–

1957–59	Central School of Art, London
1960	École des Beaux Arts, Paris, followed by setting up a workshop in Bloomsbury, London, with Robin Welch (qv)
1966–71	shares a workshop in Chippenham with Ian Auld (qv)
1971–72	travels with Ian Auld to Nigeria
1975	establishes a workshop in Camberwell, London
1976–86	part-time teaching at Camberwell and Central Schools of Art
1976–	starts experimenting with mixed media work
1979–	begins to incorporate London bricks and nichrome wire into her work
1985–	development of collages of found materials with wire, Egyptian paste etc.
1987	*Gillian Lowndes, New Ceramic Sculpture*, solo exhibition, Crafts Council, London
1989	establishes new workshop in Toppesfield, Essex

Gillian Lowndes is one of the major 'sculptural' potters whose experimentation with new form and materials has provided a continual challenge to orthodox pottery. Though her work has now largely abandoned even residual references to the vessel (the broken cup of catalogue no. 408 notwithstanding) her work is still intimately concerned with ceramic processes and materials and their validity for allusion and metaphor.

Casson (1967)
Birks (1967), (1976)
London, VAM (1968)
Sue Harley, 'Ian Auld and Gillian Lowndes', *CR*, 44/1977
Elizabeth Cameron, 'Gillian Lowndes', *CR*, 83/1983
Paisley (1984)
Angus Suttie, 'The Dangerous Edge of Things', exhibition review, *Crafts*, July/August, 1985
London, Crafts Council (1987)
Henry Pim, 'Uncertain Echoes', *CR*, 103/1987
Tanya Harrod, 'Transcending Clay', *Crafts*, January/February, 1987

405 *Three Standing Pipes*, 1968
Stoneware, handbuilt, buff matt glaze; h. 72.8 cm, d. 7.8 cm
Circ.826 to 828–1968. Source: the potter, £15

402

404

405

406

406 Vase, 1968
Stoneware, handbuilt, blue glaze; h. 38.3 cm,
d. 28.8 cm
Circ.829–1968. Source: the potter, £15

407 Sculptural form, 1968 (pl. 74)
Stoneware, hand formed, buff coloured glaze;
h. 34.3 cm, d. 58.5 cm
Circ.830–1968. Source: the potter, £25

408 Cup on base, 1986 (pl. 106)
Stoneware, handbuilt, with metal elements, and
painted mottled yellow and white; h. 18 cm,
d. 23.3 cm
C.39–1987. Source: CC (solo exhibition, 1986),
£315

Lunn, Dora 1881–c.1955

1881	born in Sheffield
1907	takes Art Class Teachers Certificate in London
1908	Ornament and Design Certificate at the Royal College of Art, London
1916–28	establishes and runs Ravenscourt Pottery, Ravenscourt Park, London, with a team of lady potters; pays rent and salaries by teaching a few days a week; initially work is cast as they have no wheel
1917	takes stall at British Industries Fair; first woman potter to exhibit; both Queen Mary and Queen Alexandra make purchases
c.1918	Pound, a potter who made a living by demonstrating throwing on the Embankment, is employed; after his death, professional throwers are engaged in their spare time to do batches of throwing
1925	exhibited at Paris International Exhibition, where she wins a Hon. Mention
late 1920s	demand for expensive wares dies down; 'Household Section' of cheaper table wares developed
1931	Ravenscourt Pottery closed; continues to teach and lecture; writes book
1933	Dora Lunn Pottery established in Chiswick; continues with individual work
c.1943–55	new workshop in Goldhawk Road, Shepherd's Bush

Dora is the daughter of Richard Lunn, potter, who was employed as a modeller on the Ceramic Staircase and Ceramic Gallery of South Kensington Museum. He eventually became Head of Ceramics at the Royal College of Art and set up the Ceramics course at Camberwell School of Art. She set up the pottery during the First World War, having already learnt much about pottery from her father except for throwing. 'I had only made it in moulds, but one day I was asked to carry out a commission for a special vase that would have to be hand thrown to get the shape. I had heard of an old man with a wheel who was doing exhibitions on the Embankment, and I got hold of him and he gave me my first lesson in throwing' (*see* Lillian Joy, cited below). Her Ravenscourt Pottery made figure groups and 'household wares' as well as decorative vases. She employed a number of assistants, and much of the work was carried out in the open air: '. . . the workers are encouraged to study graceful ways of moving and carrying the vessels, with resultant benefit to health and physique' (*The Graphic*, 3 Jan. 1920). Dora Lunn

was particularly known for her beautiful glaze colours on simple forms which were often favourably compared to the 'old Chinese'. She seems to have ceased potting during the Second World War but had resumed it by 1950. Her second pottery was in Shepherd's Bush.

Dora Lunn, *Pottery in the Making*, London, 1931
—*A Potter's Pot-Pourri*, (unpublished, V&A archive)
—*Life and the Crafts*, (1947)
The Studio Yearbook of Decorative Art, 1919–1927 and
  1950
Lilian Joy, 'Woman Potter's Work, Miss Dora Lunn's
  Decorative China', *Yorkshire Post*, 21 July, 1922

A group of Dora Lunn's papers are kept in the Twentieth Century Archive of Art and Design, Victoria and Albert Museum. They include a manuscript, *The Ravenscourt Pottery*, written by Dora Lunn in about 1951 which gives a history of her work.

Six of the items catalogued below were purchased in 1983, and had been acquired by the vendor at a house sale in Chiswick, thought to be Dora Lunn's last home.

409

412 413

409 Dish, 1916–1928
Earthenware, painted decoration in black; marks:
'RAVENSCOURT', incised; made at Ravenscourt
Pottery, London; h. 7.7 cm, d. 35.8 cm
C.287–1983

410 Vase, 1916–1928 (pl. 22)
Stoneware, blue-grey glaze; marks:
'RAVENSCOURT', impressed; made at
Ravenscourt Pottery, London; h. 19 cm,
d. 17.7 cm
C.288–1983

411 Vase, c.1919 (pl. 22)
Earthenware, mottled blue glaze; marks:
'RAVENSCOURT', impressed; made at
Ravenscourt Pottery, London; h. 24 cm,
d. 14.6 cm
C.505–1919. Source: given by Lt-Col. K.
Dingwall, DSO
Paper label on base gives the price 35/- (= £1.75).

412 Vase, 1950s
Earthenware, green glaze and a blue rim; marks:
'DHL' in monogram, incised; h. 14.9 cm,
d. 6.4 cm
C.291–1983
This may have been made at her pottery in
Goldhawk Road between 1945 and 1955. The
'H' in the seal stands for Hedges – her married
name.

413 Vase, 1920
Earthenware, with painted lines in blue and green;
marks: '1920' and 'DL' in monogram, incised;
made at Ravenscourt Pottery, London; h. 13.3 cm,
d. 9.2 cm
C.289–1983

414 Vase, 1950s
Stoneware, grey glaze with dark speckles; marks:
'DORA LUNN' in a rectangular frame, incised;
h. 9 cm, d. 10 cm
C.292–1983
This was probably made at her pottery in
Goldhawk Road.

414

415 Bowl, 1916–1928
Earthenware, yellow glaze interior, painted exterior in black; marks: 'RAVENSCOURT', incised; made at Ravenscourt Pottery, London; h. 5.8 cm, d. 9.4 cm
C.290–1983

416 Bowl, 1920
Earthenware, turquoise glaze and painting in black; marks: 'Ravenscourt', painted; made at Ravenscourt Pottery, London; h. 6.9 cm, d. 18.2 cm. Source: given by Lt-Col. K. Dingwall, DSO, through the NACF
C.402–1920.

Magson, Mal (née Withers) 1950–

1968–72   Loughborough College of Art
1973   workshop in Sheffield
1974–84   workshop in Malton, N. Yorkshire
1984–89   workshop in East Ayton, Scarborough
1989–   new workshop in Scarborough

Exhibition review, CR, 27/1974
'CPA New Members', CR, 61/1980

Magson developed the 'solid-agate' technique for which she has become known while at college, in an attempt to find a totally individual style which was not dependent on glazes. Her work, which has been largely of bowl-forms, is now developing towards wall-hung plaques.

417 Bowl, 1983
Stoneware, 'agate ware' of coloured clays, unglazed; h. 10.2 cm, d. 23.8 cm
C.212–1983. Source: Henry Rothschild Associates, Ltd., Cambridge, £55

Malone, Jim 1946–

1966–69   Teacher Training College at Bangor, N. Wales
1972–76   studies ceramics at Camberwell School of Art, London
1975   works briefly at Winchcombe with Ray Finch (qv)
1976–82   sets up workshop at Llandegla, near Wrexham in North Wales
1982   moves to Cumbria, teaching at the Cumbria College of Art, Carlisle
1984–   establishes new studio at Ainstable, Cumbria

Jim Malone is, like Batterham, something of a purist working in the oriental stoneware tradition. His work has an easy but vigorous freedom in both throwing and decoration.

Jim Malone, 'A Point of View', PQ, 14/56, (c.1983)
— Letter of resignation to the CPA, CR, 85/1984
Christopher Reid, 'Tradition and the Individual Talent', *Crafts*, July/August, 1980

418 Covered jar, 1980 (pl. 5)
Stoneware, incised decoration under a greenish-ash glaze; marks: 'JM', impressed; h. 21 cm, d. 21.5 cm
C.183&a–1980. Source: CPA, London (exhibition, November, 1980), £30

Maltby, John 1936–

1954–59   trains as a sculptor at Leicester College of Art and Goldsmith's College, London, followed by two and a half years of teaching painting and sculpture
1962–63   gives up full-time teaching to work with David Leach for two years
1964   sets up own pottery in Crediton, Devon, producing domestic and individual ware
1974   wins Gold medal at Faenza
1976–   makes only individual ware
1979–82   visiting lecturer at Kunsthandverksskole, Bergen, Norway
1987–88   teaching at Berne and Basle, Switzerland

Maltby has pursued an individual line in ceramics. Primarily interested in decoration, for which he looks to certain classes of historic Japanese wares for inspiration, he has recently started to explore vessels and is developing a somewhat conceptual approach to form.

John Maltby, 'On Decoration', CR, 78/1982
—'On Pots and Art', CR, 102/1986
—'The Leach Tradition', *Crafts*, May/June, 1986
Casson (1967)
Exhibition review, *Crafts*, July/August, 1980

419 Square dish, 1981
Stoneware, wax resist decoration with tenmoku and brown glazes; marks: 'Maltby', painted; h. 3.7 cm, d. 38.2 cm
C.70–1981. Source: V&A Craft Shop, £62.01

417

416 415

419

Margrie, Victor 1929–

1946–52 Hornsey College of Art, London
1952–56 part-time teaching at various London art colleges
1954–71 own workshop in London
1956–71 Head of Ceramics at Harrow School of Art, London
1963 founds ceramics course at Harrow School of Art with Mick Casson (qv)
1971–77 Secretary of the Crafts Advisory Committee
1977–84 Director of the Crafts Council
1984 resigns from the Crafts Council
1984 awarded CBE
1985 new workshop in Bristol
1988 moves to Moretonhampstead, Devon

Margrie has had a considerable influence on the craft world through his work with the Crafts Advisory Committee and his direction of the Crafts Council, though he is also known as a potter for his sky-pattern porcelain bowls, and later, with Mick Casson (qv) for setting up the Harrow School of Art pottery course.

Victor Margrie 'British Ceramics', *CR*, 71/1981
— 'Influence and Innovation', *CR*, 100/1986
— 'Aspects of Contemporary Ceramics', *CR*, 115/1989
Casson (1967)
Eileen Lewenstein and Emmanuel Cooper, 'Victor Margrie Talking', *CR*, 19/1973
Stephen Bayley, 'Craft, Art and Design', a discussion with Victor Margrie, David Mellor, David Queensberry and Martin Hunt, *Crafts*, May/June, 1979

420 Bowl, 1969
Porcelain, with cut and applied decoration under a transparent glaze; marks: seal, impressed; h. 7.7 cm, d. 9.1 cm
Circ.757–1969. Source: Crafts Centre of Great Britain (solo exhibition 'Porcelain Bowls', November, 1969), £17

421 Bowl, 1969
Porcelain, cut and applied decoration under a transparent glaze; marks: seal, impressed; h. 9.3 cm, d. 10.2 cm
Circ.756–1969. Source: *see* Circ.757–1969, £20
Based on a 'concept derived from sky patterns'.

Marlow, Reginald dates not known

mid-1920s attends Lowestoft and Norwich Schools of Art
1927–30 studies ceramics at the Royal College of Art, London, under William Staite Murray (qv)
1930–32 assistant art master at Christ's Hospital, Horsham
1932–34 teaches in the Department of Industrial Design, Leicester College of Art, succeeded by Sam Haile (qv)
1935– teaching design at Croydon School of Art; Head of Department by 1947, part-time teaching at Central School of Art, London
1950s Principal of Stoke-on-Trent College of Art

In 1959, William Staite Murray (qv) described Marlow as one of the few of his students, together with Henry Hammond (qv), still carrying on 'the tradition formed in those days', i.e. that of the Royal College of Art while he, Staite Murray, was Head of the School of Pottery (*see* bibliography under Heber Mathews). He is referred to with respect by those he taught, such as Henry Hammond.

Reginald Marlow, *Pottery Making and Decorating* (How to Do It series), London, 1957
Cooper (1947)
A. C. Sewter, 'Reginald Marlow – Potter', *Apollo*, October, 1947
Casson (1967)

422 Vase, 1962
Stoneware, painted decoration in blue and brown on an oatmeal glaze; marks: 'RM' in monogram, painted; h. 37 cm, d. 10.8 cm
Circ.650–1962. Source: Society of Designer Craftsmen, London, £10

Marshall, Ray 1913–1986

1913 born in Alberta, Canada
c.1940–45 comes to UK in the army, in his spare time studies at Guildford School of Art
1946 studies with Helen Pincombe (qv) at the Royal College of Art, London; works for a time with Ray Finch (qv) at Winchcombe
1946 moves to Kingswood Design and Craftsmanship, a craft workshop at Wormley, Surrey
1948 sets up Milland Pottery in Hampshire with Lester Campion and Jane Aburrow; does much of the throwing
1952 sets up a workshop at Stedham, Sussex
1957 leaves Milland; continues to work on own

Murray Fieldhouse, 'Workshop Visit: Milland Pottery', *PQ*, 2/1954
PQ, 7/1961–62 (illustrations pl. 10)

423 Vase with handles, *c.*1960
Stoneware, unglazed, applied decoration, darkened with oxide, oatmeal glaze in; marks: signature, incised; h. 21.8 cm, d. 30.7 cm
C.186–1986. Source: bequest of the potter

424 Bottle vase, dated 1961
Stoneware, oatmeal glaze with incised decoration, darkened with oxide; marks: signature and '1961', incised; h. 31 cm, d. 18.7 cm
C.187–1986. Source: bequest of the potter

420 421

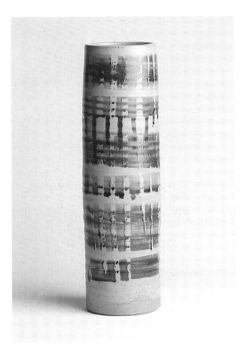

422

423 424

Marshall, William 1923–

1923 born in St Ives, Cornwall
1938 joins Leach Pottery as an apprentice
1942 conscripted into the army
1947 rejoins pottery, becomes foreman and Bernard
Leach's (qv) right-hand man
1977 leaves to set up own pottery at Lelant; teaching
at Cornwall Technical College, Redruth

William Marshall was the first of the true apprentices,
as opposed to students, taken on at the Leach Pottery.
A local boy, he came straight from school and was
trained to be a thrower for the new range of standard
ware the pottery was developing. He became the
foreman of the pottery, and after the war was
responsible for throwing, to designs done on paper, all
of Bernard Leach's larger vases. His own individual
work developed strongly, in a style much influenced
by Shoji Hamada, after he left the Leach Pottery and
set up on his own.

London, Christopher Wood Gallery (1980)
London, Tate Gallery (1985)
Exhibition reviews: *Crafts*, May/June, 1974; *Crafts*,
September/ October, 1981; *Crafts*, March/April, 1988
Godden (1988)

425 Vase, *c*.1950
Porcelain, pale celadon glaze; marks: 'WM' and
'SI'in monogram, impressed; made at Leach
Pottery, St Ives; h. 11.7 cm, d. 8.6 cm
C.120–1977. Source: Richard Dennis, London
(from the collection of Sir Edward Maufe), £10

Mathews, Heber *c*.1907–1959

1927–30 student of Staite Murray's (qv) at Royal
College of Art, having previously studied
mural painting
1930–31 year as a student demonstrator at the Royal
College of Art
1932 sets up own workshop in Lee, Kent; appointed
pottery advisor to the Rural Industries
Bureau
1932–59 teaching and eventually Head of the Art
School at the Woolwich Polytechnic

In his introduction to the pamphlet that accompanied
Heber Mathews' memorial exhibition, Staite Murray
includes Mathews as one of the '... few students who
sensed the inner meaning of potting, and that saw that
pots, when infused with vitality could be an articulating
art; they saw potting to be the genesis of all the arts,
voicing music and poetry, and when imbued with
feeling to have the moving power of sculpture.' Of
Mathews' later pots, Staite Murray remarks 'Their
inspiration I thought to be classical, with a calm dignity
that marks good breeding. They were in no way
derivative, but were highly individual, and announced
the work of a fine artist composing from within.'
   Mathews is certainly the most 'pure' of Staite Murray's
students in that his best work explores form virtually
to the exclusion of decoration. Impressive, even
monumental, pots are covered with restrained, soft and
subtle glazes.

Cooper (1947; pls. 27–32)
A. C. Sewter, 'Heber Mathews – Potter', *Apollo*, August,
1947, pp. 45–47
Wingfield Digby (1952; pl. 44))
Heber Mathews, Memorial Exhibition, Crafts Centre of
Great Britain, exhibition pamphlet with introduction
by W. Staite Murray, 1959
London, Christopher Wood Gallery (1980)

The Museum also possesses a 30-tile panel showing a
woman swimming with fish and border panels, C.193–
1985, not catalogued here.

426 Jar, *c*.1932
Stoneware, dark speckled brown glaze; h. 24.2 cm,
d. 23.6 cm
C.190–1985. Source: given by Mr R.D.G.
Mathews

427 Jar, *c*.1934
Stoneware, painting in brown in a creamy-grey
glaze; marks: 'HM', incised; h. 24.4 cm, d. 23.5 cm
C.185–1985. Source: given by Mr R.D.G.
Mathews

428 Bowl, *c*.1956
Porcelain, cut decoration; marks: indistinct seal; h.
8.7 cm, d. 10.8 cm
C.186–1985. Source: given by Mr R.D.G.
Mathews

429 Jar, *c*.1932
Stoneware, streaky brown glaze; marks: 'HM',
incised; h. 18.5 cm, d. 20.3 cm
C.191–1985. Source: given by Mr R.D.G.
Mathews

428 429

425

427 426

430 Cider jar and stand, *c.*1938
Stoneware, painting in brown in an oatmeal glaze;
marks: 'HM', incised; h. 58 cm, d. 22.8 cm
C.184–1985. Source: given by Mr R.D.G.
Mathews
A similar jar and stand is illustrated by Sewter in
his article of 1947.

431 Bowl, *c.*1955
Stoneware, painting in brown on a grey glaze; h.
34.3 cm, d. 28 cm
C.188–1985. Source: given by Mr R.D.G.
Mathews

432 Vase, *c.*1937
Stoneware, incised decoration through brown
under a thin grey glaze; marks: 'HM', incised; h.
26.7 cm, d. 20.7 cm
C.189–1985. Source: given by Mr R.D.G.
Mathews

433 Bowl, *c.*1940
Stoneware, yellow glaze; marks: 'HM', painted;
h. 16 cm, d. 33 cm
C.187–1985. Source: given by R.D.G. Mathews

434 Footed bowl, 1950s
Stoneware, speckled yellowish glaze interior, grey
glazed exterior; marks: 'HM', incised and painted
in brown; h. 26.5 cm, d. 44 cm
Circ.518–1962. Source: R. D. G. Mathews, £20

435 Bowl, 1949–1950
Stoneware, painting in brown on an oatmeal glaze;
marks: illegible oval seal, impressed and 'HM',
incised; h. 9 cm, d. 24 cm
Circ.282–1950. Source: Arts and Crafts Society
(exhibition in V&A, 1950), £3.15

436 Vase, 1958 (pl. 49)
Stoneware, combed lines under a pale oatmeal
glaze; h. 38.2 cm, d. 25 cm
Circ.263–1959. Source: Craft Centre of Great
Britain, London, £20
Peter Floud of the Circulation Department, in his
recommendation for purchase, says: 'For years we
have tried to persuade ... Mathews, the pottery
advisor to the Craft Centre, to sell us one of his
own pots. He always procrastinated on the
grounds that he would do something better later.
This spring he suddenly died. We have, however,
been allowed to pick one pot from the few he
left in his studio.' It was Mathews' brother who
agreed the purchase.

433

431 430 432

435

434

Matsubayashi, Tsuronosuke

1922–24   comes to St Ives, Cornwall to rebuild the climbing kiln at the invitation of Bernard Leach (qv)

1924–25   travels in UK and Europe, helps Pleydell-Bouverie (qv) build her kiln at Coleshill; returns to Japan

Matsubayashi was the 39th generation of the Asahi family of potters from Kyoto, Japan, who were specially famed for their technical expertise. He was asked over to the UK to help Bernard Leach (qv), whose first climbing kiln, built with the help of Hamada (qv), was inefficient and uncontrollable. Matsubayashi's kiln lasted until the 1970s. After work at St Ives, Matsubayashi helped Pleydell-Bouverie (qv) build a kiln at Coleshill. Leach was delighted with his technical help, but thought that he made terrible pots. Matsubayashi gave occasional talks on technical matters to the St Ives potters in the evenings, his wayward command of English causing great mirth. Pleydell-Bouverie recalls him with great humour in her writings.

M. Cardew, *Pioneer Potter*, London, 1988, pp. 34–37, 39–40
B. Leach (quoting Pleydell-Bouverie), *Beyond East and West*, London, 1978, pp. 149–55
London, Tate Gallery (1985)

437   Bowl, 1924
Stoneware, marbled green and white covered with a greenish glaze; marks: 'SI' and personal seal, impressed; made at Leach Pottery, St Ives; h. 9.8 cm, d. 21.3 cm
C.1370–1924. Source: given by the potter
The bowl is made from the following mixture: 1/4 native black Japanese clay (brought with him from Japan), 3/4 white clay from Devon and nearby St Ives.

McNicoll, Carol 1943–

1943   born in Birmingham
1966–67   foundation course at Solihull College of Technology
1967–70   studies Fine Art at Leeds Polytechnic
1970–73   ceramics at Royal College of Art, London
1973–76   workshop at 401½ Workshops, London, shared with Alison Britton (qv) until 1975
1976–83   new workshop in Kensington, London
1983–   new workshop in Kentish Town, London
1985   *Carol McNicoll Ceramics*, solo exhibition, Crafts Council, London

McNicoll is a remarkable potter in a number of ways. She is one of the very few non-domestic ware potters who supports herself from her work without teaching. All her work is slip-cast and assembled, the forms often being developed in other materials. She also has a continuing and beneficial connection with industry – designs of hers have, for example, been mass-produced for the Next Interiors chain of stores. She produces a range of standard ware done in series, as well as one-off pieces. Her standard ware, such as the teapot illustrated here, does actually function, in spite of its apparently eccentric nature. Her forms often imitate other materials, such as paper or cloth, but like her contemporaries Alison Britton and Jacqui Poncelet she restricts her exploration to the 'vessel' and her work always 'contains' in some way or another.

Janet Street Porter, 'Tea-Time for the Nonconformist', *Crafts*, November/December, 1980
London, Crafts Council (1985)
Piers Gough, 'Carol McNicoll Ceramics', exhibition review, *Crafts*, January/February, 1986
Henry Pim, 'Carol McNicoll – Ceramics', *CR*, 97/1986
Tanya Harrod, 'Bridging the Divide', *Crafts*, May/June, 1986
Eileen Lewenstein, 'Carol McNicoll – Slip-caster Extraordinary', *CR*, 117/1989

438   Form: *Ceramic piece*, 1980
White earthenware, cast and assembled; marks: 'Carol McNicoll', painted; h. 40.2 cm, d. 28.5 cm
C.53–1982. Source: V&A Craft Shop, £232.90

439   Bowl, 1985 (pl. 97)
White earthenware, cast and assembled, decoration in blue, black, brown and white; marks: 'Carol McNicholl', painted in script; h. 16.8 cm, d. 37.3 cm
C.38–1987. Source: CC, London (solo exhibition, 1985), £427

440   Teapot and lid, 1988
White earthenware, handbuilt, inlaid, incised and painting in blue, white and brown; marks: 'Carol McNicoll', signed in black; h. 16.8 cm, d. 34 cm
C.10&a–1989. Source: CAA, London, £129
This teapot and the following mug form part of McNicoll's series production, distinct from her one-off individual work.

441   Mug, 1988
White earthenware, handbuilt, inlaid, incised and painted decoration in blue, white and brown; marks: 'Carol McNicoll' in script and a mark, painted; h. 8.6 cm, d. 14.1 cm
C.11–1989. Source: *see* C.10&a–1989, £21.50

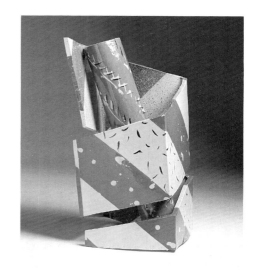

438

437

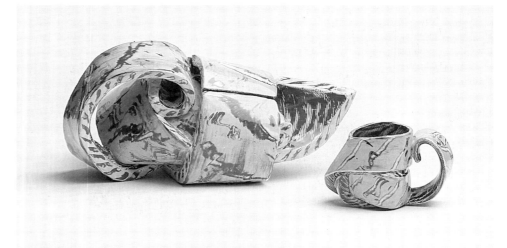

440 441

Mehornay, William 1945–

Mehornay, an American, set up a pottery in Richmond-upon-Thames, Surrey, in 1975, having worked previously at Fen Ditton near Cambridge. He specialises in fine porcelain with brilliant coloured glazes, following the model of later Chinese wares.

'Purity in Porcelain', *Collector's Guide*, March, 1981

442 Teapot, 1976
Porcelain, transparent glaze; marks: 'WNM' in monogram, impressed; h. 10.9 cm, d. 13.9 cm
C.9&a–1979. Source: given by R. J. Charleston

Mellon, Eric James 1925–

1925	born in Watford, Hertfordshire
1939–43	fine art at Watford School of Art
1941–44	Harrow College of Higher Education, weekend classes in pottery
1944–50	Central School of Art, London, studying painting, engraving, etching and lithography; part time for last three years
1951–57	sets up artistic community in Buckinghamshire with, among others, Derek Davis (qv); work in slip-painted earthenware; bathroom commissions
1958	introduced to stoneware by Rosemary Wren, becomes member of the CPA; produces some coiled figures; new workshop at Bognor Regis, Sussex
1960s	themes in painted stoneware from contemporary political events
1970s	circus themes – acrobats and trapeze artists; then themes from classical mythology – Europa and the Bull, Pluto and Persephone etc.
1980s	themes on Moon Goddess, Theme of Tenderness, Birdmaidens
1983	introduced to raku by Jill Crowley (qv), makes figures again

442

Mellon combines two unusual interests in his work – painted narrative decoration and the subtleties of ash glazing. He is a skilful decorator in placing his detailed images on the complex surfaces of his thinly thrown, rather tight forms.

Eric Mellon, 'Ash Glazes', *CR*, 42, 43 & 65/1976, 1977 & 1980
Exhibition review, *Crafts*, January/February, 1979
Ceramics, Drawing, Paintings, 1966–1986, E. J. Mellon, Bognor Regis, 1986
'Magic and Poetry', *CR*, 114/1988
London, Christopher Wood Gallery (1980)

443 Dish, 1968
Stoneware, painted decoration in blue and brown in a wood ash glaze; marks: 'Eric James Mellon/Elm Ash/1968', painted; h. 5.9 cm, d. 30.1 cm
C.59–1985. Source: Paul Rice Gallery, London, £280

444 Vase, 1984
Stoneware, painted decoration, using wood ash glazes; marks: 'Eric James Mellon 1984 34 Philadelphus Ash, Theme of tenderness and a Fox' painted in brown; h. 15.9 cm, d. 15 cm
C.200–1984. Source: Paul Rice Gallery, London, £330
The decoration includes a moon goddess, a winged woman, and various naked figures relating to the myth of Persephone; the fox symbolises the potter himself.

443

444

Mills, Donald *c.*1920–

1938–	Croydon School of Art, London
1945	employed as a thrower at the Fulham Pottery, London
1946–48	teaching at the Central School of Art, London; in collaboration with Eileen Lewenstein (qv) and Brigitta Appleby, sets up small production pottery in London (Donald Mills Pottery Ltd.) with 5 staff to make tableware; continues with own individual pieces
1948	firm driven bankrupt when cheated over an order for 250,000 electric fire elements
1948–52	continues with own work
1952–74	has to abandon potting, sets up firm (Mills and Hubball Ltd.) to supply pottery materials and equipment
1974–	resumes potting in partnership with wife, moving to Itchenor, West Sussex

Cooper (1947; pl. 33)
'Donald Mills Pottery', *Pottery and Glass*, November, 1949
The Studio Yearbook of Decorative Art, 1949, 1950, 1951 & 1952
Godden (1988)

445 Dish: *Evening Sky*, 1950
Stoneware, mottled copper-red spots in a grey glaze; h. 6.2 cm, d. 27 cm
Circ.279–1950. Source: Arts and Crafts Society (exhibition in V&A, 1950), £10.50

446 Teapot, 1951
Stoneware, painted decoration in brown, yellow and blue in a white glaze; marks: 'DM', painted; h. 16.4 cm, d. 23.6 cm
Circ.18–1952. Source: Heal & Son Ltd., London, £1.77

445

446

Moss, Vera dates not known

Vera Moss won a scholarship from Hull Art School for illumination and lettering to the Royal College of Art, London, where she studied from 1932 to 1936. She attended Staite Murray's pottery classes on Tuesdays, eventually winning the Herbert Read prize for a ceramic figure of a nun. She went to the Central School of Art in the evenings to learn glazing from Dora Billington. She abandoned pottery after her marriage, and in 1978 she emigrated to Australia, where she has recommenced potting.

These bowls were acquired to illustrate the kind of work done at a student level at the Royal College of Art under Staite Murray's tutorage.

447 Footed bowl, 1933
Stoneware, painted decoration in cream glaze with mottled green and red; made at the RCA, student work; h. 5.7 cm, d. 13 cm
C.54–1985. Source: given by the potter

448 Bowl, 1933
Stoneware, grey cream glaze with decoration in copper red; made at the RCA, student work; h. 8 cm, d. 11.4 cm
C.55–1985. Source: given by the potter

449 Bowl, 1933
Stoneware, celadon glaze with painting in brown; made at RCA, student work; h. 11 cm, d. 13 cm
C.56–1985. Source: given by the potter

447 449 448

450

Newland, William 1919–

1919	born in New Zealand
1942–45	prisoner of war in Italy and Germany; establishes art school and teaches and studies with fellow prisoners
1945–7	Chelsea School of Art, London, studying painting
1947–48	studies Art Education at Institute of Education, University of London; pottery classes with Dora Billington (qv) at Central School of Art in evenings
1948–49	appointed to part-time lecturership at London Institute of Education, where he taught pottery to trainee Art Teachers
1949	sets up studio in Bayswater with Margaret Hine (qv) and Nicholas Vergette (qv)
1950	marries Margaret Hine
1954	moves workshop to Prestwood, Bucks
1962–	full-time teaching at the Institute of Education, teaching largely takes over from making
*c.*1965	ceases teaching at Central School of Arts and Crafts
1982	retires, continues potting at Prestwood

William Newland was the key figure of the 'Institute of Education Group' which included Margaret Hine (qv), James Tower (qv) and Nicholas Vergette (qv). They were much stimulated by Picasso's ceramics which caused great excitement when shown for the first time in London after the war, and by Scandinavian ceramics, which were the dominant 'modern fashion'. They adopted tin-glazes, bright colours and a 'modern' style of decoration. Newland was especially known for his bulls, made almost entirely from wheel-thrown sections, and the tall bottles which were sought after by architects for modern interiors. He and his wife also provided panels and figures for some of the earliest coffee bars in London, helping to set a trend in their decoration. Newland's energies were eventually all but consumed in his career as a teacher; since retirement he has started working again.

William Newland, 'Recent Ceramic Art', *World Review*, December, 1952
'The Modern Potter's Craft', in London, ICA (1985)
Fennemore (1953)
The Studio Yearbook of Decorative Art, 1952, 1954
Billington (1953), (1955)
'William Newland Pottery and the Institute', *Alumnis*, Institute of Education, University of London, August, 1985
Harrod (1989)

450 Vase, 1950
Stoneware, painted decoration in a tenmoku glaze; marks: 'W.N. 1950', incised; h. 34.8 cm, d. 23.2 cm
Circ.283–1950. Source: Arts and Crafts Society (exhibition in V&A, 1950), £8.40

451 Figure of a bull, 1954 (pl. 50)
Earthenware, incised decoration showing white through a purple-brown glaze; marks: 'William NEWLAND 54', incised; h. 35.9 cm, d. 37.7 cm
Circ.57–1954. Source: the potter, £10.50

452 Vase, 1957
Earthenware, carved geometric decoration under a blue-grey glaze; marks: 'William Newland 57' and 'WN 57', painted; h. 31.6 cm, d. 36.9 cm
Circ.95–1959. Source: the potter, £12

453 Four bottles, 1958–1959
Earthenware, grey and matt brown glazes; marks: 'William Newland', painted in blue; h. (tallest bottle) 36.8 cm, d. (vase) 15 cm
Circ.96 to c-1959. Source: the potter, £6
The three bottles are dated 1958, the low vase is dated 1959.

452

453

Newman, Bryan 1935–

1953–56 Camberwell School of Art, London
1958–73 part-time teaching at Camberwell, then Bath Academy of Art, followed by Harrow School of Art
1959–64 establishes a workshop in London
1964– moves to Aller Pottery, near Langport, Somerset

Newman is particularly known for his cityscapes and models of Old London Bridge, and his inventive handbuilt teapots.

Bryan Newman, 'Ways of Working and Feeling', *PQ*, 8/29, 1963–64
—'Slab Building', in Tony Birks (ed.), *Pottery*, London, 1988
Casson (1967)
Exhibition review, *CR*, 13/1972
Birks (1967), (1976)
Cameron and Lewis (1976)
Birks, 'The Newmans at Aller', *CR*, 43/1977
'Bryan Newman – Teapot Maniac', *CR*, 51/1978

454 Form, 1969
Stoneware, assembled thrown elements under a matt yellow-brown glaze; h. 21.9 cm, d. 25.2 cm
Circ.218–1972. Source: the potter, £15

455 *Houses with Motorway*, 1973
Stoneware, hand-modelled, with a matt brownish glaze; h. 13.5 cm, d. 32.5 cm
Circ.301–1974. Source: the potter, £18

Nisbet, Eileen 1929–

1950–53 Hornsey School of Art, London
1960–63 ceramics at the Central School of Art, London, followed by part-time teaching there and at Harrow
1965 first studio in London
1965– part-time senior lecturer at Central School of Art, London
1980– new studio in Holborn, London

Eileen Nisbet's early work consisted of large modelled murals and smaller panels and tiles, and some large press moulded dishes. She currently makes free-standing sculptures and 'horizontal' pieces which explore the translucent qualities of porcelain. The sculptures are made as individual elements which are assembled and fixed together after firing.

Casson (1967)
Exhibition reviews: *Crafts*, July/August, 1977; *Crafts*, March/April, 1980
Peter Lane, 'Eileen Nisbet's Porcelain', *CR*, 61/1980

456 Form: *Horizontal Flower Sculpture*, 1983
Porcelain, hand-modelled flat elements assembled after firing; h. 21.5 cm, d. 33 cm
C.331–1983. Source: CPA, London (Decorated Porcelain exhibition, 1983), £315

Odney Pottery *see* John Bew and A. F. Spindler

Odundo, Magdalene 1950–

1950 born in Nairobi, Kenya
1969–71 studies graphic art in Nairobi
1971–73 comes to England, studies graphics at Cambridge College of Art
1973–76 studies ceramics at West Surrey College of Art and Design, Farnham
1976–79 teaches at the Commonwealth Institute
1979–82 studies ceramics at the Royal College of Art
1982–85 sets up a workshop at Ripley, Hants
1985– new workshop in Bentley, Hants

Odundo has taken the basic forms and techniques of traditional African pottery and transformed them into an individual and highly expressive artistic language.

'CPA New Members', *CR*, 83/1983
Megan Tressida, 'A Feat of Clay', *World of Interiors*, 1984
'Kenyan Heritage', *Crafts*, March/April, 1984
Katie Neville, 'Magdalene Odundo', *Observer Colour Supplement*, 2 June, 1985
New Works; Magdalene Odundo, exhibition catalogue, Swansea Museums Service, Swansea, 1987 (review, *Crafts*, May/June, 1988)

454

455

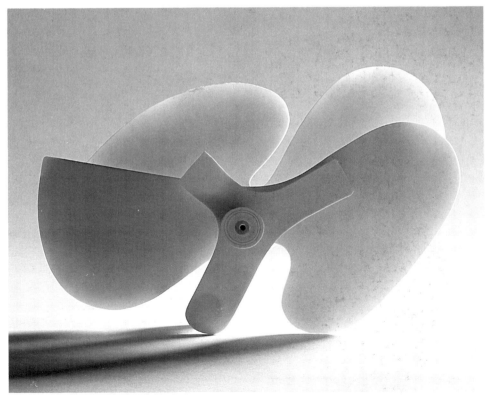

456

457 Pot, 1983
Earthenware, unglazed burnished surface, reduced black in the firing; marks: 'Odundo 83';
h. 28.6 cm, d. 23.8 cm
C.78–1984. Source: given by the Friends of the V&A
Purchased at the CPA 25th Anniversary exhibition, *Studio Ceramics Today*, held at the V&A in 1983.

O'Malley, Peter 1917–

*c.*1946 evening classes at Camberwell School of Art, London, after war service in the Far East
1947–50 studies ceramics (industrial design) at the Royal College of Art, London
1950–51 year in France drawing and working at the pottery of Carlos Fernandez in Aix-en-Provence, visiting potteries at Vallauris and Biot
1951 returns to the UK, brief period working with Anita Hoy (qv) at Buller's and nine months at Wattisfield Pottery, a traditional country pottery in Suffolk
1953–69 tutor at the Royal College of Art, senior tutor from 1967
1969 retires, sets up own workshop in Stoke-by-Nayland, Colchester, Essex
1970–79 teaches pottery part time at Colchester Technical College

O'Malley spent most of his working life as a tutor at the Royal College of Art, where he was engaged in industrial techniques. His studio pottery was done in his own time. This vase shows a similar aesthetic to Hans Coper (qv) who was a fellow tutor at the College.

PQ, 6/21, 1959, p. 38, pls. 4–5

458 Vase, *c.*1958
Stoneware, matt black glaze with abraded decoration, interior grey glaze; h. 29.3 cm, d. 19 cm
Circ.64–1959. Source: Foyles Art Gallery, London, £11.55

Owen, Elspeth 1938–

1957–60 studies History at Oxford University
1972 starts pottery at evening classes, but largely self-taught
1976– sets up workshop in Grantchester, Cambridge
1975–76 working in Papua New Guinea
1983–84 working in Devon
1986–87 working in Cornwall
1989 Artist-in-residence at Verulanium Museum, St Albans

Owen is a largely self-taught potter who started to work with clay in the early 1970s at evening classes. She works with handbuilt, unglazed clay and sees an association between her work and her environmental and social concerns.

Elspeth Owen, 'A Sense of Balance', *Crafts*, January/February, 1980
—'Rural Ride', *Crafts*, July/August, 1986
—'On Being a Potter', *CR*, 114/1988
Amanda Fielding, 'Ceramics by Elspeth Owen', exhibition review, *Crafts*, January/February, 1987
Ceramic Series, no. 30, Aberystwyth Arts Centre, 1988

459 Pot, 1983
Earthenware, handbuilt, unglazed and burnished, with smoked raku finish; h. 15.7 cm, d. 16 cm
C.213–1983. Source: Henry Rothschild Associates, Ltd., Cambridge, £38

Parkinson, Richard and Susan

Richard Parkinson 1927–1985

*c.*1949–50 Guildford School of Art with Helen Pincombe (qv)
1950 works for a summer with Harry Davis (qv) at Crowan Pottery, Cornwall
*c.*1950–51 Woolwich School of Art, London, under Heber Mathews (qv)
1951–63 pottery at Brabourne Lees, near Ashford, Kent, making slip-cast porcelain vessels and figures modelled by his first wife, Susan Sanderson
*c.*1960–1971 Head of Ceramics at Hornsey School of Art, London
1966–68 runs a pottery in Cambridgeshire, decorating industrial whitewares, mostly mugs, for the National Trust and similar customers; designs by his third wife, Dorn Parkinson
1968 moves with the pottery to London, continues production
1971 leaves teaching, moves to Wales
1971–82 pottery at Boncath, near Cardigan, Wales, casting and decorating mugs and lidded boxes

Richard Parkinson had a great interest in the technical side of pottery. He was convinced by his experience at Harry Davis' pottery that it was not feasible to produce hand-thrown tablewares at an economic price. He developed a high-temperature porcelain for slip casting and designed a kiln in which to fire it. He was one the few studio potters using porcelain in the 1950s.

Susan Parkinson 1925– (née Sanderson)

Susan Parkinson studied sculpture at the Royal College of Art, London, between 1945 and 1949 under Frank Dobson. She married Richard Parkinson in 1949. They together set up the pottery in Brabourne Lees, Kent, where Susan was responsible for the design and artistic side of the business. She produced individual work, mostly sculptures in coiled stoneware, under her maiden name, exhibiting at Primavera, London, in the early 1950s. She has continued to work since the 1960s, in portrait sculpture and general design. She has become particularly involved in teaching art to dyslexic boys.

457

458

459

Exhibition review, *PQ*, 4/1957, p. 33
Richard Parkinson, 'Porcelain', *CR*, 3/1970
Godden (1964)

460 *Cockerel and Hen*, 1954 (pl. 52)
Porcelain, cast, unglazed with incised decoration through a brown pigment; h. 30.1 cm, d. 16.2 cm
Circ.266 & 267–1954. Source: Primavera, London, £3.25

Pearson, Colin 1923–

1923   born in London
1947–52   studies painting at Goldsmith's College, discovers pottery in final year
1953–54   works with Ray Finch (qv) at Winchcombe
1954–55   works at Royal Doulton Pottery, Lambeth
1955–61   helps David Leach (qv) set up Carmelite friars' pottery at Aylesford, takes over as manager when David Leach leaves to set up Lowerdown Pottery in 1956
1961–   sets up own workshop, Quay Pottery, in Aylesford, making domestic ware; part-time lecturer at Camberwell and Medway Schools of Art
*c.*1971–   stops production of domestic ware, concentrates on individual pieces
1981   moves to Islington, London

Pearson is particularly known for his 'winged vases' – a form he has explored since the early 1970s. These can be of fine delicate form and material, or large robust pieces full of vigour and energy, with excellent glazes to match the spirit of the pieces. Inspiration comes in part from ancient Chinese bronzes. His early work was largely domestic ware.

Colin Pearson, 'Sculptural Pots', *CR*, 71/1981
Casson (1967)
Exhibition review, *CR*, 13/1972
Ceramics Monthly, April, 1974
Jeannie Lowe, 'Colin Pearson', *CR*, 33/1975
Making Good, exhibition catalogue, South East Arts, 1982; review: *CR*, 73/1982
Colin Pearson; New Ceramics, exhibition pamphlet, Amalgam Gallery, London, 1983
Tanya Harrod, 'Colin Pearson – Potter and Sculptor', *CR*, 108/1987
Angus Suttie, exhibition review, *Crafts*, March/April, 1988

461 Winged pot, 1971 (pl. 79)
Porcelain, with applied wings, transparent glaze; marks: 'CP' in monogram and seal, impressed; h. 30.3 cm, d. 22 cm
Circ.186–1972. Source: Crafts Centre of Great Britain, £21.60

462 Winged pot, 1981
Stoneware, with applied laminated wings, glazed inside; marks: 'CP' in monogram, impressed; h. 27.1 cm, d. 37.9 cm
C.155–1981. Source: CPA (solo exhibition, 1981), £170

463 Winged pot, 1981 (pl. 3)
Stoneware, with applied wings, under a grey glaze with metallic areas; marks: 'CP' in monogram and seal, impressed; h. 42.8 cm, d. 57 cm
C.12–1982. Source: the potter, £340

464 Winged pot, 1983
Stoneware, with applied wings, under a mottled cream and brown glaze; marks: seal, impressed; h. 25.4 cm, d. 27 cm
C.254–1983. Source: V&A Craft Shop, £148.50

465 Winged pot, 1984
Stoneware, slab built in flattened form, brown, cream and greenish glaze; marks: seal, impressed; h. 38.5 cm, d. 47.4 cm
C.156–1984. Source: BCC, London, £454

462

464

463

465

Pim, henry 1947–

1947	born in Sussex
1965–69	teacher training, Brighton College of Education
1969–71	travels
1971–75	works as primary school teacher, evening classes at Morley and Goldsmith's Colleges of Art
1975–79	studies pottery at Camberwell School of Art
1979–	workshop in 401½ Studios, London

Pim, like his contemporaries at Camberwell, Angus Suttie (qv) and Sara Radstone (qv), is a handbuilder. He designs his work by constructing forms from cardboard which is then used as a template for the clay slabs which are textured prior to construction. The resulting pieces, with their rich colour and dry, somewhat brittle texture, are striking; they allude to ritual and ceremonial functions and have stylistic resonances of the Classical world and Precolumbian America. His later work tends to more machine-like forms.

Henry Pim, 'Extraordinary Containers', *CR*, 89/1984
—'Lipstick on a Gorilla', *Crafts*, July/August, 1988
C. Reid 'A Culture of Doodles', Crafts, Sept/Oct, 1983
Tanya Harrod, 'Pim's', *Crafts*, September/October, 1986
Marina Vaizey, exhibition review, *Crafts*, July/August, 1988

466 Pleated Pot, 1983
Stoneware, slab built with white and metallic black glaze; h. 52.2 cm, d. 52 cm
C.332–1983. Source: BCC, London, £300

467 Form, 1988 (pl. 103)
Stoneware, handbuilt, mottled yellow, green, blue and pink surface; marks: 'HENRY PIM' impressed, '1988', painted; h. 42.7 cm, w. 67.8 cm, d. 15 cm
C.5–1989. Source: Michaelson and Orient, London, £540

Pincombe, Helen 1908–

1908	born in India; educated in Australia
1925	returns to England
1931–6	Camberwell and Central Schools of Art, London, having trained as an art teacher; six weeks at St Ives while Bernard Leach (qv) is in Japan
1937–40	student at Royal College of Art under Staite Murray (qv)
c.1940–48	teaches at Royal College of Art, evacuated during the war to Ambleside, Cumbria
1945–55	teaching at Guildford and Willesden Schools of Art
1949–72	sets up own workshop in Oxshott, Surrey
1972	retires to Cambridge, ceases to pot

Helen Pincombe took over teaching from Staite Murray when he was trapped in Rhodesia (modern Zimbabwe) during the war. She was influential in her early interest in handbuilding. While her thrown work is derived from the oriental school, her handbuilt pieces reflect a wide range of sources. She set up her studio at Oxshott in Surrey where she was a close neighbour of Denise and Rosemary Wren (qv) who followed a similar interest in handbuilt work. Pincombe's work is quiet and unassuming, but assured and poised, and of great technical skill.

Helen Pincombe, 'Coiled Pottery', *Athene*, 7/1&2, 1955, pp. 23–4
'Potter's Profile', *PQ*, 5/1958, p. 90–91
Casson (1967)
London, Hayward Gallery (1979)

468 Vase, 1939
Stoneware, tenmoku glaze; h. 31.8 cm, d. 20.9 cm
Circ.480–1939. Source: the potter

469 Vase, 1939
Stoneware, brilliant reddish crystalline tenmoku glaze; marks: 'EHP' in monogram, impressed; h. 31.4 cm, d. 20.7 cm
Circ.479–1939. Source: the potter
These two vases are student work and were purchased, for £5.77 for the pair, directly from the potter's diploma show.

470 Vase, 1958
Stoneware, coil built, unglazed with decoration in relief, interior glazed; marks: impressed seal illegible; h. 44.8 cm, d. 13 cm
Circ.12–1959. Source: Primavera, London, £4.20

471 Vase, 1958 (pl. 60)
Stoneware, coil built, white glaze inlaid into tenmoku glaze; h. 19.4 cm, d. 22.5 cm
Circ.13–1959. Source: see Circ.12–1959, £8.40
The style of this pot was inspired by ancient American pottery.

472 Bowl, c.1970
Stoneware, grey ash-glaze with painting in iron brown; marks: 'HP' in monogram, impressed; h. 10.2 cm, d. 23.5 cm
C.58–1989. Source: given by the potter

473 Vase, c.1970
Stoneware, grey ash-glaze with wax-resist painting in brushed iron brown; marks: 'HP' in monogram, impressed; h. 10.4 cm, d. 12.7 cm
C.59–1989. Source: given by the potter

474 Vase, c.1965–1970
Stoneware, press-moulded and assembled, grey ash-glaze with dark speckles; h. 12.5 cm, d. 11.6 cm
C.60–1989. Source: given by the potter

466

468 469

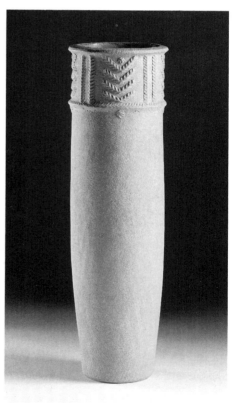

470

Pleydell-Bouverie, Katharine 1895–1985

1895	born at Coleshill, Berkshire
1921–24	studies at Central School, London, with Dora Billington (qv), at first evening classes, later full time; taught by Askam, one of the old traditional throwers
1923	sees Bernard Leach (qv) exhibition in London, applies to join pottery at St Ives
1924	pupil at the Leach Pottery, St Ives, paying 10 shillings a week
1924	sets up Cole Pottery on the family estate at Coleshill with Peter Mason
1927	Peter Mason leaves
1928	Norah Braden (qv) joins pottery
1936	Norah Braden leaves
1940–46	war disrupts work
1946	Coleshill estate sold by family; moves to Kilmington Manor, Wiltshire; installs an oil-fired kiln
1960	installs an electric kiln

Katharine Pleydell-Bouverie (Bina to her family and Beano to her friends) was one of Leach's first students at St Ives. While Michael Cardew (qv) developed a consuming interest in slipwares, Pleydell-Bouverie devoted herself to ash-glazed stoneware. She did this in partnership with Norah Braden, who joined her at Coleshill having also spent a short while at St Ives.

Pleydell-Bouverie came from an aristocratic family, and the family estate at Coleshill provided a large range of exotic and not-so-exotic trees and bushes whose prunings provided her with the material for endless glaze experiments in her wood-fired reducing kiln. Even when circumstances forced her to an oil-fired kiln, and then to an oxidising electric kiln, she sought stonewares with the same qualities as those of the first period –

soft natural colours on modest forms. In a letter to Bernard Leach in 1928 she says: 'And I want my pots to make people think, not of the Chinese, but of things like pebbles and shells and birds' eggs and stones over which moss grows. Flowers stand out of them more pleasantly, so it seems to me ... I do want the reaction of someone who sees flowers in my pots to be: "That looks natural." And it isn't so with shiny pots as a rule.' (*A Potter's Life*, 1986, p. 29)

Much of Braden's and Pleydell-Bouverie's work is designed as flower-vases, or pot-plant holders. Norah Braden is said to have had the better sense of form, but Pleydell-Bouverie herself remarked that much of their work is often indistinguishable (*A Potter's Life*, p. 27). Their pots are often marked with letters and numbers which refer to particular glaze and body recipes. Pleydell-Bouverie kept meticulous notes and her glaze-books are now preserved with other papers at the Crafts Study Centre, Holburne Museum, Bath. She was always very modest and very critical of her work and her achievement. Not having to live from her work, she charged extremely modest prices right to the end of her life.

There are many references to Pleydell-Bouverie in the writings of Bernard Leach, *see also* the bibliography for Michael Cardew.

Thorpe (1930)
Marsh (1943)
Wingfield Digby (1952)
Rose (1955), (1970)
Eileen Lewenstein and Emmanuel Cooper, 'A Visit to Katharine Pleydell-Bouverie', *CR*, 30/1974
Fiona Adamczewski, 'Katharine Pleydell-Bouverie', *Crafts*, March/April, 1976
London, Hayward Gallery (1979)

London, Christopher Wood Gallery (1980)
'Katharine Pleydell-Bouverie', *CR*, 66/1980
Katharine Pleydell-Bouverie, Bath Crafts Study Centre, 1980
David Leach, 'Katharine Pleydell-Bouverie', a tribute, *CR*, 92/1985
'Beano', a tribute, *Crafts*, July/August, 1985
Katharine Pleydell-Bouverie: A Potter's Life, Crafts Council, 1986
Mentions also in *CR* nos: 5, 6, 19, 20, 28, 50, 51, 58

475 Dish, late 1920s
Stoneware, incised decoration with brownish ash-glaze; marks: 'KPB' and 'COLE' in rectangular seals, impressed; made at Coleshill; h. 5.5 cm, d. 16.5 cm
C.72–1981. Source: Richard Dennis, London, £60

476 Vase: *Roc's Egg*, 1929–1930 (pl. 30)
Stoneware, wood-ash glaze; marks: 'KPB' in monogram, impressed; made at Coleshill; h. 25.4 cm, d. 17.2 cm
Circ.236–1930. Source: the potter, £5.25

477 Jar and cover, 1930
Stoneware, mottled green-brown wood-ash glaze; marks: 'KPB' in monogram; made at Coleshill; h. 16.7 cm, d. 14.6 cm
Circ.237&a-1930. Source: the potter, £5.25
The glaze is made from hawthorn ash.

475

472 473 474

477

478

479

480

482 481

484

485

478 Vase, *c.*1930
Stoneware, grey wood-ash glaze; made at
Coleshill; h. 19.6 cm, d. 10.5 cm
C.962–1935. Source: given by the CAS, London

479 Bowl, *c.*1930
Stoneware, unglazed, with incised decoration;
marks: 'KPB' in monogram, impressed; made at
Coleshill; h. 6.4 cm, d. 14.5 cm
C.73–1981. Source: Richard Dennis, London, £45

480 Vase, *c.*1931
Stoneware, whitish wood-ash glaze with painting
in brown; marks: 'KPB' in monogram; made at
Coleshill; h. 16.7 cm, d. 12.9 cm
Circ.252–1932. Source: the potter (exhibition at
Patterson's Gallery, London), £2.10

481 Vase, 1930
Stoneware, crystalline red-brown wood-ash glaze;
marks: 'KPB' in monogram, impressed; made at
Coleshill; h. 20.2 cm, d. 19.4 cm
Circ.763–1931. Source: the potter (shown at the
Arts and Crafts Society, Burlington House,
London, 1931), £3.15

482 Vase, 1932
Stoneware, tenmoku glaze; marks: 'KPB' in
monogram, impressed; made at Coleshill;
h. 34.3 cm, d. 19.2 cm
C.324–1983. Source: given by the potter
Given by the potter who had hoped originally to
swap it for C.71–1981 (catalogue no. 485) which
she wanted to destroy. She considered this piece
'. . . a decent example . . .' of her work. Dated 1932
in green enamel on the base.

483 Vase, 1932 (pl. 9)
Stoneware, brown wood-ash glaze with painted
bands in darker brown; marks: 'KPB' in
monogram; made at Coleshill; h. 17.3 cm,
d. 14.8 cm
C.414–1934. Source: given by the BIIA (acquired
in 1932)

484 Bowl, *c.*1935
Stoneware, grey wood-ash glaze with painted
darker bands; marks: 'KPB' in monogram,
impressed; made at Coleshill; h. 7.8 cm, d. 10 cm
C.115–1977. Source: Richard Dennis, London
(from the collection of Sir Edward Maufe), £25

485 Vase, *c.*1935
Stoneware, mottled oatmeal glaze with wax-resist
geometric decoration; marks: 'KPB' in monogram,
impressed and '187', incised; made at Coleshill;
h. 22 cm, d. 16.5 cm
C.71–1981. Source: Richard Dennis, London,
£150
The designs are based on the formations used in
sword-dancing. The potter was not happy with
this pot, wanting it to be destroyed rather than
shown. In a letter to the Museum she writes: '. . .
I was a bit horrified that you had acquired that
awful folk-dance pot for the Museum . . .'. She
eventually gave the Museum the vase no. C.324–
1983 (catalogue no. 482) in order that the
collection should have what she thought to be a
decent example of her work.

486 Dish, 1956
Stoneware, dark wood-ash glaze with decoration in trailed white slip; marks: 'KPB' in monogram, impressed; made at Kilmington; h. 33.8 cm, d. 7.3 cm
Circ.649–1956. Source: Primavera, London, £3.50
The potter's seal is larger than normal and square in shape.

487 Dish, c.1975
Stoneware, dark ash-glaze with milky streaks; marks: 'KPB' in monogram, impressed; made at Kilmington; h. 5.5 cm, d. 26.5 cm
C.19–1981. Source: Paul Rice Gallery (exhibition in November, 1981), £60

Poncelet, Jacqueline 1947–

1947 born Liège, Belgium
1951 comes to the UK with her parents
1965–69 ceramics at Wolverhampton College of Art
1969–72 ceramics at Royal College of Art
1972–75 shares a studio with Glenys Barton (qv)
1975–77 shares a studio with Alison Britton at Kings Cross, London
1974–77 teaching at Portsmouth Polytechnic
1976–77 begins to make in slab-built earthenware
1977–82 workshop in Brixton, London
1978–79 spends a year in the USA on Bicentennial Scholarship
1981 *Jacqui Poncelet – New Ceramics*, solo touring exhibition organised by the Crafts Council
1982– new workshop in East Dulwich, London
1985 *Jacqueline Poncelet: Recent Work*, solo exhibition at the Whitechapel Art Gallery, London
1985–86 works in studio at Bing and Grondahl, Copenhagen
1986– no longer works only in clay

Jacqui Poncelet is one of the most important potters of her generation. She is one of the 'Royal College Group' of women who emerged from the Royal College of Art in the 1970s, including Liz Fritsch (qv), Alison Britton (qv), Jill Crowley (qv), Carol McNicoll (qv) and Glenys Barton (qv). The nature of Poncelet's work has changed dramatically over the years. In the late 1970s she abandoned the small-scale fine work in cast bone-china that had brought her considerable success. Her new work in earthenware, geometric in shape and decoration, was larger, more ambitious and more challenging. This new work, which dismayed many of her previous supporters, was given further stimulus by a visit in 1978–79 to the USA. Her work has since become more colourful, more organic and larger in scale. It has descended from the gallery plinth to the floor, and she now no longer works in clay alone. She is married to the sculptor Richard Deacon.

The bone-china pieces were collected by the Museum for the 1977 exhibition *Six Potters*. They are all cast in plaster moulds; some are constructed in two sections joined after firing. Colour may be added to the mould before casting, or added to the liquid slip. Some pieces are carved before the firing. After firing, all are polished with wet and dry sandpaper. The later works are constructed from slabs into which decoration in different coloured clays may already be rolled. Coloured glazes are applied and fired, and enamels are added in a final firing.

Fiona Adamczewski, 'Outside Tradition', *Crafts*, May/June, 1973
London, CC (1974)
Belfast (1974)
London, VAM (1977)
London, Christopher Wood Gallery (1980)
London, CC (1981a)
'Jacqui Poncelet – New Ceramics', *CR*, 72/1981
Rosemary Pitts, 'American Graffiti', *Crafts*, May/June, 1981
Jacqueline Poncelet: Recent Work, exhibition catalogue, Whitechapel Art Gallery, London, 1985
Paul Filmer, 'Jacqui Poncelet', in London, ICA (1985)
Martina Margetts, 'Bridging the Divide' (on Poncelet's experiences working at the Bing and Grondahl factory), *Crafts*, May/June, 1986

488 Bowl, 1972
Bone china, cast, with decoration in lavender; h. 8.7 cm, d. 13.4 cm
Circ.276–1973. Source: the potter, £25

489 Bowl: *Double Circle Form*, 1974 (pl. 80)
Bone china, cast, unglazed, with yellow, green and grey staining in the body; h. 10.2 cm, d. 11.6 cm
Circ.501–1974. Source: the potter, £30

490 Pot, 1974 (pl. 80)
Bone china, cast, unglazed with green, yellow and grey staining in the body; h. 15.5 cm, d. 11 cm
Circ.500–1974. Source: the potter, £30

491 Bowl, 1974 (pl. 81)
Bone china, cast with carved geometrical decoration; h. 8.7 cm, d. 9.9 cm
Circ.366–1974. Source: the potter, £27

486 487

488

492 Bowl, 1976
Bone china, cast, with pierced and engraved
decoration; h. 8.1 cm, d. 14.5 cm
Circ.254–1976. Source: the potter, £35

493 Bowl, 1976
Bone china, cast, unglazed; h. 6.6 cm, d. 10.9 cm
Circ.255–1976. Source: the potter, £30
The piece is cast in two parts and joined before
firing.

494 Tilted form, 1976
Bone china, cast, unglazed; h. 10.3 cm, d. 13.4 cm
Circ.256–1976. Source: the potter, £25

495 Bowl, 1976
Bone china, cast, unglazed with blue staining in
the body; h. 7.6 cm, d. 13.5 cm
Circ.253–1976. Source: the potter, £35

496 Bowl, 1976
Bone china, cast, unglazed on two sides, the third
glazed with blue and yellow dots; h. 14.7 cm,
d. 8.6 cm
Circ.534–1976. Source: the potter, £30

497 Vase, 1978 (pl. 92)
Earthenware, slab built, with inlaid coloured clays;
h. 29.4 cm, d. 35.6 cm
C.30–1980. Source: Oxford Gallery, Oxford,
£115.92
This is one of Poncelet's earliest pieces in slab-
built earthenware made after she had given up
the fine bone china, but before she went to the
USA.

492

495

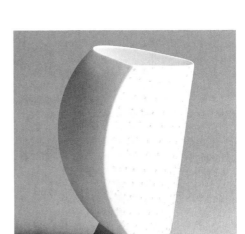

496

493

494

498

498 Vase: *Zig-Zag Pot*, 1979
Stoneware, slab built, with brown slips and white glaze; made in Claremont, USA; h. 32.6 cm, d. 39.3 cm
C.54–1982. Source: the potter, £200

499 Form, 1981 (pl. 96)
Stoneware, handbuilt, with inlaid coloured clays and low temperature enamels; h. 13 cm, d. 50 cm
C.75–1981. Source: CC, London (solo exhibition, 1981), £333

500 Dish, 1981
Stoneware, handbuilt, inlaid dark clay, turquoise glaze and overglaze enamels; h. 9.4 cm, d. 35.6 cm
C.76–1981. Source: CC, London (solo exhibition, 1981), £166

501 *Three Legged Form*, 1983
Stoneware, handbuilt, with inlaid coloured clays and low temperature enamels; h. 27.6 cm, d. 33.8 cm
C.339–1983. Source: V&A Craft Shop, £525.60

Quick, Kenneth 1931–1963

1931 born in St Ives, cousin to William Marshall (qv)
1945 joins Leach Pottery as apprentice to make standard ware
1955 sets up his own pottery at Tregenna Hill with small electric kiln
1959 spends six months in the USA
1960 rejoins the Leach Pottery in St Ives
1963 visits Hamada's pottery in Mashiko, Japan, drowns in swimming accident

Quick was regarded as one of the most promising of the local potters to be trained at St Ives. He was persuaded to return to the pottery after he had spent five years on his own. His trip to Japan, where he was drowned, was suggested and assisted by the pottery. His work in England is marked with a seal with 'K' contained within a 'Q'.

PQ, 4/1957 (illustrations of his standard ware from Tregenna Hill, pls. 9-10)
London, Christopher Wood Gallery (1980)
London, Tate Gallery (1985)

502 Jar, 1963
Stoneware, incised decoration under a green glaze; made at Hamada's Pottery, Mashiko, Japan; h. 18.3 cm, d. 18.3 cm
C.81–1981. Source: Christopher Wood Gallery, London, £300
Made shortly before the potter's death by drowning in Japan. The remains of a paper label on the base of the pot read 'Made by Kenneth ... at Maskiko ...'.

500

501

502

231

Radstone, Sara 1955–

1955   born in London
1975–76 Herefordshire College of Art
1976–79 Camberwell School of Art, London
1979–84 studio at 401½ Workshops, London
1982   teaching at West Surrey College of Art and Design
1985–   founder member of Arlington Studios, Brixton, London
1984–   teaching at Wimbledon School of Art, London
1988   awarded Unilever Prize in the Portobello Arts Festival, London
1989–   visiting lecturer, Portsmouth Polytechnic

Radstone was a contemporary at Camberwell of Henry Pim (qv) and Angus Suttie (qv). She is evidently much influenced by Ewen Henderson (qv) who taught her there. However, Angus Suttie well distinguishes her special qualities (*CR*, 100/1986): 'Her work has been compared to that by Ewen Henderson and to a shallow eye it does have similarities. However, the profound difference is that Henderson's pots allude to nature whereas Radstone's vessels are about things from our culture which have been eroded by people and time. It is the difference between something which grows and rots and something which is built and decays from use'. The two pieces catalogued here illustrate this character – both have surfaces which recall weathered sheet steel.

Richard Deacon, 'Fragile Presences', *Crafts*, May/June,

Richard Deacon, 'Fragile Presences', *Crafts*, May/June, 1983
Angus Suttie, 'Radstone and Henderson', in *Six Ways*, exhibition catalogue, Anatol Orient Gallery, London, 1988
Angus Suttie, 'Sara Radstone', *CR*, 100/1986
Alison Britton, exhibition review, *Crafts*, September/October, 1986

503 Vase, 1983 (pl. 102)
Stoneware, handbuilt, with greyish glaze; h. 34.7 cm, d. 34.1 cm
C.333–1983. Source: V&A Craft Shop, £170.10

504 Vessel, 1988
Stoneware, handbuilt, green and purple-brown surface and incised decoration; h. 62 cm, d. 45.8 cm
C.63–1988. Source: Michaelson and Orient, London, £450

Raeburn, Elizabeth 1943–

1943   born in Surrey
1968–73 works in publishing and as a teacher
1973–75 ceramics at Harrow School of Art, London, including brief period working with David Leach (qv)
1975–   sets up workshop in West Pennard, near Glastonbury, Somerset, in partnership with Rodney Lawrence

Raeburn has concentrated on raku-fired handbuilt forms whose shapes suggest ancient ritual vessels.

Nine Potters, exhibition catalogue, Fischer Fine Art, London
Elizabeth Raeburn, exhibition pamphlet, Anita Besson Gallery, London, 1989

505 Vase of flattened form, 1983
Stoneware, handbuilt, with raku-fired white crackled glaze; marks: 'ER' in a circle, plus a quatrafoil device, impressed; h. 25.3 cm, d. 19.6 cm
C.319–1983. Source: the potter, £30

Rey, Margaret 1911–

1911   born near Cardiff, Wales
1932–35 Royal College of Art, London, originally in Design Department, later moves into School of Pottery under Staite Murray (qv)
1930s   exhibited in several exhibitions in the Brygos Gallery, London
1935–39 workshop in Raynes Park, London, shared with Sam Haile (qv) from 1936
1950–   workshop in Forest Green, Surrey, but ceases to pot; works in design, painting and sculpture

Rey had some success as a potter before the war, being singled out by critics in exhibition reviews in the late 1930s. Her work was characteristic in general of the Staite Murray school – large, heavily thrown stoneware vases with abstract painting, in greys and browns.

Tanya Harrod, 'Ceramics by Margaret Rey, Paul Rice Gallery, London', exhibition review, *Crafts*, July/August, 1987
Rice (1989; pp. 78–83, 240)

506 Bowl, 1936–7
Stoneware, blue mottled glaze with brown rim; marks: 'RM' in triangular monogram, impressed and 'R95', painted; h. 7.2 cm, d. 10.5 cm
C.27–1937. Source: given by Lt-Col. K. Dingwall, DSO, through the NACF

504

505

506

Richards, Christine-Ann 1949–

1971–73 Harrow School of Art, London, under Mick Casson (qv)
1973 working for Bryan Newman (qv)
1974 six months working for David Leach (qv)
1975–83 sets up own workshop as member of Barbican Arts Group, London
1978– participates in CPA trip to China, becomes increasingly interested and involved in Chinese culture, especially modern painting; organises and leads many trips for potters and artists to China
1983– new workshop at her home in North London

Richards has long been fascinated in Chinese porcelains, and much of her work is based on later Chinese wares. She has concentrated until recently on pure form and white colour, sometimes developing a crackled glaze which is emphasised by staining with red or black Chinese ink. Her interest in modern Chinese painting has led in her latest work to a more painterly decoration in black.

'CPA New Members', *CR*, 42/1976

507 Vase, 1982
Porcelain, red-stained crackled glaze; marks: 'car', impressed; h. 25.6 cm, d. 13.6 cm
C.79–1984. Source: given by the Friends of the V&A
Purchased at the CPA 25th Anniversary exhibition, *Studio Ceramics Today*, held at the V&A in 1983.

Richards, Frances E. *c.*1869–1931

Very little is known about this potter who lived and worked in Highgate, London. She must be counted among the earliest pioneers of studio pottery, apparently working at home, with a kiln in her back garden. She was not a very successful potter, much of her work has an amateur look to it, and she is said to have lived an isolated life of poverty. She was active from at least 1916 until her death in 1931. She exhibited regularly in the Arts and Crafts Exhibition Society from 1916, and had a solo exhibition at the 3 Shields Gallery in 1928. She sold through Heal's, London, and was selected by the BIIA for inclusion in their permanent collection (catalogue nos. 508 and 509 below). Works by her were chosen for illustration in *The Studio Yearbook of Decorative Art* in 1917, 1927 and 1928. The University College of Wales at Aberystwyth have 32 pieces of her work, collected in the 1920s.

Aberystwyth (1986)

508 Honey pot and cover, 1924
Earthenware, painting in blue in a white glaze; marks: 'F.R.' in a square monogram, surrounded by '1924', painted; h. 9.8 cm, d. 12.5 cm
C.423&a–1934. Source: given by the BIIA (gift of the potter)

509 Vase, 1923
Earthenware, brown and green mottled glaze with brown stripes; marks: 'FR' in square monogram surrounded by '1 9 2 III', incised; h. 16.7 cm, d. 12.8 cm
C.422–1934. Source: given by the BIIA (gift of the potter)

510 Vase, 1927
Stoneware, mottled brown and green glaze; marks: 'FR' in square monogram, and '192VII', incised; h. 14.3 cm, d. 17 cm
C.93–1927. Source: given by Mrs J Cochrane Shanks
The same donor offered another piece as a gift in 1936, which was refused by Rackham as it did not seem '... to be so favourable an illustration of Miss Richards's skill as the vase by her you gave us some time ago. You told me, it is true, that Miss Richards herself thought very highly of it, but I sometimes think that artists are not always the best judges of their own work.'

511 Vase, 1924
Earthenware, green glaze with incised ribs; marks: 'FR' in square monogram surrounded by '1 9 2 4', incised; h. 20.2 cm, d. 15.7 cm
Circ.277–1955. Source: given by Lady Russel, MBE, from the collection of the late Francis Moore

508

510 509

507

511

Rie, Lucie 1902–

1902	born in Vienna, Austria
1922–26	studies pottery at Kunstgewerbeschule, Vienna; her teachers include Michael Powolny
1925–37	her work is shown in international exhibitions in Paris, Brussels and Milan
1938	moves to England just before the Anschluss
1939	establishes her present workshop in London
1945–47	designs and makes buttons; Hans Coper joins workshop
1947–58	shares workshop with Hans Coper; making tablewares and individual work; regular joint exhibitions at Berkeley Galleries, London
1967	Arts Council retrospective exhibition: *Lucie Rie 1926–1967*
1968	awarded OBE
1969	awarded an Honorary Doctorate, Royal College of Art, London
1981	awarded CBE
1981–82	*Lucie Rie* retrospective exhibition at Sainsbury Centre, Norwich and Victoria and Albert Museum, London
1989	solo exhibition in Japan, organised by Issey Miyake

Lucie Rie is, with Hans Coper, one of the most important potters in the post-war period. Her influence as a teacher is not as marked as that of Coper, but her work has had an enormous impact. In everything she has done she has somehow gone against the prevailing orthodoxy, yet has succeeded: before the war she made 'earthenwares with stoneware glazes'; she later produced fine stonewares with hardly a trace of the accepted classic oriental styles; she has made outstanding tablewares not country-style in a country pottery but metropolitan-style in her London mews studio; she produces rich complex glazes which are once-fired in an electric oxidising kiln. Her work is utterly individual and is based on the aesthetic of the modern movement, yet is informed by the full range of ceramic history from oriental porcelain and Islamic fritwares to prehistoric pots and the English mediaeval jugs beloved of the Leach school. She has demonstrated that it is possible to generate an entirely new and individual ceramic language of the highest expressive quality without jettisoning some of pottery's most basic traditions – practical bowl and vase shapes formed on the wheel.

Wingfield Digby (1952)
Billington (1953)
Fennemore (1953)
A.C. Sewter, 'Lucie Rie, Potter', *Apollo*, February, 1954
Melville (1954)
Rose (1955), (1970)
Tarby Davenport, 'The Pottery of Lucie Rie', *Design*, October, 1967
Birks (1967), (1976)
Casson (1967)
London, Arts Council (1967) (with good bibliography)
Tarby Davenport, 'Lucie Rie – A Potter of Our Time', *CR*, 27/1974
London, Christopher Wood Gallery (1980)
John Houston, *Lucie Rie*, Crafts Council, London, 1981 (with full bibliography)
Christopher Reid, 'Lucie Rie', *Crafts*, November/December, 1981
Emmanuel Cooper, 'Lucie Rie – Potter', *CR*, 72/1981
Emmanuel Cooper, 'Lucie Rie – Artist Potter', *CR*, 100/1986
Birks (1987) (with good bibliography), (reviewed in *Crafts*, March/April, 1988)
W. A. Ismay, 'Lucie Rie at 85', *CR*, 110/1988
Michael Dumas and Sarah Bodine, 'In Search of Form: Hans Coper and Lucie Rie', *American Ceramics*, 3/4, 1988
Issey Miyake meets Lucie Rie, exhibition catalogue, Sogetsu Gallery, Tokyo and Museum of Oriental Ceramics, Osaka, Japan, 1989.

The vessels acquired by the Museum in 1982 were shown in the Crafts Council exhibition and are illustrated in John Houston's book published in 1981.

512 Bowl, *c*.1926
Earthenware, blue, orange, white and brown splashes; made in Vienna; marks: 'L.R.G. WIEN', painted in black; h. 7.8 cm, d. 10.5 cm
C.35–1982. Source: given by the potter

513 Bowl, 1930–1938
Earthenware, blue and brown pitted glaze; made in Vienna; marks: 'L.R.G. WIEN', painted in blue; h. 9 cm, d. 27.6 cm
C.36–1982. Source: given by the potter

514 Plant pot, 1930–1938
Earthenware, turquoise and black mottled glaze, unglazed interior; made in Vienna; marks: 'L.R.G. WIEN', painted; h. 15.8 cm, d. 18.3 cm
C.37–1982. Source: given by the potter

512

513 514

515

515 Tea set, *c.*1936
Earthenware, unglazed burnished surface; made in Vienna; marks: 'L.R.G. WIEN', painted in black; h. (teapot) 11.1 cm, d. 18.2 cm
C.34–1982. Source: given by the potter
In this piece, Rie tried to achieve a terra-sigillata surface. Following a suggestion, she boiled the piece in a solution of borax after the first firing. She said that the experiment was a failure – the surface was not that which she desired, and the tea tasted of borax and was undrinkable.

516 Pot with lid, 1936–1937 (pl. 40)
Earthenware, brown and white pitted glaze, with unglazed burnished lid; made in Vienna; marks: 'L.R.G. WIEN', painted in blue; h. 11.5 cm, d. 12.5 cm
C.38&a–1982. Source: given by the potter
Lucie Rie commented on the glaze of this piece: '… too much tin oxide – which was a mistake to start with, but which I then repeated …'.

517 Vase, 1936–1937
Earthenware, brown and white pitted glazes; made in Vienna; marks: 'L.R.G. WIEN', painted in blue; h. 17.4 cm, d. 12.5 cm
C.33–1982. Source: given by the potter

518 Bowl, 1942
Earthenware, mottled brown glaze; marks: 'L./R.', painted in black; h. 8.3 cm, d. 15.5 cm
C.39–1982. Source: given by the potter
Lucie Rie made this piece soon after meeting Bernard Leach for the first time, and for a short while tried, against her own nature, to make 'weighty' pots.

519 Umbrella handles, *c.*1945–1947
Earthenware, black, white and blue glazes; h. 12.2 cm, d. 2.9 cm
C.101 to b–1982. Source: given by the potter
According to Lucie Rie, the handles had too small a hole for attaching to umbrellas and were never used.

520 Choker and bracelet, 1945–1946
Stoneware, pale glaze with gold lustre; l. (choker) 22 cm, d. (bracelet) 10 cm
C.102&a–1982. Source: given by the potter
The choker bears a label including the words: 'Theatre Leasure [sic] and fashion ware/Choker white and gold. £2/5/0' (= £2.25p).

521 Buckle, 1945–1946
Stoneware, gold lustre glaze; d. 7.7 cm
C.103–1982. Source: given by the potter

522 Earrings, 1945–1946
Stoneware, with gold lustre; d. 2.4 cm
C.104–1982. Source: given by the potter

523 Mirror frame, 1945–1946
Stoneware, unglazed red clay with white glaze and gilded border; h. 2 cm, d. 19.8 cm
C.106–1982. Source: given by the potter

524 Buttons, 1945–1946
Stoneware, with various coloured glazes; d. (largest) 5 cm
C.105 to aa-1982. Source: given by the potter

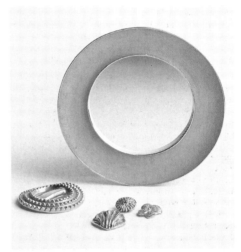

521 522 523

517

519

518

520

524

525 Bowl, 1950
Stoneware, incised decoration through a brown slip, white glaze interior; marks: 'LR' in monogram, applied; h. 11.8 cm, d. 16.4 cm
Circ.1–1951. Source: Berkeley Galleries, London, £3.15

526 Dish, 1950
Porcelain, with brown and transparent glaze; marks: 'LR' in monogram, applied; h. 8.4 cm, d. 12 cm
Circ.2–1951. Source: *see* Circ.1–1951, £3.15

527 Bowl, 1950
Porcelain, incised decoration through a brown slip band; marks: 'LR' in monogram, applied; h. 8.4 cm, d. 12 cm
Circ.3–1951. Source: *see* Circ.1–1951, £2.10

528 Tea-pot, 1951
Stoneware, interior with white glaze, exterior with black glaze; marks: 'LR' in monogram, impressed; h. 16 cm, d. 22.7 cm
Circ.20&a–1952. Source: the potter, £2.10

525

526

527

528

529 Cup and saucer, *c.*1955
Stoneware, white glaze with black rim; marks: 'LR' in monogram, applied; h. 8.5 cm, d. 13 cm
C.41&a-1982. Source: given by the potter

530 Cup and saucer, *c.*1955
Stoneware, black glaze with incised lines; marks: 'LR' in monogram, applied; h. 8 cm, d. 14 cm
C.40&a-1982. Source: given by the potter

531 Jug and two beakers, 1950–1955 (pl. 47)
Stoneware, white and black glazes; marks: 'LR' and 'HC' in monogram, applied; h. (jug) 26.5 cm
C.57 to c-1982. Source: Lady Cecilia Semphill, Sudbury
Made with Hans Coper, whose seal they also bear. According to Lucie Rie, these are probably glazed by Coper, as she herself would have applied a narrower band of cream glaze.

532 Cruet set, 1950–1955
Stoneware, white and black glazes; marks: 'LR' in monogram, impressed; h. (salt) 10 cm
C.58 to c–1982. Source: Lady Cecilia Semphill, Sudbury

533 Bowl, 1955
Porcelain, incised decoration through black glaze; marks: 'LR' in monogram, applied; h. 9.6 cm, d. 25.5 cm
Circ.336–1955. Source: the potter, £12

534 Bottle, 1959 (pl. 59)
Stoneware, white glaze with brown flecks; marks: 'LR' in monogram, applied; h. 41.6 cm, d. 13.1 cm
Circ.126–1959. Source: the potter, £18.90
In 1981, Lucie Rie deemed this piece to have a 'meek shape'.

535 Bottle, 1959 (pl. 12)
Porcelain, dark, white and blue glazes with incised decoration; marks: 'LR' in monogram, applied; h. 17.8 cm, d. 7.6 cm
Circ.127–1959. Source: the potter, £6

536 Bottle, 1959 (pl. 12)
Stoneware, dark, white and blue glazes with incised decoration; marks: 'LR' in monogram, applied; h. 12.4 cm, d. 9.9 cm
Circ.128–1959. Source: the potter, £5

537 Bottle, 1966
Stoneware, white glaze; marks: 'LR' in monogram, applied; h. 31.5 cm, d. 13.2 cm
Circ.757–1966. Source: Berkeley Galleries, London (solo exhibition, 1966), £35

529 530

532

533

537

538 Bottle, 1967
Stoneware, streaked purple-brownish glaze; marks: 'LR' in monogram, applied; h. 38.1 cm, d. 15.4 cm
Circ.1226–1967. Source: Arts Council of Great Britain (*Lucie Rie*, retrospective exhibition, 1967), £38
The colour comes from copper and manganese pigments mixed with the clay before throwing and rising through the overlaying glaze in the firing.

539 Vase, 1967 (pl. 65)
Stoneware, thick pitted grey-blue mottled glaze; marks: 'LR' in monogram, applied; h. 15.6 cm, d. 11.6 cm
Circ.1228–1967. Source: *see* Circ.1226–1967, £19
The body was incised with a hacksaw blade and coloured with cobalt and manganese before a layer of porcelain slip and the glaze were applied. The piece was fired only once.

540 Vase, 1967 (pl. 65)
Stoneware, thick pitted grey/blue glaze; marks: 'LR' in monogram, applied; h. 14 cm, d. 14.6 cm
Circ.1229–1967. Source: *see* Circ.1226–1967, £22

541 Vase, 1967 (pl. 66)
Stoneware, thrown and squared, streaked white and purple-brown glaze; marks: 'LR' in monogram, applied; h. 27.4 cm, d. 17.5 cm
Circ.1227–1967. Source: *see* Circ.1226–1967, £48
The spiral colouring comes from mixing two clays – one coloured with pigment, the other without. The spiral develops as the two pieces are thrown together and the pigments colours the overlying glaze.

542 Dish, 1967
Stoneware, mauve brown glaze with dark flecks; marks: 'LR' in monogram, applied; h. 40 cm, d. 11.4 cm
Circ.1230–1967. Source: *see* Circ.1226–1967, £38

543 Bowl, 1967
Stoneware, mauve-brown and green glaze with dark flecks; marks: 'LR' in monogram, applied; h. 14.3 cm, d. 30 cm
Circ.1231–1967. Source: *see* Circ.1226–1967, £30

544 Bottle, *c.*1979 (pl. 85)
Stoneware, swirling pattern of pinks, greys and browns in a pitted glaze; marks: 'LR' in monogram, applied; h. 38 cm, d. 17.6 cm
C.42–1982. Source: the potter, £420
Lucie Rie remarked: '... this pink comes from the chemist ...'.

545 Bowl, *c.*1976 (pl. 84)
Porcelain, bronze glaze at rim and foot, pink glaze with incised lines; marks: 'LR' in monogram, applied; h. 12 cm, d. 23.8 cm
C.43–1982. Source: the potter, £280
Lucie Rie remarked that this was one of her most successful pink bowls – an effect she had not been able to repeat satisfactorily.

546 Bowl, *c.*1978–1980
Porcelain, bronze at rim, yellow glaze; marks: 'LR' in monogram, applied; h. 11.3 cm, d. 19.7 cm
C.45–1982. Source: the potter, £220

547 Bowl, *c.*1979
Porcelain, bronze at rim, green glaze; marks: 'LR' in monogram, applied; h. 10.8 cm, d. 20.7 cm
C.44–1982. Source: the potter, £22

542 543

538

546

547

548 Bowl, 1979
   Porcelain, metallic bronze, black, brown and
   turquoise glazes; marks: 'LR' in monogram,
   applied; h. 9.9 cm, d. 22.3 cm
   C.118–1979. Source: Casson Gallery, London,
   £200

549 Bowl, c.1980
   Porcelain, white glaze with incised lines in pink;
   marks: 'LR' in monogram, applied; h. 9.4 cm,
   d. 20.8 cm
   C.46–1982. Source: the potter, £280

548

549

550

Roberts, David 1947–

1947   born in Sheffield
1966–70 trains as art teacher at Bretton Hall, Yorkshire
1970–81 works as art teacher, takes up pottery
1976–   adopts the raku technique
1981   gives up teaching to take up full-time potting;
            Yorkshire Arts Association travel award to
            visit USA to research American raku
1985–88 Chair of the CPA

Roberts is known for his handbuilt raku pots, some of
which, with simple geometrical striped designs, recalls
that of early work by Martin Smith (qv). Later pieces
are often enormous white-glazed vases with bulbous
bodies, narrow necks and flaring rims.

David Roberts, 'Raku Now', *CR*, 118/1989
'CPA New Members', *CR*, 69/1981
Stephen Brayne, 'David Roberts – Raku Potter', *CR*,
   105/1987
Stephanie Brown, exhibition review, *Crafts*,
   September/October, 1987

550 Vase: *Cornucopia*, 1983
   Stoneware, raku-fired with lustre stripes on a dark body;
   h. 37 cm, d. 31.3 cm
   C.225–1983. Source: Queensbury Hunt, London, £150

551

552

Rogers, Mary 1929–

1929   born in Derbyshire
1945–47 apprenticed to John Dickenson, studies
            graphic design part time at Watford School
            of Art
1947–49 calligraphy at St Martin's School of Art,
            London
1960–64 ceramics part time at Loughborough School
            of Art
1960–87 sets up workshop at Loughborough,
            Leicestershire
1987–   workshop near Falmouth, Cornwall

Mary Rogers achieved considerable success in the 1970s
with her handbuilt bowls, in form and decoration
reminiscent of fungi and sea-flowers.

Mary Rogers, 'Decoration through Form', *CR*, 9/1971
—'Hand Modelled or Pinched Pottery', *CR*, 38/1976
—*Mary Rogers on Pottery and Porcelain*, 1979 (reviewed
   in *Crafts*, January/February, 1980)
Exhibition review, *CR*, 36/1975
Cameron and Lewis (1976)
London, Christopher Wood Gallery, (1980)
Jon Catleugh, 'Mary Rogers – English Romantic', *CR*,
   76/1982

551 Bowl, 1979
   Porcelain, handbuilt, matt white glaze; marks:
   'MER', incised; h. 9.4 cm, d. 14.3 cm
   C.143–1980. Source: the potter, £70

552 Bowl, 1979
   Porcelain, handbuilt, with painted decoration in
   blue and brown; marks: 'MER', incised; h. 8.8 cm,
   d. 18.3 cm
   C.144–1980. Source: the potter, £80

553 Bowl, 1979
   Porcelain, handbuilt with dark spotted lines;
   marks: 'MER', incised; h. 6.5 cm, d. 10.3 cm
   C.145–1980. Source: the potter, £50

553

239

Russel, Christopher dates not known

Little is known about this potter. He was active in the 1950s at a Purbeck Pottery. Work of his in a rather ornate classical style, including a figural 'red-figure' vase, is illustrated in *The Studio Yearbook of Decorative Art*, 1953. In 1956 he went to Barbados for a year to paint.

Christopher Russel, 'The Potters of Barbados', *PQ*, 4/1957
Exhibition review, *PQ*, 2/7, 1955

554 Vase, 1955
Earthenware, tin-glazed with resist decoration and painting in brown; marks: 'CR' in monogram, painted; h. 21 cm, d. 20.5 cm
Circ.340–1955. Source: Heal and Son Ltd., London

St Leger, S.

Nothing is known of this potter, other than that she worked at Willesden School of Art. This jug, ungainly in shape and unprofessionally thrown, has all the hallmarks of student work.

It was purchased at an Arts and Crafts Society exhibition at the Museum along with other slipware by Paul Barron, Henry Hammond, Marianne de Trey and Donald Mills (qv).

555 Pitcher, 1949–1950
Earthenware, decoration in white and black slip on a dark ground; marks: cross with four dots, impressed; made at the Willesden School of Art; h. 27.4 cm, d. 21.7 cm
Circ.272–1950. Source: Arts and Crafts Society (exhibition in V&A, 1950), £2.10

Salazar, Fiona 1949–

1949	born in Athens, Greece, of English parents; educated in England
1970–75	works in Radio Drama at BBC
1875–76	foundation year at Hammersmith College of Art, London
1976–78	Central School of Art, London
1979–82	Royal College of Art, London, sets up studio in Chiswick
1982–84	workshop in Wapping, London
1984–	Kingsgate Workshops, London

Salazar specialises in vases with unglazed burnished surfaces – usually black. The shapes, and the bold coloured devices that decorate them, blend classical Greek and Central American allusions.

'Individual Touch', *Crafts*, May/June, 1985
John Gibson, 'Fiona Salazar', *CR*, 107/1987

556 Vase, 1985
Earthenware, burnished black decorated in coloured slips; marks: 'Fiona Salazar', painted in red; h. 31.3 cm, d. 30.4 cm
C.44–1985. Source: BCC, London, £355

554

555

556

Schloessingk, Micky (previously Doherty) 1949–

1949   born in London
1968–69   travels in India, first encounter with pots and pottery-making
1970   workshop experience in Mayo, Eire
1970–72   ceramics at Harrow College of Art, London
1972–74   travels and works in potteries in France and Spain
1974–86   establishes pottery at Mewith, near Bentham, North Yorkshire, producing wood-fired saltglazed stoneware
1985   short spell in a friend's pottery in the Loire valley, France
1986–   returns to UK, dismantles workshop
1987   moves to Gower, South Wales, re-establishes workshop; starts to experiment with wood-fired stoneware without saltglaze as well as developing this technique

Micky Schloessingk is one of a small group of potters producing eminently practical tablewares in saltglaze stoneware. She obtains a great richness of colour and depth of surface, and brings an inventive turn to her basically simple shapes.

'New Members', *CR*, 67/1981

557 Jug, 1988
Stoneware, brown saltglaze with brushed decoration; marks: 'M', impressed; h. 18 cm, d. 16.8 cm
C.12–1989. Source: CAA, London, £43

558 Bowl, 1988
Stoneware, brown saltglaze with brushed decoration; marks: 'M', impressed; h. 7.4 cm, d. 32.5 cm
C.13–1989. Source: *see* C.12–1989, £64.50

Scott, David 1950–

1950   born in Yorkshire
1970–73   North Staffs Polytechnic, Stoke-on-Trent
1973–76   studies ceramics at the Royal College of Art
1976–83   part-time teaching in colleges round the country
1977–83   workshop in London
1983   moves to Leicestershire, full-time teaching at Loughborough College of Art
1986–   appointed Senior Tutor in Ceramics at Loughborough

David Scott describes his work as 'interpretations of functional forms … with the emphasis on the decorative rather than the functional'.

'New Members', *CR*, 85/1984
London, CPA (1983, 1986, 1989)

559 Teapot, 1982
Earthenware, unglazed, with incised decoration and a plastic handle; marks: 'DS', impressed; h. (without handle) 11.5 cm, d. 17.4 cm
C.80–1984. Source: given by the Friends of the V&A. Purchased at the CPA 25th Anniversary exhibition, *Studio Ceramics Today*, held at the V&A in 1983.

Sharp, Alexander

Little is known about Alexander Sharp other than that he ran the Morar Pottery, at Morar in the Scottish Highlands. This piece was marketed through Highland Home Industries, an organisation set up before the war to help Scottish crafts. They had a shop in George Street, Edinburgh.

560 Vase, 1955
Stoneware, tenmoku glaze; marks: 'MP', impressed; made at Morar Pottery, for Highland Home Industries; h. 16.3 cm, d. 15.2 cm
Circ.240–1955. Source: Primavera, London, £3.25
A printed sticky label reads 'MORAR/HIH/POTTERY'.

559

558 557

560

Shelly, John 1907–

Son of a country parson, Shelly was born in Wiltshire. While in the Air Force and stationed in London during the war, Shelly attended classes at the Central School of Art under Dora Billington (qv). After short training with Ray Finch, Shelly taught for a while at various places including Corsham Court, before starting the Bath Pottery in 1951. From about 1957–1960 he worked in a pottery in Winterbourne, Dorset, and in 1961 moved to Littlehempston, near Totnes in Devon. Slipwares by him are illustrated in *The Studio Yearbook of Decorative Art*, 1953 and 1954.

Exhibition reviews, PQ, 1/1954, 5/1955
PQ, 8/30, 1963–64
Godden (1964)

561 *Dish*, 1958
Earthenware, slip-trailed decoration in white and brown under an amber glaze; marks: 'Shelly 1958', incised; made at Church Cottage Pottery, Winterbourne, Dorset; h. 6.2 cm, d. 40.7 cm
Circ.43–1959. Source: the potter, £7.35

Simpson, Peter 1943–

1943   born in Middlesex
1959–64   studies sculpture with ceramics at Bournemouth and Poole College of Art
1965–70   teaches at Bournemouth College of Art
1970–77   sets up a workshop in Sway, near Lymington, Hants.
1970–74   teaches at Wimbledon College of Art
1977   sets up a workshop at Brockenhurst, Hants.
1974–79   senior lecturer at Bristol Polytechnic
1979–85   senior lecturer, Camberwell School of Art, London
1985–   appointed Head of Ceramics, Camberwell School of Art, London

Simpson's early work, represented here, is inspired by organic forms – pomegranates, mushrooms, poppy seedpods and more enigmatic items. In the late 1970s Simpson started to make larger more formal sculptures with totemic and ritual overtones.

Peter Simpson, 'Hand-built Porcelain', CR, 5/1970
London, VAM (1972)
Belfast (1974)
Exhibition reviews: CR, 25/1974; *Crafts*, January/February, 1974; *Crafts*, July/August, 1974; *Crafts*, November/December, 1978
London, VAM (1977)
Peter Simpson – Ceramics, with an introduction by John Russell Taylor, exhibition pamphlet, Oxford Gallery, Oxford, 1981

562 *Split Form*, 1974
Porcelain, handbuilt with grey-brown glaze; marks: impressed device; h. 15 cm, d. 18.4 cm
Circ.484–1974. Source: BCC, London (exhibition with Gordon Baldwin, 1974), £31.50

563 *Fungi Form*, 1974
Porcelain, handbuilt with brown and yellowish matt glaze inside; marks: impressed device; h. 14.3 cm, d. 40 cm
Circ.485–1974. Source: *see* Circ.484–1973, £40.95

564 *Small bowl form*, 1975
Porcelain, handbuilt, with blue-grey glaze; marks: impressed device; h. 4.7 cm, d. 12.1 cm
Circ.286–1976. Source: the potter (from the *7 in 76* exhibition, Portsmouth City Museum, 1976), £25

565 *Fossil Form*, 1975
Porcelain, handbuilt, metallic copper and white glazes; marks: impressed device; h. 17.9 cm, d. 48 cm
Circ.287–1976. Source: *see* Circ.286–1976, £100

566 *Open Spinner*, 1975 (pl. 16)
Porcelain, handbuilt with green-brown glaze; marks: impressed device; h. 10.5 cm, d. 20 cm
Circ.269–1975. Source: the potter, £37

564

562

561

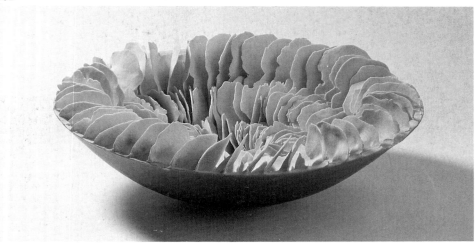

563

Slee, Richard 1946–

1946	born in Carlisle
1964–65	Carlisle College of Art
1965–70	Central School of Art, London
1971–73	employed as the Ceramic Technician, Central School of Art
1973–75	full-time teaching at Hastings College of Further Education
1973–80	sets up studio in Parsons Green and Hackney, London, part-time teaching at Harrow and Central Schools of Art
1980–	studio in Brighton
1986–88	Royal College of Art, M.A. degree by project

Slee is one of the most interesting potters of the present time. At first sight his work seems to be amusing junk – recalling the inanities of the 'funk' movement and fairground trivia. This impression is dispelled by the quality of the materials – not cheap glazes, but luscious rich ones – and the very skilled manufacture. The work takes on its full meaning with the realisation of its wide terms of historical reference: Slee draws on an extensive knowledge of historical ceramics from pompous Sèvres vases and Wedgwood teapots to 19th century fairings and curios. His work provides a witty and intelligent commentary on the foibles of ceramic production throughout history, and makes us question the role of decorative arts and antiques in our own culture.

567

569

Richard Slee, 'Richard Slee', CR, 79/1983
Janet Street-Porter, 'Slee Notes', *Design*, May, 1973
London, Christopher Wood Gallery (1980)
London, ICA (1985)
Peter Dormer, 'Routes of Exchange', *Crafts*, May/June, 1984
Richard Slee, Katherine Virgils, BCC, exhibition pamphlet, May/June, 1984

567 Jar and cover, 1981
Earthenware, with pink, yellow, blue and black glazes; marks: 'RICHARD SLEE', incised; h. 26.8 cm, d. 27 cm
C.110&a–1981. Source: the potter, £60

568 Vase, c.1981 (pl. 99)
Earthenware, pink, yellow, blue and black glazes; h. 27.6 cm, d. 15.8 cm
C.111&a–1981. Source: the potter, £60

569 Cornucopia, 1983
Earthenware, handbuilt, with white, yellow and blue glazes; marks: 'RICHARD SLEE', incised; h. 23.4 cm, d. 35.5 cm
C.253–1983. Source: V&A Craft Shop, £126

570 Corral Dish, 1984
Earthenware, handbuilt, pink and blue glazes; marks: 'RICHARD SLEE', incised; h. 8.6 cm, d. 34.9 cm
C.185–1984. Source: BCC, London, £172.80

571 Dish, 1988
Earthenware, press-moulded, with decoration in black; marks: 'RICHARD SLEE', painted; h. 5.2 cm, d. 52.5 cm
C.15–1989. Source: CAA, London, £375
This dish is made from a new earthenware clay and decorated in a technique that Slee developed during his year at the Royal College of Art in 1986–88.

570

571

Smith, Martin 1950–

1950	born in Essex
1970–71	Ipswich School of Art
1971–74	studies ceramics at Bristol Polytechnic
1974–78	workshop near Stowmarket, Suffolk
1975–77	studies ceramics at the Royal College of Art
1978–84	workshop in Rotherhithe, London
c.1978	abandons raku for red handbuilt earthenware
1977–83	teaching at Loughborough College of Art
1979–80	teaching at Camberwell School of Art, London
1980–	teaching at Brighton Polytechnic
1981–82	*Forms Around a Vessel*, Leeds Art Gallery, touring solo exhibition
1983–85	senior lecturer, Loughborough College of Art
1984–	workshop in St John's Wood, London
c.1984–	working in white earthenware
1985	*New Ceramics*, solo exhibition, BCC
1986–89	senior lecturer, Camberwell School of Art
1989–	senior tutor, Royal College of Art, London

Martin Smith's large raku bowls made a big impact at his diploma show in 1977. They introduced a new dimension in raku work – precise forms and controlled geometric decoration rather than the random effects of Japanese-inspired raku that had been usual until then. His next work explored the same theme – the geometry of the vessel – in a three-dimensional and sculptural way, and in entirely different technique. He handbuilt and assembled elements made from red clay, he used saws and polishing machines to provide the precision of form and the textures he required. He often contrasts these with clay left in a more 'natural' state, often in the interiors of the forms. After a brief period when he increasingly incorporated non-ceramic materials – slate, aluminium, stone – Smith returned to a series of vessels in white earthenware constructed from sections apparently cut from large spheres of clay, in which he defined a vessel and its space, or that of a larger architectonic form, by a few abbreviated references. He has most recently turned his attention to furniture.

Martin Smith, 'Raku Techniques', *Crafts*, November/December, 1974
London, Christopher Wood Gallery (1980)
Martina Margetts, 'Into The Red', *Crafts*, January/February, 1980
Forms Around a Vessel, exhibition catalogue, Leeds Art Gallery, 1981
Richard Deacon, 'Martin Smith: Forms Around a Vessel', exhibition review, *Crafts*, November/December, 1981
'Martin Smith: Forms Around a Vessel', CR, 75/1982
Martin Smith, New Ceramics, exhibition pamphlet by Anthony Wells-Cole, BCC, London, 1985
Tanya Harrod, 'Martin Smith', *American Ceramics*, 5/3, 1987
Diversions on a Theme, exhibition pamphlet by Alison Britton, CAA, 1988

572 Bowl, 1978 (pl. 91)
Earthenware, raku fired, geometrical pattern in white glaze on a dark ground; h. 20.5 cm, d. 35 cm
C.27–1978. Source: BCC, London, £90

573 *Baroque Wall Piece, no. 1,* 1981
Earthenware, handbuilt, cut, polished and
assembled, with black slip and slate; h. 21 cm,
d. 28.8 cm
C.15–1982. Source: the potter (from the exhibition
Forms Around a Vessel, Leeds Art Gallery, 1981–
2), £500

574 Form, 1986 (pl. 98)
Earthenware, fired, cut and reassembled, with slip
and incised decoration; h. 56.8 cm, d. 21 cm
C.278–1986. Source: BCC, London, £935

Smith, Peter 1941–

1960s	trains as a research chemist in high temperature chemistry, BSc, University of London; largely self taught in ceramics
1973–	sets up Bojewyan Pottery, Penzance, Cornwall
1983–87	part-time teaching at Cornwall College of Further Education
1987	teaching at Falmouth School of Art and Design
1987	study visit to West Coast of USA

Peter Smith is a real original in studio pottery. A man
passionately devoted to clay itself, he allows the
character of the materials and processes to speak their
fullest. At first sight crude and violent, his work hides
an almost tender and romantic approach. More recent
work includes materials such as paint and rubber as
substitutes for glaze, and forms of fired and unfired clay
with other materials and DIY products such as door-
handles.

Peter Smith was a member of a group named 'Working
Party' which staged performance and installation
artworks; Smith played percussion.

Peter Smith, technical articles in *CR*: 24/1973, 25/1974
and 96/1985
—'Controlled Uncontrolled', *Artists Newsletter*,
September, 1984
—'A Visit to California', *CPA Newsletter*, 1987
'CPA New Members', *CR*, 1980
Ceramic Series, no. 13, Aberystwyth Arts Centre, 1985

575 Dish, 1981 (pl. 117)
Earthenware, slab-formed, with slip decoration;
marks: two seals and potter's monogram,
impressed; h. 5 cm, d. 29.4 cm
C.177–1981. Source: CPA, London, £21

576 Jug, 1981 (pl. 117)
Earthenware, slip decoration; marks: 'PS' and two
decorative seals, applied; h. 29.6 cm, d. 20.2 cm
C.178–1981. Source: CPA, London, £20

Spindler, A. F. dates not known

Spindler was an associate of John Bew (qv) and worked
with him at the Odney Pottery. He is said to have
turned to boat-building after the pottery closed, and
later worked at the Chelsea Pottery (qv). These wares
represent the typical output of Odney pottery.

PQ, 4/1954 (illustrations of him decorating slipware, pls.
13–15)

577 Dish, 1949
Earthenware, painting in brown on a blue opaque
glaze over a red body; made at Odney Pottery,
Cookham; h. 3.4 cm, d. 16.2 cm
Circ.193–1949. Source: the pottery, £0.75

578 Dish, 1949
Earthenware, painting in brown on a grey glaze;
marks: 'ODNEY', impressed; made at Odney
Pottery, Cookham; h. 2.7 cm, d. 17 cm
Circ.194–1949. Source: the pottery, £0.50

579 Dish, 1949
Stoneware, incised pattern through a blue wash
over a white glaze; made at Odney Pottery,
Cookham; h. 3 cm, d. 16.5 cm
Circ.195–1949. Source: the pottery, £0.62

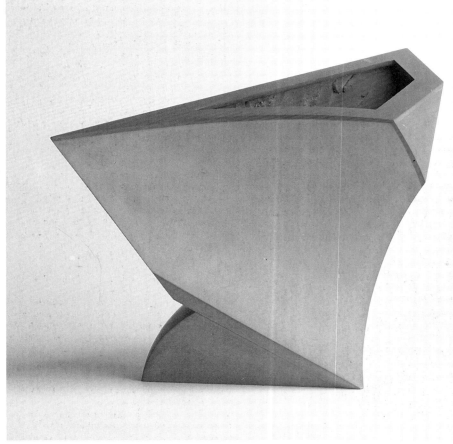

573

579 577 578

580 Dish, 1951
Earthenware (white), feather combed decoration in white and orange slip on black; marks: 'Odney', incised; made at Odney Pottery, Cookham; h. 3.5 cm, d. 29 cm
Circ.185–1951. Source: the pottery, £3.67

581 Plate, dated 1951
Earthenware, painted in coloured slips; marks: 'Odney', incised; made at Odney Pottery, Cookham; h. 4.5 cm, d. 32.2 cm
Circ.184–1951. Source: the pottery, £5.25

Stair, Julien 1955–

1974–78   ceramics at Camberwell School of Art, London
1975–76   works with Scott Marshall, Cornwall
1978–81   studies ceramics at the Royal College of Art
1981–   part-time lecturing at Bristol Polytechnic and Roehampton Institute of Higher Education
1981–85   studio in 401 1/2 workshops, London
1985–   Arlingford Studios, Brixton, London

Julien Stair, 'New Directions', CR, 104/1987

Stair, a contemporary at Camberwell with Pim (qv), Radstone (qv), and Suttie (qv), produces vases with inlaid geometric decoration. Initially working in porcelain, he has now started to use red earthenwares and a rather freer technique.

582 Vase, 1984
Porcelain, incised decoration inlaid with grey and pink; marks: 'JS' in a circle, impressed; h. 26.8 cm, d. 20.3 cm
C.122–1984. Source: Oxford Gallery, Oxford, £213.30

Staite Murray, William 1881–1962

1881   born in Deptford, London
1893–95   studies painting with cousins, professional artists
1895–1900 studies painting while travelling in Belgium, Germany and France as seed merchant
1900–03   travels in the USA
1905   marries, and sets up home in London, still in seed business
1908–09   Mediterranean cruise, visiting Italy and North Africa
c.1909–12 attends pottery classes at Camberwell
c.1912–15 experiments with potting and bronze-casting
c.1915–19 works with Cuthbert Hamilton at Yeoman Pottery, Kensington
1915–18   serves with Machine Gun Corps, Grantham
1919–24   sets up own pottery in Rotherhithe, London, on the premises of his brother's engineering and foundry firm
1923   visits St Ives, Shoji Hamada visits him in London
1924–29   sets up workshop with oil-fired kiln in Whickham Rd, London
1925   appointed, in preference to Bernard Leach, to the staff of the Royal College of Art
1926   appointed Head of Pottery Department at Royal College of Art; patents kiln design
1927   elected to 7&5 Society, proposed by Ben Nicholson, seconded by Ivor Hitchens
1929   moves to Bray, Berks
1934   elected to Art Workers' Guild
1939   visits Rhodesia with wife to see relatives; caught by war; ceases potting
1940   frustrated attempts to return to England, settles near Umtali
1955   appointed Trustee of National Arts Council of Southern Rhodesia
1957   forms Umtali Buddhist Society, contracts cancer, visits England
1958   exhibition of last of pre-war works
1959   operation for cancer

Staite Murray was without doubt the most famous and successful studio potter of the pre-war years. He was Head of Ceramics at the Royal College of Art, London, where he was chosen in preference to Bernard Leach; he was a member of the 7&5 Society and exhibited in fine-art galleries with painters and sculptors, and could, and did, charge enormous sums for his best work. His reputation has eclipsed since the war. He had ceased to pot and was retired in Rhodesia (now Zimbabwe) while Leach's influence, and that of the 'ethical' pot, grew among potters and in the art-schools. Murray considered himself a fine artist, and had distanced himself from the folkcraft attitudes of Leach. However, like Leach, he looked to the East and he found spiritual and aesthetic sustenance in Buddhism and Chinese stonewares.

Staite Murray's work is quite distinctive. He is a thrower of considerable skill, making forceful, at times almost ungainly shapes, some of enormous size, in which the marks of the throwing process are often left as expressive features – only the feet are strongly turned after throwing. Many pieces are left undecorated, covered only in rich glazes in stoney or mossy greys

580

581

582

Staite Murray

and browns. Painted, more rarely incised or inlaid decoration, usually consists of a few significant strokes which enhance the form while suggesting a motif.

Staite Murray came from an engineering family, and was technically very competent, however little he wished to give away to his students. He designed and built his own gas-fired kiln, and the control he achieved is clearly reflected in the quality of his pots. This is in sharp contrast to the technical struggles that Bernard Leach was having in the 1920s and 1930s.

Students of William Staite Murray represented in the Catalogue:

Constance Dunn 1924–30
James Dring 1927–30
Reginald Marlow 1927–30
Heber Mathews 1927–31
P.S. Wadsworth 1931–36
Sam Haile 1931–34
Vera Moss   1932–36
Margaret Rey 1932–35
Henry Hammond 1934–38
Helen Pincombe 1937–40
R.J. Washington 1937–38

Marks: until 1924 pieces bear an incised name and date; after 1924 they generally bear the impressed seal 'M' in a pentagon.

W. Staite Murray, 'Pottery from the Artist's Point of View', *Artwork*, 1/4, 1925
Bernard Rackham, 'Mr. W. S. Murray's Flambé Stoneware', *The Studio*, 1924, pp. 318–321
Ernest Marsh, 'W. Staite Murray, Studio Potter of Bray, Berkshire', *Apollo*, April, 1944
Wingfield Digby (1952)
Rose (1955), (1970)
Heber Matthews, 'William Staite Murray', exhibition review, *PQ*, 1958
'Mr Staite Murray', obituary, *The Times*, 21 February, 1962
Malcolm Haslam, 'Some Vorticist Pottery', *Connoisseur*, October, 1975
John Webber, 'William Staite Murray', *Crafts*, May/June, 1975
London, Hayward Gallery (1979)
Henry Hammond, 'A Magnetic Teacher', *Crafts*, May/June, 1975
London, Christopher Wood Gallery (1980)
Haslam (1984)
Malcolm Halsam, 'William Staite Murray's Ceramics in Context', *Antique Dealer and Collector's Guide*, March, 1984, pp. 64–66
Reggie Hynes, 'William Staite Murray – Potter and Artist', *CR*, 92/1985
Melissa Dalziel, 'The Dean's Taste', *Crafts*, March/April, 1985

584 583 585

586

588

587

589

583 Vase, February 1922
Stoneware, black lustrous glaze; marks:
'W.S.Murray 2/1922 London', incised; h. 11.3 cm,
d. 11.6 cm
C.142–1923. Source: given by Lt-Col. K.
Dingwall, DSO, through the NACF

584 Vase, 1924
Stoneware, gold-brown 'hare's fur' glaze, blue
glaze interior; marks: 'M' in a pentagon,
impressed; h. 15.8 cm, d. 19.3 cm
C.1463–1924. Source: given by Mrs H. Medhurst,
London

585 Vase, March 1922
Stoneware, mottled dark blue glaze; marks: 'W. S.
Murray 3/1922 London', incised; h. 15.7 cm,
d. 15.3 cm
C.401–1934. Source: given by the BIIA (acquired
in 1927)

586 Vase, November 1922
Stoneware, brown painting on oatmeal glaze;
marks: 'W.S.Murray 11/1922 London', incised;
made at Brockley, Kent; h. 15 cm, d. 17.7 cm
Circ.257–1923. Source: the potter, £7.35
This originally came with a wooden stand,
presumably of oriental type and manufacture.

587 Vase, 1924
Stoneware, creamy-white glaze; marks: 'W S
Murray 1924 London', incised; h. 9.5 cm,
d. 15.5 cm
C.1465–1924. Source: given by Mrs H. Medhurst,
London

588 Vase, 1924
Stoneware, mottled blue 'chun' glaze; marks: 'M'
in a pentagon, impressed; h. 16.3 cm, d. 18.2 cm
C.1464–1924. Source: given by Mrs H. Medhurst,
London

589 Bowl, 1924
Stoneware, painting in blue and brown on a
creamy-grey ground; marks: 'M' in a pentagon,
impressed and '1924', incised; h. 8.2 cm,
d. 11.7 cm
C.846–1925. Source: given by Lt-Col. K.
Dingwall, DSO, through the NACF

590 Bowl, 1924 (pl. 4)
Stoneware, thick grey-green glaze with purple
splashes; marks: 'M' in a pentagon, impressed;
h. 7.5 cm, d. 14.5 cm
C.1455–1924. Source: given by G. Eumorfopoulos

591 Vase, 1927 (pl. 4)
Stoneware, bubbled grey glaze with purple splash;
marks: 'M' in a pentagon, impressed; made at
Brockley; h. 17.5 cm, d. 16 cm
Circ.677–1927. Source: the potter, £8.40

592 Vase, 1926 (pl. 10)
Stoneware, painting in brown in a thin grey glaze;
marks: 'M' in a pentagon, impressed; h. 29.3 cm,
d. 19 cm
C.400–1934. Source: given by the BIIA (acquired
in 1927)

593 Dish, 1926
Stoneware, painting in brown in an oatmeal glaze;
marks: 'M' in a pentagon, impressed; h. 7 cm,
d. 20.4 cm
C.413–1926. Source: given by F.D. Lycett Green
(from an exhibition in Paterson's of Bond Street,
London)

594 Bowl, 1924
Stoneware, brown painting on oatmeal glaze;
marks: 'M' in a pentagon, impressed; h. 8.5 cm,
d. 15.7 cm
C.1454–1924. Source: given by Lt-Col. K.
Dingwall, DSO, through the NACF

595 Bowl, 1925–1935
Stoneware, painting in brown in an oatmeal glaze;
marks: 'M' in a pentagon, impressed; h. 14.3 cm,
d. 13.6 cm
Misc.2(54)-1934. Source: Margaret Bulley Gift

596 Bowl, 1930
Stoneware, painting on body in brown glaze,
inside brown glazed; marks: 'M' in a pentagon,
impressed; h. 10 cm, d. 12.8 cm
Circ.427–1930. Source: Lefèvre Gallery, London,
£4.20

597 Bowl, 1925–1935
Stoneware, painting in brown in an oatmeal glaze;
marks: 'M' in a pentagon, impressed; h. 9.3 cm,
d. 19 cm
Misc.2(53)-1934. Source: Margaret Bulley Gift

593

597

594 595 596

598 Vase: *Spring Song*, 1930
Stoneware, grey glaze with painting in red and
blue; marks: 'M' in a pentagon, impressed;
h. 27.8 cm, d. 17.4 cm
Circ.425–1930. Source: Lefèvre Gallery, London,
£25.20

599 Vase: *Madonna*, c.1930
Stoneware, incised decoration with painting in
copper-red in a grey glaze; marks: 'M' in a
pentagon, impressed; h. 56 cm, d. 18.4 cm
C.60–1976. Source: Richard Dennis, London,
£312
This piece was sold at the Lefèvre Gallery in
London in November 1930 for 60 gns (= £63).

600

598

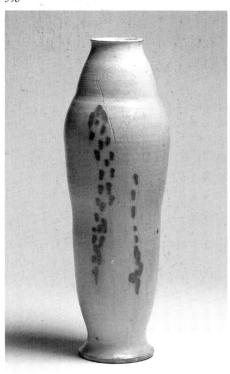

599

602

600 Vase: *Vine*, 1930
Stoneware, painting in brown on a grey glaze; marks: 'M' in a pentagon, impressed; h. 18.7 cm, d. 19.8 cm
Circ.426–1930. Source: Lefèvre Gallery, London, £12.60

601 Bowl, *c.*1930 (pl. 33)
Stoneware, painting in dark brown in an oatmeal glaze; marks: 'M' in a pentagon, impressed; h. 12.8 cm, d. 24.4 cm
C.954–1935. Source: given by the CAS (through Ernest Marsh)

602 Vase, early 1930s
Stoneware, tenmoku glaze with white mottling; marks: 'M' in a pentagon, impressed; h. 21.8 cm, d. 21.7 cm
Circ.352–1939. Source: given by the CAS (through Ernest Marsh)

603 Vase, early 1930s
Stoneware, painting in iron brown in an oatmeal glaze; marks: 'M' in a pentagon, impressed; h. 29.1 cm, d. 14 cm
Circ.353–1939. Source: given by the CAS (through Ernest Marsh)

604 Vase, early 1930s
Stoneware, grey glaze; marks: 'M' in a pentagon, impressed; h. 46.3 cm, d. 17.8 cm
Circ.351–1939. Source: given by the CAS (through Ernest Marsh)

605 Tea bowl, *c.*1930
Stoneware, mottled tenmoku glaze; marks: 'M' in a pentagon, impressed; h. 7.7 cm, d. 10.8 cm
Circ.276–1955. Source: given by Lady Russel MBE, from the collection of the late Francis Moore

606 Bowl, *c.*1930
Stoneware, brown glaze with purple flushes; marks: 'M' in a pentagon, impressed; h. 8 cm, d. 11 cm
C.114–1977. Source: Richard Dennis, London (from the collection of Sir Edward Maufe), £100

607 Vase: *Wheel of Life*, *c.*1939 (pl. 34)
Stoneware, painted decoration in shades of brown on a grey glaze; marks: 'M' in a pentagon, impressed; h. 62.8 cm, d. 30.5 cm
Circ.352–1958. Source: Leicester Galleries, London (solo exhibition in December, 1958, no. 18), £94.50

Standige, Gary 1946–

1964–67 Stoke-on-Trent College of Art
1966–81 workshop in Charing, Kent
1967–70 studies ceramics at the Royal College of Art
1970 scholarship to travel to USA and Canada studying computer technology and its influence on Art and Design
1972–74 lecturer at Southend College of Technology
1974–82 lecturer at Medway College of Design
1981– workshop in Aylesford, Kent
1981– senior lecturer in ceramics, West Surrey College of Art and Design, Farnham

Gary Standige produces work in oriental style of a highly controlled technical quality.

'CPA New Members', *CR*, 51/1978

608 Jar and lid, 1980
Porcelain, mottled brown glaze with incised decoration; marks: 'GS' in monogram, impressed; h. 16 cm, d. 15.2 cm
C.184&a–1980. Source: CPA, London (exhibition, November, 1980), £30

605 606

603

604

608

Suttie, Angus 1946–

1946	born in Tealing, Scotland
1975–79	Camberwell School of Art, London
1979–80	teacher training, Whitelands College, Putney, London
1980–	teaches at Morley College, London
1981–84	shares workshop with Sara Radstone in the 401½ workshops
1984–	new workshop in Clerkenwell, London; works now in stoneware
1986–	teaching Camberwell School of Art, returns to earthenware

Suttie is an articulate potter, both in his work and his writing. His handbuilt pottery explores ordinary functional things, in particular teapots, with an analytic and yet playful vision. Inspiration is drawn at present from Precolumbian pottery and his recent work is imbued with a ritual atmosphere. He was a fellow student of Henry Pim (qv) and Sara Radstone (qv) at Camberwell School of Art.

Angus Suttie, 'The Dangerous Edge of Things' (on Gillian Lowndes), *Crafts*, July/August, 1985
—'Sara Radstone', *CR*, 100/1986
—'Alison Britton', *CR*, 107/1987
—'Colin Pearson', *Crafts*, March/April, 1988
—'Radstone and Henderson', in *Six Ways*, exhibition catalogue, Anatol Orient Gallery, London, 1988
—'Traditions', *CR*, 117/1989
Emmanuel Cooper, 'Angus Suttie – Teasing the Imagination', *CR*, 94/1985
Peter Dormer, 'Structural Logic', *Crafts*, September/October, 1987
The Whole Works, exhibition pamphlet, Anatol Orient, July/August, 1985

Suttie's work up until 1985 is occasionally inscribed 'ANGUS MADE ME' or 'ANGUS' – sometimes with a date. After 1985 all pieces are marked 'SUTTIE'.

609 Ladle, 1987
Earthenware, handbuilt, with coloured overglaze enamels; h. 5.7 cm, d. 37.5 cm
C.100–1987. Source: Anatol Orient, London, £37.60

Swindell, Geoffrey 1945–

1945	born in Stoke-on-Trent
1960–67	studies ceramics at the Royal College of Art, London
1970–75	workshop in York and teaching at York School of Art
1975–	lecturer in ceramics, South Glamorgan Institute of Higher Education, Cardiff; new workshop in Cardiff

Swindell was acclaimed in the 1970s for his small, precisely made decorative pots, a theme he has developed for many years. Like a number of potters in the 1970s, such as Simpson (qv), Rogers (qv) and Burnett (qv), he is interested in exploring the qualities of porcelain.

Jeannie Lowe, 'Geoffrey Swindell – Press Moulded Forms', *CR*, 18/1972
Exhibition review, *CR*, 19/1973
Jeannie Lowe, 'Pressmoulding – the Technique used by Geoffrey Swindell', *CR*, 27/1974
London, CC (1974)
'CPA New Members', *CR*, 34/1975
Cameron and Lewis (1976)
London, Christopher Wood Gallery (1980)
Peter Lane, 'The Precise Forms of Geoffrey Swindell', *CR*, 67/1981
Ceramics Monthly, September, 1981
Ceramic Series, no. 24 bis, Aberystwyth Arts Centre

610 Bowl, 1978
Porcelain, sprayed coloured glazes; marks: 'S', impressed; h. 7.6 cm, d. 11.2 cm
C.116–1978. Source: CPA, London, £84.60

611 Vase, 1978
Porcelain, sprayed coloured glazes; marks: 'S', impressed; h. 9.1 cm, d. 8.6 cm
C.115–1978. Source: CPA, London, £94

610 611

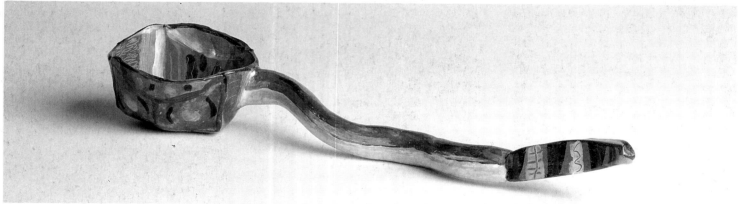

609

Sykes, Steven 1914–

1933–36 trained as a designer of stained glass and mosaics at the Royal College of Art, London
1937–39 assistant to Herbert Hendrie, Head of Design at Edinburgh College of Art, who ran a stained-glass business from his college studio
1946–79 teaches at Chelsea School of Art, London
1947–60 workshop in Kew, Surrey, making ceramics
1960–68 workshop in Fulham, London, making sculpture
1968–   workshop at Bepton, Midhurst, Sussex
1979   retires from teaching

Sykes took part in the post-war revival of tin-glaze, coloured decoration and figural modelling such as was also being explored by Newland (qv), Hine (qv) and Vergette (qv). Sykes's most important works, however, are large architectural commissions. He designed a large mural for the Gethsemane chapel at Coventry Cathedral in 1960. Other work included decorative tiles in the Lion and Unicorn pavilion for the Festival of Britain, the US National War Memorial Chapel in the Cathedral in Washington (DC), USA, and a large fibreglass fountain group outside the British Pavilion at Expo 67 in Montreal, Canada.

Margaret Costa, 'Tableware', October, 1950
Hugh Wakefield, 'The Ceramics of Stephen Sykes', *Image*, 6, Spring 1951
C. G. Tomley, 'An English Potter', *Graphics*, 44, 1952
Floud (1953)
Billington (1953)
PQ, 1/1954 (illustrations pl. 15), 2/1954 (illustrations pls. 11–12)
Warwick (1987)

612 Dish, 1950
Earthenware, relief decoration and lustre on a transparent glaze; h. 7.6 cm, d. 30.5 cm
Circ.180–1950. Source: the potter, £4.50

613 Dish: *Signs of the Zodiac*, 1950
Earthenware, relief decoration and green painting in a white glaze; marks: 'Steven Sykes' and '15.2.50', incised; h. 7.3 cm, d. 29.5 cm
Circ.181–1950. Source: the potter, £4.20

614 *Trumpeting Angel*, 1950 (pl. 53)
Earthenware, relief decoration and painting in green in a white glaze; marks: 'Steven Sykes' and '1950', incised; h. 4.6 cm, d. 30 cm
Circ.182–1950. Source: the potter, £4

615 *Tripod Bird*, 1951
Earthenware, painting in black and green under a white tin glaze; marks: 'Steven Sykes 51', incised; h. 33.9 cm, d. 40 cm
Circ.75–1952. Source: the potter, £12.60

616 *Daphne*, 1951
Earthenware, unglazed, with hair and flowers in green, black and blue under a white tin glaze; h. 43 cm, d. 30 cm
Circ.74 to b–1952. Source: the potter, £12.60

617 Panel of four tiles, 1955
Earthenware, modelled in relief, green glaze; h. 44.5 cm, d. 41.5 cm
Circ.97 to c–1963. Source: the potter, £35
A note in the Museum records explains that these tiles were purchased for a Circulation Department tile exhibition: '... this panel of tiles by Steven Sykes [is justified] as being some of the only modern English tiles of sufficient quality to share a screen with the Rut Bryk panel'. Rut Bryk is a noted designer and artist working at the Arabia factory in Finland.

612

613

615

616

617

Tacon, Pamela

Pamela Tacon studied pottery at the Royal College of Art, London just before the war. The piece in the collection is a student work, purchased at the same diploma show as those by Helen Pincombe (qv) and Gwilym Thomas (qv). She went with Helen Pincombe to Ambleside where the Royal College of Art was evacuated during the war. She is not thought to have continued potting afterwards.

618 Jug, 1939
Stoneware, cream and brown mottled glaze; h. 38 cm, d. 2 cm
Circ.481–1939. Source: the potter (purchased from a diploma show at the Royal College of Art), £4.20

Taylor, Sutton 1943–

1943	born in Yorkshire
1964–69	teaching in Manchester and Kingston, Jamaica, during which he discovers clay; becomes a self-taught potter
1966–70	sets up a pottery in Jamaica
1971–76	returns to the UK, sets up a studio at Temple Newsam, Leeds
1976–78	new studio at the Almshouses, Aberford, Leeds
1978–	new studio at Lotherton Park, Aberford, Leeds

Sutton Taylor has concentrated on decoration in polychrome reduced lustre – a very difficult technique, similar to that used by Caiger-Smith (qv), and one that he has most impressively mastered. His vessels, generally large open bowls, are decorated with a rich over-all pattern that gives full play to the brilliant metallic lustre reflections.

Sutton Taylor, 'Lustred Earthenware', *CR*, 82/1983
Sutton Taylor: Lustreware, exhibition pamphlet, Craft Centre and Design Gallery, Leeds, 1988

619 Bowl, 1982–1983
Earthenware, in-glaze lustre with gold and red on pale red-speckled ground; marks: 'ST' and 'LH', impressed; h. 15.2 cm, d. 37.8 cm
C.224–1983. Source: Queensbury Hunt, London, £225

Tchalenko, Janice 1942–

1942	born in Rugby, Warwickshire
1965–67	diploma at Putney School of Art, London, after six years in the Foreign Office
1967–69	part-time teaching and workshop assistant
1969–71	studies ceramics at Harrow College of Art
1971–88	workshop in East Dulwich, London
1972–87	teaches part time at Camberwell and Croydon Schools of Art, London
1979	starts experimenting with decorated pots in bright colours
1981–	tutor at the Royal College of Art
1982–	solo exhibition of work made in co-operation with the textile designer J. Hinchcliffe, Crafts Shop, Victoria and Albert
1984–	designs new range of wares for Dart Pottery
1987	made a fellow of the Royal College of Art
1988–	new studio in Camberwell, London

In years of making domestic ware Janice Tchalenko developed a formidable throwing technique and very strong sense of form. Her domestic ware was brown or yellow-brown glazed and was usually undecorated – she was particularly known for her nests of stacking pouring bowls. She had always wanted to use brighter colours and began to experiment with high-fired coloured glazes in 1979, a Crafts Council bursary in 1980 giving her further time to do this. Her first decorations were restricted to trailing as she was somewhat fearful of her skill as a painter. An exhibition with the textile designer John Hinchcliffe in 1982 marked a turning point which showed Tchalenko to

618

619

what effect her colouristic talents could be put. She has since developed into one of the most powerful potters of the 1980s; she bridges the gap between purely domestic potters and the 'new ceramics'. Her wares are all basically functional in form, but with an ever increasing sculptural force, and a unique exuberance, boldness and richness of decoration.

From about 1984, she has worked with Dart Pottery (qv) to design a new range of shapes and designs for their standard ware. These have been commercially very successful and the venture won Radio 4's Enterprise award in 1988.

'CPA New Members', *CR*, 30/1974
Emmanuel Cooper, 'Janice Tchalenko', *CR*, 80/1983
Peter Dormer, 'Tchalenko, Eclectic', *Crafts*, January/February, 1985
Rachael Sherratt, 'Dart/Tchalenko: Designer Workshop', exhibition review, *Crafts*, July/August, 1987
'Janice Tchalenko – New York Pots', *CR*, 96/1985
Peter Dormer, 'Tchalenko, Eclectic', *Crafts*, January/February, 1985
Ceramic Series, no. 2, Aberystwyth Arts Centre

620 Jug, 1980
Stoneware, painting in blue, yellow and green glazes on a grey ground; h. 29.2 cm, d. 20.3 cm
C.43–1980. Source: CPA, London, *Jugs* exhibition, 1980, £20
This was an early piece in her new coloured style – a brightness of colour that was almost shocking for the time, but which seems very restrained in view of her later developments.

621 Dish, 1982
Stoneware, painting in black, green and red glazes on a grey ground; h. 5.8 cm, d. 49.5 cm
C.91–1982. Source: V&A Craft Shop, £80
Part of a group of pieces made in partnership with John Hinchcliffe, a textile designer, which were shown in an exhibition in the V&A Craft Shop, May–June, 1982.

622 Bowl, 1983
Stoneware, painting in red, yellow, blue and green glazes on a grey ground; h. 18.1 cm, d. 38.3 cm
C.312–1983. Source: Bohun Gallery, Henley-on-Thames (solo exhibition, 1983), £200

623 Bowl, 1983 (pl. 120)
Stoneware, painting in red, green yellow and blue glazes on a grey ground; h. 11.8 cm, d. 35.3 cm
C.313–1983. Source: Bohun Gallery, Henley-on-Thames (solo exhibition, 1983), £110

624 Teapot, 1983 (pl. 19)
Stoneware, painting in coloured glazes; h. 13 cm, d. 20.5 cm
C.314&a-1983. Source: Bohun Gallery, Henley-on-Thames (solo exhibition, 1983), £50

621

620

622

Thomas, Gwilym dates not known

Thomas was a student at the Royal College of Art just before the war, a contemporary of Helen Pincombe (qv) and Henry Hammond (qv). He was a conscientious objector during the war and afterwards taught at Hammersmith School of Art. Little is known of his activities in the post-war period.

625 Bowl, 1938
Stoneware, painting in brown on an oatmeal glaze; h. 11.7 cm, d. 16 cm
Circ.98–1939. Source: Brygos Gallery, London, £1.25

626 Bowl, 1938
Stoneware, painting in brown on a green-grey glaze; marks: 'G', incised on foot; h. 7.6 cm, d. 10.5 cm
Circ.99–1939. Source: Brygos Gallery, London, £0.37

627 Teapot, 1939
Stoneware, painting in brown on a mottled green-grey glaze; h. 15.4 cm, d. 19.5 cm
Circ.482&a–1939. Source: the potter (purchased from a diploma show at the Royal College of Art), £1.57

Tower, James 1919–1988

1919   born in Sheerness, Kent
1938–40   studies painting at the Royal Academy Schools, London
1940–46   war service, works on camouflage and mapping
1946–49   studies painting at the Slade School of Fine Art, London
1949–50   Institute of Education, London, studies ceramics with William Newland (qv) and attends evening classes at Central School of Art under Dora Billington (qv)
1949–66   teaching at the Bath Academy of Art, Corsham Court, concentrating at first on pottery
1950–65   workshop at Corsham, Wilts.
1951   first shows work at Gimpel Fils, London
1959–78   largely abandons pottery for sculpture in bronze
1965–88   workshop at Barcombe, near Lewes, Sussex
1966–86   appointed head of Fine Art, Brighton College of Art, sets up sculpture department
1978–   resumes potting
1986   retires

James Tower is associated with the 'Institute of Education' group in the 1950s along with Newland (qv), Hine (qv) and Vergette (qv), who were contemporaries at London University after the war. Together they developed their own method of tin-glaze decoration, which involved a second layer of dark glaze with incised decoration fired over a layer of white glaze (or reversed: a layer of white fired over a layer of dark glaze). Tower used this technique all his life, though from about 1959 to the late 1970s he abandoned ceramics as he felt they could not fetch a high enough price to justify the work involved. He returned to sculpture, producing large terracottas destined for casting in bronze. His work in the 1950s was on varied forms including leaf-shaped dishes. By the late 1950s he had developed the flattened vase which was, in various formats, to remain his prime form. The vase of 1957 catalogued here is an interesting precursor of the 'optical pots' with similar plays on perspective that were developed by Liz Fritsch (qv) and others in the 1970s and 1980s.

Floud (1953)
Billington (1953)
Melville (1954)
Exhibition review, *PQ*, 1/1954
Paul Atterbury, 'Ceramics by James Tower', exhibition review, *Crafts*, March/April, 1979
'Making Good', *CR*, 73/1982
Peter Lane, 'James Tower – Artist Potter', *CR*, 88/1984
Obituaries: *The Times*, 15 April 1988; *Crafts*, July/August, 1988; *CR*, 112/1988
James Tower, 1919–1988, exhibition pamphlet, Hove Museum and Art Gallery, 1989 (review, *Crafts*, May/June, 1989)

628 Vase, 1957 (pl. 55)
Earthenware, white glaze decoration over black; marks: 'James Tower 57', incised; h. 38 cm, d. 46.5 cm
Circ.7–1958. Source: Gimpel Fils, London, £18

629 Dish, 1958
Earthenware, black and white glazes; marks: 'James Tower 58', incised; h. 6.8 cm, d. 46.3 cm
Circ.16–1959. Source: Gimpel Fils, London, £22.48

630 Pot: *Glacier II*, 1982
Earthenware, dark manganese over a white tin glaze; marks: 'James Tower 82', incised; h. 53.5 cm, d. 54 cm
C.328–1983. Source: Gimpel Fils, London, £450

625

626

627

629

Uusman, Beatrice dates not known

Virtually nothing is known of this potter. She exhibited in the 14th Arts and Crafts Exhibition Society exhibition held at the Royal Academy in 1928 alongside Leach, Staite Murray, Cardew, Braden, Dalton, Billington, Harding, Finnemore, Frances Richards and Lunn (qv). Uusman showed two vases at £5.25 and £3.15, and a number of models – a frog for £0.52 and two fish for £0.75 and £0.52 in both stoneware and earthenware. She is listed at an address in Queen's Gate, SW7, London.

A label on the base of this vase says: Mrs Uusman, Camberwell 38/- (or 58/-; £1.90 or £2.90). Mrs Uusman may have moved, or may have been a pupil of Alfred Hopkins (qv) at Camberwell School of Art.

631 Vase, c.1930
Stoneware, with brown mottled glaze; h. 11.7 cm, d. 15.6 cm
C.958–1935. Source: given by the CAS

Vergette, Nicholas 1923–1974

1923	born in Market Deeping, Lincs.
1941–46	does service as an RAF pilot in Europe and Far East
1946–50	Chelsea School of Art
1950–51	teacher training at the Institute of Education, London University, introduced to pottery by William Newland (qv)
1951–58	lecturer at Camberwell and Central Schools of Art
1958	moves to USA, Rochester NY, then University of Southern Illinois

Vergette is one of the 'Institute of Education' group in the 1950s with Newland (qv), Hine (qv) and Tower (qv). They were contemporaries at London University after the war and explored handbuilding, including figural work, and colourful tin-glaze decoration. Vergette was the most adventurously sculptural of the group, gaining admiration for his seated figures cut from a single thrown vase. The bowl catalogued here shows a skilful decorative talent. After he left for the USA, Vergette's work increasingly inclined to environmental ceramics and full-blown sculpture.

The Studio Yearbook of Decorative Art, 1952 and 1954
Fennemore (1953)
Billington (1953), (1955)
Craft Horizons: March, 1956; July, 1962; September/October, 1963; March/April, 1968; July/August, 1969; September, 1969; October, 1973; April, 1974; August, 1974
Ceramics Monthly: April, 1971; September, 1973; April, 1974
Vergette, exhibition catalogue, University Galleries, Southern Illinois University at Carbondale, June–July, 1962
Nicholas Vergette, exhibition catalogue, Mitchell Museum, Mt. Vernon, Illinois, April–May, 1974

632 Bowl, 1954 (pl. 54)
Earthenware, coloured painting on a white glaze, with dark incised lines; marks: 'N 54', painted; h. 16.8 cm, d. 20 cm
Circ.278–1954. Source: Crafts Centre of Great Britain, London, £3.15

Vyse, Charles 1882–1971

1882	born in Staffordshire
1896	apprenticed to Doulton's as modeller and designer
1905–10	wins scholarship from Hanley Art School to Royal College of Art
1909	travelling scholarship to Italy
1911	elected member of the Royal Society of British Sculptors
1919	sets up studio in Cheyne Walk, Chelsea; working with his wife, Nell, who is exceptionally knowledgeable in ceramic chemistry; production of cast figures and experiments with high-fired Chinese wares
1940	studio damaged by air raids
1940–	modelling and pottery instructor at Farnham School of Art
post-war	working with assistant Barbara Waller, a former student at Farnham School of Art, producing stonewares with a variety of chinese glazes, and animal figures
1963	retires to Deal, Kent

Vyse occupies an important position in the history of British studio pottery as one of the pioneers in experimenting with high-fired stonewares of Chinese type. His work is technically of a very high order, though his shapes and decoration are somewhat timid and over-refined in comparison to the work of Staite Murray (qv), Leach (qv), Pleydell-Bouverie (qv) or Braden (qv). He is at his best in brush-decorated work in non-Chinese style. Before the war, Vyse ran a business in slip-cast figures of 'local characters', made and decorated by a small team of local women employees, which gained considerable success; after the war he continued figure production with his assistant Barbara Waller.

Vyse held annual exhibitions from 1928–1939 and 1950–1963 at Walker's Galleries, London, which are reviewed annually in December by Ernest Marsh in *Walker's Monthly* from 1928–38.

Charles Vyse, 'The Craftsman in Pottery', in Blunt (1973) (originally published in 1924; with an interesting account by one of Vyse's employees added in the new edition of 1973)
Bernard Rackham, 'The Pottery Figures of Mr Charles Vyse', *Studio*, 81/1921, pp. 184 ff.
Ernest Marsh, 'Charles and Nell Vyse, Studio Potters of Chelsea', *Apollo*, May, 1943
'The Chelsea Potters', *The Sphere*, June 30, 1951

631

630

Figures and Stoneware Pottery by Charles Vyse, exhibition
catalogue, arranged by Richard Dennis at the Fine Art
Society, London, 1974
Malcolm Haslam, 'Charles Vyse, 1882–1971, Potter',
Connoisseur, exhibition review, December, 1974
Emmanuel Cooper, 'Charles Vyse – Figures and Pots',
exhibition review, *CR*, 32/1975
Marigold Coleman, 'Charles Vyse', *Crafts*,
January/February, 1975
London, Hayward Gallery (1979)

The Museum has a collection of figures produced by
Vyse dating from both before and after the war. These
semi-industrial wares are not catalogued here.

633 Bowl, *c.1930*
Stoneware, incised decoration through a white
slip under a celadon glaze; marks: 'TO E M FROM
THE A-M SOCY FEB 1931.', incised; h. 7.4 cm,
d. 25.2 cm
C.83–1984. Source: given by Mr Christopher
Marsh, son of Ernest Marsh
The inscribed motto 'adsum pene ademall' is a
Latin-esque jocular spoof: 'had some, almost had
them all'. This is a reference to the collecting of
Martin wares. The bowl was presented to Ernest
Marsh, an avid collector of Martin ware, by his
friend and rival collector Francis Berry, who
styled himself the Anti-Marsh society in
recognition of their good-humoured competition.

634 Bowl, *c.1932*
Stoneware, painting in green in a grey glaze;
marks: 'CHARLES VYSE CHELSEA', incised;
h. 13.4 cm, d. 21.5 cm
C.132–1977. Source: Richard Dennis, London
(from the collection of Sir Edward Maufe), £100

635 Jug, 1934 (pl. 37)
Stoneware, painting in brown in a grey speckled
glaze; marks: '19 VYSE 34', incised; h. 24.5 cm,
d. 24.4 cm
C.63–1980. Source: Richard Dennis, London,
£300 (with the following mug)
The inscription reads:
  'This is the Jug
  That holds the beer
  To fill the mug
  And bring us cheer'

636 Mug, 1936 (pl. 37)
Stoneware, painting in blue in a grey glaze; marks:
'VYSE 1936', incised; h. 15 cm, d. 15.3 cm
C.64–1980. Source: Richard Dennis, London
The inscription reads:
  'All the fun of the fair'

637 Bowl, *c.1931*
Stoneware, mottled rust glaze, interior with pale
lavender glaze; marks: 'C. VYSE', incised;
h. 6.7 cm, d. 13.3 cm
C.284–1976. Source: D. M. Booth, £60

638 Bowl, *c.1950*
Stoneware, carved decoration under a pale blue
glaze, interior brown-glazed; marks: 'CHARLES
VYSE, CHELSEA', incised; h. 11.6 cm, d. 17.5 cm
Circ.16–1951. Source: Walker's Galleries Ltd.,
London, £10.50

639 Jug, *c.1950*
Stoneware, painted decoration in brown in a grey
glaze; marks: 'CHARLES VYSE, CHELSEA',
incised; h. 18.1 cm, d. 22.5 cm
Circ.17–1951. Source: *see* Circ.16–1951, £6.30

640 Bowl, 1934
Stoneware, painted decoration in brown on an
oatmeal glaze; marks: 'VYSE 1934', incised;
h. 11.5 cm, d. 21.7 cm
C.61–1976. Source: Richard Dennis, London, £69

637 638

633

634

639 640

641 Bowl, *c.*1935
Stoneware, cut decoration under a celadon glaze;
marks: 'CHARLES VYSE, CHELSEA', incised;
h. 13.7 cm, d. 14.4 cm
C.116–1977. Source: Richard Dennis, London
(from the collection of Sir Edward Maufe), £50

642 Vase, 1935
Stoneware, incised decoration through a slip under
a grey-white glaze; marks: 'CV' in monogram,
incised; h. 17.1 cm, d. 16.8 cm
C.955–1935. Source: given by the CAS

643 Small vase, 1931
Stoneware, lavender-blue glaze with purple
flushes; marks: 'C.V. 1931', incised; h. 11.3 cm,
d. 11 cm
C.285–1976. Source: D. M. Booth, £60

644 Bowl, *c.*1935
Stoneware, blue and purple glaze; marks:
'CHARLES VYSE, CHELSEA', incised; h. 8.5 cm,
d. 13.5 cm
C.117–1977. Source: Richard Dennis, London
(from the collection of Sir Edward Maufe), £40

645 Bowl, 1939
Stoneware, blue mottled glaze; marks: 'VYSE
1939' and 'SW', incised; h. 11.6 cm, d. 17.8 cm
C.118–1977. Source: Richard Dennis, London
(from the collection of Sir Edward Maufe), £70

Wade, Constance E. *see* Constance **Dunn**

Wadsworth, Philip S. 1910–

1910   born in Cheshire, son of Art Director at
        Minton's
1931–36 studies ceramics at the Royal College of Art
        under William Staite Murray (qv)
1936–40 part-time teaching at Kingston and Leicester
        Schools of Art
1940–45 war service in the army
1946–49 teaches at Leeds School of Art
1949–66 teaches at Poole School of Art, teaching full
        time, makes little pottery of own
1966   retires, ceases to pot

Wadsworth's work catalogued here was made shortly
after he graduated from the Royal College of Art. It
shows how Staite Murray's students produce work both
recognisably similar to that of their tutor, and yet
developing their own characteristics.

646 Lidded jar, 1939
Stoneware, crackled transparent glaze over a grey
body; marks: 'PSW', incised; h. 16.8 cm,
d. 11.4 cm
Circ.170&a-1939. Source: the potter, £1.05

647 Lidded jar, 1939
Stoneware, oatmeal glaze; marks: 'PSW', incised;
h. 15 cm, d. 12.7 cm
Circ.171&a-1939. Source: the potter, £1.50

648 Lidded jar, 1939
Stoneware, mottled grey glaze flecked with
brown; marks: 'PSW', incised; h. 11.7 cm,
d. 12.8 cm
Circ.172&a-1939. Source: the potter, £2.10

644 643 645

641

647 648 646

642

257

649

649 Jar, 1939
Stoneware, grey glaze with dark bands; marks:
'PSW', incised; h. 15.7 cm, d. 22.3 cm
Circ.173–1939. Source: the potter, £5.25

650 Vase, 1939
Stoneware, thin grey glaze; marks: 'PSW', incised;
h. 19.7 cm, d. 10.8 cm
Circ.174–1939. Source: the potter, £0.77

651 Vase, 1939
Stoneware, tenmoku glaze; marks: 'PSW', incised;
h. 30 cm, d. 25 cm
Circ.175–1939. Source: the potter, £6.30

652 Jug, 1939
Stoneware, reddish glaze; marks: 'PSW', painted;
h. 19.8 cm, d. 17.2 cm
Circ.176–1939. Source: the potter, £1.05

Walford, James 1913–

1931–	studies painting at the Slade and Royal College of Art, London
c.1945–	takes up pottery, evening classes at Kingston School of Art, London, with Dora Billington (qv), then at Woolwich School of Art with Heber Mathews (qv)
1947	purchases a small gas kiln from Bernard Leach (qv) (described in Leach's *A Potter's Book*)
1948	started potting at South Nutfield, Surrey
1958	founder member of the CPA
1959	moves to Crowborough, Sussex
1959–77	forced by illness to abandon potting
1977–	resumes pottery on a small scale; sells through auction houses and privately

The Times review praises him for his close copies after Chinese Song wares, their 'exceptional virtuosity', but wondering if 'so devout an affection for the past is a mark of good sense'.

Walford is interested in materials and technology. The porcelain bowl is an early example of a 'throwable' porcelain which he developed, made with the help of a white fuller's earth from Africa. David Leach (qv) was experimenting with various recipes to obtain a porcelain useful for studio potters at about the same time. The three brown stoneware pieces, described by Walford as 'routine test pieces' in 'porcelaneous stoneware', were experiments to reproduce the earliest Chinese stoneware glazes. The glaze is a mixture of red clay and elm ash in proportions respectively of 1:3, 1:1 and 3:1. The effects are very similar to original Chinese pieces, and it was this that interested Lane, Keeper of the Ceramic Department. In a memo to the Director recommending the acquisition he says: 'Mr. Walford has very successfully reproduced the effect of the glazes on one of the earliest classes of Chinese glazed stoneware ... as unsound theories have been put forward about their technique, Mr Walford's experiments provide a useful material piece of evidence. He has given us the formula of the composition of glaze, degree of firing etc., all of which might easily have been adopted by the Chinese potters.'

650

652

651

655 654 653

James Walford, 'Fuller's Earth', *CR*, 60/1979
'Technique in Art', exhibition review, *The Times*, 19 October, 1955
'Celadon Pottery and Porcelain, Berkeley Galleries', exhibition review, *PQ*, 2/7, 1955

653 Vase, 1954
Stoneware, mottled brown ash glaze; marks: 'JW' in monogram, impressed; h. 12 cm, d. 10.7 cm
C.6–1954. Source: the potter, £4.20
This is the first piece purchased by, as opposed to given to, the Department of Ceramics.

654 Jar, 1954
Stoneware, mottled brown glaze; marks: 'JW' in monogram, impressed; h. 9.2 cm, d. 12.2 cm
C.5–1954. Source: given by the potter

655 Vase, 1954
Stoneware, mottled brown ash-glaze; marks: 'JW' in monogram impressed; h. 11.3 cm, d. 10.5 cm
C.7–1954. Source: the potter, £4.20

656 Bowl, 1951
Porcelain, white glaze; marks: 'JW' in monogram, impressed; h. 6.9 cm, d. 10.9 cm
Circ.310–1951. Source: Berkeley Galleries, London, £3.15
A note in recommendation of purchase says that Walford is: 'one of the few contemporary potters of any interest whose work is not represented in our collections ... almost unique among the present generation of studio potters in that he works mainly in porcelain rather than stoneware or earthenware'.

657 Bowl, 1957
Stoneware, very pale blue glaze; marks: 'JW' in monogram impressed; h. 11 cm, d. 23.8 cm
Circ.203–1957. Source: Berkeley Galleries, London, £15.75

658 Vase, 1957
Stoneware, slip decoration under a green glaze; marks: 'JW' in monogram, incised; h. 19 cm, d. 16.7 cm
Circ.204–1957. Source: Berkeley Galleries, London, £16.80

Wallwork, Alan 1931–

c.1955   teacher training at Goldsmith's College, London, taking pottery classes in the last year
1957   first workshop in Forest Hill, London
1959–   working from Alan Gallery, Forest Hill, London, producing both standard ware and individual pieces
1960   moves to Greenwich
1964   sets up a pottery in Marnhull, Dorset; with a team of assistants produces a wide range of products – in particular tiles, but also garden pots, lamps and sculpture
1970–   tile production expands until business hit by inflation in late 1970s
early 1980s   tile business wound down and abandoned
1984   moves to new workshop in Lyme Regis, Dorset; makes only individual pieces, organic in inspiration, mostly handbuilt

Alan Wallwork has had a long interest in handbuilt work which he carried on alongside his more commercial activities. This large rugged jar was made at about the same time as potters like Ruth Duckworth (qv) and Louis Hanssen (qv) were making similar handbuilt forms.

Alan Wallwork, 'Workshop', *CR*, 8/1981
—'A Potter's Day', *CR*, 115/1989
London, CPA (1989)

659 Vase, 1965
Stoneware, handbuilt, oval in section, with mottled blue-brown glaze; marks: 'W', roughly incised; h. 43.7 cm, d. 31.7 cm
Circ.353–1965. Source: the potter (from a Design Centre exhibition *Hand and Machine*), £14.70

658

657 656

659

Walton, Sarah 1945–

1945   born in London
1960–64   studies painting at Chelsea School of Art
1965–71   trains and works as a nurse
1971–73   studies pottery at Harrow School of Art
1973–74   works for the potter Zelda Mowat
1975–   sets up own workshop at Selmeston in Sussex

Sarah Walton produces an unusual richness and depth of colour from saltglaze on satisfyingly solid and well-based forms. She has recently made bird-baths and large fish as garden sculptures.

Sarah Walton, 'Salt Glaze', *Crafts*, November/December, 1976
—'Nursing the Kiln', *Crafts*, January/February, 1979
—'Salt Glaze', *CR*, 104/1987
'CPA New Members', *CR*, 50/1978
'Profile', *Ceramics Monthly*, November, 1983
Ceramic Series, no. 14, Aberystwyth Arts Centre, 1986

660   Tea caddy, 1981 (pl. 114)
Stoneware, grey body with saltglaze over incised decoration; marks: 'SW', impressed; h. 17.7 cm, d. 18.3 cm
C.180&a–1981. Source: CPA, London, £40

661   Jug, 1988
Stoneware, with a pinky-brown saltglaze outside, green-grey interior; marks: 'SW' in monogram, impressed; h. 22.6 cm, d. 16.7 cm
C.6–1989. Source: CAA, London, £75.25

662   Dish with handles, 1988
Stoneware, saltglaze with pink flushes outside, pink glaze inside; marks: 'SW' in monogram, impressed; h. 9 cm, d. 29.7 cm
C.9–1989. Source: CAA, London, £76

Ward, John 1938–

1938   born in London
1965–66   studies ceramics part time at East Ham Technical College, London
1966–70   trains at Camberwell School of Art, London
1970–79   teaches part time in various Institutes, and has various other jobs including TV cameraman
1971–76   first workshop in South East London
1976–79   moves workshop to Charlton, London
1979–   new workshop near Newport, Dyfed, Wales

Ward has gained a devoted following for his quiet pots which depend on their sensitive shapes and subdued surfaces and decoration for their impact.

'CPA New Members', *CR*, 65/1980
Stephen Brayne, 'The Pottery of John Ward', *CR*, 96/1985
David Sexton, 'John Ward', *Daily Telegraph Colour Magazine*, 25 March, 1989
A large private collection of pieces by John Ward were sold at auction at Bonham's, London, on 27 February, 1989, lots 110–137 (illustrated catalogue)

663   Vase, 1985
Stoneware, green painted lines in a matt white glaze; marks: 'JW' in monogram, impressed; h. 20.3 cm, d. 21.3 cm
C.25–1986. Source: Henry Rothschild Associates, Cambridge (from the exhibition *European Ceramics and Wall Textiles*, Fitzwilliam Museum, Cambridge), £120

Washington, R. J. 1913–

1930–33   studies painting at Goldsmith's College, London
1933–36   painting at Royal College of Art, London
1936–37   art teachers diploma at Goldsmith's and Royal College of Art
1937–38   pottery at Royal College of Art under William Staite Murray (qv), attending evening classes at the Central School of Art with Dora Billington (qv)
1938–46   teaches painting and pottery at Derby School of Art; work interrupted by war
1940–45   war service in the RAF
1946–48   appointed Deputy-principal, Margate School of Art
1948–49   appointed Principal, Dewsbury School of Art
1949–74   works as Inspector for Art Education, Essex Education Committee
1954–79   sporadically returns to potting in a studio at his home in Little Badow, Essex
1979   retires, resumes potting full time

Most of Washington's earlier work consisted of tall vases in stoneware with brushed decoration. In the post-war period these forms develop into a distinct profile of the female torso or figure, though some large bowls are also produced. His most recent work in the 1980s has consisted of stoneware and mixed media wall-hung plaques decorated with themes inspired by the elements, and more recently of large panels where clay is treated in painterly techniques in a fine-art manner.

Washington was little seen since his pre-war exhibitions at the Brygos Gallery until he started to exhibit work again in the 1980s.

Wingfield Digby (1952; pp. 77–8, pl. 45)
London, Hayward Gallery (1979)

662 661

663

664 Vase, 1938 (pl. 35)
Stoneware, painting in dark brown iron-oxide in a grey-brown glaze; marks: 'RJW', impressed; h. 50.7 cm, d. 16.5 cm
Circ.96–1939. Source: Brygos Gallery, London, £7.35
Tripod marks on the wall of this and the following vase indicate that they were fired on their sides.

665 Vase, 1938 (pl. 35)
Stoneware, mottled yellow and brown glaze; marks: 'RJW', impressed; h. 58.8 cm, d. 17.2 cm
Circ.97–1939. Source: Brygos Gallery, London, £5.25

666 Vase, 1964
Stoneware, painting in brown in a cream glaze; marks: 'RJW' and '64', incised; h. 79.8 cm, d. 14 cm
C.49–1979. Source: given by the potter

667 Vase: *Uranus*, c.1965
Stoneware, painting in brown in a cream glaze; h. 70.6 cm, d. 16 cm
C.48–1979. Source: given by the potter
The colour comes from the use of uranium oxide, which gives the pot its name.

668 Vase: *Satyr and Pryad*, from the series *Satyrnalia*, 1981
Stoneware, painting in brown in a cream glaze; marks: 'RJW 81', incised; h. 49.1 cm, d. 21.1 cm
C.32–1985. Source: the potter, £350
The pot comes from a small series entitled *Satyrnalia*. The profile of the pot is intended to evoke the outline of a woman's torso.

Welch, Robin 1936–

1936	born Nuneaton, Warwickshire
1952–53	Nuneaton School of Art
1953–59	Penzance College of Art, works part time at Leach Pottery, St Ives
1959–60	Central School of Art, London
1960	sets up pottery in London
1962–65	three years in Australia
1965	returns to UK, sets up pottery in Stradbroke, Suffolk
1968–	develops standard ware using jolleying and press-moulding techniques
1980	teaching tour to Australia, where landscape inspires new work
1980–	makes individual ware in raku

Welch first made his name with a series of domestic tableware based on simple cylindrical shapes and produced by 'jigger and jolleying', and other industrial means, and with colourful matt glazes in varied browns, yellows, greens and blues. Individual pieces in this general style were also produced. After a trip to tropical Australia, much looser individual forms were made with organic encrusted surfaces (catalogue nos. 671–2).

Birks (1967), (1976)
Exhibition review, CR, 36/1975
Peter Lane, 'Robin Welch', CR, 69/1981

669 Dish, 1962
Stoneware, blue, yellow and brown matt glazes; marks: 'Robin Welch', painted; h. 6.5 cm, d. 33.6 cm
Circ.648–1962. Source: Crafts Centre of Great Britain, London, £4.75

666 668 667

669

670 Sculpture: *Cylinder with Split Centre*, 1968
Stoneware, white, black and brown mottled matt
glazes and blue acrylic paint; marks: 'Robin
Welch/1968', painted; h. 63 cm, d. 12.7 cm
Circ.529–1969. Source: Crafts Centre of Great
Britain, London (solo exhibition entitled *Robin
Welch – Sculpture*), £25

671 Bowl, 1983
Stoneware, raku fired with low-temperature
coloured glazes; marks: 'ROBIN WELCH',
impressed; h. 17 cm, d. 22.5 cm
C.329–1983. Source: JK Hill & Co., London (solo
exhibition, 1983), £79

672 Pod pot, 1983
Stoneware, raku fired with low-temperature
coloured glazes; marks: 'ROBIN WELCH',
impressed; h. 11.7 cm, d. 9 cm
C.330–1983. Source: *see* C.329–1983, £38

Wells, Reginald 1877–1951

1890s	trains as sculptor at Royal College of Art, London; brief flirtation with the designing of aircraft; studies ceramics later at Camberwell School of Art under W. B. Dalton (qv) and Richard Lunn
*c.*1900	sets up pottery producing slip earthenwares at Coldrum, near Wrotham, Kent
1909–14	sets up Coldrum Pottery in Keppel Street, Chelsea, London
1914–18	workshop discontinued for period of war – Wells Aviation Company established on the same site
1919–24	pottery resumed at Kings Road, Chelsea, London, called the London Pottery Co., and making 'SOON' ware
1923	first exhibition held with William Staite Murray at Gièves Gallery, London
1925–51	moves to Storrington, Sussex, continues to make 'SOON' ware

Reginald Wells is the earliest potter in this catalogue.
He lays claim to be the first 'studio potter' in that his
interests lay exactly in those areas which were to
preoccupy studio potters in later decades – English
slipware, and Chinese stonewares. Wells' work has a
somewhat amateur and experimental look compared
to that of Leach, Cardew and Staite Murray who were
to follow in his path.

The Museum's register entry for the pieces
accessioned in 1919 reads: 'Mr Reginald F. Wells, the
maker of this and the ten following pieces, informed
Mr Rackham verbally that he was formerly a student
at the Royal College of Art and that he owed most of
his ideas as to pottery to the study of the exhibits,
specially early Chinese, in the Victoria and Albert
Museum. He set up his first kilns at Coldrum Farm,
near Wrotham, Kent, employing the same bed of clay
as the 17th century Wrotham potters. Afterwards he
moved to what he named the "Coldrum Pottery",
Keppel Street (later Draycott Avenue), Chelsea; the
factory was discontinued in 1914, when Mr Wells
established the Wells Aviation Company with works
on the same site.'

According to Marsh (1925), Wells' wares up to 1914
were known as 'Coldrum Wares'. They were attractive
pots with delicately coloured glazes and many were
fairly large in size. The SOON wares of the post-1919
period were made with new mixtures of clays, new
glazes and working more along the lines of the 'Chinese
traditions'. However, the name of the ware, SOON, '. . .
had no intention of suggesting the old "Sung" wares
of China, but . . . arose from a purely personal and
sentimental incident quite apart from this'. We are not
told what the sentimental incident was.

670

672 671

The Studio Yearbook of Decorative Art, 1913, 1927 and
1928

Ernest Marsh, 'R. F. Wells – Sculptor and Potter', *Apollo*,
1925

Bernard Rackham, 'The Pottery of Mr. Reginald Wells',
The Studio, 90/1925

Rose (1955), (1970)

Blunt (1973)

London, Christopher Wood Gallery (1980)

673 Bowl, 1909
Earthenware, green-brown glaze, decorated with
white slip and applied relief; marks: 'R.F.W',
incised and 'COLDRUM 1909', painted in white
slip; made at Coldrum Pottery, Wrotham, Kent;
h. 7.3 cm, d. 14.9 cm
C.952–1917. Source: given by Herman Hert
The clay contains chalky particles that have caused
the glaze to spall. The glaze is very uneven, rough
and missing in parts. This suggests that the piece
was made in Kent at Wells' country pottery rather
than at Chelsea.

674 Handled pot, *c.*1909
Earthenware, slip decoration under a muddy green
glaze; marks: 'COLDRUM', painted in slip; made
at Coldrum Pottery, Wrotham, Kent; h. 12.7 cm,
d. 17.5 cm
C.743–1923. Source: given by W. Ridout
The technical roughness suggest that this piece
was also made in Kent.

675 Jug, 1909
Earthenware, slip decoration on a red clay under
a transparent glaze; marks: 'COLDRUM
CHELSEA 1909', painted in slip; made at Coldrum
Pottery, Chelsea, London; h. 20.9 cm, d. 24 cm
C.82–1981. Source: Christopher Wood Gallery,
London, £250
This must have been an early work at Wells' new
pottery in Chelsea. The clay is smooth and well
prepared and the glaze is uniform, shiny and well
fired. This contrasts with the previous two pieces
which were probably made at his country pottery
in Kent.

676 Jar with three handles, 1910–1914
Stoneware, greenish glaze with brown flecks;
made at Coldrum Pottery, Chelsea, London;
h. 23.3 cm, d. 15.6 cm
C.521–1919. Source: given by Victor Ames,
Norfolk
Paper label on pot gives price as 15/6d (= £0.77).

677 Jar with three handles, 1910–1914
Earthenware, transparent glaze with green streaks
over a red body; made at Coldrum Pottery,
Chelsea, London; h. 29.4 cm, d. 18.8 cm
C.530–1919. Source: given by Victor Ames,
Norfolk

678 Vase, *c.*1910–1914
Earthenware, green mottled glaze with brown
streaks; made at Coldrum Pottery, Chelsea,
London; h. 13.9 cm, d. 13.5 cm
Circ.515–1919. Source: given by Victor Ames,
Norfolk

679 Vase, *c.*1910–1914
Earthenware, greenish glaze with brown mottling;
marks: 'COLDRUM', impressed; h. 29.9 cm,
d. 19.2 cm
Circ.517–1919. Source: given by Victor Ames,
Norfolk

673 674

675

679 676 678 677

680 Jug, 1910–1914
Stoneware, mottled brown and green glaze; made at Coldrum Pottery, Chelsea, London; h. 19.7 cm, d. 14 cm
C.522–1919. Source: given by Victor Ames, Norfolk

681 Vase, *c.*1910–1914
Stoneware, shiny black glaze; marks: 'COLDRUM', impressed; made at Coldrum Pottery, Chelsea, London; h. 32.2 cm, d. 26 cm
Circ.908–1967. Source: given by Miss Prunella Clough

682 Vase, *c.*1920
High-fired earthenware, pale opaque green glaze; marks: 'SOON', incised; h. 24.2 cm, d. 18.9 cm
Circ.11–1927. Source: given by A. E. Anderson

683 Jar, 1910–1914
Stoneware, finely mottled grey glaze; marks: 'COLDRUM', impressed; made at Coldrum Pottery, Chelsea, London; h. 28 cm, d. 24.4 cm
C.531–1919. Source: given by Victor Ames, Norfolk

684 Jar, 1910–1914
Stoneware, finely mottled grey and black glaze; made at Coldrum Pottery, Chelsea, London; h. 10.6 cm, d. 12.7 cm
C.523–1919. Source: given by Victor Ames, Norfolk
The price 6/6d (= £0.32) is written in ink on the base.

685 Jar, 1910–1914
Stoneware, finely mottled greenish-grey and black glaze; made at Coldrum Pottery, Chelsea, London; h. 18.7 cm, d. 14.6 cm
C.526–1919. Source: given by Victor Ames, Norfolk

686 Jar, 1910–1914
Stoneware, pale-blue streaked glaze; made at Coldrum Pottery, Chelsea, London; h. 14.4 cm, d. 10.3 cm
C.525–1919. Source: given by Victor Ames, Norfolk

687 Vase, 1910–1914 (pl. 6)
Stoneware, lavender blue glaze with red mottling; made at Coldrum Pottery, Chelsea, London; h. 19.7 cm, d. 14.4 cm
C.527–1919. Source: given by Victor Ames, Norfolk

688 Vase, 1910–1914 (pl. 6)
Stoneware, plum-red glaze with blue streaks; made at Coldrum Pottery, Chelsea, London; h. 18.9 cm, d. 14.3 cm
C.524–1919. Source: given by Victor Ames, Norfolk

689 Vase, *c.*1910–1914 (pl. 6)
High-fired earthenware, opacified glaze with blue and red mottling; marks: 'COLDRUM', impressed; h. 20 cm, d. 15.1 cm
Circ.516–1919. Source: given by Victor Ames, Norfolk

690 Vase, *c.*1925
Stoneware, white glaze with crackle and green speckles; marks: 'SOON', incised; made at Storrington; h. 26.8 cm, d. 19.5 cm
C.791–1925. Source: given by A. E. Anderson through the NACF

691 Vase, *c.*1925
Stoneware, opaque yellow-green glaze; marks: 'SOON', incised; made at Storrington; h. 20.8 cm, d. 17.3 cm
C.790–1925. Source: given by A. E. Anderson through the NACF

692 Vase, *c.*1925
Earthenware, grey-cream crackled glaze; marks: 'SOON', incised; h. 22.5 cm, d. 17.3 cm
C.339–1926. Source: given by A. E. Anderson

693 Vase, 1910–1914
Stoneware, pale grey-white glaze with turquoise flecks; marks: 'COLDRUM CHELSEA', impressed; made at Coldrum Pottery, Chelsea, London; h. 31 cm, d. 16.9 cm
C.529–1919. Source: given by Victor Ames, Norfolk

680

682

681

683

685 684 686

694 Vase, 1910–1914
Stoneware, crackled white glaze; marks:
'COLDRUM', impressed; made at Coldrum
Pottery, Chelsea, London; h. 19.4 cm, d. 16 cm
C.528–1919. Source: given by Victor Ames,
Norfolk

695 Vase, *c.*1910–1914
Stoneware, opaque white glaze with black crackle;
marks: 'COLDRUM CHELSEA', impressed; made
at Coldrum Pottery, Chelsea, London; h. 20.3 cm,
d. 22.1 cm
Circ.907–1967. Source: given by Miss Prunella
Clough

696 Vase, *c.*1910–1914
Stoneware, streaky blue glaze; h. 7.1 cm,
d. 7.6 cm
C.12–1924. Source: given by Victor Ames,
Norfolk

697 Bowl, *c.*1925
Stoneware, blue mottled glaze; marks: 'SOON',
incised; h. 7 cm, d. 21.5 cm
Circ.274–1955. Source: given by Lady Russel,
MBE, from the collection of the late Francis
Moore

690 691 692

695 694 693

697 696

265

698 Bowl, *c.*1925 (pl. 21)
Stoneware, opaque white glaze; marks: 'SOON', incised; h. 6 cm, d. 9.3 cm
Circ.513–1925. Source: given by Bernard Rackham
The bowl originally had a carved wooden stand.

699 Vase, *c.*1924 (pl. 21)
Stoneware, opaque white glaze with crackle; marks: 'S', incised; h. 15 cm, d. 10 cm
C.60–1925. Source: given by Sir Amhurst Selby-Bigge, Ernest Marsh and Bernard Rackham (purchased by the donors for £7.82)
This piece is described by Marsh in 1925 as follows: 'The horizontal ribbings running well down over the shoulder of the vase give the necessary distinction to a simple shape, and the glaze, with its delicate crackle, completes a very perfect little vase.'

700 Vase, 1928
Stoneware, white glaze mottled with black; marks: 'SOON', cut in relief; h. 20.9 cm, d. 13.4 cm
Circ.108–1959. Source: given by Wing-Commander H. D. Wells
This piece was lent to the BIIA (then housed in the V&A) in 1928. It was given to the Museum after Wells' death by his son.

701 Vase, 1928
Stoneware, copper-red mottled glaze; marks: 'SOON', cut in relief; h. 20.4 cm, d. 15.5 cm
Circ.109–1959. Source: *see* Circ.108–1959

702 Vase, *c.*1924
Stoneware, 'chun' glaze with purple mottling; marks: 'SOON', cut; h. 7.7 cm, d. 7.8 cm
Circ.991–1924. Source: given by W. Winkworth

703 Vase (with wooden stand), *c.*1925
Stoneware, grey glaze mottled with black; marks: 'SOON', incised; h. 26.8 cm, d. 17.7 cm
Circ.273&a–1955. Source: given by Lady Russel, MBE, from the collection of the late Francis Moore

704 Figure: *Runner Duck, c.*1923
Stoneware, hand-modelled, blue, yellow and green in a transparent glaze; h. 18.9 cm, d. 12 cm
Circ.438–1934. Source: given by the BIIA (gift of the potter in 1923)
This was shown as part of the British Section at the International Exhibition in Paris in 1925.

705 Figure: *Mother and Child,* 1924
Stoneware, brownish glaze; h. 39.5 cm, d. 16.5 cm
Circ.272–1955. Source: given by Lady Russel, MBE, from the collection of the late Francis Moore

706 Figure of a horse, 1926
Stoneware, hand-modelled, with a mottled blue-grey glaze; marks: 'SOON' (twice) and 'R. F. Wells', incised; h. 29.6 cm, d. 35.8 cm
Circ.10–1927. Source: given by R. Mond
This piece originally came with a wooden stand.

703

705

701 702 700

704

706

White, Mary 1926–

1926	born in Monmouthshire, Wales
1948	studies design at Hammersmith College of Art, London
1949	studies at Newport College of Art
1950	takes Art Teachers Diploma at Goldsmith's College of Art, London
1950–62	teaches in schools and art schools
1962–73	moves to Canada with her husband who is appointed Head of Art at Atlantic College, St Donats; builds up graphic design department, and initiates ceramic workshop
1973	return to UK, sets up workshop in Wales
1975–80	new workshop in Malmesbury, Wilts.
1980–	leaves for West Germany, sets up studio in Wonsheim

While Mary White's earlier work often includes calligraphic decoration, her latest work, mostly in porcelain, consists either of small sculptures or of organic vessel forms using land, sea and sky as inspiration.

Mary White, 'A Potter in Paradiesgarten', *CR*, 84/1983
'CPA New Members', *CR*, 30/1974
Keramik Creativ, 4/1981, 4/1982, 1/1983, 1/1986, 1/1988
Kunst und Handwerk, 5/1983
Keramik Magazin, 1/1985
Neue Keramik, 6/1988

707 Bottle, 1977
Porcelain, blue grey and cream glazes with an inscription in silver lustre; h. 16 cm, d. 18.4 cm
C.181–1977. Source: given by the potter
Presented by the potter after being exhibited in the Jubilee exhibition at the V&A in 1977; chosen by Lady Casson.

Whiting, Geoffrey 1919–1988

1930s	trains as an architect at Birmingham School of Architecture
1939–48	army service in India, encounters village potters
1949	teaches himself pottery with help from Herbert Read; sets up workshop in Worcestershire at Avoncroft where attached to Adult Education college
1954	moves workshop to Hampton Lovett, Worcs.
1971	trip to Lesotho
1972	workshop in Canterbury, teaching at Kings School, Canterbury; lecturing at the Medway College of Art and Design

Whiting is very much a potters' potter. His work is quiet and restrained, and in style is in the best Leach tradition of oriental stonewares. He was particularly noted for his teapots.

Geoffrey Whiting, 'Making Teapots', *PQ*, 2/7, 1955
—'Avoncroft Pottery', *PQ*, 5/1958
—'Quality in Glazes', *PQ*, 10/37, 1971–73
—'Workshops and the Future of Potting', *CR*, 15/1972
—'Quo Vadis?', *CR*, 84/1983
—'Showman Potter', *CR*, 106/1987
Rose (1955), (1970)
Casson (1967)
W.A. Ismay, 'Geoffrey Whiting – Potter', *CR*, 100/1986
Exhibition reviews: *CR*, 29/1974, 59/1979
Obituary: *CR*, 110/1988
Geoffrey Whiting, Potter, exhibition catalogue, Aberystwyth Arts Centre, 1989
David Whiting, 'Geoffrey Whiting—a Personal View', *CR*, 120/1989

708 Vase, 1973
Stoneware, deep blue glaze with poured brown glaze decoration; marks: 'GW' in monogram and 'A' in a circle, impressed; h. 17.5 cm, d. 14 cm
C.284–1987. Source: given by the potter

709 Vase, 1959
Stoneware, grey and brown mottled glaze; marks: 'A' in a circle and 'GW' in monogram, impressed; h. 23 cm, d. 17.8 cm
Circ.327–1959. Source: the potter, £4

710 Teapot, 1959
Stoneware, tenmoku glaze; marks: 'A' in a circle and 'GW' in monogram, impressed; h. 12.1 cm, d. 20.3 cm
Circ.328&a-1959. Source: the potter, £2.10

711 Bottle, 1987
Stoneware, thrown, cut and squared, with grey and brown glazes; marks: 'A' and 'G' in circles, impressed; h. 21.5 cm, d. 13.5 cm
C.16–1988. Source: CPA, London (exhibition: *The Leach Tradition, a Creative Force*, 1985), £85.50

710

707

709 708

711

Whittall, Eleanor 1900–?

Eleanor Whittall is recorded as having trained at the
Central School of Art, London, in the 1940s. She
worked in London from 1944 onwards, first at a studio
in North London, later in Kensington. She made
stonewares, and after 1958 porcelains, and was
interested in glazes, mostly brightly coloured and ash-
fluxed. It is said that she gave up potting when the
change to North Sea gas in the 1960s prevented her
reducing in her accustomed way. She is illustrated in
The Studio Yearbook of Decorative Art regularly from
1950 to 1957 and again in 1963. Her mark consists of
an impressed owl, originally made up of the initials
'EEW'.

Eleanor Whittall, 'Vegetable Ash Glazes', *PQ*, 2/1954
Exhibition review, *PQ*, 1/1954
Godden (1964), (1988)

712 Bowl, 1956
Stoneware, pale blue glaze; h. 10.3 cm, d. 25 cm
Circ.108–1957. Source: the potter, £15.75

Wolstencroft, Barbara *see* Barbara **Cass**

Wren, Denise 1891–1979

1891	born in Western Australia (née Tuckfield)
1899	leaves with family for England
1900	family settles in East Molesey, Surrey
1907–12	Kingston-upon-Thames School of Art under Archibald Knox, takes up pottery
1911	learns to throw pots by watching a Mr Mercer, flower-pot maker of Norbiton Potteries
1912	following Knox's resignation, helps set up Knox Guild of Design and Craft; buys kick wheel from Mr Mercer
1915	marries Henry Wren
1920	buys plot in Oxshott, Surrey; attends pottery evening class at Camberwell School of Art under Henry Hopkins; builds house and workshop in Oxshott, installs American Drakenfield gas-fired muffle kiln
1920–39	makes earthenware decorated with slips and glazes: 'pots for flowers'
1922	daughter Rosemary (qv) born
1922–50	two-week summer courses taught at Oxshott
1924–26	teaches evening classes at Teddington School of Art
1925–68	designs and builds coke-fired kilns and offers design for sale to studio potters
1932–38	teaches at Weybridge Hall School

c.1937	rebuilds and extends workshops
1937	starts to design textiles
1941	ceases potting temporarily; gardening schemes for war effort
1945	entered in National Register of Industrial Art Designers as textile designer
1946	resumes pottery
1947	Henry Wren dies; Rosemary takes over his workshop; first power wheel
1950	first saltglaze firing for Rosemary's Diploma show; Rosemary joins pottery full-time
1953	Francine Delpierre and Albert Diato work briefly at Oxshott; Denise makes her first elephant
1954	the coke kiln is converted to gas
1954–68	makes glazed pottery 'stones' for mounting in pewter
1958–59	designs and builds larger coke-fired kiln for saltglazing; involved in setting up of CPA
1959–67	saltglazed stoneware produced
1968	unavailability of suitable coke leads to abandoning of saltglazing
1969–75	makes raku-fired elephants
1979	dies in Devon

(Most information taken from *The Oxshott Pottery*, Bath
Craft Study Centre, 1984.)

Denise and Henry Wren, *Oxshott Handmade Pottery*
(exhibited at the Central Hall, Westminster, May),
London, 1924
—*Handcraft Pottery, for Workshop and School*, London,
1928
—*Pottery, the finger-built methods*, London, 1932

Denise and Rosemary Wren, *Pottery Making*, London,
1952
Rose (1955), (1970)
Casson (1967)
'Coke and Pottery', *Gas Coke News*, October, 1959
Rosemary Wren, 'Denise K. Wren, Sixty-one Years a
Potter', *CR*, 15/1972
Obituary: *CR*, 59/1979
London, Christopher Wood Gallery (1980)
Margot Coatts, 'Denise and Henry Wren – Pioneer
Potters', *CR*, 87/1984
The Oxshott Pottery, Bath Craft Study Centre, Bath, 1984
(with detailed biography and bibliography)

Not catalogued here are a sherd of a tobacco jar dated
1921 (C.54–1981) and a plant-pot by Henry Wren of
about 1938 (C.133–1985).

713 Vase, 1913
Earthenware, handbuilt, decoration cut through a
dark slip to a white body, amber glaze; marks:
'DKT 1913' incised; made at Knox Guild of Design
and Crafts, Kingston; h. 11.3 cm, d. 9.5 cm
C.102–1980. Source: Rosemary Wren, £500
The design is the view from a window of the
potter's family home by Molesey Lock on the
Thames. It shows her younger brother Charlie
fishing.

714 Dish, 1927
Stoneware, white slip trailed on a red body,
unglazed; marks: 'D. K. WREN OXSHOTT 1927',
incised; made at Oxshott Pottery, Surrey; h. 7 cm,
d. 30 cm
C.49–1981. Source: Rosemary Wren, £200
See Wren (1932, p. 23) and (1928) where a similar
dish is being decorated.

712

713

714

715 Jar and cover, *c.*1930
Stoneware, handbuilt, mottled blue glaze; marks: 'OXSHOTT', incised; made at Oxshott Pottery, Surrey; h. 15.5 cm, d. 14.7 cm
C.50&a–1981. Source: Rosemary Wren, £500

716 Dish, *c.*1930
Stoneware, painted decoration in blue, brown, red and purple; marks: 'DENISE WREN' and 'M:M:', painted and 'OXSHOTT', incised; made at Oxshott Pottery, Surrey; h. 7 cm, d. 26.7 cm
C.48–1981. Source: Rosemary Wren, £250

717 Vase, *c.*1930–1935 (pl. 39)
Earthenware, handbuilt, from moulded slabs, blue-green glaze; marks: 'Denise K. Wren Oxshott', incised; made at Oxshott Pottery; h. 33.2 cm, d. 21 cm
C.51–1981. Source: Rosemary Wren, £350

718 Dish, *Ikebana pot*, *c.*1960
Stoneware, mottled green and brown saltglaze; marks: 'DKW Oxshott', incised; made at Oxshott Pottery; h. 7.5 cm, d. 19.4 cm
C.53–1981. Source: Rosemary Wren, £150
A paper label bears the price '£10'.

719 Vase, *c.*1913
Stoneware, incised decoration through a greenish transparent glaze; marks: 'DKW Oxshott' incised; made at Oxshott Pottery; h. 13.7 cm, d. 6 cm
C.52–1981. Source: Rosemary Wren, £45

720 Jar, 1967
Stoneware, grey saltglazed, mottled brown; marks: 'DKW Oxshott', incised; made at Oxshott Pottery; h. 25.4 cm, d. 12.3 cm
Circ.1221–1967. Source: Commonwealth Institute Art Gallery (exhibition of 'batiks and ceramics', 1967), £5

721 Elephant, 1971
Stoneware, unglazed, raku fired; made at Oxshott Pottery; h. 25.5 cm, d. 29.8 cm
Circ.238–1971. Source: Briglin Studio, London, £32

715

718

720

716

719

721

Wren, Rosemary 1922–

1922	born, daughter of Henry and Denise Wren (qv), at Oxshott, Surrey
1941–45	joins Women's Land Army, working with animals
1945–47	attends Guildford School of Art studying sculpture and ceramics under Helen Pincombe (qv)
1947–50	studies ceramics at Royal College of Art ('industrially orientated and ceramically unhelpful'); takes over her father's workshop in Oxshott
1950	sets up own workshop in Oxshott
1954	major influence from the French potter, Francine Delpierre, and the Algerian, Albert Diato, starts to make animals using their handbuilding techniques
1956	founder member of CPA
1970	begins partnership with Peter Crotty
1979	moves workshop to Hittisleigh, Devon
1983	moves workshop to Lustleigh, Devon, Peter Crotty now responsible for infilling of glaze decoration
1989	moves workshop to Strathpeffer, Ross-shire, Scotland

Rosemary Wren, *see* Denise and Rosemary **Wren**
'Why Raku?', *CR*, 1/1970
—'Potters' Aches and Pains' (with Peter Crotty), *CR*, 93/1985
—'All Creatures Great and Small', *CR*, 98/1986
The Studio Yearbook of Decorative Art, 1951, 1955, 1957, 1959, 1961, 1963, 1966 and 1967
Exhibition review, *CR*, 22/1973
'Rosemary Wren – Animals and Birds', *CR*, 67/1981

722 Vase, 1957
Stoneware, grey-green glaze with resist decoration; made at Oxshott Pottery; h. 32.6 cm, d. 17.5 cm
Circ.126–1957. Source: Heal and Son Ltd., London, £15.75

723 Figure of a hen, 1957
Stoneware, hand modelled with brown and black painting; made at Oxshott Pottery; h. 21.7 cm, d. 21.3 cm
Circ.127–1957. Source: *see* Circ.126–1957, £3.57

722

724 Figure of a nanny goat, 1969
Stoneware, hand-modelled with orange and white glazes, raku fired; marks: a wren in a square, impressed and 'OXSHOTT', incised; made at Oxshott Pottery; h. 24.7 cm, d. 20 cm
Circ.754–1969. Source: Briglin Studio, London, £8

725 Pigeon, 1980
Stoneware, hand-modelled with coloured glazes; marks: a wren in a square, impressed; made at the Oxshott Pottery; h. 21.2 cm, d. 29.4 cm
C.191–1980. Source: Casson Gallery, London, £49

723

724

725

Wyne Reeves, Ann 1929–

1929	born in London
1948–51	Willesden School of Art, London
1951–54	Central School of Art, London
1954	married, and began working with, Kenneth Clark, potter and designer
1954–80	various workshops (Kenneth Clark Pottery) in London producing tiles, murals and individual pieces
1980–	moves to new workshop (Kenneth Clark Ceramics) in Lewes, Sussex, continues work

Ann Wyne Reeves in the 1950s made vessels in a thoroughly contemporary style, and in the 'contemporary' technique – tin-glazed earthenware; in this she forms part of a group with Newland (qv), Hine (qv), Vergette (qv) and Tower (qv). Her later work consisted of decoration and designs for tilework.

The Studio Yearbook of Decorative Art, 1954, 1959 and 1961
Exhibition reviews, *PQ*, 3/1954, 2/8 1955
Casson (1967)

The Museum has a large group of tiles from the Kenneth Clark Pottery, including designs by Wyne Reeves, which are not catalogued here.

726

727

726 Dish on three legs, 1958
Earthenware, press-moulded, with incised
decoration and painting in green, turquoise and
black; marks: paper label: 'HANDMADE &
DECORATED/By ANN WYNE REEVES'; made
at the Kenneth Clark Pottery, London; h. 8.8 cm,
d. 36.5 cm
Circ.279–1958. Source: the pottery, £7.50

727 Bowl, 1957
Earthenware, incised decoration and painting in
green on a dark mottled glaze; made at Kenneth
Clark Pottery, London; h. 7.7 cm, d. 13.3 cm
Circ.280–1958. Source: the potter, £2

Yasuda, Takeshi 1943–

1946   born in Tokyo, Japan
1963–66 apprenticed at the Daisei Pottery, Mashiko,
        Japan
1966–73 established own workshop in Mashiko, Japan
1973   moves to UK
1973–75 workshop at Monk Sherbourne, Hants.,
        shared with Sandy Brown (qv)
1975–   new workshop near South Molton, Devon,
        shared with Sandy Brown
1977   marries Sandy Brown
1978   appointed Craftsman in Residence,
        Bergenskunsthandverksskole, Bergen,
        Norway
1978–85 teaches at West Surrey College of Art and
        Design, Farnham

1982   Research Fellow at the South Glamorgan
        Institute of Higher Education, Wales
1984–86 appointed to the Cleveland Ceramic
        Residency, Middlesborough
1984–86 teaches at Camberwell College of Art
1987   solo touring exhibition, Cleveland Crafts
        Centre, Middlesborough

Takeshi, Japanese born and trained, has settled in the
UK. His work is powerfully thrown and decorated;
particularly impressive is the way he manages to retain
the plastic qualities of soft clay in the finished pot. He
has developed a series of strong functional forms
decorated with splashed colours inspired by Chinese
T'ang ware. He has introduced to the British scene an
authentic Japanese approach to the handling of clay
and decoration.

Sandy Brown, 'The Sensuous Pots of Takeshi Yasuda',
 CR, 93/1985
'Japanese Treasure', *Crafts*, September/October, 1985
Takeshi Yasuda Ceramics, exhibition pamphlet,
 Cleveland Crafts Centre, 1987
'Takeshi Yasuda Ceramics', exhibition review, CR,
 87/1987

728 Dish, 1984
Stoneware, celadon glaze with white splashes;
h. 10 cm, d. 60 cm
C.228–1985. Source: BCC, London, £337.50
This piece was made at the Devon Pottery shortly
before Yasuda went as potter-in-residence to
Cleveland.

Young, Andrew and Joanna
Andrew 1949–; Joanna 1950–

1970–73 train at West Surrey College of Art and
        Design, Farnham, where they meet
1973–74 six months' work with Gwyn Hanssen (qv)
        in France
1974   training at Goldsmith's College
1975   take over and develop a workshop in North
        Norfolk
1981–   new workshop at Gresham, Norfolk
1988   design a range of ware produced in Stoke-
        on-Trent for Next Interiors

Andrew and Joanna Young are known for their range
of elegant, but eminently practical domestic wares. The
designs are characteristic in their precise and sharp-
edged forms turned and worked after throwing, but
softened by a thin but rich glaze. These wares were
adopted, amongst others, by David Mellor for his chain
of shops, in which they remain a best seller.

'CPA New Members', CR, 51/1978
Stephen Brayne, 'Andrew and Joanna Young – Country
 Potters', CR, 104/1987
Ceramic Series, no. 24, Aberystwyth Arts Centre

729 Jug, 1981
Stoneware, incised decoration and green glazed
interior; marks: 'A & J YOUNG 1981', impressed;
h. 24.9 cm, d. 16.7 cm
C.179–1981. Source: CPA, London, £20

728

729

730 Bowl, 1982
Stoneware, interior with pale orange glaze; marks:
'A & J YOUNG', impressed; h. 11.6 cm,
d. 21.6 cm
C.81–1984. Source: given by the Friends of the
V&A
Purchased at the CPA 25th Anniversary
exhibition, *Studio Ceramics Today*, held at the
V&A in 1983.

731 Lemon squeezer, 1988
Stoneware, thin brown glaze; marks: 'A & J
YOUNG GRESHAM', impressed; h. 7.5 cm,
d. 13.6 cm
C.17&a–1989. Source: David Mellor, Kitchen
Shop, London, £12.96

732 Tureen, cover and ladle, 1988
Stoneware, incised decoration and ash flashings,
interior glazed; marks: 'A & J YOUNG
GRESHAM', impressed; h. 18.2 cm, d. 28.3 cm
C.19 to b-1989. Source: David Mellor, Kitchen
Shop, London, £24.11

730

731 732

ARTISTS

Bell, Quentin 1910–

Quentin Bell, Vanessa Bell's son, spent most of his career teaching art history, finishing as Professor of Art Theory at University of Sussex. He is probably best known as the biographer of his aunt Virginia Woolf. He had originally learnt pottery before the war to provide the wares for Vanessa Bell and Duncan Grant to decorate. These had been made in the 1930s by Phyllis Keyes, a skilful mould-maker and slip-caster. In her London workshop she would take casts from Italian and Spanish peasant pottery brought to her by Bell and Grant. However, they found her a woman of strong opinions, not always the easiest to work with, and they encouraged Quentin Bell to learn pottery in order to have a more 'domesticated' potter at hand. He had been a painter and sculptor sporadically for most of his life. His interest in pottery was rekindled after retirement by association with the Fulham Pottery, who were interested in drawing artists into ceramics. They provided Bell with an assistant to help with basic tasks in Bell's studio in Sussex. Bell threw his own ware, but is mostly concerned with decoration.

Quentin Bell, 'Vanessa Bell and Duncan Grant', *Crafts*, January/February, 1980
—*Techniques of Terracotta*, London, 1983

Dan Klein, 'Fired with enthusiasm', *Connoisseur*, June, 1981
Philip Rawson, 'Review – Quentin Bell Ceramics', *Crafts*, September/October, 1981
Isabelle Anscombe, 'When Joy is Put First', *The Times Review*, 28/2/1981

733 Bowl, *c.*1981
Earthenware, painted and sprayed decoration in blue, green and purple; marks: 'fulham [sic] Pottery, Quentin Bell', incised; fired at Fulham Pottery; h. 10.1 cm, d. 17.7 cm
C.109–1981. Source: Dan Klein Ltd., London, £45

734 Vase, 1981
Earthenware, painted and sprayed decoration in blues, greens and purples; indistinct marks; fired at Fulham Pottery, London; h. 29.3 cm, d. 24 cm
C.117–1982. Source: Dan Klein Ltd., London, £150

734

Dernbach, Jupp 1905–

Dernbach is an artist who works primarily as a painter, sculptor and mosaicist. Born in Mayen in the Rheinland, he studied art in Berlin, before moving to Paris in 1937. He came to Britain in 1939. He was a life-long friend of Hans Coper whom he met while both were interned as alien refugees during the war. They met again in 1947 at Lucie Rie's studio, where both had been advised to seek work. They made buttons together, and helped design and build Lucie Rie's top-loading kiln. This is one of the few pieces of his own work that he made while working for Lucie Rie.

Birks (1983; pp. 13, 15, 20–21, 55)

735 Dish, *c.*1949
Stoneware, painted in yellow and brown on a white glaze; marks: 'JD' in monogram, painted; made at Lucie Rie's pottery; h. 4 cm, d. 35.6 cm
Circ.60–1951. Source: the potter, £15.75

Flanagan, Barry 1941–

Flanagan is a noted contemporary sculptor who trained at St Martin's School of Art in the 1960s. Earlier Flanagan had translated simple hand-formed shapes of clay into large stone pieces, contrasting and creating tension between the natural qualities of each material. This seemingly simple pot uses one of clay's most basic techniques, coiling, to produce an imaginative and somewhat enigmatic object.

Barry Flanagan, in 'Sculptors in Limbo?', *Crafts*, July/August, 1978
Barry Flanagan, Sculpture, exhibition catalogue, British Council, London, 1982–83

736 Pot and cover, *c.*1975–1976
Earthenware, coil built, unglazed; h. 19.3 cm, d. 13 cm
C.171&a–1984. Source: Anthony Stokes Ltd., London, £1437
Published: *Barry Flanagan, Sculpture*, British Council, 1982–83, pl. 70

733

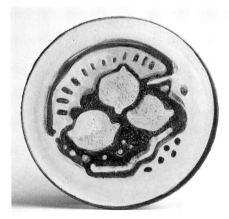

735

736

Hamilton, Cuthbert 1884–1959

Hamilton was a Vorticist painter, member of the Camden Town group, and friend and contemporary of Wyndham Lewis. With Lewis he joined the Omega Workshops briefly in 1913 and the Rebel Arts Centre in 1914. He served as a Special Constable during the war, and by 1916 he was pre-occupied with pottery, which he had possibly learnt with Staite Murray (qv) or at the Camberwell School of Art. He established 'Yeoman Pottery' in Yeoman's Row, London, which he shared for a while with William Staite Murray. It is not clear whether Staite Murray made the pots for Hamilton when he worked there; this piece is certainly decorated by Hamilton. After a successful marriage in 1919, Hamilton gradually abandoned his artistic career.

Richard Cork, *Vorticism*, London, 1970, pp. 545–6
Haslam (1975)
Haslam (1984, pp. 10–13)
The Omega Workshops, Alliance and Enmity in English Art, 1911–1920, exhibition catalogue, Anthony d'Offay, London, 1984

737 Plate, c.1919
Stoneware, painted decoration in blue-black in a cream glaze; marks: 'CH' in monogram, painted; h. 3.6 cm, d. 17.7 cm
C.120–1984. Source: Anthony d'Offay Gallery, London, £1500
A price £1.5.0 (£1.25) is marked in pencil on the base.

McLean, Bruce 1944–

The painter Bruce McLean first turned his attention to clay in 1986, when he decorated bowls and jugs made for him at the Fulham Pottery. He uses colour and incised designs in a typically bold manner. From 1977 he designed the jugs himself and took a more active part in their making. The jug shapes seem to derive from earlier forms of Alison Britton (qv).

'Bruce McLean; Painter Potter', *CR*, 100/1986
Mel Gooding, 'McLean's Pots', *Crafts*, May/June, 1986
Oliver Watson, 'Critic's Choice', *Crafts*, September/October, 1989

738 Jug, 1987 (pl. 104)
Earthenware, incised decoration through orange, black, green and blue; h. 94 cm, d. 54 cm
C.98–1987. Source: D'Offay Gallery, London, £1863

Piper, John 1903–

In addition to his multifarious other artistic talents – painting, stained glass, theatre design etc. – Piper began to work in ceramics in 1968. He was helped in the technical ceramic processes by the potter Geoffrey Eastop with whom he shared one of his studios. Piper gradually developed his own practical skills through working with Eastop on technical developments.

Martina Margetts, 'A Piper Portfolio', *Crafts*, January/February, 1979
'John Piper's Studios', *Studio*, 1981, pp. 92–3
Exhibition review, *Crafts*, May/June, 1974

739 Dish, June 1974
Earthenware, blue-black glaze with overglaze painting in white; marks: 'JP' and 'VI 74', painted; h. 68 cm, d. 48 cm
C.64–1976. Source: given by the artist
The plates were both made and decorated by Piper. The original moulds were made with the help of the potter Geoffrey Eastop.

740 Dish, August 1974
Earthenware, press-moulded, with decoration incised through the dark slip, with; marks: 'JP VIII 74', painted; h. 40 cm, d. 61 cm
C.65–1976. Source: given by the artist

Richards, Ceri 1903–1971

Ceri Richards was a well-known painter and lithographer, and though his artist output was varied, he rarely turned his hand to ceramic decoration. This dish was made in the studio of, and probably by, John Erland, a potter who taught at the Central School of Art, London.

741 Dish, 1949
Earthenware, painting in blue, yellow, green and brown on a white glaze; marks: painting signed 'CR49'; made at workshop of John Erland, London; h. 6.4 cm, d. 40.5 cm
Circ.476–1970. Source: Marlborough Fine Art Ltd., London, £135

737

740

739

741

Appendix: Potters' Marks

The numbers after each name refer to the catalogue. For some potters, who normally mark their pieces, those pieces in the Museum either happen to have no marks or the marks are not distinct enough to be photographed. In these cases, for the sake of completeness, a drawn mark has been substituted.

ARBEID 4

AULD 11

BARRETT-DANES 22

BARRON 24

BARRY 27

BARTON 30

BAYER

BERGNE 41

BEW 42

BILLINGTON 46

BRADEN 55

BRITTON 58

BURNETT 66

CAIGER-SMITH 68

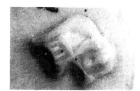

CAMPAVIAS 75

M CARDEW (WINCHCOMBE) 93

M CARDEW (WENFORD BRIDGE) 100

M CARDEW ('ABUJA') 108

S CARDEW 111

CASS 112

CASSON 118

CHAPPELL 119

CHELSEA (DRUMMOND) 124

CLARKSON 126

CLINTON 127

COLE 129

COOK 133

COOPER

COPER 142

COPER 147

CROWLEY 148

DALTON 151

DART POTTERY

276

HARRY DAVIS

DEREK DAVIS 159

DE TREY 165

DE TREY 166

DODD 179

DRING 182

DUCKWORTH 183

DUNN 189

EL NIGOUMI 191

EPTON 194

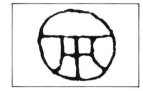

FEIBLEMAN

FIELDHOUSE 198

FINCH (WINCHCOMBE) 199

FOURNIER 208

FRANKLIN 211

FRITH 213

GARLAND 213

GORDON 231

GREGORY

GROVES 237

HAILE 245

HAILE 246

HAMADA 248

HAMLYN 254

HAMMOND 262

GWYN HANSSEN 264

HARDING 267

HINE 277

HOMOKY

HOPKINS 287

HOY 288

IONS 289

277

KALAN 296

KALINDJIAN 297

KEELER 301

KEMP 309

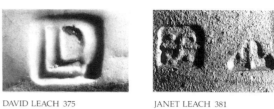

KING 310

BERNARD LEACH 318

BERNARD LEACH 348

BERNARD LEACH 363

DAVID LEACH 375

JANET LEACH 381

JOHN LEACH 388

MARGARET LEACH 389

MICHAEL LEACH 394

LEWENSTEIN 398

LLOYD-JONES 401

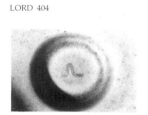

LORD 404

LUNN 414

MALONE 418

MALTBY 419

LUNN 412

MARGRIE 421

MARLOW 422

R MARSHALL 423

W MARSHALL 425

MATHEWS 432

McNICOLL 438

MEHORNAY 442

MELLON 443

MILLS 446

MATSUBAYASHI 437

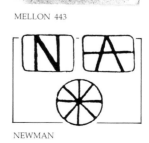

NEWLAND 451

ODUNDO 457

NEWMAN

278

NISBET

PEARSON 461

PEARSON 463

PINCOMBE 468

PLEYDELL-BOUVERIE 475

PLEYDELL-BOUVERIE 481

PLEYDELL-BOUVERIE 482

RAEBURN 505

REY 506

CHRISTINE-ANN RICHARDS 507

FRANCES RICHARDS 508

RIE 546

ROBERTS

RUSSEL 554

ST LEGER 555

SALAZAR 556

SCHLOESSINGK

SCOTT 559

SHARP 560

SHELLY 561

SIMPSON 562

SLEE 567

PETER SMITH 575

SPINDLER 580

STAIR 582

STAITE MURRAY 585

STAITE MURRAY 603

STANDIGE 608

SWINDELL 610

SYKES 613

TAYLOR 619

TOWER 629

VYSE 634

VYSE 642

WADSWORTH 648

WALFORD 656

WALTON

WARD 663

WASHINGTON 665

WELCH 669

WELLS 693

WELLS 702

WHITE

WHITING 709

DENISE WREN 713

DENISE WREN 716

ROSEMARY WREN 723

YOUNG 730

BELL 733

DERNBACH 735

PIPER 739

Concordance

of Museum and catalogue numbers

MUS. NO.	CAT. NO.	NAME	MUS. NO.	CAT. NO.	NAME	MUS. NO.	CAT. NO.	NAME
C.952–1917	673	Wells, Reginald	C.413–1934	152	Dalton, W. B.	C.79–1976	73	Caiger Smith, Alan
C.505–1919	411	Lunn, Dora	C.414–1934	483	Pleydell-Bouverie, Katharine	C.247 & a–1976	53	Braden, Norah
C.521–1919	676	Wells, Reginald						
C.522–1919	680	Wells, Reginald	C.415–1934	188	Dunn, Constance E.	C.283–1976	382	Leach, Janet
C.523–1919	684	Wells, Reginald	C.416–1934	207	Finnemore, Sybil	C.284–1976	637	Vyse, Charles
C.524–1919	688	Wells, Reginald	C.417–1934	194	Epton, Charlotte	C.285–1976	643	Vyse, Charles
C.525–1919	686	Wells, Reginald	C.418–1934	209	Fox-Strangeways, Sylvia	C.292–1976	131	Constantinidis, Joanna
C.526–1919	685	Wells, Reginald	C.419–1934	210	Fox-Strangeways, Sylvia	C.114–1977	606	Staite Murray, William
C.527–1919	687	Wells, Reginald	C.422–1934	509	Richards, Frances E.	C.115–1977	484	Pleydell-Bouverie, Katharine
C.528–1919	694	Wells, Reginald	C.423 & a–1934	508	Richards, Frances E.	C.116–1977	641	Vyse, Charles
C.529–1919	693	Wells, Reginald				C.117–1977	644	Vyse, Charles
C.530–1919	677	Wells, Reginald	C.424 & a–1934	78	Cardew, Michael	C.118–1977	645	Vyse, Charles
C.531–1919	683	Wells, Reginald				C.120–1977	425	Marshall, William
C.402–1920	416	Lunn, Dora	C.488–1934	284	Hopkins, A. G.	C.132–1977	634	Vyse, Charles
C.742–1921	312	Leach, Bernard	C.954–1935	601	Staite Murray, William	C.181–1977	707	White, Mary
C.1040–1922	317	Leach, Bernard	C.955–1935	642	Vyse, Charles	C.27–1978	572	Smith, Martin
C.142–1923	583	Staite Murray, William	C.956–1935	82	Cardew, Michael	C.111–1978	247	Hall, William R.
C.743–1923	674	Wells, Reginald	C.957–1935	79	Cardew, Michael	C.115–1978	611	Swindell, Geoffrey
C.12–1924	696	Wells, Reginald	C.958–1935	631	Uusman, Beatrice	C.116–1978	610	Swindell, Geoffrey
C.63–1924	352	Leach, Standard Ware	C.959–1935	51	Braden, Norah	C.9 & a–1979	442	Mehornay, William
C.106–1924	249	Hamada, Shoji	C.960–1935	52	Braden, Norah	C.48–1979	667	Washington, R. J.
C.1370–1924	437	Matsubayashi, Tsurunosuke	C.962–1935	478	Pleydell-Bouverie, Katharine	C.49–1979	666	Washington, R. J.
C.1454–1924	594	Staite Murray, William				C.99–1979	57	Britton, Alison
C.1455–1924	590	Staite Murray, William	C.963–1935	324	Leach, Bernard	C.100–1979	58	Britton, Alison
C.1463–1924	584	Staite Murray, William	C.27–1937	506	Rey, Margaret	C.115–1979	29	Barton, Glenys
C.1464–1924	588	Staite Murray, William	C.73–1937	130	Cole, Vivian	C.117–1979	127	Clinton, Marjorie
C.1465–1924	587	Staite Murray, William	C.74–1937	129	Cole, John	C.118–1979	548	Rie, Lucie
C.60–1925	699	Wells, Reginald	C.31–1943	55	Braden, Norah	C.119–1979	279	Homoky, Nicholas
C.790–1925	691	Wells, Reginald	C.19–1946	43	Billington, Dora	C.120–1979	278	Homoky, Nicholas
C.791–1925	690	Wells, Reginald	C.47–1946	334	Leach, Bernard	C.139–1979	268	Henderson, Ewen
C.846–1925	589	Staite Murray, William	C.48–1946	335	Leach, Bernard	C.157–1979	348	Leach, Bernard
C.148–1926	321	Leach, Bernard	C.49–1946	336	Leach, Bernard	C.160 & a–1979	215	Fritsch, Liz
C.149–1926	323	Leach, Bernard	C.73–1953	122	Chelsea Pottery, (Daphne Corke)			
C.339–1926	692	Wells, Reginald				C.3 to d–1980	297	Kalindjian, Sona
C.413–1926	593	Staite Murray, William	C.74–1953	125	Chelsea Pottery, (Joyce Morgan)	C.24 & a–1980	21	Barrett-Danes, Ruth
C.93–1927	510	Richards, Frances E.				C.25–1980	16	Baldwin, Gordon
C.474–1927	285	Hopkins, A. G.	C.5–1954	654	Walford, James	C.26 & a–1980	280	Homoky, Nicholas
C.2–1933	286	Hopkins, A. G.	C.6–1954	653	Walford, James			
C.3–1933	287	Hopkins, A. G.	C.7–1954	655	Walford, James	C.30–1980	497	Poncelet, Jacqueline
C.400–1934	592	Staite Murray, William	C.29–1968	344	Leach, Bernard	C.42 & a–1980	289	Ions, Neil
C.401–1934	585	Staite Murray, William	C.61–1970	281	Hopkins, A. G.			
C.402, 404 & 409–1934	327	Leach, Bernard	C.84 & a–1972	314	Leach, Bernard	C.43–1980	620	Tchalenko, Janice
						C.44–1980	253	Hamlyn, Jane
C.403–1934	326	Leach, Bernard	C.58–1973	328	Leach, Bernard	C.56–1980	191	El Nigoumi, Siddig
C.405 & a–1934	316	Leach, Bernard	C.59–1973	49	Braden, Norah	C.63–1980	635	Vyse, Charles
			C.60–1976	599	Staite Murray, William	C.64–1980	636	Vyse, Charles
C.406–1934	319	Leach, Bernard	C.61–1976	640	Vyse, Charles	C.68–1980	402	Locke, Donald
C.407–1934	251	Hamada, Shoji	C.64–1976	739	Piper, John	C.69–1980	211	Franklin, Ruth
C.408–1934	320	Leach, Bernard	C.65–1976	740	Piper, John	C.102–1980	713	Wren, Denise
C.410–1934	325	Leach, Bernard	C.66–1976	343	Leach, Bernard	C.116–1980	148	Crowley, Jill
C.411–1934	252	Hamada, Shoji	C.67–1976	313	Leach, Bernard	C.117–1980	238	Gunn-Russell, Linda
C.412–1934	151	Dalton, W. B.	C.68–1976	333	Leach, Bernard	C.124–1980	399	Lloyd-Jones, David

MUS. NO	CAT. NO.	NAME	MUS. NO.	CAT. NO.	NAME	MUS. NO.	CAT. NO.	NAME
C.125–1980	400	Lloyd-Jones, David	C.39–1982	518	Rie, Lucie	C.70–1984	159	Davis, Derek
C.126–1980	401	Lloyd-Jones, David	C.40 & a–1982	530	Rie, Lucie	C.71 & a–1984	204	Finch, Ray
C.143–1980	551	Rogers, Mary						
C.144–1980	552	Rogers, Mary	C.41 & a–1982	529	Rie, Lucie	C.72–1984	213	Frith, David
C.145–1980	553	Rogers, Mary				C.73–1984	290	Ions, Neil
C.152–1980	262	Hammond, Henry	C.42–1982	544	Rie, Lucie	C.74–1984	300	Keeler, Walter
C.172–1980	376	Leach, David	C.43–1982	545	Rie, Lucie	C.75–1984	310	King, Ruth
C.173–1980	377	Leach, David	C.44–1982	547	Rie, Lucie	C.76–1984	398	Lewenstein, Eileen
C.174–1980	378	Leach, David	C.45–1982	546	Rie, Lucie	C.77–1984	192	El Nigoumi, Siddig
C.175–1980	379	Leach, David	C.46–1982	549	Rie, Lucie	C.78–1984	457	Odundo, Magdalene
C.180–1980	235	Gregory, Ian	C.51–1982	135	Cooper, Emmanuel	C.79–1984	507	Richards, Christine-Ann
C.183 & a–1980	418	Malone, Jim	C.53–1982	438	McNicoll, Carol	C.80–1984	559	Scott, David
			C.54–1982	498	Poncelet, Jacqueline	C.81–1984	730	Young, A. & J.
C.184 & a–1980	608	Standige, Gary	C.57 to c–1982	531	Rie, Lucie	C.82–1984	263	Hammond, Henry
			C.58 to c–1982	532	Rie, Lucie	C.83–1984	633	Vyse, Charles
C.191–1980	725	Wren, Rosemary D.	C.82–1982	269	Henderson, Ewen	C.120–1984	737	Hamilton, Cuthbert
C.13–1981	216	Fritsch, Liz	C.84–1982	149	Crowley, Jill	C.122–1984	582	Stair, Julien
C.19–1981	487	Pleydell-Bouverie, Katharine	C.91–1982	621	Tchalenko, Janice	C.151–1984	118	Casson, Michael
			C.101 to b–1982	519	Rie, Lucie	C.152–1984	270	Henderson, Ewen
C.40–1981	66	Burnett, Deidre				C.153–1984	303	Keeler, Walter
C.43–1981	195	Feibleman, Dorothy	C.102 & a–1982	520	Rie, Lucie	C.154–1984	304	Keeler, Walter
C.44–1981	26	Barry, Val				C.155–1984	17	Baldwin, Gordon
C.45–1981	27	Barry, Val	C.103–1982	521	Rie, Lucie	C.156–1984	465	Pearson, Colin
C.46–1981	31	Batterham, Richard	C.104–1982	522	Rie, Lucie	C.161–1984	196	Feibleman, Dorothy
C.48–1981	716	Wren, Denise	C.105 to aa–1982	524	Rie, Lucie	C.171 & a–1984	736	Flanagan, Barry
C.49–1981	714	Wren, Denise						
C.50 & a–1981	715	Wren, Denise	C.106–1982	523	Rie, Lucie	C.172 & 173–1984	404	Lord, Andrew
			C.108–1982	298	Keeler, Walter			
C.51–1981	717	Wren, Denise	C.109–1982	299	Keeler, Walter	C.185–1984	570	Slee, Richard
C.52–1981	719	Wren, Denise	C.110 & a–1982	302	Keeler, Walter	C.186–1984	221	Gaunce, Marion
C.53–1981	718	Wren, Denise				C.187–1984	219	Garland, David
C.70–1981	419	Maltby, John	C.111–1982	301	Keeler, Walter	C.200–1984	444	Mellon, Eric James
C.71–1981	485	Pleydell-Bouverie, Katharine	C.117–1982	734	Bell, Quentin	C.32–1985	668	Washington, R. J.
C.72–1981	475	Pleydell-Bouverie, Katharine	C.148–1982	220	Gaunce, Marion	C.36–1985	388	Leach, John
C.73–1981	479	Pleydell-Bouverie, Katharine	C.211–1983	132	Constantinidis, Joanna	C.44–1985	556	Salazar, Fiona
C.75–1981	499	Poncelet, Jacqueline	C.212–1983	417	Magson, Mal	C.45–1985	32	Batterham, Richard
C.76–1981	500	Poncelet, Jacqueline	C.213–1983	459	Owen, Elspeth	C.46–1985	33	Batterham, Richard
C.79–1981	30	Barton, Glenys	C.224–1983	619	Taylor, Sutton	C.47–1985	34	Batterham, Richard
C.81–1981	502	Quick, Kenneth	C.225–1983	550	Roberts, David	C.51–1985	217	Fritsch, Liz
C.82–1981	675	Wells, Reginald	C.251–1983	383	Leach, Janet	C.54–1985	447	Moss, Vera
C.87–1981	59	Britton, Alison	C.252–1983	384	Leach, Janet	C.55–1985	448	Moss, Vera
C.88–1981	385	Leach, John	C.253–1983	569	Slee, Richard	C.56–1985	449	Moss, Vera
C.89 & a–1981	386	Leach, John	C.254–1983	464	Pearson, Colin	C.57–1985	110	Cardew, Michael
			C.262–1983	288	Hoy, Anita	C.59–1985	443	Mellon, Eric James
C.90–1981	387	Leach, John	C.287–1983	409	Lunn, Dora	C.60–1985	77	Cardew, Michael
C.109–1981	733	Bell, Quentin	C.288–1983	410	Lunn, Dora	C.184–1985	430	Mathews, Heber
C.110 & a–1981	567	Slee, Richard	C.289–1983	413	Lunn, Dora	C.185–1985	427	Mathews, Heber
			C.290–1983	415	Lunn, Dora	C.186–1985	428	Mathews, Heber
C.111 & a–1981	568	Slee, Richard	C.291–1983	412	Lunn, Dora	C.187–1985	433	Mathews, Heber
			C.292–1983	414	Lunn, Dora	C.188–1985	431	Mathews, Heber
C.152–1981	111	Cardew, Seth	C.312–1983	622	Tchalenko, Janice	C.189–1985	432	Mathews, Heber
C.155–1981	462	Pearson, Colin	C.313–1983	623	Tchalenko, Janice	C.190–1985	426	Mathews, Heber
C.177–1981	575	Smith, Peter	C.314 & a–1983	624	Tchalenko, Janice	C.191–1985	429	Mathews, Heber
C.178–1981	576	Smith, Peter				C.228–1985	728	Yasuda, Takeshi
C.179–1981	729	Young, A. & J.	C.319–1983	505	Raeburn, Elizabeth	C.230–1985	395	Lee, Jennifer
C.180 & a–1981	660	Walton, Sarah	C.322 & a–1983	60	Britton, Alison	C.231–1985	396	Lee, Jennifer
						C.25–1986	663	Ward, John
C.12–1982	463	Pearson, Colin	C.324–1983	482	Pleydell-Bouverie, Katharine	C.76–1986	243	Haile, Sam
C.14 & a–1982	212	Frith, David				C.77–1986	242	Haile, Sam
			C.328–1983	630	Tower, James	C.78–1986	240	Haile, Sam
C.15–1982	573	Smith, Martin	C.329–1983	671	Welch, Robin	C.79–1986	241	Haile, Sam
C.33–1982	517	Rie, Lucie	C.330–1983	672	Welch, Robin	C.80–1986	239	Haile, Sam
C.34–1982	515	Rie, Lucie	C.331–1983	456	Nisbet, Eileen	C.81 & a–1986	181	Dring, James
C.35–1982	512	Rie, Lucie	C.332–1983	466	Pim, Henry			
C.36–1982	513	Rie, Lucie	C.333–1983	503	Radstone, Sara	C.82–1986	182	Dring, James
C.37–1982	514	Rie, Lucie	C.339–1983	501	Poncelet, Jacqueline	C.83–1986	180	Dring, James
C.38 & a–1982	516	Rie, Lucie	C.68–1984	47	Bowen, Clive	C.107–1986	40	Bergne, Suzanne
			C.69–1984	126	Clarkson, Derek	C.108–1986	41	Bergne, Suzanne

MUS. NO.	CAT. NO.	NAME	MUS. NO.	CAT. NO.	NAME	MUS. NO.	CAT. NO.	NAME
C.176–1986	271	Henderson, Ewen	Circ.993–1924	318	Leach, Bernard	Circ.193–1949	577	Spindler, A. F.
C.186–1986	423	Marshall, Ray	Circ.513–1925	698	Wells, Reginald	Circ.194–1949	578	Spindler, A. F.
C.187–1986	424	Marshall, Ray	Circ.10–1927	706	Wells, Reginald	Circ.195–1949	579	Spindler, A. F.
C.278–1986	574	Smith, Martin	Circ.11–1927	682	Wells, Reginald	Circ.33 & a–1950	95	Cardew, Michael
C.38–1987	439	McNicoll, Carol	Circ.646–1927	322	Leach, Bernard			
C.39–1987	408	Lowndes, Gillian	Circ.677–1927	591	Staite Murray, William	Circ.156–1950	236	Groves, Lewis
C.83–1987	65	Buck, Steve	Circ.236–1930	476	Pleydell-Bouverie, Katharine	Circ.157–1950	237	Groves, Lewis
C.98–1987	738	McLean, Bruce	Circ.237 & a–1930	477	Pleydell-Bouverie, Katharine	Circ.160–1950	389	Leach, Margaret
C.100–1987	609	Suttie, Angus				Circ.161–1950	390	Leach, Margaret
C.102–1987	272	Henderson, Ewen	Circ.425–1930	598	Staite Murray, William	Circ.162–1950	392	Leach, Margaret
C.233–1987	61	Britton, Alison	Circ.426–1930	600	Staite Murray, William	Circ.163–1950	391	Leach, Margaret
C.284–1987	708	Whiting, Geoffrey	Circ.427–1930	596	Staite Murray, William	Circ.164–1950	393	Leach, Margaret
C.16–1988	711	Whiting, Geoffrey	Circ.144–1931	329	Leach, Bernard	Circ.165–1950	309	Kemp, Dorothy
C.60–1988	64	Brown, Sandy	Circ.145–1931	331	Leach, Bernard	Circ.166–1950	306	Kemp, Dorothy
C.63–1988	504	Radstone, Sara	Circ.147–1931	330	Leach, Bernard	Circ.167–1950	305	Kemp, Dorothy
C.2–1989	74	Caiger Smith, Alan	Circ.763–1931	481	Pleydell-Bouverie, Katharine	Circ.168–1950	307	Kemp, Dorothy
C.3–1989	62	Brown, Christie	Circ.765 & a–1931	50	Braden, Norah	Circ.169–1950	308	Kemp, Dorothy
C.4–1989	150	Crowley, Jill				Circ.170 & a–1950	368	Leach, Standard Ware
C.5–1989	467	Pim, Henry	Circ.766 & a–1931	193	Epton, Charlotte			
C.6–1989	661	Walton, Sarah				Circ.171–1950	363	Leach, Standard Ware
C.7–1989	48	Bowen, Clive	Circ.252–1932	480	Pleydell-Bouverie, Katharine	Circ.172–1950	371	Leach, Standard Ware
C.8 & a–1989	218	Fuller, Geoffrey				Circ.173–1950	366	Leach, Standard Ware
C.9–1989	662	Walton, Sarah	Circ.438–1934	704	Wells, Reginald	Circ.174–1950	367	Leach, Standard Ware
C.10 & a–1989	440	McNicoll, Carol	Circ.333–1935	54	Braden, Norah	Circ.175 & a–1950	369	Leach, Standard Ware
			Circ.37–1938	83	Cardew, Michael			
C.11–1989	441	McNicoll, Carol	Circ.304–1938	56	Braden, Norah	Circ.176–1950	370	Leach, Standard Ware
C.12–1989	557	Schloessingk, Micky	Circ.310–1938	87	Cardew, Michael	Circ.177–1950	364	Leach, Standard Ware
C.13–1989	558	Schloessingk, Micky	Circ.311–1938	88	Cardew, Michael	Circ.178–1950	365	Leach, Standard Ware
C.14–1989	22	Barrett-Danes, Ruth	Circ.312–1938	85	Cardew, Michael	Circ.179–1950	362	Leach, Standard Ware
C.15–1989	571	Slee, Richard	Circ.313–1938	86	Cardew, Michael	Circ.180–1950	612	Sykes, Steven
C.16–1989	254	Hamlyn, Jane	Circ.314 & a–1938	90	Cardew, Michael	Circ.181–1950	613	Sykes, Steven
C.17 & a–1989	731	Young, A. & J.				Circ.182–1950	614	Sykes, Steven
C.18–1989	206	Finch, Winchcombe Pott	Circ.315–1938	91	Cardew, Michael	Circ.186–1950	229	Gordon, William
C.19 to b–1989	732	Young, A. & J.	Circ.316–1938	92	Cardew, Michael	Circ.187–1950	230	Gordon, William
			Circ.317–1938	81	Cardew, Michael	Circ.188–1950	233	Gordon, William
C.20 & a–1989	39	Bayer, Svend	Circ.318–1938	89	Cardew, Michael	Circ.189–1950	228	Gordon, William
C.21 & a–1989	205	Finch, Winchcombe Pott	Circ.319–1938	84	Cardew, Michael	Circ.272–1950	555	Saint Leger, S.
			Circ.93–1939	255	Hammond, Henry	Circ.273–1950	133	Cook, G. F.
C.22 & a–1989	153	Dart Pottery	Circ.94–1939	256	Hammond, Henry	Circ.274–1950	259	Hammond, Henry
C.23–1989	154	Dart Pottery	Circ.95–1939	257	Hammond, Henry	Circ.275–1950	260	Hammond, Henry
C.24–1989	155	Dart Pottery	Circ.96–1939	664	Washington, R. J.	Circ.276–1950	24	Barron, Paul
C.25–1989	156	Dart Pottery	Circ.97–1939	665	Washington, R. J.	Circ.277–1950	23	Barron, Paul
C.26–1989	157	Dart Pottery	Circ.98–1939	625	Thomas, Gwilym	Circ.278–1950	165	De Trey, Marianne
C.27–1989	158	Dart Pottery	Circ.99–1939	626	Thomas, Gwilym	Circ.279–1950	445	Mills, Donald
C.28 & a–1989	35	Batterham, Richard	Circ.170 & a–1939	646	Wadsworth, P. S.	Circ.280–1950	338	Leach, Bernard
C.29–1989	36	Batterham, Richard				Circ.281–1950	339	Leach, Bernard
C.30–1989	37	Batterham, Richard	Circ.171 & a–1939	647	Wadsworth, P. S.	Circ.282–1950	435	Mathews, Heber
C.31–1989	38	Batterham, Richard				Circ.283–1950	450	Newland, William
C.34–1989	128	Cohen, David	Circ.172 & a–1939	648	Wadsworth, P. S.	Circ.419–1950	200	Finch, Ray
C.37–1989	25	Barron, Paul				Circ.420–1950	201	Finch, Ray
C.38–1989	179	Dodd, Mike	Circ.173–1939	649	Wadsworth, P. S.	Circ.421–1950	202	Finch, Ray
C.39–1989	273	Henderson, Ewen	Circ.174–1939	650	Wadsworth, P. S.	Circ.422–1950	203	Finch, Ray
C.40–1989	18	Baldwin, Gordon	Circ.175–1939	651	Wadsworth, P. S.	Circ.423 & a–1950	96	Cardew, Michael
C.41–1989	294	Jupp, Mo	Circ.176–1939	652	Wadsworth, P. S.			
C.58–1989	472	Pincombe, E. H.	Circ.346–1939	93	Cardew, Michael	Circ.424 & a–1950	97	Cardew, Michael
C.59–1989	473	Pincombe, E. H.	Circ.347–1939	94	Cardew, Michael			
C.60–1989	474	Pincombe, E. H.	Circ.351–1939	604	Staite Murray, William	Circ.425–1950	98	Cardew, Michael
Circ.515–1919	678	Wells, Reginald	Circ.352–1939	602	Staite Murray, William	Circ.426–1950	99	Cardew, Michael
Circ.516–1919	689	Wells, Reginald	Circ.353–1939	603	Staite Murray, William	Circ.427–1950	100	Cardew, Michael
Circ.517–1919	679	Wells, Reginald	Circ.478–1939	258	Hammond, Henry	Circ.428–1950	101	Cardew, Michael
Circ.257–1923	586	Staite Murray, William	Circ.479–1939	469	Pincombe, E. H.	Circ.429–1950	102	Cardew, Michael
Circ.542–1923	248	Hamada, Shoji	Circ.480–1939	468	Pincombe, E. H.	Circ.430 & a–1950	103	Cardew, Michael
Circ.1278–1923	315	Leach, Bernard	Circ.481–1939	618	Tacon, Pamela			
			Circ.482 & a–1939	627	Thomas, Gwilym	Circ.431–1950	104	Cardew, Michael
Circ.991–1924	702	Wells, Reginald				Circ.432 & a–1950	105	Cardew, Michael
Circ.30–1940	361	Leach, Standard Ware						
Circ.31–1940	360	Leach, Standard Ware	Circ.433–1950	106	Cardew, Michael			
Circ.992–1924	250	Hamada, Shoji	Circ.11–1941	199	Finch, Ray			

MUS. NO.	CAT. NO.	NAME
Circ.434 & a–1950	44	Billington, Dora
Circ.436–1950	45	Billington, Dora
Circ.437 & a–1950	46	Billington, Dora
Circ.1–1951	525	Rie, Lucie
Circ.2–1951	526	Rie, Lucie
Circ.3–1951	527	Rie, Lucie
Circ.5–1951	169	De Trey, Marianne
Circ.6–1951	168	De Trey, Marianne
Circ.7–1951	173	De Trey, Marianne
Circ.8-1951	172	De Trey, Marianne
Circ.9–1951	171	De Trey, Marianne
Circ.10 & a–1951	170	De Trey, Marianne
Circ.11–1951	167	De Trey, Marianne
Circ.12–1951	175	De Trey, Marianne
Circ.13–1951	176	De Trey, Marianne
Circ.14–1951	166	De Trey, Marianne
Circ.15–1951	174	De Trey, Marianne
Circ.16–1951	638	Vyse, Charles
Circ.17–1951	639	Vyse, Charles
Circ.46–1951	311	La Salle, Vivian Neil
Circ.54–1951	136	Coper, Hans
Circ.60–1951	735	Dernbach, Jupp
Circ.61–1951	160	Davis, Harry and May
Circ.62 & a–1951	161	Davis, Harry and May
Circ.84–1951	340	Leach, Bernard
Circ.184–1951	581	Spindler, A.F.
Circ.185–1951	580	Spindler, A.F.
Circ.286–1951	244	Haile, Sam
Circ.287–1951	245	Haile, Sam
Circ.288–1951	246	Haile, Sam
Circ.310–1951	656	Walford, James
Circ.18–1952	446	Mills, Donald
Circ.19 & a–1952	162	Davis, Harry and May
Circ.20 & a–1952	528	Rie, Lucie
Circ.74 to b–1952	616	Sykes, Steven
Circ.75–1952	615	Sykes, Steven
Circ.76–1952	231	Gordon, William
Circ.136–1952	341	Leach, Bernard
Circ.137–1952	342	Leach, Bernard
Circ.138–1952	372	Leach, David
Circ.406–1953	123	Chelsea Pottery, (Daphne Corke)
Circ.407–1953	124	Chelsea Pottery, (John Drummond)
Circ.57–1954	451	Newland, William
Circ.58 & a–1954	277	Hine, Margaret
Circ.266 & 267–1954	460	Parkinson, Richard and Sue
Circ.278–1954	632	Vergette, Nicholas
Circ.311–1954	267	Harding, Deborah H.
Circ.240–1955	560	Sharp, Alexander
Circ.272–1955	705	Wells, Reginald
Circ.273 & a–1955	703	Wells, Reginald
Circ.274–1955	697	Wells, Reginald
Circ.276–1955	605	Staite Murray, William
Circ.277–1955	511	Richards, Frances E.
Circ.335–1955	42	Bew, John
Circ.336–1955	533	Rie, Lucie
Circ.337–1955	137	Coper, Hans

MUS. NO.	CAT. NO.	NAME
Circ.338–1955	189	Dunn, Constance
Circ.339–1955	190	Dunn, Constance
Circ.340–1955	554	Russel, Christopher
Circ.116–1956	232	Gordon, William
Circ.117–1956	234	Gordon, William
Circ.498–1956	345	Leach, Bernard
Circ.649–1956	486	Pleydell-Bouverie, Katharine
Circ.108–1957	712	Whittall, Eleanor
Circ.126–1957	722	Wren, Rosemary D.
Circ.127–1957	723	Wren, Rosemary D.
Circ.203–1957	657	Walford, James
Circ.204–1957	658	Walford, James
Circ.7–1958	628	Tower, James
Circ.112 & a–1958	107	Cardew, Michael
Circ.113–1958	108	Cardew, Michael
Circ.115–1958	346	Leach, Bernard
Circ.131–1958	75	Campavias, Estella
Circ.154–1958	138	Coper, Hans
Circ.155–1958	139	Coper, Hans
Circ.279-1958	726	Wynn Reeves, Ann
Circ.280–1958	727	Wynn Reeves, Ann
Circ.352–1958	607	Staite Murray, William
Circ.354–1958	283	Hopkins, A.G.
Circ.355–1958	282	Hopkins, A.G.
Circ.1–1959	63	Brown, Paul
Circ.6–1959	76	Campavias, Estella
Circ.12–1959	470	Pincombe, E.H.
Circ.13–1959	471	Pincombe, E.H.
Circ.16–1959	629	Tower, James
Circ.18 & a–1959	164	Davis, Harry and May
Circ.40–1959	197	Fieldhouse, Murray
Circ.41–1959	198	Fieldhouse, Murray
Circ.42–1959	163	Davis, Harry and May
Circ.43–1959	561	Shelly, John
Circ.59–1959	67	Caiger Smith, Alan
Circ.64–1959	458	O'Malley, Peter
Circ.95–1959	452	Newland, William
Circ.96 to c–1959	453	Newland, William
Circ.108–1959	700	Wells, Reginald
Circ.109–1959	701	Wells, Reginald
Circ.126–1959	534	Rie, Lucie
Circ.127–1959	535	Rie, Lucie
Circ.128–1959	536	Rie, Lucie
Circ.129–1959	261	Hammond, Henry
Circ.157–1959	1	Arbeid, Dan
Circ.241–1959	183	Duckworth, Ruth
Circ.242–1959	184	Duckworth, Ruth
Circ.263–1959	436	Mathews, Heber
Circ.327–1959	709	Whiting, Geoffrey
Circ.328 & a–1959	710	Whiting, Geoffrey
Circ.129–1960	347	Leach, Bernard
Circ.240–1960	10	Auld, Ian
Circ.22–1961	337	Leach, Bernard
Circ.255 to b–1961	178	De Trey, Marianne
Circ.256–1961	177	De Trey, Marianne
Circ.263–1961	112	Cass, Barbara
Circ.297–1961	2	Arbeid, Dan
Circ.440–1962	394	Leach, Michael
Circ.454–1962	265	Hanssen, Louis
Circ.487–1962	19	Ballantyne, David
Circ.488 & a–1962	20	Ballantyne, David

MUS. NO.	CAT. NO.	NAME
Circ.518–1962	434	Mathews, Heber
Circ.617–1962	185	Duckworth, Ruth
Circ.648–1962	669	Welch, Robin
Circ.650–1962	422	Marlow, Reginald
Circ.97 to c–1963	617	Sykes, Steven
Circ.375–1963	380	Leach, Janet
Circ.551–1963	349	Leach, Bernard
Circ.88–1964	355	Leach, Standard Ware
Circ.89–1964	357	Leach, Standard Ware
Circ.90–1964	356	Leach, Standard Ware
Circ.91–1964	358	Leach, Standard Ware
Circ.92–1964	359	Leach, Standard Ware
Circ.93 & a–1964	353	Leach, Standard Ware
Circ.94–1964	354	Leach, Standard Ware
Circ.304–1965	266	Hanssen, Louis
Circ.351–1965	11	Auld, Ian
Circ.352–1965	381	Leach, Janet
Circ.353–1965	659	Wallwork, Alan
Circ.45–1966	121	Chappell, John
Circ.46–1966	120	Chappell, John
Circ.47–1966	119	Chappell, John
Circ.757–1966	537	Rie, Lucie
Circ.880–1966	373	Leach, David
Circ.763–1967	186	Duckworth, Ruth
Circ.764–1967	187	Duckworth, Ruth
Circ.907–1967	695	Wells, Reginald
Circ.908–1967	681	Wells, Reginald
Circ.1192–1967	350	Leach, Bernard
Circ.1206 & a–1967	274	Hepburn, Anthony
Circ.1219–1967	295	Kalan, Stephanie
Circ.1220–1967	296	Kalan, Stephanie
Circ.1221–1967	720	Wren, Denise
Circ.1226–1967	538	Rie, Lucie
Circ.1227–1967	541	Rie, Lucie
Circ.1228–1967	539	Rie, Lucie
Circ.1229–1967	540	Rie, Lucie
Circ.1230–1967	542	Rie, Lucie
Circ.1231–1967	543	Rie, Lucie
Circ.587–1968	332	Leach, Bernard
Circ.592–1968	68	Caiger, Smith, Alan
Circ.820 & a–1968	69	Caiger, Smith, Alan
Circ.821–1968	70	Caiger, Smith, Alan
Circ.822 & a–1968	71	Caiger, Smith, Alan
Circ.823–1968	72	Caiger, Smith, Alan
Circ.826–1968	405	Lowndes, Gillian
Circ.829–1968	406	Lowndes, Gillian
Circ.830–1968	407	Lowndes, Gillian
Circ.831–1968	275	Hepburn, Anthony
Circ.832–1968	276	Hepburn, Anthony
Circ.836–1968	4	Arbeid, Dan
Circ.837–1968	3	Arbeid, Dan
Circ.838–1968	5	Arbeid, Dan
Circ.839–1968	6	Arbeid, Dan

MUS. NO.	CAT. NO.	NAME	MUS. NO.	CAT. NO.	NAME	MUS. NO.	CAT. NO.	NAME
Circ.840–1968	7	Arbeid, Dan	Circ.237–1971	264	Hanssen, Gwyn	Circ.501–1974	489	Poncelet, Jacqueline
Circ.841–1968	8	Arbeid, Dan	Circ.238–1971	721	Wren, Denise	Circ.517–1974	114	Casson, Michael
Circ.842–1968	9	Arbeid, Dan	Circ.186–1972	461	Pearson, Colin	Circ.269–1975	566	Simpson, Peter
Circ.204–1969	140	Coper, Hans	Circ.218–1972	454	Newman, Bryan	Circ.408–1975	214	Fritsch, Liz
Circ.205–1969	141	Coper, Hans	Circ.422 & a–1972	224	Godfrey, Ian	Circ.8–1976	115	Casson, Michael
Circ.206–1969	143	Coper, Hans				Circ.9–1976	116	Casson, Michael
Circ.207–1969	142	Coper, Hans	Circ.423–1972	223	Godfrey, Ian	Circ.253–1976	495	Poncelet, Jacqueline
Circ.208–1969	144	Coper, Hans	Circ.154 & a–1973	403	Lord, Andrew	Circ.254–1976	492	Poncelet, Jacqueline
Circ.474–1969	109	Cardew, Michael				Circ.255–1976	493	Poncelet, Jacqueline
Circ.529–1969	670	Welch, Robin	Circ.163–1973	374	Leach, David	Circ.256–1976	494	Poncelet, Jacqueline
Circ.540–1969	291	Jupp, Mo	Circ.276–1973	488	Poncelet, Jacqueline	Circ.286–1976	564	Simpson, Peter
Circ.541–1969	292	Jupp, Mo	Circ.277 to 279–1973	28	Barton, Glenys	Circ.287–1976	565	Simpson, Peter
Circ.661–1969	208	Fournier, Sheila				Circ.398–1976	145	Coper, Hans
Circ.754–1969	724	Wren, Rosemary D.	Circ.290–1973	293	Jupp, Mo	Circ.399–1976	147	Coper, Hans
Circ.756–1969	421	Margrie, Victor	Circ.293–1973	375	Leach, David	Circ.530–1976	15	Baldwin, Gordon
Circ.757–1969	420	Margrie, Victor	Circ.332–1973	351	Leach, Bernard	Circ.531–1976	117	Casson, Michael
Circ.767–1969	146	Coper, Hans	Circ.4–1974	113	Casson, Michael	Circ.532–1976	226	Godfrey, Ian
Circ.57 to dd–1970	222	Godfrey, Ian	Circ.301–1974	455	Newman, Bryan	Circ.533–1976	227	Godfrey, Ian
			Circ.366–1974	491	Poncelet, Jacqueline	Circ.534–1976	496	Poncelet, Jacqueline
Circ.461–1970	12	Baldwin, Gordon	Circ.484–1974	562	Simpson, Peter	Misc.2(53)–1934	80	Cardew, Michael
Circ.466 & a–1970	13	Baldwin, Gordon	Circ.485–1974	563	Simpson, Peter			
			Circ.486–1974	14	Baldwin, Gordon	Misc.2(54)–1934	595	Staite Murray, William
Circ.476–1970	741	Richards, Ceri	Circ.491 & a–1974	225	Godfrey, Ian			
Circ.490–1970	134	Cooper, Emmanuel				Misc.2(53)–1934	597	Staite Murray, William
Circ.125–1971	397	Lewenstein, Eileen	Circ.500–1974	490	Poncelet, Jacqueline			

Bibliography

This is not a full bibliography. Works which are specific to, or are written by, particular potters are listed in the main catalogue under their names. Works listed here are of more general interest which are referred to more than once in the main text. Other references will be found in full in the footnotes.

Aberystwyth
1979 *Aberystwyth Ceramics*, ed. Moira Vincentelli, University College of Wales, Aberystwyth
1986 *Catalogue of Early Studio Pottery*, compiled by M. Vincentelli and A. Hale, University College of Wales, Aberystwyth

Belfast
1974 *New Ceramics*, exhibition catalogue, Ulster Museum

Billington, Dora M.
1953 'The Younger English Potters', *The Studio*, 145
1955 'The New Look in British Pottery', *The Studio*, 149

Birks, Tony
1967 *The Art of the Modern Potter*, London
1976 *The Art of the Modern Potter* (2nd edn.), London
1983 *Hans Coper*, London
1987 *Lucie Rie*, London

Blunt, Reginald (ed.)
1973 *The Cheyne Book of Chelsea China and Pottery*, 1924, with a new introduction by J. V. G. Mallet, EP Publishing, Wakefield, Yorkshire

Cameron, Elizabeth and Lewis, Philippa
1976 *Potters on Pottery*, London

Casson, Michael
1967 *Pottery in Britain Today*, London

Cooper, Emmanuel and Lewenstein, Eileen
1974 *New Ceramics*, London

Cooper, R. G.
1947 *The Modern Potter*, London

Dormer, Peter
1986 *The New Ceramics, Trends and Traditions*, London

Floud, Peter
1953 'The Crafts Then and Now', *The Studio*, 145, pp. 127 ff.

Frayling, Christopher
1987 *The Royal College of Art; One Hundred and Fifty Years of Art and Design*, London

Godden, Geoffrey
1964 *Encyclopaedia of British Pottery and Porcelain Marks*, London
1988 *Encyclopaedia of British Porcelain Manufacturers*, London

Gotleib, Rachel
1987 'The Critical Language and Aesthetic Criteria of Art-Pottery Manufacturers and Studio-Potters 1914–1934,' thesis presented for the degree of MA V&A/RCA Course in the History of Design and Decorative Art (unpublished)
1988 'The Critical Language and Aesthetic Criteria of Art-Pottery Manufacturers and Studio-Potters 1914–1934', *Apollo*, March

Greenhalgh, Paul
1989 'Art and Craft: a Dichotomy of Falsehood', *CR*, 116/1989

Harrod, Tanya
1989 'The Forgotten '50s', *Crafts*, May/June
1989a 'From "A Potter's Book" to "The Makers Eye": British Studio Ceramics 1940–1982', *The Harrow Connection*, Northern Centre for Contemporary Art, Sunderland

Haslam, Malcolm
1975 'Some Vorticist Pottery', *The Connoisseur*, October, pp. 98–101
1984 *William Staite Murray*, Crafts Council and Cleveland County Museum Service

London, British Council
1942 *Exhibition of Modern British Crafts*, exhibition catalogue, 14 sites in Canada and the USA in 1942–45, London

London, Crafts Advisory Committee, *see* London, Crafts Council

London, CC (Crafts Council)
1965 *Craftsmanship*, exhibition catalogue
1974 *Ceramic Forms, Recent Work from Seven British Potters*, exhibition catalogue
1974a *The Work of the Committee, 1971–1974*
1976 *Craftsmen of Quality*, guide to Council–registered craftworkers

1976a *Michael Cardew*, a collection of essays with an introduction by Bernard Leach
1977 *Domestic Pottery*, exhibition catalogue
1977a *Jill Crowley*, exhibition catalogue
1977b *Glenys Barton at Wedgwood*, exhibition catalogue, with an introduction by J. V. G. Mallet
1979 *The Work of Alison Britton*, exhibition catalogue
1981 *The Maker's Eye*, exhibition catalogue
1981a *Jacqui Poncelet – New Ceramics*, exhibition catalogue
1984 *Tableware*, introduction by Alison Britton, exhibition booklet
1985 *Carol McNicoll Ceramics*, exhibition catalogue
1987 *Gillian Lowndes: New Ceramic Sculpture*, exhibition catalogue
1988 *Craft Classics Since the 1940s*, ed. J. Houston, a collection of historical articles to accompany an exhibition of the same name

London, CPA (Craftsmen Potters Association)
1972 *Potters*, London (1st edn.) (2nd edn., 1973; 3rd edn., 1975; 4th edn., 1977; 5th edn., 1980; 7th edn., 1986; 8th edn. 1989
1983 *Studio Ceramics Today*, (includes *Potters*, 6th edn.), exhibition catalogue of the 25th anniversary exhibition held at the VAM

London, Christopher Wood Gallery
1980 *British 20th Century Ceramics*, ed. Ian Bennett

London, Hayward Gallery
1979 *The Thirties*, exhibition catalogue, Arts Council

London, ICA (Institute of Contemporary Arts)
1985 *Fast Forward, New Directions in British Ceramics*

London, Tate Gallery
1985 *St Ives*, exhibition catalogue, with section on the Leach Pottery by Oliver Watson

London, VAM
1936 *English Pottery, Old and New*, book of an exhibition held in 1935
1968 *Five Studio Potters*, exhibition pamphlet
1972 *International Ceramics*, exhibition catalogue
1973 *The Craftsman's Art*, exhibition catalogue
1977 *Six Studio Potters*, exhibition pamphlet

Marsh, Ernest
1943 'Studio Potters of Coleshill, Wilts: Miss K. Pleydell-Bouverie and Miss D. K. N. Braden', *Apollo*, December

Milner-White, Eric (Dean of York)
1971 *Modern Stoneware Pottery, Select Handlist of the Milner-White Gift*, Corporation City Art Gallery and Museum, York

Newland, William
1952 'Recent Ceramic Art', *World Review*, December

Paisley
1984 *The Studio Ceramics Collection at Paisley Museum and Art Galleries*, ed. Robert A. Saunders

Rice, Paul and Gowing, Christopher
1989 *British Studio Ceramics in the 20th Century*, London

Rose, Muriel
1955 *Artist-Potters in England*, London
1970 *Artist Potters in England*, London

Sunderland
1989 *The Harrow Connection*, Northern Centre for Contemporary Art, Sunderland, with essays by Tanya Harrod and others

Thorpe, W. A.
1930 'English Stoneware Pottery by Miss K. Pleydell-Bouverie and Miss D. K. N. Braden', *Artwork*, VI, pp. 257–65

Warwick
1987 *To Build a Cathedral, Coventry Cathedral, 1945–1962*, ed. Louise Campbell, University of Warwick

Wingfield Digby, G.
1952 *The Work of the Modern Potter in England*, London

Woodhead, Kate
1989 'Muriel Rose and the Little Gallery', MA thesis, RCA/V & A Course in the History of Design and Decorative Art (unpublished)

York City Art Gallery
1983 *Michael Cardew and Pupils*, exhibition catalogue, York City Art Gallery and Arts Centre

Index

With a few exceptions, this index relates only to the Introduction.